Always try the problem that matters most to you.
- Andrew Wiles

The SAT Math 2 Prep Black Book

"The Most Effective SAT Math 2 Strategies Ever Published"

By Mike Barrett

Dedication

If you're reading this, you probably plan to take the Math Level 2 SAT Subject Test, which suggests that you may someday want to enter a field that emphasizes exacting, technical thinking. I hope the concepts and strategies we'll discuss in this Black Book will be an immediate help to you as you prepare to clear one of the early hurdles in your journey by taking this test.

Beyond that, I hope the ideas in this Black Book can also—in some small way—help you develop skills that are more subtle and more important in your educational career. These are the skills of identifying a problem, determining which questions should be asked to help you solve the problem you've identified, and finding the most elegant and satisfying answers to the questions you've asked. These skills are the foundation of math and of so many other disciplines, and the foundation of the approach that you'll learn in this Black Book.

This book is dedicated to the people who remember that foundation.

Free Video Demonstrations And Calculator Downloads

If you'd like to see video demonstrations of some of the concepts and solutions in this Black Book—and to download a version of the cheatsheet at the end of this book that's formatted for your calculator on test day—then please visit www.Math2PrepVideos.com. A selection of free downloads and videos is available there for readers of this book.

Table Of Contents

Read This First!

I know how a lot of people read test prep books, and I don't want you to read this Black Book like that :)

For a lot of readers, test prep material isn't the most exciting. On top of that, they often feel like they already know most test prep advice before they start to read, because they've often received tips and guidance from teachers and friends. And when you're reading something you're not too excited about, and you think you already know what it's going to say anyway, you tend not to read too carefully.

But here's the thing: I promise that you don't already know exactly what I'm going to say in this Black Book.

The advice in this book really is different from traditional test prep advice, and it really has been successfully taught to a large number of people.

If you pay attention to the techniques I teach you, and make an effort to implement them by following my advice on training, you'll find that you understand the Math Level 2 Test much better than most people do—and that's actually pretty exciting, when you think about it. It means you can spend less time preparing and still get better results on a test that can have a serious impact on your college admissions opportunities.

So the material in this Black Book actually can be worth your time and energy, if improving on the SAT Subject Test in Mathematics Level 2 is something you care about.

The material in this Black Book is unique.

It probably won't do you much good to flip through this book and try to get a general idea of what it's about. You can't just skim a few sections, see a diagram with a triangle or something, and think, "Yeah, okay, learn some trigonometry, I get it. I already knew that . . ."

You really need to read this Black Book carefully and pay attention to what it actually says, instead of just expecting me to say what your math teacher has already said, because I'm not going to do that.

On the SAT Subject Test in Mathematics Level 2, the details of individual questions (and of the test's overall design) are much more important than details tend to be on a math test in high school. Because of this important distinction, you'll find that the details of your training for the test will be very important too.

So remember to pay close attention to what you see in this Black Book, and think about how you'll be able to apply it for yourself on test day.

Of course, you'll probably find that some sections of this Black Book are more helpful for you than others, because everybody has different strengths, weaknesses, and goals. But you won't know for sure which sections are the most helpful for you until you read them. So read them! :)

Your goal is to get a great score on the Math Level 2 Test, and my goal is to help you do that. So please work with me. If you promise to read this book carefully and think about what we discuss, I promise I'll tell you everything you need to know about the Math Level 2 Test.

Reading isn't all it takes

But wait—there's one more thing. Doing well on the Math Level 2 Test isn't just a matter of memorizing a list of facts that you'll spit back on test day. In fact, memorization plays a much smaller role on this test than most people think. Instead, the key to preparing for this test is to train yourself to develop a certain skill: the ability to figure out which concepts a real Math Level 2 question is actually testing, and then to respond appropriately.

So, while reading this Black Book is critical, you also need to do more than read—you actually need to take what you'll learn here and practice it against real test questions from the College Board. You need to try out these techniques for yourself before you use them for real on test day. (Refer to the section of this Black Book called "How To Train For The SAT Subject Test in Mathematics Level 2" for more ideas on ways to practice the techniques in this Black Book.)

Before you get started with this book and your preparation, I need you to commit to the idea that you're going to pay careful attention to what you find in this Black Book. I also need you to commit to the idea that you're going to practice these techniques against real Math Level 2 questions from the College Board until you feel comfortable with them. Those two activities will put you in the best possible position on test day.

A note on my writing style . . .

You may have already noticed that I use an informal, conversational writing style in this Black Book. I do this because my students tend to find it much easier to read and digest.

This means I might do a few things your English teacher wouldn't love, such as starting sentences with conjunctions like "and" or "but." Most teachers will tell you not to do that in formal writing, even though famous and respected authors like John Locke, W. E. B. DuBois, and Jane Austen did it all the time.

But I don't think of my Black Books as examples of formal writing (see? I just did it again . . . and now I'm putting an ellipse inside parentheses . . . and I'm not sure how to punctuate the end of this sentence). I prefer to write in a way that feels less like a textbook and more like a conversation. In my experience, students find this approach to be much more engaging and ultimately much more effective—which is the whole point.

Frequently Asked Questions

When people come to me for help with a test, they often already have questions on their minds. This section of the Black Book is meant to address those common questions in a way that will allow you to refer to more detailed explanations if you feel you need them right away. Otherwise, I'd encourage you to keep reading through the sections of this Black Book in the order in which I've presented them.

What's the difference between a trained test-taker and an untrained one? How do I become a trained test-taker?

I'll frequently call your attention to the differences between trained test-takers and untrained test-takers. Here are my explanations for those terms:

- A trained test-taker is someone who understands the purpose, structure, and inherent weaknesses in the Math Level 2 Test, and who knows how to exploit those things to score high on the test. A trained test-taker understands that the Math Level 2 Test doesn't really reward advanced math knowledge; instead, it rewards a detail-oriented, creative approach to test-taking in which relatively basic concepts are combined in unusual ways to answer questions that seem more advanced than they really are. A trained test-taker frequently finds solutions to questions in under 30 seconds, and these solutions often involve unorthodox approaches such as analyzing answer choices. A trained test-taker also understands the importance of certainty when taking the Math Level 2 Test, and avoids guessing on the test.

- An untrained test-taker, on the other hand, is someone who has a difficult time on the Math Level 2 Test because he doesn't understand what the test is actually designed to do. Because of this misunderstanding, an untrained test-taker typically approaches the Math Level 2 Test in the same way he would approach a high school math test. Untrained test-takers usually have a difficult time scoring high on the Math Level 2 Test; even if they do manage to score high, they usually expend significantly more effort than necessary in achieving that score. Untrained test-takers are more likely to be frustrated by all aspects of test-taking than trained test-takers are.

One way to become a trained test-taker is to analyze the Math Level 2 Test on your own, which can take a significant amount of time and effort. But a much easier way to become a trained test-taker is to read this Black Book and apply what you learn.

What does "MSTB" mean?

Throughout this Black Book, I use the acronym MSTB to refer to the College Board publication *The Official SAT Subject Tests in Mathematics Levels 1 & 2 Study Guide*, which is an essential part of your preparation. That name is extremely clumsy to repeat over and over again, so I use the abbreviation "MSTB" to stand for the phrase "Math Subject Test Book," which is what a lot of people call the book.

For more on why you'll need a copy of that book in addition to this Black Book, and on how to use the MSTB in your preparation, see the section of this Black Book called "Why You'll Need A Copy Of The Official SAT Subject Tests in Mathematics Levels 1 & 2 Study Guide."

What kind of schedule should be used to prepare for the Math Level 2 Test?

The short answer to this question is that there's no one-size-fits-all approach to preparing for the Math Level 2 Test, because different test-takers will have different situations, which can depend on any of the following factors, among others:

- the amount of time until the next test-date

- the number of times the test can be re-taken before college application deadlines

- the test-taker's comfort level with the math concepts necessary for the test

- the amount of free time the test-taker has, which is influenced by things like extra-curricular activities and homework

- the test-taker's willingness to focus on preparation

- how quickly the test-taker can learn to implement the concepts in this Black Book

- the importance of the test score in the test-taker's overall admissions campaign (some programs expect high scores on SAT subject tests, while other programs might not require the scores, or might use them to grant course standing, etc.)

By the time a test-taker is considering taking the Math Level 2 Test, she should be more than capable of evaluating her own situation, determining an effective preparation timeline, and then adjusting that timeline as necessary.

I lay out the key considerations for developing a preparation timeline in the part of this Black Book called "How To Train For The SAT Subject Test In Mathematics Level 2."

Do test-takers need to know advanced math for this test?

In order to score high on the Math Level 2 Test, you do need to be familiar with areas of math that some people would consider advanced for a high school student, such as trigonometry, logarithms, probability, and so on.

But these different areas of math are NOT all equally important in the context of the test! Some concepts will appear far more frequently on test day than others, and some concepts may not appear at all on a given test day.

You'll also find that some questions might seem advanced to an untrained test-taker, even though they can be answered by combining fairly basic concepts in unusual ways. You'll learn how to identify these simplified approaches as you read through this Black Book, and you'll see several examples of such solutions in action when we get to the question walkthroughs later on.

See the section of this Black Book called "The Secrets Of The SAT Subject Test In Mathematics Level 2" to learn more about why the College Board has designed the test to reward more basic math knowledge than most people realize.

See Part I of the Math Toolbox in this Black Book for a basic run-down of the concepts that appear most frequently on test day.

See Part II of the Math Toolbox in this Black Book for a discussion of the types of concepts that appear less frequently on test day.

What kind of calculator is best for the test?

I highly recommend that you bring a graphing calculator with you on test day. The particular model of calculator isn't important as long as you know how to use it effectively, and as long as it's allowed by the College Board. In my experience, most clients use a calculator by Texas Instruments or Casio.

For information on necessary calculator functions, along with recommended ways to use the calculator, see the section of this Black Book called "Your Calculator For The Math Level 2 Test."

What should a test-taker do if she runs out of practice tests?

The MSTB contains 2 practice tests. To most people, that doesn't seem like very much to work with. After all, some test-takers want to prepare by doing as many practice tests as possible, but this is never the best strategy in itself for any standardized testing situation.

Believe it or not, if you had a complete and total understanding of just one real Math Level 2 Test written by the College Board, you'd know enough to get a perfect score on test day. Let me clarify what I mean by that, though—I'm not saying that simply being able to answer every question on a real test from the College Board would serve as a guarantee that you'd be able to answer every question on all future tests. Instead, I mean that if you understood all aspects of the design of one real practice test in the same way that the College Board understood it—in terms of things like subject matter, answer choices, patterns, rules, and so on—then you'd be able to answer enough questions on test day to get a perfect score.

So how do you get to that level of understanding? You get there by understanding the concepts in this Black Book and reviewing real test questions from the College Board until you thoroughly understand how the College Board has designed them. You would only really need to use one test for this process, and you've got two tests to work with in the MSTB, so that's actually plenty.

Of course, I understand that some students will want more questions to work with. If you find yourself in that position, please find the section of this Black Book called "How To Train For The SAT Subject Test In Mathematics Level 2," and then read the sub-section called "Looking For Additional Practice Material?"

Are the questions easier at the beginning of the test and harder at the end?

There's a common myth about College Board math tests (such as the Math part of the SAT 1, the SAT Math Level 2 Test, and so on) that says that easier questions come at the beginning of a section, and harder questions come at the end of a section.

While some people will find that *many* questions toward the beginning of a section are easier for them than *many* questions toward the end of a section, it's important not to let this impact your mindset or approach.

First of all, the fact that many other people find something easy (or difficult) has no bearing on whether you, personally, will find it easy (or difficult). Different people have different strengths and weaknesses, and might respond differently to the same question. You'll find this to be especially true as you come to understand the way the test is designed—it often happens that questions that might seem unsolvable to an untrained test-taker can actually be answered in a few seconds by a trained test-taker.

Secondly, it doesn't really matter whether a question is easy or hard, in terms of the correct approach. Either way, we still need to read carefully, consider answer choices and diagrams, come up with an efficient solution, execute that solution, check our work, and try to understand the question from the College Board's standpoint.

If you start to expect questions in one part of the test to be hard or easy, you could start to overthink what you're doing and get yourself into trouble. For example, if you don't solve one of the earlier questions right away, you might panic, even if you're able to find the answer eventually. You might also make a careless mistake if you assume a question is easier than it really is, just because you're still in the first half of the test.

Similarly, you might assume that a later question must be challenging, and never realize that there's a very quick and easy way to solve it if you apply the kinds of techniques you'll learn in this Black Book. So the best approach is to take every question seriously, and approach them all with an open mind and an awareness of how the test is designed: every question might potentially trick you if you're not careful, and many questions have simple solutions that aren't obvious to most test-takers, no matter where they appear on the test.

If anything, it might be accurate to say that questions that appear earlier tend to be a little more concrete, involving numbers and calculations that might reflect practical scenarios, like using simple trigonometry to calculate the height of a tree, while later questions tend to be more abstract. But even that statement is just a broad generalization, not a hard and fast rule. So, again, remember that you always need to approach each question with the same mindset, and take the test one step at a time.

How should I approach Roman numeral questions?

For a trained test-taker, the best approach to a Roman numeral question isn't really any different from the best approach to any other question on the test. Instead of considering which individual answer choice is correct before choosing our answer, we evaluate each individual Roman numeral to see which ones are valid, and then pick the answer choice that accurately reflects our findings. Just as with any question, it's extremely important to pay attention to small details and to insist on finding an answer choice that fits exactly with our understanding of the question, rather than giving up and guessing if we can't find an answer choice that we think is correct.

If you'd like to see solutions for real test questions that involve Roman numerals, take a look at this Black Book's walkthroughs of the following questions:

- Question 40 on page 136 of the MSTB
- Question 28 on page 169 of the MSTB
- Question 48 on page 176 of the MSTB

Why You'll Need A Copy Of *The Official SAT Subject Tests in Mathematics Levels 1 & 2 Study Guide*

One of the most important parts of your preparation for any standardized test is the idea of working with real test questions written by the company that makes the test.

As you'll soon see, the College Board follows specific, standardized rules and patterns when it creates questions for the Math Level 2 Test. These rules and patterns often have little to do with actual math concepts, and much more to do with things like the following:

- when it might be possible to answer questions with a graphing calculator in non-obvious ways

- what kinds of shortcuts are encouraged, and which kinds should be avoided

- how answer choices can relate to one another

- the maximum amount of time that can be required for the fastest solution to a question

The rules and patterns that I'm talking about are generally NOT obvious to most people, including most math teachers (and, unfortunately, most test preparation companies). But understanding these rules and patterns—and the weaknesses that they create—is one of the most important parts of maximizing your success on test day, while minimizing the effort you'll need to put into your preparation.

It's true that other companies besides the College Board publish practice tests for the Math Level 2 Test as well, but I strongly recommend that you avoid working with those fake practice tests. There's simply no way to guarantee that those fake tests will follow the same rules and patterns that real practice tests from the College Board must follow, and that you'll see on test day. In fact, I've seen several unfortunate situations in which fake practice tests from well known companies included questions that could literally NEVER appear on a real test from the College Board, because those questions violated the design principles of the real test. Similarly, I've seen fake practice tests that don't reward the same kinds of shortcuts and streamlined approaches that the College Board's practice tests do.

Companies that make these fake Math Level 2 practice tests might do so for any of the following reasons, among others:

- They don't know the College Board's standards.

- They don't think it's important for test-takers to be aware of the College Board's standards.

- They think their fake tests are better for preparation than the real thing.

- They need to create scenarios to make their test-taking strategies seem more relevant than they really are.

So the bottom line is that working with fake tests can set you back in two ways:

1. Fake tests can reward strategies that the College Board punishes in real tests.

2. Fake tests can punish strategies that the College Board rewards in real tests.

As it turns out, the only easily available published source of real practice tests for the Math Level 2 Test is the College Board's book *The Official SAT Subject Tests in Mathematics Levels 1 & 2 Study Guide*, because those questions are created and owned by the College Board. That book contains two real

Math Level 2 practice tests. You'll need them for your training if you want to get the maximum benefit out of this Black Book.

(As I mentioned earlier, since the name of *The Official SAT Subject Tests in Mathematics Levels 1 & 2 Study Guide* is awkward to keep repeating, I'll call the book the MSTB, for "Math Subject Test Book," instead of writing out the whole name each time I refer to it in this Black Book.)

You can buy a copy of the MSTB from Amazon.com, from a local bookstore, or from wherever you generally buy your books. You may also be able to find a copy in a school library or a public library (although library copies often have markings on the test questions, unfortunately).

Why I didn't include any practice questions in this Black Book

People sometimes ask why I don't include my own fake practice questions in my Black Books—if I claim to understand the hidden design principles of all these standardized tests, then why don't I feel qualified to write my own practice questions?

This is a good question. As it turns out, there are two good answers to it:

1. As sure as I am that I understand how a test is written, it's still the case that working with real test questions from the College Board is the only way to be totally, completely CERTAIN that you're focusing on things that might appear on test day. So even if I wrote my own questions, smart test-takers would still refuse to use them anyway, because they could just use real College Board questions and remove all doubt that they were practicing correctly.

2. Some of the things that I teach my students are so surprising and effective that I want to make sure the students see them in action against real test questions, so they never have to wonder if what I'm showing them will actually work on test day. They know it will work, because they see it working on real questions from a real, previously administered test, and they understand how standardization works in testing.

So this Black Book contains no practice tests.

What it does contain is a set of thorough walkthrough explanations for every question in the two Math Level 2 practice tests in the MSTB. These walkthroughs will show you exactly how to use the strategies and concepts from the first part of this Black Book against real test questions from the College Board, so you can model that behavior on test day.

But what about "harder" practice questions?

Some third-party prep companies have a reputation for writing fake tests that are supposed to be more difficult than the real thing; the idea behind this kind of practice is that it should make the real test seem easy by comparison. My students sometimes ask if it's a good idea to practice with these harder fake tests, because they want to go above and beyond in their preparation.

Unfortunately, the basic problem underlying all fake test questions still applies: the fake questions will end up training you to do things that the real test won't reward. Whether those fake tests are harder than the real test is beside the point, which is that the fake tests are *different* from the real test.

On top of that, it's a mistake to think that improving your performance on a harder task will always result in improved performance on an easier task, just because one is harder than the other. In order for that kind of hardship training to work, the harder task has to be similar to the easier task in a meaningful way. For example, if you're training for a sport that requires you to run 90 feet in a given period of time, then you might benefit from training to run 110 feet in the same amount of time, because the task of running 90 feet is highly similar to the task of running 110 feet—pretty much all the techniques and tactics that would help a person run 110 feet would also help that person run 90 feet, and you'd be getting yourself used to a higher level of stress in training, so that the actual event would seem more relaxed in comparison.

But using harder questions to get ready for a standardized test isn't like that, because the whole point of training for a standardized test is to get used to exploiting the *standardization*. Harder questions fall outside the standards of the test by definition (since part of the test's standardization includes the difficulty level of the material in the question).

So training with harder test questions to get ready for the Math Level 2 Test would be more like training to do a standing backflip so you can get better at swimming. Doing a backflip is harder than swimming for most people, but the two things are so unrelated that learning to do backflips doesn't really affect your swimming ability, even though they're both sort of exercise-related.

If you want to get good at backflips, you should work on backflips. If you want to be a better swimmer, you should work on swimming. Similarly, if you want to get better at taking some test prep company's practice test, then you should work on their practice tests. But if you want to get better at the Math Level 2 Test—the same one you'll actually take on test day, administered by the College Board—then you should only practice with real Math Level 2 practice tests from the College Board.

(Just so we're clear here, I'm not saying that anyone who works with a practice test from another company will get a terrible score. There are lots of people who use these practice tests and still get good scores for other reasons. What I'm saying is that working with third-party tests isn't a good use of your time, and there's a chance that working with them could even hurt your score. Your best option is always to work with real practice questions from the College Board.)

Why you shouldn't just rely on the College Board's test-taking advice and explanations for its own questions

Although the MSTB is the only printed source of practice tests for the Math Level 2 Test, it's NOT the best source of test preparation advice! In fact, I'd call it a mediocre resource for actual strategies.

This actually makes sense, if you think about it. For one thing, the College Board probably doesn't want to give the world an effective way to beat its tests. If every test-taker knew the best way to approach the Math Level 2 Test, then everybody would get great scores, and the test wouldn't be helpful to colleges anymore—the whole point of a standardized test is that it reliably generates a range of scores from the test-taking population, so that those scores can be compared to one another in a meaningful way by an admissions department. If nearly everyone who took the test answered nearly all of the questions correctly, there would be no further need for the test to exist. Another reason not to explain the best approach to the test is that the most effective approach—the one you'll learn in this Black Book—actually makes the test look a little silly. The College Board probably doesn't want to come forward and call your attention to the fact that almost every question can be answered in under 30 seconds, or that the trigonometry questions can be answered with only a basic understanding of trig, or that it's typically possible to leave roughly 10% of the test blank and still score a "perfect" 800, and so on.

I think you'll find that the College Board's test-taking advice, and its explanations for its own questions, tend to make the Math Level 2 Test sound more advanced and complicated than it really is.

But I'm getting ahead of myself a bit—we'll cover all of this stuff in the rest of this Black Book, and you'll see lots of examples of what I'm talking about.

For now, just make sure you have access to a copy of the College Board's book *The Official SAT Subject Tests in Mathematics Levels 1 & 2 Study Guide*. The real test questions in that book are absolutely essential to your training. I recommend you use that book as your only source of test questions, and this Black Book as your only source of test-taking advice. (If you find yourself wanting more practice material to work with, I recommend you find the section of this Black Book called "How To Train For The SAT Subject Test In Mathematics Level 2" and read the subsection called "Looking For Additional Practice Material?")

The Secrets Of The SAT Subject Test In Mathematics Level 2

In order to beat the College Board at its own game, you need to understand what game the College Board is playing in the first place.

So before we can start talking about the best ways to approach this test, you need to understand that this test is fundamentally different from the math tests you take in school. If you don't appreciate these differences, then you won't fully understand how to exploit them later on, and you won't be able to approach this test in the most effective way possible.

We're going to cover a lot of concepts here. I'll try to make it as painless as possible—in fact, you might even find this discussion interesting, because we're going to pull back the curtain on how the College Board thinks when it creates an SAT math test. This important background information will make the rest of your preparation much easier and more effective. Let's get started.

Why does the Math Level 2 Test even exist?

Nearly all American colleges and universities consider standardized test scores as part of their admissions process, and a high percentage of those schools accept scores on SAT subject tests like the Math Level 2 Test.

Why do they do that? Why don't schools just look at an applicant's math grades? It might seem silly to make all those people take an extra math test, since their applications already include transcripts with information about their math classes. But colleges spend a lot of time and energy collecting and reviewing standardized testing data from applicants—in fact, the Math Level 2 Test has existed (in one form or another) since the 1930s! So colleges must think the test is useful. But why?

There are probably 3 main reasons that colleges trust the Math Level 2 Test—and when we know them, they lead us to an inescapable, and very important, conclusion about the way the test is designed, and how to beat it. Here are the 3 reasons:

1. The Math Level 2 Test is objective.

One of the main reasons for the existence of standardized testing in general is the fact that admissions departments want a reliable way to compare applicants from vastly different backgrounds. If two applicants have different math classes with different teachers in different schools in different cities, how can a college make a meaningful comparison between one applicant's B in statistics and another applicant's A in analytical geometry? The short answer is that it can't be done. The Math Level 2 Test provides a level playing field that allows some kind of objective comparison to be made across the entire applicant pool. And that leads us to the next reason . . .

2. The Math Level 2 Test is consistent without repeating questions all the time.

The Math Level 2 Test is given multiple times a year, and applicants can re-take it as many times as they want. But the scores from the test are still reliable for colleges—a college can compare a score of 800 from one test date to a score of 800 from another test date, and have a high degree of confidence that the two scores represent the same level of ability, instead of wondering if one of the applicants just got lucky and caught the test on an "easier" day. Colleges know that the College Board uses a strict process for designing its tests and standardizing the results of those tests. (As it turns out, our whole approach to the test will be based on exploiting the weaknesses of this strict standardization process. But we'll get into that later.)

3. The Math Level 2 Test creates a spectrum of results.

In addition to the test's objectivity and reliability, colleges seem to appreciate that tests like the Math Level 2 Test assign a precise score from a fairly wide range of possible scores. This means, for example, that colleges trust there is a meaningful difference between a score of 700 and a score of 800—both test-takers are clearly talented, but the 800-scorer did something extra on the test that the 700-scorer failed to do. In other words, the test doesn't just indicate that a test-taker passed or failed; instead, it allows very subtle comparisons to be made among test-takers, which means the admissions department has a lot more information to use when it makes its decisions.

In short, the Math Level 2 Test exists because colleges and universities trust it to give them useful information about their applicants. The College Board knows this, and goes to serious lengths to ensure that the test maintains its high standard of reliability, so that it consistently generates objective, reliable data about the testing performances of applicants from all over the world.

So now, as strategic thinkers who are analyzing the Math Level 2 Test so that we can beat it as easily as possible, we need to think like the College Board for a minute. Ask yourself a very important question: How is it possible to administer a reliable, objective test to a large number of people from a wide range of backgrounds?

How the test is designed, and why

The Math Level 2 Test is given to over 100,000 people from a variety of math backgrounds every year, but the College Board still manages to keep the test results reliable and objective. This is actually a very impressive accomplishment for the College Board, if you stop to think about it. It means the test must be designed very carefully, because the reliability of the results could never be achieved just by luck.

As it turns out, there are 4 major aspects of the test's design that allow the College Board to achieve these goals. You need to know about all of them, because they'll have a tremendous impact on your training and your performance.

1. The test relies on relatively basic math ideas.

Believe it or not, the concepts that you'll encounter on the Math Level 2 Test are actually much more basic than most untrained test-takers would assume. Many of those test-takers have taken classes in calculus, statistics, and other advanced areas of math, but the Math Level 2 Test often asks questions based on topics like arithmetic and basic algebra. In fact, questions on this test can never require you to know about derivatives, margins of error, and other concepts that would be considered fundamental in a lot of advanced high school math classes. (By the way, I'm not saying that the test questions on basic concepts are always *easy*. It's very possible to build challenging questions out of basic concepts—but we'll talk about that below.)

The test needs to limit itself to relatively simple concepts because it's going to be taken by people with different backgrounds. Some of them will have studied advanced calculus or stats, and some will have taken trigonometry, or pre-calculus. But the Math Level 2 Test exists because colleges want a meaningful way to compare all the people who are choosing to emphasize their math skills in their applications, so it needs to be theoretically possible that nearly all the questions have subject matter that's accessible to nearly all the test-takers—otherwise, a bad result on the test might just indicate that the test-taker knew a lot about an area of advanced math that didn't appear on the test, which would make the test results much less useful for colleges.

So we can see why the College Board needs to make sure that the subject matter on the test isn't advanced—relatively speaking, at least. But if the test relies on basic concepts, why doesn't it seem easier? Well, that leads us to the next point.

2. The test often presents basic ideas strangely.

As we just saw, it's true that the College Board needs to limit itself to less advanced ideas in order to ensure that the results reflect a test-taker's ability more than her curriculum. But this creates another problem for the College Board: if the questions can only cover relatively basic concepts, how can the test still be hard enough to allow for a distribution of results across all test-takers? After all, the test would also be useless to colleges if nearly everybody got a great score on it because it was too easy.

The College Board's solution to this issue is to create difficult questions *by presenting less advanced concepts in strange ways.* That's extremely important, so I'm going to say it again, and give it its own line on the page and everything:

Most of the challenging questions on the test are actually asking about relatively basic concepts in strange ways.

When I say the questions are written strangely, what I mean is that they're not written the way a math teacher would usually write them. We'll talk about that in more detail below, but, for now, the key thing to realize is that Math Level 2 questions rarely rely on obscure formulas and detailed calculations; instead, they're more likely to focus on definitions and properties, and small details. We'll talk a little more about that in the next point.

3. The test is more detail-oriented than most test-takers are.

Another facet of the College Board's approach to test design is a strong focus on small details. Of course, math is already a detail-oriented field of study, but the Math Level 2 Test is generally even more detail-oriented than math teachers in high school and college tend to be. We'll see several examples of this principle elsewhere in this Black Book, especially in the question walkthroughs, but one of the biggest ways the College Board does this is by including wrong answer choices that deliberately anticipate the mistakes that test-takers are likely to make on most questions. This allows untrained test-takers to work through a question and arrive at one of the wrong answer choices without ever realizing they've done something wrong. This is especially effective because most untrained test-takers never realize that the College Board cares so much about details in the first place.

Of course, if you make a small mistake on a math test in school, many teachers will give you partial credit, especially if they can tell from your work that you were on the right track. But that's impossible on the Math Level 2 Test, because the College Board will never review your work. In fact, there's no such thing as partial credit on this test—you're either right or you're wrong, with no consideration of how you reached your conclusion. And that's only one way that the College Board uses the multiple-choice design of the test questions to affect the difficulty level of the test. Let's talk about another way.

4. The test uses multiple-choice questions for further control over question difficulty.

The multiple-choice format allows the College Board to accomplish a lot of things, from an administrative standpoint. The format allows questions to be graded more quickly and with near-perfect objectivity and accuracy.

But it also allows the College Board to control how difficult a question actually is, no matter how strange the prompt seems to be. If the answer choices are highly similar to one another in some way, then it becomes harder for a test-taker to distinguish among them, and more likely that the test-taker can make a small mistake without catching it; on the other hand, if the answer choices are clearly different from one another in the context of the question, then it sometimes becomes possible for a test-taker to identify the correct answer with total certainty, without even picking up a pencil. The multiple-choice format also allows the College Board to write questions that might *seem* to require advanced math knowledge, but that actually don't require anything more than basic algebra once the test-taker notices she can plug the answer choices into an equation and see which one must be right.

As it turns out, the College Board has fairly detailed rules and patterns that it follows when creating the answer choices for a question. We'll talk about those later, and you'll see several examples of ways that the design of the answer choices can be exploited when we go through the walkthroughs. For now, the key thing is to keep in mind that the College Board's use of the multiple-choice format can make the test harder for untrained test-takers to understand . . . but the multiple-choice format actually makes the test much easier for trained test-takers who know how to exploit it.

As you're starting to see, the College Board does a lot of unique things when it creates the SAT Math Level 2 Test. This is part of the reason why the best approach to this test has little in common with the best ways to approach school tests. It's very important to be aware of these differences, so let's explore them now.

Differences between school math and the Math Level 2 Test

We've been talking for a little while now about what the College Board is trying to achieve with the Math Level 2 Test. We saw that some of the key goals and methods for the College Board include the following things:

- The test is designed to be given to a large number of people from a wide variety of backgrounds.

- Objectivity and consistency of the testing data are the most important things for the College Board.

- The test needs to generate a good distribution of scores, so colleges can compare a large number of applicants in precise ways.

- The test is limited to asking about relatively basic ideas.

- The test uses strange presentations of ideas to make questions seem harder than they are.

- The test focuses more on attributes and definitions than on obscure formulas.

- The test is highly detail-oriented.

- The test is completely multiple-choice.

- No partial credit is possible on the test.

If you look back over that list, you'll notice that your math tests in high school have almost none of those attributes. A school test is usually written for a single classroom of students, and it doesn't matter if the results of the test are spread out across a range of scores, or if those results can be meaningfully compared to results for another class from 10 years ago. School math tests usually focus on two or three formulas at a time, and pay almost no attention to properties and definitions. Most teachers will check over your work, and some will give partial credit if they can tell you were on the right track with your solution. And math classes generally tend to cover one area of math pretty deeply, instead of surveying all areas of math in a relatively basic way.

In short, if we really think about it, we see that the Math Level 2 Test doesn't reward the same things that school math tests reward. In fact, the two types of tests couldn't possibly be similar, since they're designed by different people to be given to different groups of test-takers for different purposes. All of these differences probably seem obvious to you now, because we've just gone through the reasons for them in some detail . . .

. . . but most test-takers never, ever realize the difference. And that's a big problem for them.

If you try to approach the Math Level 2 Test like it's a regular high school math test, you'll be extremely frustrated. You'll think the test is much harder than it is, because you won't be looking for opportunities to exploit the weaknesses of the College Board's standardization. You'll wonder why you never learned the formulas for so many things, without realizing that many questions on the test can't be answered with formulas. You'll miss questions you think you understand because you'll overlook some detail like a minus sign in your own calculations, and find a wrong answer choice that matches your result. You'll guess on questions you don't understand at all and wind up losing even more points.

But none of this is because the Math Level 2 Test is actually *harder* than a school test. The two things are just *different*—and now, you know why.

All of this probably also helps explain why colleges aren't only interested in your scores on standardized tests. Colleges are interested in your test scores *and* your transcripts. So it's pretty safe to conclude that colleges think your grades in high school math classes must be measuring something different from what your standardized test scores are measuring. And colleges are right to think that, because it's true.

This also makes sense when we remember that some people who do really well in math classes struggle on standardized math tests, and some people who do really well on standardized math tests might not get very good grades in math classes.

So one of the most important things you can do at this point is to realize that the math you do in a high school classroom is often very different from the specific techniques and calculations you'll be doing on the Math Level 2 Test. There's some overlap in the subject matter, of course, but the material is tested in such different ways that it's best to think of the two tests as separate things.

Conclusion

You now understand something very important, and very fundamental, about the way the Math Level 2 Test works. This understanding will help everything that comes next make a lot more sense to you, which means you'll be able to retain it better, until it becomes second nature to you. You may not realize it yet, but if you internalize the ideas we just talked about, you'll already have a significant advantage over the vast majority of test-takers, who have no idea how the test works or what its objectives actually are.

Of course, we're not done yet, though :) In fact, we're only getting started.

Now that we've laid the groundwork and explained some of the general tendencies of the test, it's time to discuss the most efficient ways to prepare to learn the details of exploiting the test, and how to put that knowledge into action on test day.

How To Train For The SAT Subject Test In Mathematics Level 2

Of course, this entire Black Book is about training for the Math Level 2 Test, but in this section we'll deal with the best ways to spend your time as you get ready for test day. We'll start with the most important guiding principles for you to keep in mind, and then I'll suggest some priorities for your preparation, and, finally, we'll discuss some drills and other exercises you can work on.

There's no one-size-fits-all approach to scheduling.

Sometimes a student will want me to give her an exact schedule to follow as she gets ready for a test. But there are several reasons why I can't really do that. Different test-takers will have different backgrounds, different amounts of time until their tests, different obligations outside of test preparation, different attention spans, and so on.

Instead of telling you there's only one way to schedule your preparation, I prefer to trust your intelligence. So I'm going to lay out the principles I'd recommend you keep in mind as you prepare, and then you can incorporate those principles into your schedule as you see fit.

I've found that each individual student is usually the best judge of what her preparation schedule should be. In fact, for a lot of students, there's no real need for a formal schedule—once they understand the principles we'll discuss in this section, they find they can work their prep sessions into their free time without laying out a strict plan in advance.

So don't worry about trying to follow someone else's schedule as you prepare. Instead, use the ideas in this section of the book to work out your own approach, and remember to adjust it as the process continues. You may find that you need to spend more time reviewing your practice work than you originally planned, or that you don't need to spend as much time brushing up on the Math Toolbox as you thought you would, and so on.

Remember that your time is an investment.

One of the most important things to understand about time management—for any purpose, not just test-taking—is that time is precious, and we should use it in ways that are most likely to bring us the results we want.

So at every moment during your preparation and on test day, you should be asking yourself, "What could I be doing right now that has the greatest chance of increasing my test score?" The answer to that question is what you should be doing. If you can spend an hour of your time on an activity that's likely to help you answer 5 more questions correctly on test day, then that activity should be prioritized over something that will probably only help you answer 1 more question correctly on test day. (This advice may sound obvious to you, but my experience with test-takers has shown me that most of them don't understand the fundamentals of time management because nobody has ever really allowed them to manage their own time before. So it's good to start with the basics.)

In other words, there's no magic number of hours that you can spend on any particular activity to ensure that you've mastered it, or that you've earned the right to focus your energies somewhere else. Instead, you should work on the things that seem important until you've gotten so good at them that it makes sense to start working on the next most important thing. Keep the ultimate goal of maximizing your score in the front of your mind, and base all of your decisions on that.

Now, I realize that you probably want me to give you some guidance on what's most important in your preparation, and I'll do that in a moment. For now, I want to establish that our primary goal when it comes to planning your training for this test is to prioritize the activities that will get you the most points in return for the time you invest.

Before we get into more detail on what those activities are, I want to make sure you understand something fundamental about this test, which we'll discuss now.

Every question has the same overall impact on your score.

A lot of untrained test-takers assume they should work harder to understand the questions they find more difficult, because they're making the mistake of approaching the Math Level 2 Test in the same way they'd approach a high school math test. In a high school test, it's normal for the teacher to award more points for harder questions . . . *but every question on the Math Level 2 Test has the same overall impact on your final score*[1]. So, as you decide how to invest your preparation time, it makes sense to prioritize the concepts and strategies that are relevant to the greatest number of questions on the test—and these are NOT necessarily the concepts and strategies that are hardest for you.

So don't feel bad if you're not preparing for the test by cramming new, obscure formulas into your memory (or your calculator's memory, as we'll discuss later in this Black Book). In fact, I'd say that the majority of test-takers already know enough math to score very well on the Math Level 2 Test, or even to get a perfect score, so it's usually a bad idea for them to focus on learning more math. Instead, they should invest more time on understanding and exploiting the design of the test. And that leads me to our next topic.

Recommended ranking of priorities

As I've just said, it's important to focus on the concepts and strategies that are most likely to improve your score, rather than just mindlessly trying to memorize more math, which is how most untrained test-takers approach their preparation.

With that in mind, here's a guideline for how to prioritize the different aspects of your preparation. Of course, you're free to modify it as you see fit, but I recommend you strongly consider following it more or less exactly as I've laid it out.

---

[1] Technically speaking, every question on the test counts for exactly one raw point if you answer it correctly, and every question will cost you one-quarter of a raw point if you get it wrong, no matter how hard the question seems to you. The College Board will determine your scaled score (from 200 to 800) by using a conversion chart like the ones on pages 145 and 180 of the MSTB, which translate a raw score into a scaled score. Some test-takers get confused because a difference of one raw point can correspond to a difference of 0, 10, or 20 scaled points, which makes some test-takers think that different test questions could be worth different numbers of points. But the key thing to keep in mind is that the calculation for the raw score doesn't take into account how hard a question was to answer. For example, on the conversion chart from page 180 of the MSTB, a raw score of 42 corresponds to a scaled score of 790, a raw score of 43 corresponds to a scaled score of 800, and a raw score of 44 also corresponds to a scaled score of 800; but correctly answering any 42 of the test questions (with zero wrong answers) from that day would give you a scaled score of 790, while answering any 43 of the questions correctly (with zero wrong answers) would give you a scaled score of 800, and answering any 44 of the questions correctly (with zero wrong answers) would also give you a scaled score of 800. The bottom line is that if you're trying to decide whether to invest your time in an easier question or a harder question, you should choose the easier question first, because you'll get exactly one raw point for answering either question correctly. It doesn't matter *which specific questions* you answer correctly or incorrectly—it only matters *how many total questions* you answer correctly or incorrectly.

First priority: Learn how the Math Level 2 Test actually works.

One of the most important things for you to understand is that the Math Level 2 Test has less in common with a traditional math test than most people realize. If you want to improve your score as efficiently as possible, you need to know what the Math Level 2 Test actually rewards, and this Black Book is one of the best ways to learn that. So I strongly recommend that you begin your preparation by reading most or all of this Black Book, including some of the walkthroughs (but not necessarily all of them right away—see below). All the material in here is important, but I recommend you pay particular attention to the rules, patterns, and techniques we'll discuss, and familiarize yourself with the Math Path and the logic behind it.

Second priority: Commit to avoiding mistakes.

As you come to understand how this test works, you'll see that most untrained test-takers end up throwing away a lot of points on questions they actually understand because they don't make themselves focus on the fundamentals. In fact, a lot of test-takers could come close to their target scores (or maybe even exceed them) if they could eliminate careless mistakes from their performance on the test, without making any other change. Your improved understanding of how the College Board writes the Math Level 2 Test will help you anticipate where mistakes are likely to occur, and will give you a stronger set of tools for avoiding them.

Third priority: Make sure you know the concepts in Part I of the Math Toolbox.

This Black Book has a section called the Math Toolbox, which contains the math concepts you'll need to know on test day. (As you'll see, the inventory of ideas that can be tested is actually much more simple, and much less advanced, than most untrained test-takers would think.) The toolbox is divided into two major parts:

- Part I contains the concepts that appear more frequently on the test and account for the large majority of questions. These tend to be more fundamental than the concepts in Part II of the Math Toolbox. A test-taker who only mastered the ideas in Part I of the toolbox could hit a perfect or near-perfect score on most days, but would probably still need to leave some questions blank on test day (remember that it's typically possible to skip five questions or so and still make a "perfect" 800 on the test if all the other questions are answered correctly). Most people who are considering taking the Math Level 2 Test have covered the majority of the concepts in Part I in school.

- Part II contains the more obscure kinds of concepts that can appear on the test, which account for a significantly smaller number of questions on any given day. In fact, there are some concepts in Part II that won't show up at all for you on test day. (There's no way for us to know which particular concepts won't appear on a given day, but it's extremely unlikely that any one test would contain all of the Part II concepts).

I'd strongly recommend that you have a solid command of all the concepts in Part I of the toolbox, because they're probably already pretty familiar, and because they can appear in a significant number of questions on test day, so that a lack of knowledge in those areas could cause you to miss out on a fair number of questions. But I wouldn't necessarily worry about the concepts in Part II at this stage of your preparation, because there are other things you could be working on that would be more likely to improve your score to a greater degree, while taking less of your time.

Fourth priority: Focus on the act of test-taking itself, using official questions from the College Board.

The Math Level 2 Test rewards a lot of behaviors that don't necessarily get rewarded in regular math classes, as you'll see throughout this Black Book. These kinds of behaviors include things like approaching the test in passes, looking for informal solutions, paying very close attention to details, and so on. For most test-takers, it's one thing to read about these approaches, and another thing to practice them on real test questions. I'd recommend you try to take at least one of the practice tests in the MSTB in test-like conditions, as though it were the real thing—although some test-takers find it's enough just to go through the questions in the MSTB and think about them in conjunction with the walkthroughs in this Black Book. (See below for advice on how to use the two practice tests in the MSTB, and see the section of this Black Book called "Why You'll Also Need a Copy Of The Official SAT Subject Tests In Math Levels 1 & 2 Study Guide" for more information on the necessity of using real test questions in your practice.)

Fifth priority: Review your practice work carefully.

Carefully reviewing your practice work and analyzing your remaining areas of weakness is actually one of the most important things you can do to improve your performance on test day, even though I made it fifth in a list of six priorities. The thing is that your review and analysis won't really help you much if you haven't handled the four priorities above—if you don't understand how the test works on a fundamental level, then you won't be in a good position to evaluate your remaining areas of weakness. Still, I STRONGLY recommend that you carefully review any practice work you decide to do. In fact, for most people, the review of the practice work should take at least as long as the practice work itself. (See below for more on how to review your practice work effectively.)

Sixth priority: Review the concepts in Part II of the Math Toolbox, and memorize (or record in your calculator) any math you still feel like you need to know.

After you've made sure that you understand the concepts in Part I of the Math Toolbox in this Black Book, *and* you feel like you understand the fundamentals of this test's design, *and* you've done some practice with official test questions, *and* you've reviewed that practice in a meaningful way . . . then you can shift your attention to any math concepts you feel like you still need to know. You'll probably find all the other concepts you need in Part II of the Math Toolbox, but you might also decide that you want to brush up on some other stuff, too. That's up to you, but I'd caution that it's almost definitely not necessary. (You may be wondering how there could be any disagreement over which math concepts can be involved in the test, but the issue here is that the College Board often writes questions in ways that make an untrained test-taker think the question is covering a more advanced topic than it really is. For an example of this, see this Black Book's walkthrough of question 43 on page 138 of the MSTB. A lot of test-takers think the question requires them to understand the law of sines, but it actually doesn't, as my walkthrough explains. You could use the law of sines to find the answer, but you can also find the answer without knowing the law of sines at all.)

Note that memorizing obscure math concepts is the LAST thing I advise you to do as you prepare, but it's the FIRST thing that most untrained test-takers try to do when they prepare! This, again, goes back to the fact that most test-takers don't understand what the test is really about.

Now that we've discussed these priorities, let's talk about a few practical concerns when it comes to doing practice questions, and reviewing your practice.

How to Use The Two Practice Tests In The MSTB

Some students are concerned that they won't have enough test questions to practice with, because there are only two full-length sample tests available in the MSTB, and I strongly recommend that you only use real test questions from the College Board when you prepare for the test. (I discussed the reasons for this policy in the section of this Black Book called "Why You'll Also Need A Copy Of The Official SAT Subject Tests In Math Levels 1 & 2 Study Guide.")

But there's really no need to be concerned.

Remember that the whole key to beating this test is to understand the rules and patterns it follows, and how we can exploit the weaknesses inherent in that standardized design. To accomplish this, all you really need is a single official sample test . . . provided you have access to someone who can use that official test as a platform for a thorough explanation of how the Math Level 2 Test is standardized and what to look out for on test day, which is what you have in this Black Book. Really, we could say that we actually have *more* sample material than we need, since the MSTB gives us two full-length tests.

Many untrained test-takers make the mistake of thinking that the best way to attack this test is to do a dozen or more sample tests, because they expect that the questions on test day will look just like the questions in sample tests—after all, this is how most math tests work in school. But, for reasons we discussed earlier when we talked about how the test is designed, you'll find that the questions you see on test day will follow the same deep design principles as the questions you see in the MSTB, but they won't appear similar to questions from the MSTB on the surface. In other words, when you see a difficult question in the MSTB, there's no guarantee that you'll see a question on test day that will seem similar to it in any obvious kind of way. This means that the kind of drilling you could do to get ready for a final exam in math class will be pretty useless when we're talking about preparing for the Math Level 2 Test. So, again, the goal is to develop an understanding of how the questions are designed and how they can be attacked successfully, so you can apply this knowledge in a flexible way on test day.

With all of that in mind, I find that most of my students can hit their target scores (which frequently means a perfect 800 on this test) after working with only the two sample Level 2 tests in the MSTB. I often take the following steps with them—you'll notice that this process follows closely with the priorities I just laid out for you above:

1. We discuss the standardized design of the Math Level 2 Test, including how it differs from math tests in school, and how attacking difficult questions successfully will often involve being aware of rules, patterns, and key phrases in the prompt and the answer choices. These discussions can take an hour or so, and involve using some of the questions in the MSTB as examples. You can develop the same understanding of the test's design by reading the parts of this Black Book before the Math Toolbox and the walkthroughs, especially the following sections:

   - The Unwritten Rules Of The SAT Subject Test In Mathematics Level 2

   - Answer Choice Patterns

   - Special Technique: Backsolving

   - Special Technique: Ruling Out Answer Choices Without Calculations

   - Rounding On The SAT Subject Test In Mathematics Level 2

   - Decimals, Fractions, And Percentages

- The Math Path

2. We discuss some of the key aspects of the ideal test-taking process for the Math Level 2 Test, including managing time and avoiding guessing. You can find my advice on these topics in the following sections of this Black Book:

    - Guessing On The Math Level 2 Test

    - Time Management On Test Day

3. I ask the student to do the first 25 questions from one of the two sample Math Level 2 Tests in the MSTB. Before the student does this, I remind her that the stakes are very low, and that we're not viewing her performance on these first 25 questions as an indication of her final score on test day; all we're doing is helping her get her feet wet with the test. The student does the first 25 questions from one of the tests without any concern for time limits, and she tries to look for ways to apply the concepts we've been discussing. The next time we speak after she's done, we have a long conversation about how she approached the different questions, what she could have done to finish individual questions more quickly, how she might have been able to avoid any mistakes she made, and so on. In general, we end up spending more time reviewing and discussing this first batch of questions than the student spent actually doing them in the first place. The goal is to help the student understand how the test is constructed, and how the answer choices, wording, diagrams, and other elements of the questions can be understood according to the rules and patterns described in this Black Book. You can develop a similar understanding of the questions you work on in the MSTB by consulting the walkthroughs for them in this Black Book.

4. Once the student feels that she understands how the College Board constructed the first 25 questions and the optimal ways she could have been able to attack each of them, I ask her to complete the remaining 25 questions from the same test. I explain that the remaining 25 questions aren't necessarily easier or harder (on an individual basis) than the ones she's already done, even though some untrained test-takers incorrectly think the questions are strictly arranged from easiest to hardest. Just like with the first 25 questions, her job is to work through the remaining 25 questions and look for opportunities to apply the techniques she's been learning. The next time we speak after she's completed this task, we have another detailed discussion of the questions—how she approached them, what she might have done differently, and so on. We look for trends and patterns in her approach across all 50 questions. (Is she more likely to miss questions that involve more text? Does her accuracy drop as time goes by? Is she remembering to use the calculator to graph functions where appropriate?) Again, you can gain the same kinds of insight by reading the question walkthroughs in this Black Book, and analyzing your own performance.

5. Now that the student has completed all the questions from one of the practice tests in the MSTB, I often do a general review of all of the test-taking concepts we've covered so far, reminding her of the various ways that those concepts appeared in the practice work she's done. If there are any specific math concepts that she feels challenged by at this point, then we discuss them; I might also suggest that she speak to a math teacher if there are concepts that still seem especially challenging to her. If I know that a concept only appears on the test infrequently (say, less than once per test on average), then I advise her not to spend too much energy worrying about that concept unless she feels totally confident in all the other aspects of

her preparation, and has literally nothing else to work on. You can simulate these kinds of discussions and review by making sure you're familiar with the concepts in Part I of the Math Toolbox of this Black Book, and also by revisiting the parts of this Black Book that you've read through at this point, including the walkthroughs for the questions you've already done. At this point, you should feel that you have a strong understanding of how the test works and how to approach it.

6. When the student feels that her understanding of the test is significantly more developed than it was originally, and when she feels like she understands any mistakes she's made up to this point, and how to look out for them in the future, I ask her to try taking the remaining official test in the MSTB. She should treat the experience of taking this sample test as something very close to what she'll encounter on test day. I advise most test-takers to try to observe the one-hour time limit they'll have on test day, but not to worry too much if they end up going over the time limit by 5 minutes or so—at this point, we're still trying to get the student used to the process of taking the test, rather than trying to imitate testing conditions exactly. Our next couple of conversations after she takes the test will focus on her performance: how she was able to apply the ideas we discussed from her first test, how she was able to manage her time, what went well, what can be improved, and so on. We discuss and review *every* question from the second test, not just the ones she missed, so that she's fully aware of all the different ways the questions could be attacked, and able to judge which approaches would work best for her. You can read the relevant walkthroughs in this Black Book for the same kind of analysis.

7. At this point, my students are generally ready for test day. If they want to keep practicing, I typically recommend that they continue to review the practice tests they've done. If they can look at any question and figure out the College Board's motivation for designing the question, and remember the best way for them to attack it, and what elements it contains that they might see in other questions on test day, then they're ready to go. You can simulate this by revisiting the walkthroughs and advice in this Black Book.

So this, in general, is how I recommend that you use the sample material available in the MSTB, and combine it with the advice and strategies in this Black Book.

But my experience has shown that some test-takers just aren't comfortable with the idea of only having two practice tests to work with, even when I assure them that 100 official practice questions are more than enough if they follow the advice I give them and work to understand the test's design, rather than mindlessly drilling as they often would for a math class. So I've put together some ideas you can use if you want to look for practice questions outside the two official Math Level 2 practice tests available in the MSTB. We'll discuss those ideas now.

Looking For Additional Practice Material?
As we just discussed, I firmly believe that the two official College Board tests in the MSTB should provide enough material for you to understand how to attack questions on test day if you combine them with the analysis and discussion in this Black Book. And, as I said in the section of this Black Book titled "Why You'll Also Need A Copy Of The Official SAT Subject Tests in Mathematics Levels 1 & 2 Study Guide," I strongly advise that you work with real practice questions written by the College Board, rather than using fake questions from other companies, because questions from the College Board are the only ones that are guaranteed to follow the same design principles you'll encounter on test day. If you work with

fake questions, you might end up not developing the correct instincts for what the real test will punish or reward.

So if you want more practice material than the two sample tests from the College Board, you'll have to compromise on the desire to work with authentic questions. Fortunately, though, some compromises are smaller, and more acceptable in my opinion, than others.

There are three printed sources that could be worth considering for people who want more practice questions, and I'll explain the advantages and shortcomings of each source now:

1. The practice tests for the Math Level 1 Subject Test in the MSTB

The two practice tests in the MSTB for the Math Level 1 test are actually much more similar to the Level 2 tests than most people think. While they're not identical in terms of subject matter, there's still a significant overlap between them, and most of the rest of the rules, patterns, and strategies in this Black Book apply to the Level 1 test as well. In addition, the number of questions and the time limit are the same. The "curve" for generating the scaled results from the raw score is less generous at the top—for a perfect 800 on the Math Level 1 Test, you can usually only leave one question blank, or even no questions blank on some days, though you can typically leave 5 or 6 questions blank on the Math Level 2 Test and still score a perfect 800 if everything else is correct. But you shouldn't really use questions from a different test to try to draw inferences about your likely score on the Math Level 2 Test anyway. The Level 1 tests are usually the best option for people who are getting ready to take the Math Level 2 Test and want extra practice material.

2. The math sections of the ACT

The math sections on the ACT are also broadly similar to the questions you can be asked on the Math Level 2 SAT Subject Test. Both tests involve similar rules and patterns, both tests depend heavily on details in prompts and answer choices, and both tests involve trigonometry to some extent. Of course, the exact rules and patterns followed by ACT math questions are different from the ones you'll see on the Math Level 2 Test when it comes to specifics, but they're still fairly close in a lot of ways. Another nice benefit is that the number of questions on an ACT math section is close to the number of questions on the Math Level 2 Test, making ACT math a decent option if you want to practice doing 50 consecutive questions and you've already exhausted the Math Level 1 tests from the MSTB.

3. The math sections of the SAT 1 from March 2005 to January 2016

(Please note that the math portion of the SAT 1 underwent a significant change in 2016 that makes it less similar to the Math Level 2 Test than the version of SAT 1 Math that existed from March 2005 to January 2016.)

The good thing about the old SAT 1 Math section, for our purposes, is that it follows many of the same rules and patterns as the Math Level 2 Test, because both tests were designed by the College Board for similar purposes. You'll find that the College Board writes questions on both tests that combine relatively simple ideas in strange ways. The main drawback of SAT 1 math from that time, for our purposes, is that it included less advanced concepts than the Math Level 2 Test does, as I explain in the section of this Black Book called "The Differences (And Similarities) Among The Math Level 2 Test, SAT 1 Math, And ACT Math." Another minor drawback is that the math mini-sections on the old SAT 1 are designed with fewer than 50 questions each, so you'll have to combine multiple mini-sections together if your goal is to practice doing 50 math questions in one session.

I still recommend that you avoid tests written by test prep companies.

For the reasons I discussed in the part of this Black Book called "Why You'll Also Need A Copy Of The Official SAT Subject Tests in Mathematics Levels 1 & 2 Study Guide," I recommend you avoid tests by third-party companies, even if you do decide to branch out from the two Math Level 2 Tests available in the MSTB. The main reason for this is that the sources I list above still involve authentic test questions written by official testing companies for the purpose of generating reliable data from a large number of real test-takers, so they still have certain elements in common with the Math Level 2 Test. If you take a fake test written by a test prep company, you don't even have that level of similarity to rely on.

An important reminder!

Even if you decide to use some of the sources I just mentioned to supplement the Math Level 2 questions available in the MSTB, it's still important to make sure that you come back to the Math Level 2 questions periodically and review them, along with the walkthroughs in this Black Book, so you can make sure you don't lose track of the specific details of this test as you prepare with slightly different questions.

I also want to repeat once more that it should be possible for most students to train effectively for the Math Level 2 Test using only the two Level 2 tests that are available in the MSTB, along with the strategies and walkthroughs in this Black Book. Of course, your approach to this issue is ultimately up to you.

Guessing On The Math Level 2 Test

Before we get any further into the specific tactics and strategies you can use against different kinds of questions, I want to address one of the most important execution issues that most untrained test-takers get completely wrong when it comes to this test.

That issue is the habit of guessing on the test, which is one of the most harmful things you can do if your goal is to score high.

If you've never read any of my other Black Books before, you may be wondering if you're understanding me correctly, because this piece of advice directly contradicts most of the test prep advice available from other sources. So let me say it again, to be totally clear:

If your approach to the Math Level 2 Test involves guessing—even the so-called "educated" guessing we'll discuss below—then you'll have a very hard time maximizing your score. High-scoring test-takers generally don't guess, and guessers generally don't score high.

In a moment, I'll explain what I mean, and then I'll explain what you should do instead. But first, let me walk you through the argument *in favor* of guessing, in case you're not familiar with it, and then I'll explain why that argument is wrong, so you'll be prepared if a mis-informed friend or teacher ever tells you that guessing is a good idea.

The misguided argument for guessing . . .

The most common single piece of test prep advice is the idea that you should guess on a question if you can eliminate at least one answer choice first. The idea is that eliminating answer choices will turn the College Board's wrong answer penalty in your favor.

To understand why this is supposed to be true, we need to understand the wrong answer penalty and the common guessing "strategy" in a little more detail.

On the Math Level 2 Test (and on other SAT Subject Tests at the time of this writing), you get one "raw point" for every question you answer correctly. (These raw points are added up to determine your "raw score," which is later converted to the "scaled score." The scaled score is the three-digit score from 200 to 800 that gets reported to colleges. The raw score goes up to 50, and doesn't get reported to colleges.)

For every question you answer incorrectly, you lose one-quarter of a raw point.

For every question you leave blank, you don't gain any points, and you don't lose any points.

You may be wondering why the College Board takes away a fraction of a point when you're wrong. The reason is that this wrong answer penalty is meant to counteract the effect of random guessing on your score. Since each question has 5 answer choices, and 4 of them are wrong, the probability of randomly selecting a wrong answer is 4/5. So if you guessed randomly on 5 questions, the odds are you'd pick 4 wrong answers, and 1 right answer. With the College Board's wrong answer penalty, you'd lose $\frac{1}{4}$ of a raw point for each of the 4 wrong answers, resulting in an overall loss of 1 whole raw point, exactly off-setting the 1 raw point you could expect to score by guessing randomly on 5 questions.

So this wrong answer penalty is intended to stop test-takers from gaining points through guessing randomly.

But the common guessing strategy says you should guess on a question IF you can eliminate at least one answer choice from consideration, because guessing in this way should allow you to beat the wrong answer penalty, which is fixed at $\frac{1}{4}$ of a raw point, no matter how many choices you're actually guessing from.

If you can guess randomly from 2, 3, or 4 choices instead of 5, then you should be right more often than 1 time in 5 guesses—even though you still only get penalized $\frac{1}{4}$ of a point for your wrong answers.

So, in theory, your score should improve if you guess on questions where you're able to eliminate one or more answer choices from your guessing.

This sounds like perfectly correct math, doesn't it? Guessing from fewer things should lead you to be right more often, even though you're still only being penalized as though you were right less often.

The problem with this idea is that it relies on two assumptions that aren't actually correct. Let's discuss them now.

. . . and why there's no such thing as reliable educated guessing on this test

As we just saw, the traditional guessing advice makes mathematical sense in theory.

But there's a difference between theory and practice in this case. The traditional guessing strategy makes two critical assumptions, and it turns out both assumptions are wrong:

1. The answer choices you eliminate are assumed to be wrong. (If, on the other hand, you mistakenly eliminate the right answer from consideration, then your chance of guessing correctly on that question is zero.)

2. Your guesses are assumed to be random. (But if your guess isn't random, then probability goes out the window, and the approach has no mathematical basis.)

Let's explore the first assumption. It's important to realize that the College Board deliberately creates most of the wrong answers on the test so that they'll appeal to people who don't fully understand a question, or who think they understand it but don't check their work carefully. As we discussed in the section of this Black Book on the secrets of the test, the questions you'll see on test day are likely to seem strange in a lot of ways, and to be much more detail-oriented than most test-takers realize. Under these circumstances, it actually happens quite frequently that test-takers accidentally "rule out" answers choices that are really correct, because the issue that keeps them from answering the question correctly in the first place is also the issue that causes them to be wrong when they try to rule out answer choices. And every time you accidentally eliminate the correct answer before you guess, your chance of randomly picking the right answer drops to zero.

Now, let's talk about the second assumption, which is that the guessing happens randomly. Be honest with yourself—have you ever *randomly* picked an answer choice on a multiple choice question? Guessing randomly means exercising no judgment at all, and making no attempt to consider any meaning in the question whatsoever. It means picking randomly from the remaining letters every time, no matter what happens. In my experience, nobody actually does this for every single question they guess on.

Instead, here's what most people actually do when they say they're using the guessing strategy. They start out by reading the question and realizing they don't know the answer. Then they decide they sort of have a feeling that one of the answer choices is more likely to be right, even though they've admitted that they don't know what's going on in the question. So they find some reason to justify eliminating some of the other answer choices, and then they mark the choice they liked from the beginning.

Of course, there's nothing random about answering questions in this way. It just boils down to picking an answer choice you like, even when you don't know how to answer the question. And remember, again, that the wrong answer choices on the test are often specifically designed so that somebody who understands the question a little bit—but not completely—will want to pick them. So the odds are good that when you do this kind of "educated" guessing, you're really doing exactly what the College Board wants you to do: you're talking yourself into picking the wrong answer on a question you don't understand, and you're lowering your raw score by a fraction of a point each time you do it.

Further evidence against "educated" guessing

As I mentioned earlier, you won't find people who make a habit out of guessing on the test and still score high, and now you know why.

But there's more evidence to suggest that the traditional guessing approach is a bad idea. Consider the fact that the College Board itself *actually advises you to guess* in the MSTB if you feel you can eliminate any of the answer choices. That might sound like a reason to try guessing, but think about it for a minute. The College Board doesn't want you to benefit from guessing—that's the whole reason there's a wrong answer penalty in the first place. So it makes no sense that the College Board would give people a little trick for getting around its own wrong answer penalty, so they could score higher than they otherwise would. If the College Board really believed this type of guessing were effective, it would make more sense to keep quiet about the whole thing. (As we'll discuss later in this Black Book, the College Board does seem to keep quiet about many other aspects of test design that actually do give an advantage to people who notice them.)

So what should you do if you don't guess?

So far we've talked about what happens when you answer correctly, and when you answer incorrectly. But there's one option we haven't covered: leaving a question blank.

When you leave a question blank, you don't gain or lose any raw points. So you should leave a question blank when you don't know the answer—that stops you from losing the hard-earned raw points you get from the answers you do know.

Consider the score conversion table on page 145 of the MSTB. We can see from the table that if we answered 39 questions correctly on this test and left the remaining 11 questions blank, we'd get a 750 on the test. But if we had answered the same number of questions correctly and got the other 11 wrong (instead of leaving them blank), we'd end up with only a 710. That's a 40-point drop in our score for not having the discipline to leave questions blank when we aren't sure of the answers. (Of course, this is only one example—conversion tables change slightly on each test date, and different regions of the scoring conversion table can vary in how sensitive they are to gaining or losing a raw point. The idea is that the difference between a wrong answer and a blank question adds up quickly over the course of the test.)

As I said before, people generally don't guess their way to high scores, just like people generally don't gamble their way into being wealthy. Protect your hard-earned points. Don't lose them by taking chances on questions you don't understand well enough to answer correctly.

Of course, in addition to not losing points from guessing anymore, I'm also going to teach you how to gain more raw points in the first place by understanding the test better. So I don't want you to think that my advice stops at leaving things blank—I'm just saying right here that leaving things blank is preferable to getting them wrong and losing points. We'll talk about how you earn more points in just a little while. And this leads me to my next topic, which is that there's a hidden cost of guessing that goes beyond the raw points it can cost you.

Other drawbacks to guessing . . .

There's another very important concept at work here that has to do with your mindset when you approach the test.

In order to do well on this test, it's critical to understand each of these concepts:

1. Each question has EXACTLY one correct answer.

2. The correct answer to each question is completely correct, and the wrong answers are completely wrong[2].

3. You, personally, can use the information provided in the question to find the correct answer with total certainty.

4. If you fail to find the correct answer to a given question, it's not because the question is vague or poorly written, as might happen in a math class. It's just because you didn't manage to find the solution.

But the "guessing" approach gives you the wrong attitude about the test, because it encourages you to view the test in shades of grey, when the test is actually very black-and-white.

The moment when you get stuck trying to figure out a question is the moment you should step back, carefully read the question and answer choices again, and try to find another perspective or angle of attack—or considering skipping the question for the time being.

Unfortunately, most untrained test-takers treat the whole test as though it's open to interpretation and subjectivity, even though it's a multiple-choice math test. They never feel totally certain on anything; instead, they view each question as an opportunity to make a guess with varying degrees of certainty. This makes success on the test practically impossible.

Of course, when you do get really stuck on test day (which happens to all of us at least once, because nobody's perfect), you should skip the question and move on to something else for the time being; you can always come back to the challenging question later if you have time. But, especially during your training, you should avoid the urge to "just guess" and be done with a hard question.

---

[2] I realize that some official test questions are occasionally successfully challenged for being defective, and the College Board removes them from scoring consideration. But this happens so rarely that it's not worth thinking about during your training or on test day. For our purposes, we have to treat every question as though it's perfectly valid, because having this mindset is the only way we can move through the questions efficiently and with certainty, maximizing our results.

Page 43

Time Management On Test Day

In this section, I'll lay out the important aspects of managing your time on test day; for a discussion of how time management applies to your preparation, see the section of this Black Book called "How To Train For The SAT Subject Test In Mathematics Level 2."

I recommend you read this section carefully, even if you feel like you don't need help with time management right now. Improving your time management on test day is one of the fastest and easiest ways to raise your score. My experience with students has shown me that everyone can improve their time management to some degree, no matter how good they think they already are when it comes to that aspect of testing performance.

We'll start out by discussing a couple of key underlying concepts to keep in mind as you make decisions on test day. Then we'll go over the general process I recommend you follow on test day in order to decide which question you should be answering at any given time. Finally, we'll discuss some other aspects of time management that might still be an issue after you've tried to implement everything else.

Key concepts

Remember that time is an investment.

As we discussed in the section of this Black Book called "How To Train For The SAT Subject Test In Mathematics Level 2," we always want to spend our time in the ways that are most likely to increase our raw score in the most efficient way possible. For example, we don't want to spend 90 seconds on a question that seems difficult to us if we could have spent those 90 seconds correctly answering 2 or 3 questions that seem easier to us. If we have time to go back and try the harder question later, that's great—but we should take care of the ones we find easier first.

Working on a question and leaving it blank is a waste of time . . . but getting a question wrong is an even bigger waste of time.

Since our goal is to maximize the number of points we score on the test, it's a bad idea to invest our time in questions that we ultimately leave blank—or, worse, get wrong—because those questions don't help us increase the number of points we get on the test (remember that questions we leave blank don't add any points to our score, and questions that we miss will lower the raw score).

At the same time, if we end up working hard on a question but we still don't feel confident in the answer, our best option AT THAT POINT IN THE PROCESS is to leave the question blank, rather than marking an answer choice that's probably going to be wrong (if the choice were correct, you'd probably be confident it was correct after putting in all that work). Remember that the College Board imposes a wrong answer penalty on this test (at the time of this writing), which means that you'll lose one-quarter of a raw point for marking a wrong answer on the test. In other words, if you imagine a set of 5 questions in which you answer 1 question correctly and 4 questions incorrectly, your overall score is exactly the same as if you'd left all 5 questions blank—which means that all the time you spent on answering those 5 questions was wasted, even though you got one right, because the wrong answers on the other ones undid the right answer you had. So remember that it's never a good idea to mark an answer choice unless you're sure it's right—even if you've spent more time on a given question than you'd like.

Catching and fixing a mistake is the most valuable thing you can do.

This may sound strange, but catching and fixing a mistake you've already made is actually more valuable than answering a blank question correctly, in terms of the impact on your final score.

Like many of the most intelligent time-management strategies for taking the Math Level 2 Test, this one is a result of the College Board's wrong answer penalty (which, again, subtracts one-quarter of a raw point from your raw score before the raw score is converted to a scaled score of 200-800). It may sound counter-intuitive at first, but let's think about it:

- Every wrong answer you submit impacts your raw score by -0.25 raw points.

- Every correct answer you submit impacts your raw score by +1 raw point.

- Every blank question you submit has no impact on your raw score.

- Submitting one wrong answer and one right answer has a net effect of gaining 0.75 raw points (because 1 raw point plus -0.25 raw points is a net of 0.75 raw points).

- Changing a wrong answer to a correct answer and leaving another question blank has a net effect of gaining 1.25 raw points (because you keep yourself from submitting the wrong answer that would have cost you 0.25 raw points, and you also submit an answer that earns you 1 raw point).

So catching and fixing a mistake is actually more valuable than leaving the mistake in place and answering another question correctly. (Of course, the best course of action is to avoid making mistakes in the first place, as we discuss throughout this Black Book.)

All of this leads to the following conclusions:

- We want to invest time in questions that we'll be able to answer correctly.

- We want to avoid working on questions that we'll end up having to leave blank.

- If we're not sure about an answer, we should leave the question blank, no matter how much time we've invested in it (for more on leaving questions blank, see the section of this Black Book called "Guessing On The Math Level 2 Test.")

Now that we've discussed these key ideas underlying time management, let's talk about some of the ways we can apply them practically.

Answer questions in the order you choose, not in the order they're presented.

Most untrained test-takers answer questions in the order that the College Board chooses to present them, instead of prioritizing the questions they find easier. This is almost always a bad idea—sticking to the College Board's order can't possibly help your score, and the only way it could fail to hurt your score is if you're so good at this test that you know you'll finish every question quickly and correctly, in which case you wouldn't need to be reading this Black Book in the first place.

So instead of just accepting the order that the College Board chooses for its questions, we should decide on our own whether to answer each question as we first encounter it, or skip it for the moment. To help us make that decision, we should keep in mind the fundamentals of time management:

- Every question has the same overall impact on your score.

- Working on a question and leaving it blank is a waste of time.

- Getting a question wrong is an even bigger waste of time.

- Catching and fixing a mistake is the most valuable thing you can do.

When we first come to a question, we shouldn't assume that we have to try to answer it right away. We're the ones who decide what we'll work on next, not the College Board. Instead of just diving right in and trying to find a solution, we should read the question and decide quickly if we think we'll be able to find the correct answer with total confidence in a fairly short time. My general rule of thumb is that I give myself 10 seconds to see if I can figure out how to find a solution that I can execute in 30 seconds or less. In other words, I spend 10 seconds reading through the question and trying to figure out how I could solve it in under 30 seconds. If 10 seconds have gone by and I still have no idea how to attack the question, I skip it for the time being. I can always come back to it later if I want to, but it's silly to invest more time in it now, when I could be working on other questions that will probably be easier for me. I always have to keep in mind that every question has the same impact on my score, so I should ideally be working on the easiest unanswered question at any given moment.

All of this leads to the next idea, which is VERY important, and which most untrained test-takers don't seem to realize.

Approach the test in multiple passes.

I've mentioned the idea of skipping questions if we don't think we'd be able to answer them with certainty, but there's a bit more to this idea than we've discussed so far.

A trained test-taker should approach the Math Level 2 Test with the expectation of doing at least three or four passes through the test. This allows us to be fairly certain that we're not wasting time on questions that are more challenging for us when we could be scoring points on easier questions that we haven't seen yet.

Here's the basic idea—of course, you should feel free to modify this as you see fit, but this is roughly how I divide up the passes when I take a standardized test:

First pass: low-hanging fruit and information-gathering

I have two primary goals in mind the first time I go through the test:

1. I want to mark down correct answers for all the questions I feel I can work through pretty quickly and easily.

2. I want to get an idea of what the harder questions look like.

I start the first pass by reading the first question on the test. If I can figure out a quick, easy way to attack the question and find the answer, then I do that—making EXTREMELY sure, as always, that I don't take the question for granted and fall for some kind of trick that causes me to mark the wrong answer. If I've looked at the first question for 10 seconds or so and I still don't feel like I have an idea of how to answer the question by following the Math Path (which is a way of approaching SAT Math 2 questions that we'll discuss later), then I skip it. I can always come back to it in a later pass if I want.

After I handle the first question, either by finding the answer quickly and easily or by deciding to skip it for the moment, I go on to the second question, and repeat the process: if I think I can answer with total certainty by working on the question for 30 seconds or less, then I do; if not, I skip it and save it for later.

I repeat this process until I've gone through every question on the test.

After the first pass, I've marked correct answers to all the questions that seemed pretty easy to me . . . and I've also put my eyes on *every single question on the test*, even if it was only to glance at the question and decide quickly that it was something that would require more time than I wanted to spend on my first pass.

I'm going to use my knowledge of the various questions on the test on the next pass.

Second pass: questions that require a little more thought

Keeping in mind what I saw during my first pass, I go back to the beginning of the test booklet and find the first question that I skipped during my first pass. I read it a bit more carefully and apply the Math Path a bit more deliberately than I might have done on my first pass, when I was just trying to answer the questions whose solutions seemed obvious to me.

Just like on the first pass, I don't let myself get too bogged down on any question; it's just that, now, I'm more willing to invest a few extra seconds trying to figure out how to approach a question. (Notice that I'm NOT willing to spend several minutes doing calculations for a single question, or anything like that, because I know that the College Board never sets up a question in a way that would require me to do calculations for several minutes. I'm willing to spend more time analyzing the wording of a question, the relationships among the answer choices, and the other kinds of things we consider as part of the Math Path, but I still know that when I figure out how to execute a solution, that solution will usually take less than 30 seconds per question.)

Unlike my first pass, though, I have some idea of what the other questions on the test look like when I go through my second pass, and I use that information to help me decide which questions I should skip again, and which of the remaining questions seem easier to me. I let that knowledge guide me.

I always keep in mind that my goal at any given moment is to invest my time in the activities that are most likely to result in getting me more raw points, which generally means answering the remaining questions that seem easiest to me, and making sure I don't make any careless errors.

When I've reached the end of my second pass, the only questions left unanswered are the ones that seem the most challenging, because I've now looked through the whole test twice and still decided not to attack those questions yet. Now it's time for the third pass.

Third pass: remaining upbeat and remembering my training

Most untrained test-takers would be very discouraged at the thought of focusing on the questions that seemed hardest initially, but we know two things that untrained test-takers don't know:

1. The College Board generally makes questions seem challenging by combining basic concepts in weird ways, not by writing questions that require us to know obscure formulas or do complicated calculations.

2. On most days we can leave 5 or more questions blank and still score a perfect 800 if everything else is answered correctly. This means we never need to worry about the 5 or 6 questions on the test that seem hardest to us, as long as we're careful to answer all the other questions correctly.

So on the third pass through the test, we need to keep in mind that our goal is basically to identify the unanswered questions that we're most likely to be able to answer correctly with a little extra attention and reflection. In general, these will be the questions that contain words and concepts we feel like we're familiar with, as opposed to questions that include phrases we may not recognize—but it's important to keep in mind that you'll sometimes find you can work out the meaning of an unknown phrase if you stay calm and analyze the parts of the question that make sense to you. (We'll see examples of this in the walkthroughs later in this Black Book, such as the walkthrough for question 18 on page 128 of the MSTB.)

By the time you start this third pass, you're likely to have used up half of your allotted time on the test, or maybe even three-quarters of it, or more. You may only have enough time to expect to answer 10 or fewer additional questions, so it's especially important to tackle the remaining questions in the order that you want. If you feel like the last question on the test is likely to be the easiest remaining question to figure out, then start there. Start this pass on the question that seems like the one that's most likely to result in a correct answer in the shortest possible time, and then go on to the question that seems the next most likely to result in a right answer in the shortest possible time, and so on.

At some point, you may be ready for a fourth pass, either because you've answered all the questions on the test, or you've decided that there are some questions on the test you shouldn't even attempt, because you don't think you'll be able to figure them out in the remaining time. This is when we might consider shifting our focus a little bit.

Fourth pass: review and clean-up

I usually start my last pass through the test when I've answered all the questions that I think I can answer with certainty, or when there are about 5 or 10 minutes left, whichever comes first.

On this last pass, my goal is to go quickly back through all the work I've done and make sure that I haven't made any mistakes in the answers that I marked. I check for all the little kinds of mistakes that the College Board likes to trick us into—stuff like finding sine instead of cosine, forgetting to multiply by negative 1 when I should, finding perimeter instead of area, and so on.

I often like to check my work by seeing if I can figure out the kinds of mistakes the College Board was trying to anticipate with the wrong answers that it set out. If I can do that for a particular question, I can usually be pretty sure I've answered it correctly.

Of course, I've also been very careful to avoid mistakes during the other passes, so this last pass usually doesn't turn up too many mistakes. But I'm always on the lookout for them, because I always remember that one of the College Board's main goals in writing the test is to trick me into answering questions incorrectly even when I think I understand what they're asking. I never forget that rigorous attention to detail is the main thing that separates top-scoring test-takers from everybody else—not advanced math knowledge!

Make it your own and remember what counts.

As I mentioned earlier, you should feel free to modify this idea of approaching the test in passes, and make it your own. The key thing to keep in mind is that you should always be investing your time in the activities that are most likely to improve your score, instead of mindlessly tackling whatever the College Board decides to throw at you next.

Below, I'd like to address a few other important considerations when you approach the test in this way.

Don't mis-bubble the answer sheet!

As you're skipping questions and working in passes like this, it's important to make sure that the answers you do fill in are marked in the proper place on your answer sheet. For example, if you skip question 17 to work on question 18, make sure that you mark the answer for 18 next to the 18 on your answer sheet—not next to the 17. This idea of working in passes will save you a lot of time and frustration if you do it right, but if you end up having to erase a bunch of answers and re-grid them, you'll undo a lot of the benefits you've gotten. So pay attention, and make sure you're always marking each answer next to the right number.

Remember that you REALLY don't need to answer all the questions.

As we've discussed elsewhere, it's important to keep in mind that the College Board's scoring process allows us to skip roughly 5 or 6 questions per test and still get a "perfect" 800 on the test, assuming we answer all the other questions correctly. (The actual number of questions or raw points necessary to achieve a scaled score of 800 varies a little from test to test, as part of the College Board's standardization process.) So we really don't need to attempt every question on the test, no matter what score we need, because it's possible to get a perfect score on the test while only getting about 90% of the questions right, assuming we leave the other questions blank. (For more on the issue of leaving questions blank, see the section of this Black Book called "Guessing On The Math Level 2 Test.") This is especially important to keep in mind as you're reaching your final passes, because there will probably be at least a question or two that you can't figure out before time runs out—and, again, there's nothing wrong with that, because you don't need to answer every question correctly to get a perfect score.

It's never a good idea to mark a wrong answer, no matter how little time is left.

For some reason, some test-takers lose their nerve as the test draws to a close, and feel like they should fill in their best guesses on the questions that are still blank. This is a bad idea, and it comes from panicking and forgetting their training. We always have to remember the way the College Board writes these questions: the correct answers are clear and unambiguous *if you understand how the question works*, but many questions are set up to trick a confused test-taker into marking a wrong answer, which is why most test-takers who make a habit of guessing will do poorly on the test. Because of the College Board's wrong answer penalty on this test, it's better to leave a question blank than to mark an answer when you're not certain.

Again, for more on the issues related to leaving questions blank, take a look at the part of this Black Book called "Guessing On The Math Level 2 Test."

Don't lose track of time.

As we've discussed, the idea of approaching the test in passes is an essential part of optimal test-taking, because it allows us to make sure we invest our time on the questions that are easiest for us. But we still have to make sure we move through each pass with an appropriate sense of urgency. Sometimes, finishing a pass can make us feel like we're done with the test overall, because we find ourselves considering how to answer the last few questions of the test much earlier than untrained test-takers will see them. But it's important to remember that we're not trying to answer every question on the test when we complete a pass! We're just looking for the easiest remaining questions on each pass, even though it might feel like we're completing the test multiple times. So we can't take breaks during passes or between passes, even though it might be tempting to pause and reflect sometimes. When I finish one pass, I go right back to the questions that are still unanswered and start the next pass, and I repeat this process until time is called—even after I've finished answering the questions I'm going to answer, I can keep re-checking my work, because I know how important it is to make sure I avoid mistakes on this test.

Mistakes will undo your hard work. Don't make them.

You've probably noticed by now that I constantly remind you of the importance of avoiding small mistakes. This is because every wrong answer costs you in two ways:

1. You lose the time you invested in the question, which you could have invested in a question you would have answered correctly.

2. You lose one-quarter of a raw point for every wrong answer that you mark.

So when you're going through your passes, you want to make sure to remain thorough and diligent on the questions that you answer, because it doesn't help you to work on a question and get it wrong.

Similarly, you should take your final review passes seriously, because correcting a question that you'd previously marked wrong has an even bigger net effect on your score than leaving the mistake in place and marking a correct answer on a blank question.

Other Time-Management Issues

Up until now, we've been discussing general time-management strategies that apply to all trained test-takers. But you may still feel that you have other concerns when it comes to timing, and we'll address some of those now.

Actually, a lot of test-takers worry about having enough time on the Math Level 2 Test, because they're used to having timing issues on regular high school math tests, and they don't know that high school tests tend to be slower, more methodical, and more repetitive than the kinds of questions we see on the Math Level 2 Test. Then these test-takers open up their booklets on test day, and find a lot of questions that look more complicated and advanced than they actually are. And, on top of that, they think they need to answer 50 of these difficult questions in roughly one minute per question, and they start to panic . . . none of which helps with their time-management issues.

But my first piece of advice for a student in this position is to put the issue aside until after you learn about everything else in this Black Book. You might very well find that you no longer have any issues with time management after you adopt my approach to the Math Level 2 Test.

In most situations, test-takers who worry about time are approaching the test the wrong way in the first place. So they don't need to get quicker at the old approach—instead, they need to start using a method that's more efficient and, therefore, inherently faster. I'll teach you this kind of efficient approach in this Black Book. This kind of approach takes less time and generally produces better results than the traditional approach that most untrained test-takers will use.

So, again, the first thing I'd recommend you do is ignore your timing issues at the beginning of your preparation, and see if they go away on their own as you come to understand how the test really works. They often do.

If they don't go away, though, there's still plenty of stuff we can work on. Read on.

Remember that you don't need to answer every question.

As we've discussed several times now, it's possible to skip 5 questions or so on each test and still get a "perfect" 800 if all the other questions are answered correctly, because of the College Board's scoring process. As you continue to work on your time management, remember that the goal isn't necessarily to answer every question on the test; in fact, it's perfectly normal for people who get a perfect score to find that they can't answer a few questions in the allotted time. There's nothing wrong with having some blanks on your answer sheet at the end of the test.

You may need to work on deciding to skip questions faster.

If you're using the multiple-pass approach that I described earlier in this section, but still having difficulties with time, you may need to make a conscious effort to get better at recognizing when to skip a question during a pass. My general recommendation is that students should move on to the next question if ten seconds have gone by and they still can't figure out how to approach the question they're looking at. You may want to play around with trying to make that decision even faster.

(To be clear, I don't try to *solve* the question in ten seconds. I'm just saying that I try to figure out what my approach is going to be within the first ten seconds of reading a question. For example, it might take me ten seconds to read a question, look at the answer choices, and think "I could find the answer by graphing each answer choice and comparing it to the text in the prompt." I haven't actually found the answer yet, but I know how to approach the question, and would probably do so right then, rather than saving the question for a later pass. This is an important distinction.)

If I can't see how I'm going to approach a question within the first ten seconds of reading it, I immediately forget about that question for the time being, and go on to the next one. I recommend you do the same thing. Remember that our goal is to invest our time in the easiest questions available.

Everyone runs into questions that just don't "click." This is a completely normal part of taking a standardized test, and you need to train yourself to act accordingly.

So it's important to learn to skip questions as soon as you realize that you're not able to work productively on them. There's no shame in it—in fact, skipping questions like this is a major part of smart, disciplined test-taking.

Don't think about the average time per question.

A lot of untrained test-takers try to maintain a constant pace throughout the test. These test-takers usually figure that the test is an hour long and has 50 questions, so they should plan on spending a little more than a minute on each question. Then, as they go through the test, if they find a question they can answer quickly, they slow down a little so that the question still takes them roughly a minute; if they find a question that seems harder for them, they panic and rush because they still want to try to get it done in a minute.

This approach might make sense if most of the questions on the test were similar to one another in terms of subject matter and complexity, but they aren't. Some questions will naturally take you 10 or 15 seconds to figure out with total certainty (especially as you get better at implementing the strategies in this Black Book, as you'll see in the question walkthroughs later on). In these situations, it would be silly to spend forty or fifty extra seconds once you've checked your solution and made sure you're right. On the other hand, sometimes you'll misunderstand a question, or keep making a small mistake that causes you not to arrive at any of the answer choices, or you'll have some other issue on a question that causes you to skip it twice and then finally do a more time-consuming backsolving approach, and you'll end up needing to spend two minutes or more on one question. For these kinds of questions, it makes no sense to try to cram all of that thinking into an arbitrary one-minute window.

So the smart way to approach the test is to realize that some questions take much less than a minute, and some questions might take you more than a minute. You should try to handle every question as quickly as you can without sacrificing accuracy—whether that means solving it on your current pass, saving it for later, or deciding to skip it altogether. If you keep this attitude, you'll find that the questions you answer quickly will help you have enough time to devote extra energy to the occasional question that stumps you in the later passes.

Analyze and adjust your performance.

If you're still having timing issues, you may need to do some analysis on the specific questions that are slowing you down. When you practice, make a mark next to questions that take you a lot of time. Go back to them after your practice session is over, and try to identify the elements they have in common that made them take so long. Every test-taker has different triggers that might cause him to spend more time than necessary on some questions, and your goal is to figure out what causes it to happen to you. You might think about issues like the following, just as examples:

- Do you have trouble reading the prompt carefully if it involves more than two or three lines of text?

- Do you re-check work on your calculator more than necessary because you're worried that you'll enter something incorrectly?

- Do you panic when questions ask about trig concepts?

Try to pinpoint the kinds of things that generally slow you down. Then do some untimed review of relevant practice questions from the College Board, along with the walkthroughs from this Black Book, and really analyze and break down the aspect of solving that question that takes you the most time. Keep in mind what you've learned when you do your next timed practice, and try to modify the behavior that was costing you extra time before.

Breaking down your performance like this, and thinking about how you react to different elements of official practice questions from the College Board, can give you some insights into where you should focus as you try to increase your speed. For example, if you find that certain calculations take a lot of time for you to do by hand, consider using your calculator a little more; if you find that you're frequently re-reading long blocks of text in word problems, focus on trying to absorb all the necessary information in one or two tries. You'll find that identifying the causes of your issues as precisely as you possibly can will make it a lot easier to figure out likely solutions to your problems.

Remember that the College Board rewards us for finding informal solutions.

Sometimes, a test-taker will waste time unnecessarily writing out extra steps to a solution as though she were going to submit the work to a teacher, forgetting that the College Board will only grade her on the bubbles she fills in on the answer sheet. In fact, as we'll see in the walkthroughs in this Black Book, the fastest solutions to many questions don't involve formulas, or even written solutions at all.

If you find yourself writing out a lot of steps for most questions, then give yourself permission to be more efficient, and focus on finding answers without doing so much writing. As we'll discuss in more detail later on, these solutions might involve analyzing the answer choices as part of the question, using a calculator, noticing a shortcut that's possible because of a diagram, and so on.

Consider petitioning the College Board for accommodations.

If you've been working on implementing the ideas in this Black Book, and particularly in this section, but you're still feeling totally overwhelmed by the time limit on the test, then you may want to consider contacting the College Board for special timing accommodations. The requirements of the conditions for getting these accommodations can change at any time (as can the nature of the accommodations themselves), so I won't mention the current ones right here. If you're interested in more information on these accommodations, you can look them up on the Internet, or ask a teacher or guidance counselor for advice.

The Differences (And Similarities) Between The Math Level 2 Test, SAT 1 Math, And ACT Math

If you're preparing to take the Math Level 2 Test, I'm guessing you're familiar with at least one other standardized math test, whether it's the math section of the SAT 1 or of the ACT (or of both).

You may be wondering what the difference is between the Math Level 2 Test and the other tests. What's the point of creating a Math Level 1 Test and a Math Level 2 Test if the regular SAT 1 and ACT already test math?

As it turns out, the style of questions on the Math Level 2 Test is fundamentally the same as the style of many questions on the Math section of the SAT 1—which, in turn, is actually pretty similar to the math section of the ACT. The topics will be presented in a similar way, there will be similar patterns in the answer choices and diagrams, and so on.

If you already do well on the math sections of the ACT and/or the SAT 1, you should have a good foundation to build on for the Math Level 2 Test. On the other hand, if you struggle with those other math sections, you should expect to run into some of the same challenges on this test. But don't worry too much about any struggles with other math sections, especially if you're not already familiar with my general approach to the ACT and the SAT 1. Most test-takers simply approach those tests with the wrong mindset, and they find that everything makes a lot more sense once they learn how the test really works.

But there are a few other elements of the SAT Math Level 2 exam that aren't really reflected in the math sections of other tests. (Of course, we'll cover *all* the elements of the Math Level 2 Test in this Black Book—right now, I'm just interested in discussing the differences between this test and other standardized math tests you might have taken recently.)

You should use a graphing calculator more

One pretty big difference between the Math Level 2 Test and the other two tests is that a graphing calculator plays a significantly larger role on this test. You'll see a fair number of Math Level 2 questions on test day that require the use of a graphing calculator, and several that are much, much easier if you use one.

This isn't because questions on the Math Level 2 are harder, necessarily; it's just that Math Level 2 questions sometimes involve decimal approximations of things like the sine or cosine of an angle, or they might ask you about the behavior of a graph in a way that you don't really see on the other tests. In short, having a graphing calculator and knowing how to use it will make your experience on this test much, much better. I wouldn't think of taking the test without one.

(For more on calculators, see the section of this Black Book called "Your Calculator For The Math Level 2 Test," as well as the section on Backsolving; also look at the question walkthroughs for several examples of solutions that make use of calculators.)

Slightly more advanced subject matter

Another difference between this test and the math sections of the ACT and SAT 1 is that the Math Level 2 Test focuses on some different subject matter, although much of the subject matter overlaps among the three tests.

Concepts like trigonometry, logarithms, and functions are tested more rigorously on the Math Level 2 Test than on the SAT 1 and the ACT. Many test-takers think of these as advanced topics, but we'll see that the College Board tests them in ways that are actually pretty simple and straightforward if we know the basic concepts related to those areas of math.

The Math Level 2 Test can include several other areas of math that untrained test-takers might think of as advanced, such as complex numbers, matrices, and so on. But, again, you'll see that the test deals with those areas in a relatively basic way—and, on top of that, they come up relatively infrequently.

(We've talked about this already, and we'll get into it more later, but I want to remind you that when I say something is covered in a "basic way," I don't mean that the College Board comes right out and directly asks for basic information. We have to remember that the College Board makes this test challenging by asking about basic concepts in ways that we're not used to seeing. The difficulty generally comes from having to figure out what the question is asking and which concepts are being combined, not from having to understand advanced or obscure math concepts, or apply complicated formulas.)

So this is a subject test that sometimes involves more "advanced" math than we'd find on the SAT 1 or the ACT—but the design of this test is broadly similar to the design of the math sections on the SAT 1 and the ACT. We still expect to see most of the same kinds of patterns and the same unusual presentation of math concepts, and we'll see that the Math subject tests still reward a different overall approach from the approach that gets rewarded in math classes.

You have more time per question than on the ACT, less time per question than on the SAT 1, and fewer questions overall than on either test

The Math Level 2 Test gives you 50 questions in an hour. The ACT, on the other hand, gives you 60 questions in an hour, while the two SAT 1 Math sections give you a total of 58 questions in 80 minutes.

But I'd recommend you not worry too much about time management unless you absolutely have to, because most trained test-takers should find that they have plenty of time no matter which of those three tests they're taking. I just wanted you to know that the timing on this test is really no worse than it is for the other tests—in fact, you could make an argument that the Math Level 2 Test offers the most favorable combination of the number of questions and the amount of time allotted. (I realize that this kind of analysis doesn't take into account the difficulty levels and subject matter of the different tests, but I'd also argue that those apparent differences will disappear to a large extent as you come to understand what all of these tests actually reward.)

(For more on dealing with timing issues, please see the section of this Black Book called "Time Management On Test Day.")

Your Calculator For The Math Level 2 Test

As I've already mentioned, one of the primary challenges of the Math Level 2 Test is to read carefully and then set up clever, efficient solutions that exploit the weaknesses in the test's design . . . but you'll sometimes find that executing those solutions requires a calculator. For example, you probably can't find the sine of 37° or the natural log of 6.91 in your head, but these are the kinds of calculations you might have to do for *some* questions on the Math Level 2 Test (definitely not for every question, but for some).

Beyond that, there are questions that could be solved without a calculator, but that are much easier and faster to solve with a calculator—and not just because calculators are fast at calculating, but because the calculator can sometimes provide us with another way of looking at a question altogether. For example, we'll often find that a question about the behavior of a function or a curve has an obvious answer if we use a calculator's graphing function, or that a trig question can be answered much more easily if we evaluate expressions in the answer choices, and so on. (We'll see concrete examples of these kinds of solutions later in this Black Book.)

So your calculator will need to play a larger role in your attack on the Math Level 2 Test than it would on other tests. There are certain things that your calculator *must* be able to do in order for you to get the full benefit of using a calculator on test day.

Beyond the standard functions of all calculators, your calculator should be able to do the following:

- find the values of trigonometric functions in both radian mode and degree mode
- find the values of inverse trigonometric functions in both radian mode and degree mode
- find the common log (log) and natural log (ln) of a number
- graph functions
- find the square root or cube root of a number
- raise a number to a given exponent

(Incidentally, you can find the College Board's rules for calculators on the Math Level 2 Test on page 19 of the MSTB.)

One type of question that responds very well to graphing

You've probably had math teachers who asked you to graph functions, or who asked you to identify features of a function like its period or domain. Teachers generally don't let you use a graphing calculator for those kinds of tasks, because a graphing calculator makes them too easy. Your teacher wants you to understand how functions actually work, but a graphing calculator makes it possible to graph a function and identify its features without having any real idea of the underlying math.

Many untrained test-takers get so used to working out these kinds of graph-related questions with a pencil in class that they forget they're allowed to use their calculators when they take the Math Level 2 Test. As a result, they end up spending unnecessary time and energy on questions about graphs when they could often just read the answer right off their calculator screens instead.

So, as a general rule, I always advise my students to answer any question about the behavior or features of the graph of a function by using their calculators to graph the function, and then consulting the graph directly to find the correct answer. This approach is faster and easier than trying to work out an answer on your own, and far less likely to result in a mistake.

For a few examples of real Math Level 2 Test questions that can be attacked with this graphing approach, please see the walkthroughs in this Black book for the following questions from the MSTB, among others:

- Page 133, Question 31

- Page 133, Question 33

- Page 136, Question 40

Where to get specific instructions for your specific calculator
Of course, it's one thing to own a calculator with the functions that will be necessary for the test, and another thing for you to know how to operate the calculator properly, so you can get it to do what you need. So you need to be comfortable with using your calculator to do all the tasks in the list above.

Every model of graphing calculator is a little different, so I won't be training you on your specific calculator in this Black Book. But there are three reasons not to worry too much if you're not feeling like a whiz at the calculator at this moment:

1. The most important reason not to worry over your calculator skills is that you'll find the best approach to the Math Level 2 Test doesn't actually require fancy calculator techniques, formulas, or programming. In fact, I often find that people who struggle with the test are trying too hard to use their calculators in places where the calculator isn't really relevant. As you'll see later on in this Black Book, when we get to the walkthroughs of real test questions, your calculator use is likely to be limited to relatively basic things like graphing functions, finding trig values like sine, and so on. And that leads me to the next reason . . .

2. You'll find that your math classes have probably already given you the calculator skills you'll need for the Math Level 2 Test. As you'll see throughout this Black Book, the key skills for doing well on this test are related to using basic ideas in new ways without making mistakes, and that still applies when it comes to calculator usage. The kinds of calculator issues that might trip you up on this test are things like accidentally using radian mode instead of degree mode, as opposed to being able to use or modify some kind of advanced program or something.

3. Finally, if you do discover during your practice that you need to learn a new calculator technique, you can always go to the Internet and search for a quick article or video that explains what you need. The best way to do this is usually by searching the model of your calculator and then a short description of what you need help with, such as "TI-84 graph a function" or "Casio FX-9750GII find arcsin," and so on.

A use for your calculator besides calculating . . .
As you probably know, the graphing calculators that the College Board encourages you to use have memory functions that allow a user to store information. This memory capacity is usually used for

storing programs, but it can also be used to store a "program" of notes that you might want to refer to while you take your test. In other words, it's possible to store any information you want in your calculator before test day, and then access that information while you're taking the test.

Before I go any further into this discussion, I want to make it very clear that what I'm about to suggest is fully consistent with the College Board's rules for calculator use on the Math Level 2 Test! In fact, the College Board's calculator policy, which (at the time of this writing) is available at https://collegereadiness.collegeboard.org/sat-subject-tests/taking-the-test/calculator-policy , specifically says that you don't have to erase your calculator's memory before taking the test. (We'll talk about the important implications of this policy in a moment.)

The easiest way to make a note file on your calculator is to follow the same steps that you would follow to create a program on the calculator, and then type your notes straight into the program file. Don't worry about trying to follow the rules of the calculator's programming language! The goal here isn't to create a working calculator program; the goal is simply to save your notes as though they were a program. Of course, when you try to access this "program" through the calculator later on, you won't be able to run it, because it doesn't use calculator code. But you *will* be able to edit the "program," which means you can easily read through the text of all the notes you've entered. In other words, all you're doing is using the calculator's program features to store and access the text of your notes, with no intention of ever actually running them like a program.

This technique can be used to store any kind of obscure formula or fact that you're worried you might forget on test day. This way, you never have to worry that you'll forget something.

At this point, you might be wondering why the College Board allows you to take the test with a calculator that can contain any math information you want, right at your fingertips. That's an important question to ask, and the answer to that question goes back to a theme that comes up very frequently in this Black Book: *The Math Level 2 Test isn't really a test about how much math you can memorize.* Instead, the test rewards skills like reading carefully and being flexible enough to combine basic concepts in new ways to answer a question. These key skills can't really be recorded in a calculator, which is why the College Board doesn't care what information you bring into the test with you.

So you should think of this tactic as more of a security blanket than a secret key to acing the test easily. If you're worried that you'll forget how to find the area of a triangle or something, then it can be worthwhile to store that formula as text in your calculator, just so you'll know that you have it handy. But you shouldn't expect the Math Level 2 Test to focus heavily on memorized facts, as we'll discuss repeatedly throughout this Black Book.

Don't have a graphing calculator?

If you don't have a graphing calculator, consider asking a friend if you can borrow one. If that's not an option, explain to your math teacher that you need a graphing calculator for the Math Level 2 SAT Subject Test. Your teacher may be able to work something out so you can borrow a calculator ahead of time and get used to it, and then have it with you on test day.

If it's absolutely not possible for you to get your hands on a graphing calculator for the test (and for your training), I'd still recommend having at least a scientific calculator. That way you'll still be able to do everything on the list above, other than graph functions. But I seriously advise you to do everything you can to get your hands on a graphing calculator, because it will make a tremendous difference.

The Unwritten Rules Of The SAT Subject Test In Mathematics Level 2

Most test-takers realize that this test follows certain obvious rules related to things like the number of questions per test, the time limit, and so on. But trained test-takers know that the College Board's standardization process involves a lot more rules than that, and most of them are never discussed publicly by the College Board. We can learn these rules by carefully analyzing real test questions from the College Board, and we can use our knowledge of these rules to give us a huge advantage in training, and in our performance on test day.

After we lay out these rules in this section, we'll discuss answer choice patterns and a variety of special techniques for the test, and then we'll pull all of that together in a step-by-step process you can follow for each question on the test. After that, we'll briefly review the kinds of math concepts you'll need for test day in the Math Toolbox. Finally, you'll have the chance to see all of this in action against every question in the two Math Level 2 Tests in the MSTB. So let's get started—and remember that you'll see all of this stuff in action later on, so there's no need to worry if it seems vague or abstract right now.

Rule 1: The Words Are Critical.

On the Math Level 2 Test, you'll find that not knowing the meanings of mathematical terms like "diameter," "prime," or "asymptote" will leave you with very little chance of correctly answering questions that contain those unknown terms. On top of that, since the vocabulary of technical terms in math is fairly limited, you can be pretty sure that any challenging math term you see while training with real questions can also show up on test day. This is especially important on this test, as opposed to a high school math test, because so many of the questions on this test rely on the definitions and properties of specific words and phrases, as we'll see later on.

So if you encounter a word or phrase that you're not familiar with in an official Math Level 2 practice test, ask a math teacher what it means, or look it up in a resource like the Math Toolbox in this Black Book. It could come up again on test day. (It's true that you can sometimes work around an unknown term in a question on the Math Level 2 Test, but, in general, you don't want to leave yourself in the position of needing to do that if you can possibly avoid it. So make an effort to familiarize yourself with the properties and definitions of any unknown terms you run across in official practice tests from the College Board.)

Rule 2: Formulas Matter, But Not Nearly As Much As Most People Think.

In a classroom setting, we often answer math questions by relying exclusively on formulas—but this is NOT the way we should expect to answer most questions on the Math Level 2 Test! Instead, we'll find that questions on this test tend to rely on an understanding of properties and definitions. Formulas do come up occasionally, but they're rarely the only way (or the easiest way) to answer a question.

Even though many test-takers think the Math Level 2 Test often requires complicated or advanced formulas, the most commonly used formula on the test is probably the Pythagorean theorem. Also, remember that the first page of your test booklet has the formulas for the volume of a right circular cone, a sphere, and a pyramid, as well as the formula for the surface area of a sphere. These formulas aren't used too often, but it's good to know where they are if you need them.

So when you come across a question that doesn't seem to fit any formula you ever learned, don't panic! It's normal for questions on this test not to depend on formulas.

Rule 3: Calculations Are Often Pretty Simple.

Although test-takers often think of this as an advanced math test, the actual calculations you'll be doing will often be pretty simple, for the most part. The challenge on this test isn't usually in the actual calculations, as it might be in math class in school.

Instead, the challenge is usually in figuring out what the question is even asking you to do. Once you understand that, actually doing the calculations to execute the solution (if there even are any calculations) is often pretty simple, like adding 3 and 9, or knowing that 4 times 0 is 0.

When a question does call for a calculation with a non-terminating decimal or something, it will almost always be something you were going to need to use your calculator for anyway. In other words, if you find yourself doing tedious calculations or long algebraic solutions by hand, then you're probably not approaching the question in the most efficient way—in fact, there's a good chance you could be headed down the wrong path altogether.

Rule 4: Your Calculator Will Definitely Play A Role, But It Can't Take The Test For You.

The Math Level 2 Test is designed in a way that requires occasional calculator use, but it's very important not to fall into the trap of expecting your calculator to do the heavy lifting for you!

Sometimes the only efficient approach to a question will involve math that's nearly impossible to do in your head, such as graphing a third-degree expression or finding the inverse sine of a given decimal. You'll also find that some questions that don't strictly *require* a calculator are easier for you if you use one. On the other hand, you'll see plenty of questions on test day that can't possibly be answered with a calculator, and plenty of questions whose solutions only require one simple calculation that's probably faster to do in your head, such as multiplying two single-digit numbers.

In short, it's important to view the calculator as a critical tool on this test, without forgetting that the major factors affecting your score will be your abilities to read carefully, combine relatively simple ideas in new ways, and pay attention to small details.

Rule 5: The Difference Between Radians And Degrees Is Usually Important.

The SAT Math Level 2 Test involves trigonometry, and there will be times when you have to use your calculator to find the sine, cosine, or tangent of a given number, or to graph a trig function.

MAKE SURE YOUR CALCULATOR IS IN THE RIGHT MODE WHEN YOU DO ANYTHING RELATED TO TRIG! There are two ways that having your calculator in the wrong trig mode can negatively affect you. In some cases, it will cause your calculation to result in one of the wrong answer choices; even when it doesn't lead to a wrong answer, though, it will usually lead to some number that isn't in the answer choices at all, which means you'll spend time trying to figure out your mistake and then re-doing the question.

It would be a shame to miss a question that you otherwise understood because your calculator was in degree mode when it needed to be in radian mode, or vice-versa.

When a question involves finding sine, cosine, tangent, or another trigonometric function, and the values in the question are in degrees, your calculator should be in degree mode. (If the values are in degrees, they'll use the degree symbol, like this: 90°, 15°, 39°.)

When a trig question doesn't use degrees, your calculator should be in radian mode. If the values are in radians, they'll often (but not always!) be expressed in terms of π, like this: $2\pi, \frac{\pi}{2}, \frac{2\pi}{3}$. A radian value could also just be a number with neither a π symbol nor a degree sign, like 0.307.

(This may sound like kind of an obvious thing to look out for if you've ever taken a trig class, because most math teachers harp on it all the time. But there's a reason they do that, and a reason I'm bothering to point it out, and the reason is that it's very, very easy to have your calculator in the wrong mode and not realize it. So pay attention!)

Rule 6: The Subject Matter Necessary For A Perfect Score Is Limited.

Many people who take the SAT Math Level 2 Test think that they have to be ready to answer questions about every obscure, advanced math topic if they want to score a perfect 800 on the test. But this isn't the case—as we discussed earlier, the test is standardized so that it produces reliable data, which means the concepts you have to know to get an 800 are standardized as well.

So don't make the common mistake of reviewing all the math content from any random source you can get your hands on as you prepare for this test. Instead, make sure you focus on the math concepts you'll need to know in order to get a perfect score. You can learn these concepts by reviewing the Math Toolbox and walkthroughs in this Black Book. If you're thoroughly familiar with this material, then you're ready for the subject matter you'll need to score an 800. (See the next rule for more on what it means to score a "perfect" 800).

Rule 7: You Can Leave Some Questions Blank And Still Get A "Perfect" Score.

The College Board's scoring process for this test generally allows you to skip 5 questions or so and still receive a score of 800 if you answer all the other questions correctly. The official sample tests in the MSTB bear this out:

- You can skip 6 questions on the first Math Level 2 practice test in the MSTB and still score 800 if everything else is correct, as we see in the conversion chart on page 145 of the MSTB.

- You can skip 7 questions on the second Math Level 2 practice test in the MSTB and still score 800 if everything else is correct, as we see in the conversion chart on page 180 of the MSTB.

So if you encounter a few questions on test day that you just don't feel like you can answer, you can leave them alone and still get a great score—even a perfect score—as long as you perform well on the other questions.

(Note that the conversion table will NOT be exactly the same for every single test. In fact, you can see that it's different for the two practice tests in the MSTB. So you can't be absolutely certain that it's possible to get a perfect score while leaving 6 or 7 questions blank on test day—but you can be confident that you can leave a handful of questions blank and still get a near-perfect or perfect score if you execute correctly on all the other questions. Either way, the best policy is to answer everything you feel confident about, and leave questions blank if you don't feel confident about them, as we discussed when we talked about guessing. This is why it's so important to make sure that you avoid mistakes on all the questions you DO answer. Read carefully and pay attention to details!)

Rule 8: Questions Can Usually Be Answered In 30 Seconds Or Less.

If you're familiar with my preparation material for the ACT and the SAT 1, you probably remember that all the math questions on those tests can be answered in 30 seconds or less. This 30-second rule is *almost* true on the Math Level 2 Test as well: The *majority* of the questions on an official Math Level 2 Test from the College Board really can be answered in 30 seconds or less.

Sometimes a question on the Math Level 2 Test will take a little more time, but questions like that are definitely in the minority, and even those generally don't require much more than a minute if we attack them in the most efficient ways possible.

It's important that you understand that I'm not saying you HAVE to answer questions in 30 seconds or less! Instead, I'm saying that it's POSSIBLE to answer most questions in 30 seconds or less. As we'll see in the walkthroughs, the main challenge on this test is to read each question carefully, think in terms of properties and definitions, find the most efficient solution that we can, and execute it carefully. The challenge is NOT to do a dozen complicated calculations on each question, or to spend two minutes trying recall an obscure formula.

I want you to get used to looking for solutions that tend to take fewer steps, rather than solutions that take more steps. Once you adopt this kind of thinking, you'll be able to answer a lot of questions in 30 seconds or less. That will free up time for those other questions whose solutions just take a little bit more time.

(Again, we'll see many examples of solutions that take 30 seconds or less in the walkthroughs later in this Black Book.)

Rule 9: Wrong Answers Aren't Random.

Some untrained test-takers might be aware of this idea to a limited extent, but they're generally not aware of how important it is: the wrong answer choices for questions on the Math Level 2 Test just as standardized as every other part of the test.

When the College Board comes up with wrong answer choices for questions on the Math Level 2 Test, it generally tries to anticipate the mistakes that a test-taker is most likely to make, and then position the incorrect answer choices to attract test-takers who make those mistakes.

So if a question asks you to find the area of a circle, then one wrong answer might be the circumference of the circle, because the College Board knows that a lot of test-takers will confuse the two concepts. If a question asks you for the *x*-value in a coordinate pair, then one wrong answer might be the *y*-value in that coordinate pair.

It's not the case that every single wrong answer choice will relate back to an obvious mistake, but many will. It can be helpful to pick up on these connections; you can be more confident that you've understood the question from the College Board's viewpoint if you can see where the wrong answer choices are coming from.

We'll also see that some sets of answer choices will follow common patterns we can learn to identify, because the College Board has decided to incorporate these patterns and relationships as part of the standardization of the test. These patterns are often unrelated to the concepts and relationships in the prompt, but being aware of them can help us diagnose what the College Board is trying to test in a particular question. We'll talk about this idea in more detail in the next section of this Black Book, and you'll see several examples of it throughout the question walkthroughs later on.

Answer Choice Patterns

Recognizing patterns in the answer choices is a key part of learning to attack the SAT Math Level 2 Test in the most efficient and effective way possible. Remember that when the College Board creates wrong answer choices, it doesn't just generate random numbers. Instead, the wrong answers often relate to ideas in the prompt, and to other answer choices, in ways that are likely to make them attractive to test-takers who don't understand what a question is asking, or who make some small mistake.

This might seem like a pretty sneaky thing for the College Board to do—and it is.

But, as trained test-takers, we can actually turn the College Board's own sneakiness against it. We can do this once we realize that *the relationships among the wrong answers usually indicate important details of the question.*

Let me be clear here. Answer choice patterns on their own aren't completely reliable, and you should NEVER pick an answer based purely on an answer choice pattern that you think you've observed. But an awareness of these patterns can point you in the right direction if you aren't sure how to get started on a question, and it can also help you to check your work from another perspective, to make sure you haven't made any mistakes.

If you've understood the question correctly, you should usually be able to understand where some or all of the wrong answer choices came from. If you can't figure out the mistakes that might have led to some of the wrong answer choices, then you probably want to reconsider your own solution, to see if *you* made a mistake. In other words, if you can't see why any of the other answer choices might be tempting to other test-takers, then there's a chance you've failed to understand the question in some way, and have actually fallen for one of the wrong answers that was designed to look attractive to someone who made a particular mistake. This doesn't mean you're definitely wrong, but it does mean you should take a few seconds to double-check your approach to the question.

You can also use the answer choices to help figure out what "kind" of an answer you're looking for, and what kinds of concepts must be involved in the question. For example, if all the answer choices involve π, then you know that the question must involve concepts related to π, such as circles, radians and so on, which means that your approach needs to account for those kinds of ideas. Similarly, if all the answer choices involve variables, or are decimal expressions, or are fractions, or start with "*y =,*" for example, then you know that your approach will need to produce an answer with that characteristic. (These are often things you could have figured out on your own if you thought about the question for a while, but you can reach these conclusions much more quickly, and with total certainty, when you notice that the College Board has laid them out in front of you.)

Patterns aren't everything!

The possible relationships among answer choices on the Math Level 2 Test are standardized, like every other important aspect of the test. If we can learn these answer choice patterns ahead of time, we'll be in a better position to recognize them on test day. When we recognize them, we can gather information from them that can help us answer the question more quickly, and with more confidence.

At the same time, it's important to remember that you should NEVER pick an answer choice solely because you think it's indicated by a pattern! The patterns we're about to discuss *often* indicate correct answers, but they *don't always* indicate correct answers. As trained test-takers, we should use these patterns to help us think about real test questions in new ways, which can help us work through questions more quickly, and with a higher degree of accuracy.

(If some of this sounds a little strange, remember that you'll see several examples and discussions of all of these patterns in the walkthroughs later in this Black Book.)

With all of that in mind, let's take a look at some common answer choice patterns on the Math Level 2 Test.

Answer Choice Pattern 1: Halves And Doubles

When you look at a set of answer choices, you may notice that some of the choices are half as much or twice as much as the values of other choices.

One reason that this pattern appears frequently is that it's common for a solution to involve multiplying or dividing by 2. The College Board expects that a test-taker might accidentally forget to do that, or do it one time too many, and end up with half or twice the correct answer. So that makes sense, as far as it goes.

But this answer choice pattern even appears in questions that have nothing to do with multiplying or dividing by 2! For some reason, the College Board sometimes just likes to include wrong answers that are half as much or twice as much as the correct answer choice.

So when you see a pair of answer choices where one choice is half as much as the other choice, you should be aware that the correct answer is slightly more likely to be one of the choices involved in that pattern, all other things being equal. As with any answer choice pattern, we should know never to pick an answer choice solely because we think we recognize this pattern, but it can often be a strong hint from the College Board that you should pay attention to one or both of the answer choices in the pair.

Similarly, if the answer choices contain a pair like this, and your solution tells you that the right answer isn't one of the answer choices in the pair, then you might want to take a moment to make sure you've really understood the question before you move on. If you're still confident in your choice, that's fine, and you can move on to the next question, of course. No answer choice pattern is guaranteed to apply unfailingly in every single question. But you can often catch a mistake when you find that the answer choice you were going to pick doesn't really explain a pattern you see in the other answer choices.

Answer Choice Pattern 2: Opposites

You may also encounter a question with some answer choices that are opposites of other choices. For example, a question might have the answer choices 12 and -12, or $\frac{1}{5}$ and $-\frac{1}{5}$.

Untrained test-takers commonly lose track of negative signs when they're doing their calculations. The result can be that the test-taker comes up with an answer that's the opposite of the correct answer: if the right answer is -9, the test-taker might come up with 9, or vice versa. So you'll commonly see two answer choices that are opposites of one another, and the correct answer is slightly more likely to be one of those two choices than it is to be an answer choice whose opposite isn't present in the other choices.

If you see this pattern in a set of answer choices, you should be especially careful to double-check your work for any mistake that could result in choosing the opposite of the correct answer. Possible mistakes could involve things like the following:

- multiplying an expression by -1 instead of 1, or vice versa

- going in the wrong direction on a number line

- going in the wrong direction on the unit circle

As with any pattern in the answer choices, seeing a pair of opposites doesn't guarantee that one of the opposites is correct, but noticing this pattern can often help you be alert to potential mistakes.

Answer Choice Pattern 3: "On The Way" Answer

The College Board often gives us questions that involve multiple steps. When this happens, we'll sometimes find that one of the wrong answers is a number we arrived at during an earlier step, before reaching the correct solution.

For example, a question might ask for the value of *y* in a situation where we first need to find the value of *x* in one equation, and then use *x* to find the value of *y* in another equation. Some untrained test-takers in that scenario would read the question, start to work on the solution, find *x*, and then notice that *x* is one of the answer choices, and forget to do the rest of the solution. They would pick the value of *x* as the correct answer to the question and move on, completely forgetting that they were supposed to find the value of *y*, and not the value of *x*!

While this pattern can easily trick an untrained test-taker, it's actually something that can also help us out a lot once we're aware of it. If we notice that one of the answer choices reflects a number that we had to find on the way to finding the correct answer, then this pattern can help reassure us that we followed the right sequence of steps in our solution, because we see that the College Board anticipated that test-takers would need to pass through the earlier step on the way to the right answer.

Answer Choice Pattern 4: Wrong Trig Function

When Math Level 2 questions involve trig functions, a common wrong answer choice will reflect the result of using the wrong trig function. For example, if a question requires the sine of 60°, one wrong answer choice might involve the *cosine* of 60°, and another might involve the *tangent* of 60°.

Remember that paying careful attention to details is very important on this test! Otherwise, it's easy to press the wrong button on your calculator, forget to double check for small mistakes, and end up losing points on something like this even though you actually understood how to answer the question.

Answer Choice Pattern 5: Beware The First And Last Numbers In A Series

For the purposes of this answer choice pattern, there are a variety of different types of series that you could see in the answer choices for a question on test day, and this pattern could apply to any of them. You might see a set of answer choices that form a classic arithmetic or geometric series. The "series" might also be something a bit more abstract in the context of the question, such as one answer choice with a triangle, another choice with a square, and a third choice with a pentagon; in that case, the series would be formed by the number of sides in each successive shape. (Don't expect to see this exact kind of "shape series" on test day, because you almost certainly won't. I'm just using it as a made-up example to show that the College Board can find a variety of ways to work the idea of a series into a set of answer choices.)

When you see a series in a set of answer choices, you'll generally find that the correct answer choice is NOT the first or last number in the series—it tends to be one of the other numbers.

There's a reason for this. The College Board often includes a series of numbers in the set of answer choices if a question involves some kind of repeated process, because it's hoping that you'll accidentally repeat the process one time too many, or one time too few. So the question includes one wrong answer to reflect the mistake of repeating the process one time too many, and one wrong answer to reflect the mistake of repeating it one time too few, and the result is that the correct answer ends up being the middle value in a series. In these situations, if the College Board made the correct answer be the first or last number in the series, it would be giving up the chance to provide you with a wrong answer to pick if you're off by a step in one direction. On the other hand, if the correct answer isn't on either end of the series, then test-takers can be off by a step in either direction and still find a wrong answer that matches their mistake.

So, for example, if a series of answer choices had values like $\frac{1}{9}, \frac{1}{3}$, 1, 3, where each choice is three times as much as the number before it, then we might expect the correct answer to be $\frac{1}{3}$ or 1, but probably not $\frac{1}{9}$ or 3, because if the correct answer is one of the numbers towards the middle of the series, test-takers still have a chance to miscalculate in either direction and arrive at one of the answer choices, which means that untrained test-takers would be more likely to miss the question.

(To be clear, if the answer choices for a question involve a series, then it's still possible that the correct answer could be the first or last number in that series, or the correct answer might not even be part of the series at all. It's just a little more likely that the correct answer is part of the series, and that it's neither the first nor the last number in that series.)

Again, no answer choice pattern is always reliable, so this pattern on its own isn't enough to justify picking an answer choice or eliminating an answer choice. But noticing a series in a set of answer choices might help reassure you that you've answered a question correctly if the choice you like is part of the series without being on the end of the series; it could also help suggest that you might have overlooked something if you want to pick an answer choice that doesn't fit the pattern.

The relationships among the numbers in the series can also suggest which concepts are involved in the solution to the question in the first place. For example, if the answer choices increase by a factor of 5 (such as 3, 15, 75), then this pattern strongly suggests that finding the correct answer is likely to involve multiplying or dividing something by 5. Figuring out that detail and looking back at the question might give you an idea of how to get started on your solution, even if you were stuck before.

Answer Choice Pattern 6: Wrong Answers Imitate Right Answers
This pattern could potentially come into play on almost any question, but it's especially common on questions whose answers involve variables.

Before I tell you about this pattern, I should warn you that a lot of test-takers get really excited about it when they first see it in action a few times against real questions from the College Board. But we always have to remember that this is just a pattern that we'll *frequently* see followed in real test questions—it's NOT a rule that must *always* be followed in real questions!

The basic idea behind the pattern is that the College Board often tries to trick us by designing the wrong answers to a question so that they incorporate some elements of the right answer. The College Board seems to do this in the hope that some untrained test-takers might correctly work out some part of the right answer, but not the whole thing, and then guess and pick a wrong answer; alternatively, a test-taker might understand the question correctly but misread one of the wrong answers and choose it. In other words, the College Board's goal is to make the wrong answers be as similar to the right answer as possible, to increase the likelihood of fooling a test-taker into picking the wrong thing.

As an example, imagine that the correct answer to a question is the equation $y = 2x + 7$. If you worked for the College Board and you needed to come up with some wrong answer choices to tempt untrained test-takers, what kinds of equations do you think you might use? Remember that you need to think of choices that test-takers might actually pick.

Well, if the correct answer is $y = 2x + 7$, one good wrong answer choice might be $y = 2x - 7$. Notice that we changed the "plus 7" at the end of the right answer choice to a "minus 7" at the end of the wrong answer choice. We can probably imagine how a test-taker might make a small mistake that would cause the sign to be wrong at the end of the expression.

Another tempting wrong answer choice might be $y = \frac{1}{2}x + 7$. As you can see, in this case we've changed the coefficient of x from 2 in the correct answer to $\frac{1}{2}$ in the wrong answer. While we're at it, another wrong answer choice could be $y = \frac{1}{2}x - 7$, which would incorporate the changed coefficient of x *and* the minus sign.

Do you see how this works? We're changing one or two elements of the correct answer to come up with something that's similar to the right answer so it can be tempting for untrained test-takers.

Here are a few other wrong answer choices that the College Board might come up with if the correct answer were $y = 2x + 7$:

$y = 7x + 2$

$y = 7x - 2$

$y = x + 7$

$y = x - 7$

Like the other wrong answer patterns, this one is a pretty tricky ploy by the College Board. But it can also be really helpful for trained test-takers once we know to watch out for it.

Think about it: if the wrong answer choices are sometimes created by making small modifications to the correct answer, then the correct answer is likely to be the choice that has the most in common with the other choices.

That might sound a little confusing at first, so let's try a made-up example.

Imagine that we see a question with the following answer choices:

(A) $y = 3x + 1$

(B) $2y = 3x + 1$

(C) $2y = 3x - 1$

(D) $y = x + 1$

(E) $y = x - 1$

These answer choices all have three main elements:

- All the choices start with either y or $2y$.

- All the choices have an x-term that's either x or $3x$.

- All the choices end by either adding or subtracting 1.

Now, as trained test-takers, we'd want to consider each of the above elements individually, and ask ourselves which version of each element appears most frequently. If a single answer choice turns out to include all of the most common elements from the whole set of answer choices, then that choice is likely to be correct.

So here's what we'd find if we analyzed the elements we've identified in this imaginary set of answer choices:

- More of the answer choices incorporate y than $2y$.

- More of the answer choices incorporate $3x$ than x.

- More of the answer choices incorporate + 1 than - 1.

So if there's an answer choice that includes y, $3x$, and +1, we'd expect that choice to be correct. In this case, that would be choice (A).

As we've discussed repeatedly in this section, it's important to remember that you want to use these patterns to help diagnose a question, not as a way to answer a question blindly without actually understanding it, because these patterns aren't 100% reliable. In the question walkthroughs in this Black Book, we'll discuss a number of official test questions that follow this pattern, and we'll also see some that don't.

Answer Choice Pattern 7: The Right Answer To The Wrong Question

This answer choice pattern takes advantage of situations where the test-taker gets mixed up about what the question is asking, either through careless reading or through losing track of the steps in a question.

A classic example of this type of answer choice is when a question about the *area* of a figure includes an answer choice that's the *perimeter* of the figure. In this case, we can imagine that a test-taker who gets caught up in executing the solution to the question might not realize that he mixed up area and perimeter when he read the question. The answer he ends up with seems right to him, *but it's the right answer to the wrong question.*

Other examples of this kind of thing could include an answer choice with the slope of a parallel line when the question asked for the slope of a perpendicular line, an answer choice that provides the y-intercept of a graph when the question asked for the x-intercept, and so on.

The two best ways to protect yourself against making this kind of mistake are the following:

1. Re-read what the question asks one more time before you mark your answer. For example, you might think to yourself, "Okay, I've found the perimeter of the figure, and I see that it's an answer choice. Let me make sure that's what the question actually wanted, because I know the College Board sometimes includes answer choices that reflect a concept related to the correct answer, for people who aren't paying close attention." Then take an extra look to confirm that you found the value the prompt was actually asking for.

2. Look back over the other answer choices and see if any of them might represent values that are related to the values in the question. For example, if you find the perimeter of a figure as part of a solution, and you go over the answer choices and notice that one of them is the area for the same figure, that should cause you to re-check yourself.

Once you're confident that the value you've found is actually what the question asks for, mark it and move on.

Conclusion

As trained test-takers, we don't learn about answer choice patterns because we hope they'll let us find the correct answer without doing any work. We know that these patterns are largely reliable, but not perfectly reliable. We learn about them so we can develop a better understanding of each Math Level 2 question we encounter.

When you start to be aware of the answer choice patterns the College Board likes to use, you'll find that you can use the relationships among the answer choices to gain added insight into the best ways to attack a given question. Beyond that, though, you'll have a much stronger understanding of the way the College Board creates questions. At that point, the College Board will have a much tougher time trying to trick you.

So when you train for the test, watch for these answer choice patterns in action. We'll see many examples of these patterns when we look at the walkthroughs later in this Black Book.

Also keep in mind that the single best way to learn to identify these patterns and use them to your advantage is to practice careful reading at all times. I keep bringing this up because it's really, really important :)

Now that we've discussed answer choice patterns, we'll cover some special techniques and other important concepts that you'll find useful on test day. After that, we'll wrap all of these concepts into an organized approach you can use on any official test question. Then we'll change gears slightly and review the kinds of math concepts that can appear on test day. Finally, we'll go through the official test questions in the MSTB and see all of the ideas from this Black Book in action against them.

Special Technique: Ruling Out Answer Choices Without Calculations

It's sometimes possible to rule out all four of the wrong answer choices on a Math Level 2 question without actually doing the calculation that the question seems to be asking us to do, allowing us to identify the correct answer with total certainty in pretty short order.

In other words, based on the context of a given question, we can sometimes tell for sure that one of the answer choices is right, without doing the math that most untrained test-takers would do to approach the question. This can be useful for two reasons:

- It can save us the time and frustration of doing the calculation that the question seems to be asking for.

- It can often give us a very high degree of confidence that we're right, because the techniques for ruling out some answer choices are often more simple than the calculation we would have to do otherwise.

There are potentially many different scenarios that might allow us to rule out an answer choice, because official Math Level 2 questions can combine basic math concepts in a wide variety of ways, as we've discussed. But the most common way to rule out answer choices is to determine that the correct answer must be above or below a certain value. Once we know that the correct answer must fall within a certain range (or outside of a certain range, depending on the question), we can sometimes rule out four of the answer choices if they're too small or too large.

Before I go any further with this idea, I'd like to address something that might seem like a contradiction to you. Earlier in this Black Book, we talked about the problems with the common—but bad—guessing strategy, which involves "ruling out" some answer choices and then guessing "randomly" from the remaining choices. There are important differences between that misguided approach and this technique! In the common guessing tactic we discussed earlier, test-takers who DON'T understand a question resort to making up reasons to eliminate a few choices so they can pick from what's left. But we only use the strategy of ruling out answer choices when we DO understand the question, and when we know that we can rule out all 4 of the wrong answer choices for concrete reasons. This is a very critical difference, and it's important for you not to forget it!

Question 18 on page 128 of the MSTB is one example of a real Math Level 2 question from the College Board that allows us to rule out four wrong answer choices without doing the math that seems to be required by the question. This question is worded in a way that can allow a trained test-taker to realize that choices (B), (C), (D), and (E) must all be too large, perhaps even before the test-taker would realize that (A) must be correct on its own. (For a detailed discussion of this question, see the walkthrough for it later in this Black Book.)

We can see a similar use of this general technique in this Black Book's walkthroughs for the following questions in the MSTB, among others:

- Page 165, Question 15

- Page 140, Question 48

Of course, you won't be able to use this technique on every question you see on test day. In fact, you probably won't be able to apply it more than a few times on any one test. But it's still a good idea to keep this kind of approach in mind, because it will save you a lot of time and hassle when you do get the opportunity to use it. As you continue to read through this Black Book and practice on your own, you'll continue to improve your instincts for figuring out the best way to approach a given question. And if you do accidentally try a technique like this on a question where it can't be used, you'll find that you've only lost a couple of seconds, and you can continue working on a different approach to the question.

Special Technique: Backsolving

"Backsolving" is the common name for a set of techniques that allows us to find the correct answer to a question by plugging numerical values into algebraic expressions in order to tell whether those expressions might be equivalent. It's kind of a way to work backwards from information in the answer choices to see which one is correct. Sometimes we plug in the answer choices themselves, and sometimes we choose other values to plug in, as we'll discuss shortly.

Many test-takers are aware that backsolving exists, but most don't realize the extent to which we can use it on this test, so I strongly recommend that you pay attention to this section, even if you think you're already familiar with backsolving.

There are two main kinds of backsolving that we can do:

- Backsolving when there are no variables in the answer choices
- Backsolving when the answer choices include variables

Backsolving when there are no variables in the answer choices

This type of backsolving is useful on some questions that ask for the value of a variable in a given expression. We can often just take the numbers from the answer choices and plug them into the given equation to see which one makes a true statement.

You can see an example of this type of backsolving in question 4 on page 123 of the MSTB. Question 4 gives us some expressions involving x, y, and z, and then asks for the value of y. One way to approach this question is to set y equal to each answer choice in turn—the answer choice that creates a true statement in the prompt is the correct answer. To see the full solution, read the walkthrough of question 4 on page 123 of the MSTB in the question walkthroughs section later in this Black Book.

Here are a few more examples of questions in the MSTB whose solutions involve this type of backsolving:

- Page 135, Question 37
- Page 168, Question 25
- Page 169, Question 27

Backsolving when the answer choices include variables

This type of backsolving can get a little more complicated, but it's still a valuable tactic on some questions. When the answer choices are expressions involving variables, we can pick an arbitrary value to plug in for the variable in the expressions from the answer choices, and see which expression gives the result that the question is looking for.

You can see an example of this type of backsolving in question 43 on page 174 of the MSTB. That question gives us an expression involving n, and asks us to pick the answer choice with an equivalent variable expression. One way to solve this question is to follow these steps:

1. Choose an arbitrary value for n.
2. Plug this arbitrary value into the original expression from the prompt, and determine the numerical value of the expression.

3. Plug the same *n*-value into each expression in the answer choices, and determine the numerical values of each of those expressions.

4. See which answer choice yields the same numerical value as the expression in the prompt. That answer choice is the correct answer.

(For the full solution to question 43 from page 174 of the MSTB, read its walkthrough in this Black Book.)

There are two things we must keep in mind when backsolving like this:

1. Any value we decide to pick for the variable must meet the requirements given in the question.

For example, if the question says *x* must be greater than 6, then we have to pick a value greater than 6 for *x*; we can't pick 5. If the question says the variable must have a value between 0 and π, then we have to pick a value like π/2, and not 2π. If the question requires an odd integer, then we pick an odd integer. And so on. You get the idea—if the number we use to backsolve doesn't meet the requirements given by the question, then our conclusions won't be reliable. This might seem like a silly thing to point out, but I bet you'd be surprised how many times I've seen a very intelligent test-taker miss a question because he tried to backsolve with a number that didn't meet the written requirements of the prompt.

2. We should generally avoid picking numbers that are likely to result in false positives.

Depending on how a question is set up, and on what number we decide to use for backsolving, it can sometimes happen that more than one answer choice will give us a result that matches the result from the expression in the prompt, just by sheer coincidence, even when two expressions aren't algebraically equivalent. I call these coincidental matches "false positives."

To understand how we might get a false positive, consider the following different algebraic expressions:

- x
- $2x$
- x^3

If we plugged 0 into these expressions as *x*, we'd get the same result for all three, even though the expressions themselves aren't algebraically equivalent for all values of *x*. If we plugged 1 into all three expressions as *x*, then the first and third expressions would produce the same result as one another. On the other hand, if we plugged in 2, 3, 4, 5, or most other numbers, we'd get three different results from the three different expressions.

Generally speaking, we're more likely to produce false positives on the Math Level 2 Test when we backsolve with 0, 1, -1, or any number that appears in the question, so we should avoid picking those numbers when we backsolve.

But don't worry too much if you accidentally do create a false positive in your backsolving. You can fix the problem by picking another value to backsolve with, and then plugging that value into each answer choice. The correct choice will be the only one whose value matches the value from the prompt no matter which number is used to backsolve. (By the way, the odds are usually pretty small that you could pick two numbers in a row that would coincidentally give you a false positive when you backsolve with them.)

Since running into a false positive means you'll have to do all your backsolving work again with different numbers, you can potentially save time on test day by avoiding false positives in the first place. Again, the easiest way to prevent these kinds of issues is to make a habit of avoiding 0, 1, -1, and any number from the question when we pick an arbitrary number for backsolving.

Here are a few more examples of questions from the MSTB that involve backsolving when there are variable expressions in the answer choices:

- Page 128, Question 16

- Page 160, Question 2

- Page 176, Question 50

Remember that you can see my full explanations of those questions in the question walkthroughs in this Black Book.

Backsolving and rounding

When we backsolve, we need to keep in mind that we'll sometimes encounter situations in which the correct answer causes two expressions to have values that *almost* match, but don't match exactly. This happens because the College Board sometimes rounds off values in the answer choices, or even in the prompt. It will usually still be obvious which answer choice is the correct one in these situations, but I wanted to make sure you were aware of the possibility of these slight inconsistencies before you encountered them in your training. For more on issues related to rounding on this test, see the section of this Black Book called "Rounding On The SAT Subject Test In Mathematics Level 2."

Catching and fixing mistakes by evaluating every answer choice

As trained test-takers, we understand the importance of avoiding small mistakes on the Math Level 2 Test, and we know that the College Board often designs wrong answers to attract people who make those mistakes. There are two types of mistakes that a test-taker could be likely to make when backsolving, and there's a single technique that can help us eliminate both.

The first mistake is to backsolve with a number that happens to have a unique property relative to the question, and results in more than one answer seeming to correct. We discussed ways to avoid this situation in general above, but it can still come up on some questions even if you don't backsolve with -1, 0, or 1, or a number in the question. If there are two or three answer choices that coincidentally all work out to the same result for a particular value that you plug in during your backsolving, you run the risk of accidentally selecting the wrong answer choice if you don't realize the situation.

The second type of potential mistake is to make a small error in your calculations while you're backsolving. As you might imagine, this can easily cause an incorrect answer to seem correct if you don't realize your mistake.

We can greatly reduce the likelihood of either kind of backsolving mistake by making sure that we *always evaluate all the answer choices whenever we backsolve*. This will give us a better chance of noticing when more than one answer choice seems to work out to the target value. For example, if a trained test-taker is working through a backsolving solution and finds that (C) seems to be correct, she doesn't just stop working on the question and pick (C) as her answer! She continues to evaluate (D) and

(E) as well, to make sure that neither of them seems to work out to the desired value. If she finds that more than one answer choice seems to result in the desired value, then she knows she needs to re-evaluate her work. It might be that she's picked a number that results in more than one choice having the same value, or it might just be that she's miscalculated. In either situation, one of the best ways to try to find the correct answer is to retry the backsolving with a different number plugged in, if possible. If the initial mistake was choosing a bad number to plug in, then choosing a new number will usually solve the problem, because it's unlikely that two different numbers will result in the same false positives; if the initial mistake was a miscalculation, then the test-taker will often avoid the mistake on a second approach with new values.

If you want to score high on this test, it's very important to commit to the idea of testing out every answer choice whenever you backsolve! This is why you'll always see me go through every answer choice whenever I use a backsolving approach in the walkthroughs in this Black Book.

Conclusion
Backsolving can be a very useful technique, and it can be applied in a lot of different ways on real Math Level 2 practice questions from the College Board. The best way to get more comfortable with backsolving is to see it in action before trying it yourself, so make sure you read this Black Book's walkthroughs of the listed example questions for examples of both types of backsolving.

Make sure you keep the possibility of backsolving in mind when we discuss the Math Path in a few pages.

Rounding On The SAT Subject Test In Math Level 2

Rounding numbers is an important concept on the Math Level 2 Test that doesn't really come up on the Math section of the SAT 1 or the ACT.

On the Math section of the SAT 1, if the test talks about the square root of two, that expression will typically look like this: $\sqrt{2}$. On the Math Level 2 Test, it might also look like $\sqrt{2}$ . . . but the same value might be expressed in a decimal approximation, instead, such as 1.414, or something like that.

On the Math Level 2 Test, we sometimes do things like the following:

- take square roots or cube roots of numbers that aren't perfect squares or cubes

- approximate values of trig functions

- find natural logs

Basically, the test sometimes makes us use our calculators to come up with "ugly" decimals, like 1.409324524, instead of the kinds of "clean" numbers that appear in the majority of math questions on the SAT 1 and the ACT.

On the Math Level 2 Test, decimal approximations will typically be rounded to 1, 2, 3, or 4 decimal places, but you might find that decimals are rounded off to integers, or other values. Questions usually won't state directly that the answer choices are rounded off. Instead, they'll typically just say something like "what's the value of x?" as opposed to "which value is closest to x?" It's up to us, as trained test-takers, to account for the rounding when it appears.

Potential issues with rounding

There are two potential ways in which this kind of rounding might keep you from realizing a particular answer choice is correct:

1. Rounding during your own calculations

2. Back-solving with rounded numbers

Let's talk about them both briefly.

When you perform calculations for a question whose answer choices involve decimal expressions, be careful about rounding numbers off while you're doing calculations on your way to the final answer, because you might throw off your result by too much. For example, if you round a number like 6.14989940236843 to 6.1, and then perform a couple of operations on your rounded amount, you could end up changing the final result enough that you won't know which answer choice is correct.

So if you have to round off the numbers you're working with before you complete your final calculation, I recommend rounding off to 6 digits, because doing that will preserve more digits than the College Board preserves when it rounds, which minimizes the chance that your rounding will prevent you from recognizing the correct answer choice. You might see a very slight difference between the outcome of your calculations and the right answer, but it should be quite clear which answer choice is correct if you've done your math correctly.

Also be aware that if you backsolve on the Math Level 2 Test (that is, if you try plugging the answer choices back into the expression to see which one is correct, as we discussed in the previous section), then you might find that the correct answer choice only creates results that are very close to the result from another expression, instead of being identical to it, when the choice is plugged into the expression from the prompt. This can happen if the College Board has rounded off the answer choices, because the answer choice value you're plugging in is the rounded version of the correct answer, instead of being the actual value of the correct answer. It won't fit "perfectly" when you plug it back in because it's not the exact answer, but it should be close enough that you'll easily be able to tell which choice is correct, especially when comparing the result to what you get from the other answer choices.

You'll see examples of all of these ideas in the walkthroughs of real College Board questions from the MSTB that we'll do later on in this Black Book, including the following, among others:

- Page 124, Question 5
- Page 135, Question 37
- Page 168, Question 25
- Page 170, Question 32

Dealing With Questions That Feature More Than One Variable

As we've discussed several times, and as you'll see on test day, the Math Level 2 Test loves to exploit an untrained test-taker's "school math" instincts. One of the test's favorite ways to do this is to show us a problem that involves several variables. If we saw a question like this in math class, we would most likely solve it by trying to find the values of each individual variable. But on the Math Level 2 Test, we'll often discover that the values of some variables just cannot be found separately from one another, which means that trying to solve for them on their own is a confusing waste of time.

In other words, imagine that the prompt of a math question mentions that $(a + b)^3 = 8$. If the prompt then asks us for the value of $a + b$, most people will waste time in an effort to identify the individual values of a and b, so they can add them together and find the value of $a + b$. In this situation, though, it's completely impossible to identify a single value for either variable. Either one can have more than one solution.

But this doesn't mean that we can't figure out the value of $a + b$!

We're still able to know that $a + b = 2$, because $(a + b)^3 = 8$, and $2^3 = 8$. So we can know the value of the sum of a and b, even if we can never know the value of either variable by itself.

Do you see how much easier the solution becomes once we stop focusing on the concept of finding each individual variable, and think about what the math question is actually looking for, instead?

So be on the lookout for questions that ask you to find the value of an expression with more than one variable, such as $a + b$, as opposed to directly testing you on the value of a single, specific variable. When the College Board does this, it's often a big hint that it's impossible to find the values for all the variables individually, even if it's still possible to find the value of the overall expression.

The following walkthroughs in this Black Book cover questions from the MSTB that require us to find the value of an overall expression even when it wouldn't be possible to find the values of each component of the expression:

- Page 167, Question 22
- Page 172, Question 38

Decimals, Fractions, and Percentages

We know that one of the College Board's primary strategies in writing Math Level 2 questions is to present familiar material in unfamiliar ways. This tactic can be very effective for the College Board, as we'll see repeatedly when we get to the question walkthroughs in this Black Book.

One way that the College Board will try to make familiar concepts seem strange is by expressing a value as a decimal when you would normally expect to see it as a fraction with a numerator and denominator. For example, most high school math teachers would represent the slope of a line as an expression with a fraction bar, but the College Board might show you some slope values in decimal form.

The College Board might apply the same basic idea in any other direction—probabilities might be expressed as decimals instead of percentages, and so on.

So it's often useful to be able to convert percentages to decimals or fractions, and vice versa. We'll discuss some things to keep in mind for each type of expression in this section.

Percentages

To make a percentage into a fraction, just give the original percentage a denominator of 100, and then simplify if necessary. For example, 47% is the same as $\frac{47}{100}$.

To make a percent value into a decimal expression, just divide the original percentage by 100. For example, 3% is the same as 0.03, because 3/100 = 0.03.

Decimals

To make a decimal value into a percentage, we multiply the original decimal expression by 100 and add the percent sign. For example, 0.895 is the same as 89.5%.

Making a decimal value into a fraction can be a little more complicated, and it doesn't come up very often, because the multiple-choice format of the test means that we never have to enter a fraction on our own; we can always just check whether a fraction in a question is equal to a particular decimal. To do this, we use a calculator to divide the denominator by the numerator and see if the result is the decimal that we're looking for. For example, if our calculations give us 0.45, but all the answer choices are fractions, we can just divide the numerator of each answer choice by its denominator to find the equivalent decimal expression; if 0.45 is correct, one answer choice would have to be equivalent to 9/20. When we divide 9 by 20 we get 0.45, so we know 9/20 and 0.45 are equivalent.

But if you do want to convert a decimal to a fraction on your own, you need to know there are basically three kinds of decimal numbers for this purpose:

1. Decimals that terminate.

2. Decimals that don't terminate, but do repeat.

3. Decimals that don't terminate and don't repeat.

The easiest ways to convert the first two types of decimals are different from each other, so we'll discuss them separately, on the off chance that you feel you need to do these kinds of conversions on test day. The third type of decimal can't be converted to a fraction.

For decimals that terminate, all we have to do is make the decimal number the numerator in a fraction, and make the denominator of the fraction a number consisting of the digit 1 followed by as many zeros as there were digits after the original decimal point. For example, the decimal 0.12668 is equal to the fraction $\frac{12668}{100000}$.

For decimals that don't terminate, but do repeat, the easiest approach is to use a function on your calculator. To do this, enter a portion of the number that you want to convert, and then use your calculator's fraction conversion tool to find the equivalent fraction (on TI calculators, the tool is called FRAC, and it's in the MATH menu; on HP calculators, use the →Q command; and on Casio calculators, enter the decimal and press the S←→D button). Some calculators require you to include at least 10 digits of the repeating part of the fraction! For example, to convert the number $0.\overline{6}$, we'd enter 0.6666666666, and then convert, and the calculator would show us the equivalent was $\frac{2}{3}$. (There's another way to convert repeating decimals without a calculator, of course, but in my experience it's not worth learning for this test if you don't already know it, because it's harder than just checking for the decimal value of a fraction that appears in a question, as we discussed above.)

It sometimes also helps to be able to recognize some decimal expressions and their equivalent fractions:

- $0.1 = \frac{1}{10}$
- $0.\overline{1} = \frac{1}{9}$
- $0.2 = \frac{1}{5}$
- $0.25 = \frac{1}{4}$
- $0.\overline{3} = \frac{1}{3}$
- $0.5 = \frac{1}{2}$
- $0.\overline{6} = \frac{2}{3}$
- $0.75 = \frac{3}{4}$

Remember that you can use your calculator to confirm the fraction equivalent of a decimal expression. For example, if you see the value 0.125, and you think it's equal to $\frac{1}{8}$, you can just use your calculator to divide 1 by 8 and make sure you're right—the decimal equivalent will be displayed on the calculator.

Decimal expressions that don't terminate and don't repeat are called irrational numbers. That literally means they can't be described as a ratio of two integers—in other words, they can't be converted to fractions. For that reason, you won't have to worry about making this type of decimal expression into a fraction.

Fractions

To make a fraction into a decimal, divide the numerator by the denominator—remember that you can use a calculator if you want. For example, $\frac{3}{16} = 3 \div 16 = 0.1875$.

To make a fraction into a percentage, divide the numerator by the denominator, and then multiply the result by 100 and add a percent symbol. For example, $\frac{3}{5}$ = 3 ÷ 5 = 0.6 = 60%.

Examples In The MSTB

Here are two examples of questions that raise the issue of converting among decimals, fractions, and percentages for most test-takers:

- Page 123, Question 3
- Page 129, Question 21

Remember you can find my solutions for these questions in the walkthroughs later in this Black Book.

The Math Path

When I train my students to attack math sections of standardized tests, I recommend that they follow something I like to call the "Math Path." It's kind of a silly name, but I call it that mostly because it rhymes and I hope it'll stick in your head.

There are seven steps on the Math Path. That might sound like a lot, but many of the steps can be done in just a few seconds, and the whole thing will be second nature once you start using it on practice questions.

Bear in mind that you don't necessarily need to execute every single one of these steps on each question! In fact, as you get more familiar with the test, you'll probably find that you work through most questions without consciously referring to the math path, even though you'll use most of these steps in some form. That's fine, of course, as long as you're consistently able to answer real practice questions correctly. The goal here isn't to make you memorize a set of steps for no reason—it's just to provide a framework to help you start incorporating your awareness of the unique rules and patterns of the Math Level 2 Test into your approach.

With all of that in mind, let's take a look at the steps of the Math Path.

1. Read the question prompt carefully.

This might sound like a simple and obvious step, but it's something that most test-takers do poorly—and it's also one of the most important aspects of test-taking.

Think about it this way: how are you going to have any shot at answering a question if you misread part of it in the very beginning? Overlooking even one word can make the difference between choosing a right answer and a wrong answer, so always read carefully—for example, if you overlook the word "odd" in a question with the phrase "consecutive odd integers," then you won't answer the question correctly.

On top of that, we'll find that it's very important to be aware of the key words and phrases in the question when we're trying to figure out the best way to attack it in later steps. So the bottom line is that it will be almost impossible to succeed on the Math Level 2 Test if you don't commit to reading each question very carefully.

2. Read the answer choices.

Most test-takers don't bother to read the answer choices for a question until they've already attempted their solution. At that point, they're just looking to see if the answer they came up with is one of the choices.

This can potentially be a huge mistake.

I'll admit that solving a question and then looking for the answer choice that matches your result could work out fine in theory . . . *if* you manage to answer every question quickly and correctly.

But a trained test-taker knows that the answer choices often contain valuable information, so she always takes the time to read them before she starts working on a solution. As we discussed earlier in this Black book, the College Board often likes to create a question's answer choices according to patterns—and you're not going to be able to use any of those patterns if you don't read through the choices before deciding on a plan of attack.

And do you remember our discussion of the unwritten rules of the Math Level 2 Test, when I said that most Math Level 2 questions can be answered in 30 seconds or less? Those quick solutions are often only possible if you incorporate the answer choices in your approach.

This step is also important because it can give you a clue about the types of concepts that might be relevant to the question. For example, if every answer choice includes π, then you know the question probably involves circles or radians in some way. Noticing these details can help you figure out how to tackle a strange question.

3. Consider any diagrams that appear in the question.
Diagrams can be very important on the Math Level 2 Test. Remember that every diagram is drawn to scale unless it includes a note saying it's not to scale.

If the diagram is drawn to scale, then looking at the diagram will usually improve your understanding of the situation described in the question. Sometimes—but definitely not always—a diagram will even provide enough information to allow you to answer a question with complete certainty, without doing any calculations.

If a diagram's not drawn to scale, I'd recommend that you try to identify the part (or parts) that are out of scale, and consider re-drawing the diagram to scale. When the College Board provides you with a diagram that's not to scale, the reason is often that drawing the diagram to scale would have made the answer to the question too obvious. For this reason, thinking about how the diagram would look if it were properly scaled can also give you useful information about what's going on in the question.

At this stage of the process, looking at a diagram is like reading the prompt and the answer choices: it's just another way of taking in information about the concepts in the question and the way they're presented before you attempt to answer it.

Also remember to pay close attention when looking at a diagram that is drawn to scale—don't assume an unlabeled angle is 45° just because you think it looks like a 45° angle, for example. Similarly, don't assume that two lines are the same length just because they might look pretty close to the same length. Instead, use scaled diagrams to tell when one line segment is *clearly* longer or shorter than another line segment, or when one angle is *clearly* larger or smaller than another angle, and so on, without trying to assign specific numerical values to those kinds of things. If you can't be sure about a measurement or comparison just from eyeballing a diagram, then rely on some other analysis, such as the rules of geometry or trigonometry, to figure out what you need to know.

4. Think about the mathematical concepts that could be related to the question.
Once you've read the prompt and the answer choices, and you've taken a look at any diagrams in the question, you should try to identify the specific math concepts that could be related to the concepts you've seen in the question.

This is a critical step, because it sets up the approach you'll take in the next step. Unfortunately, this critical step is one that most test-takers omit completely, or do badly.

In my experience, when untrained test-takers encounter a challenging question, they have a tendency to panic and try to recall all the math concepts they've ever learned in their lives, looking for ways to apply all of them to the question at once—which is obviously impossible. This is an undisciplined reaction to their frustration and anxiety, and it will almost never lead to a good solution.

So instead of panicking and trying to apply every math concept you know to the question at once, you should try to focus as *narrowly* as you can on the *specific* mathematical concepts that might be directly related to the question, based on your understanding of its wording, answer choices, and diagrams.

We do this by identifying the math concepts that are directly related to what we've seen so far. For example, if a question contains words like "radius" or "diameter," then the solution to the question probably involves concepts related to circles. If we see the word "sine" in a question, then the solution to the question might involve the unit circle, SOHCAHTOA, inverse sine, and so on.

Let's reflect for a moment on why this part of the Math Path is so important. Mathematical processes (such as algebraic solutions, geometric proofs, and so on) generally proceed in a step-by-step manner, in which each step builds on the previous step with some small, incremental change. For this reason, the first step in a process that will lead to an answer to the question must be closely related to the concepts that were used to ask the question. This is why it's so important that we deliberately *narrow* our focus to the specific concepts in the question, and the concepts that are immediately related to those specific concepts, instead of panicking whenever we're not sure where to start.

(At this stage, it can be helpful to be aware of the concepts that are in the Math Toolbox in this Black Book, because they give you an indication of what could potentially appear on test day. If you can limit yourself to that set of ideas as you look for concepts related to the things you've identified in the question, then you can be sure that you're not wasting your time by worrying about math ideas that the College Board has made off-limits for this test.)

5. Look for an efficient solution—one that involves as few steps as possible, and ideally takes 30 seconds or less. Remember that your solution doesn't have to be something your math teacher would recommend!

Now that you've read the entire question, and thought about which areas of math are directly relevant to it, you can actually start to think about possible solutions in an effective way.

We want to train ourselves to look for the most efficient and direct solutions that we can, which means we'll often find ourselves attacking questions in a variety of unorthodox ways, rather than relying on formulas, as we've discussed at various points in this Black Book so far. It may be that backsolving is the fastest way to answer a question, or it may be that we can eyeball a scaled diagram and tell that only one answer choice is anywhere near the appropriate value, and so on. The important thing to remember is that the Math Level 2 Test doesn't always reward us for doing "school math," because the test is designed for a unique purpose, as we've discussed. So our job is just to find the correct answer, with total certainty, by any means except cheating.

Most Math Level 2 questions can be answered in 30 seconds or less. Of course, your solution doesn't *have* to take 30 seconds or less, but it's good to approach each question with the goal of finding an efficient, fast solution. This will remind you that SAT Math isn't always like classroom math, and that you should be looking for straightforward solutions rather than messy, complicated ones.

Remember to stick to the areas of math you identified in the previous step, and think about how you could apply your knowledge of those concepts to the question.

(By the way—if around ten seconds go by and you can't think of an efficient way to answer the question, I'd recommend skipping the question and coming back to it later if you have time, as we discussed in the section of this Black Book called "Time Management On Test Day.")

6. Execute your solution. Always be aware of the possibility of making a small mistake if you're not careful.

Now that you've gone through the first five steps and figured out how to solve the question, it's time to implement your solution.

Most untrained test-takers on the Math Level 2 Test will try to apply a formula as soon as they can think of one—which often means they jump right into attempting a bad solution before they've even finished reading the prompt. This is because most high school math classes encourage that kind of mindless, automatic approach: students cram some formulas the night before a test, and then the test presents them with formulaic questions that allow the students to demonstrate that they remember the formulas.

But we have to break this habit when we train for the Math Level 2 Test! Each question on this test is going to be different from all the other questions, and probably at least a little different from anything you've ever seen before. This is why we train ourselves to consider all aspects of a question and think about which math concepts might be related to it before we begin our solution.

It's also important to remember to take the solution itself one step at a time, and think carefully about what you're doing. As we've discussed repeatedly, and as you'll see in the walkthroughs later in this Black Book, the College Board deliberately creates opportunities for a careless test-taker to make mistakes that will cause her to answer questions incorrectly, even if she understands them. This is why trained test-takers always guard against small mistakes.

7. Re-check your work. Try to consider the question from the College Board's perspective.

Now that we've reflected on all aspects of the question, identified an efficient approach to the question, and executed our solution carefully, we need to take a few seconds to make sure we're certain about the answer we've chosen. We re-read the prompt to make sure we haven't overlooked or misread anything. We look back through the answer choices and see if we notice any patterns that fit (or don't fit) with the way we approached the question. We ensure that any diagrams make sense in the context of our answer.

In short, before we move on to the next question, we look back over our work for the current question and see if we can figure out what the College Board was trying to accomplish when it created the question. If we can understand how the question follows the rules and patterns that we've seen in our training for the test, then there's a very good chance we've answered the question correctly. On the other hand, if we finish working on the question and can't really see how it follows the College Board's general game plan, then there's a good chance that we might be about to miss the question if we don't go back and fix things.

Similarly, if we can see how an untrained test-taker might have been able to make small mistakes in math or reading that would have led to any of the answer choices we think are wrong, then that's another good sign we've answered the question correctly. On the other hand, if we can't see how anyone could make small mistakes that would lead to some of the wrong answers, then we might have made a mistake ourselves! When I find myself in this position, I always quickly re-check my reading and my solution to make sure I'm still certain that my answer is correct.

When we run into any mistakes, we go back and fix them quickly if we can. If we get stuck on a question, we move on and come back to it later if we have time, as we discussed in the section of this Black Book called "Time Management On Test Day."

When we're confident that we've found the right answer choice, we mark it on our answer sheet and move on.

(By the way, you should DEFINITELY expect to find and fix some mistakes in this last step! You probably won't find mistakes on every single question, but everyone makes careless errors sometimes, and we always have to keep in mind that the College Board goes out of its way to give us lots of opportunities to get things wrong. This final step is just as important as any other step on the Math Path, so don't skip over it! Almost everyone who gets perfect or elite scores on standardized tests makes mistakes on several questions per test—they're just disciplined enough to catch those mistakes and correct them, while average test-takers leave their mistakes uncorrected. It would be a shame to put so much effort into your preparation for the test and then throw points away on test day because you're too lazy to check over your work. So check your work!)

Conclusion

We've discussed the Math Path in terms of rigid steps here, but I don't want you to think that you have to follow these steps strictly on every single question on test day. Instead, you'll probably find that the principles of the Math Path become second nature to you whenever you attack a new question on the Math Level 2 Test, and you won't need to think about each step consciously in most situations. For that reason, you'll find that most of the question walkthroughs in this Black Book don't specifically refer to each step of the Math Path, even though the key elements of the Math Path are present in each walkthrough. Still, if you'd like to see an example of an approach to a question from the MSTB that explicitly describes going through the steps of the Math Path, you can check out this Black Book's walkthrough of question 35 from page 135 of the MSTB.

The important thing to take away from our discussion of the Math Path is that you must always read the whole question carefully (including the answer choices and any diagrams), think about which concepts appear in the question or are immediately related to the content of the question . . . and only decide your plan of attack after taking in that information. Then you execute your solution and check your work, with the overall goal of being certain of your answer, and of trying to see the question from the College Board's perspective.

Now that you've seen the Math Path discussed in general terms, it's time to shift our focus a little bit and cover the basic math concepts you'll need to know for test day. Then we'll get started with our question walkthroughs, so you can see all of these concepts in action against real test questions written by the College Board.

SAT Subject Test In Mathematics Level 2 Toolbox

There are two primary components to our approach to the Math Level 2 SAT Subject Test:

- We need to be familiar with the math concepts that can appear on the test.

- We need to be aware of the strategic considerations involved in approaching real Math Level 2 questions written by the College Board.

At this point, we've addressed all of the strategic considerations for the test in an abstract sense; in a little while, you'll see them applied against every single Math Level 2 Test question in the MSTB. But first we'll review the math concepts you'll need for test day in the Math Toolbox.

I'd recommend that you read through this Math Toolbox twice to be sure that you're familiar with all the concepts it covers. Most students feel much more comfortable with the material after reading it a second time.

Keep in mind that the Math Level 2 Test will require an understanding of properties and definitions, not just the application of formulas! This is different from what's required by most high school math tests. Make sure you're fully comfortable with Part I of this toolbox before you take the test (keep reading for an explanation of the two different parts of the Math Toolbox).

Some concepts show up more than others

You'll see that the toolbox is divided into two sections: Part I and Part II. The material covered in Part I comes up far more often on the test than the material covered in Part II does. It's also generally less advanced than the material in Part II.

Untrained test-takers tend to worry most about the more advanced, obscure material they expect to see on test day, because they think the Math Level 2 Test is similar to a challenging math test in school. But, as trained test-takers, we know that it's much more important to have a thorough understanding of the more "basic" concepts you'll find in Part I than it is to know the more "advanced" material in Part II, because the material in Part I accounts for a much larger portion of the points you can score on test day.

I'll say it one more time to make sure we're on the same page: get completely comfortable with everything in Part I before you spend any time learning the material in Part II.

Organization of the Math Toolbox

While the goal of the Math Toolbox in this Black Book is to show you which math concepts you'll need to know for the Math Level 2 Test, I should note that the Math Toolbox isn't really designed to teach you these concepts from scratch if you've never taken a single math class.

Instead, the goal is to remind you of the key details of math concepts that you might not have used in a long time, and to explain some related concepts that you may never have encountered before. It's definitely possible to learn some new math concepts from the Math Toolbox, but the Math Toolbox does assume a basic knowledge of things like simple arithmetic, solving an algebraic equation, and so on.

Math Toolbox Part I

This first part of the Math Toolbox contains the math concepts that come up most frequently on the Math Level 2 Test. Although you should familiarize yourself with all the material in this section, pay extra attention to the first four topics, because they tend to account for the majority of issues that most test-takers have with the subject matter of this test:

- functions

- triangles

- trigonometry

- logarithms

The other topics that appear in Part I of the Math Toolbox also occur frequently on the test, but they tend to be less troublesome for most test-takers.

Functions

Concepts related to functions appear frequently on the Math Level 2 Test. Make sure you're thoroughly comfortable with the material in this section before test day, and see the question walkthroughs later in this Black Book for examples of how these concepts are tested in real questions.

A function is a type of equation that allows us to enter one value (often called x) and generate another value (often called y, or $f(x)$).

The values we enter into the function can be referred to as "inputs" or "x-values" (if the function is written in terms of x).

The values generated by the function can be referred to as "outputs" or "y-values" (if the function is written in terms of y) or "$f(x)$ values" (if the function is called f and written in terms of x-values).

There are many different ways we can write a function, but one of the most common ways we'll encounter on the Math Level 2 Test is probably by using $f(x)$:

> Example:
>
> $$f(x) = x + 3$$

Even though the most common way that functions are expressed on the test is in terms of f and x, any other two letters can also be used.

> Example:
>
> $$f(x) = 2x + 3$$
> $$g(h) = 2h + 3$$
> $$E(\theta) = 2\theta + 3$$
> $$A(x) = 2x + 3$$
> $$r(N) = 2N + 3$$

All of these functions refer to the same process; they just use different letters as variables.

In the example function above, the function $f(x)$ is equal to $x + 3$. In other words, for any x-value that we enter into the function above, we find $f(x)$ by adding 3 to the x-value. For example, entering $x = 8$ will produce an $f(x)$ value of 11. We could write this in the following way: $f(8) = 11$.

The expression in parentheses immediately after the f is the thing we'll be plugging into the function:

- If the expression in parentheses after the f is a variable, such as x, then we're using it to represent the idea of *any* expression being plugged into the function.

- If the expression in parentheses after the f is a specific value, such as 8, then the notation describes the idea of that specific value being plugged into the function.

Example:

$f(x) = x + 3$ **(equation defining function f)**

$f(8) = 8 + 3$ **(plug in 8 for x)**

$f(8) = 11$ **(add 3 and 8 to find $f(8)$)**

We can also plug in more complicated expressions. For example, we can plug in something like $(x^2 + 4)$ and find $f(x^2 + 4)$. Let's do that in the example function we've been using.

Example:

$f(x) = x + 3$ **(equation defining function f)**

$f(x^2 + 4) = (x^2 + 4) + 3$ **(plug in $x^2 + 4$ for x)**

$f(x^2 + 4) = x^2 + 7$ **(combine like terms)**

As we can see, any term in parentheses after f simply replaces the x term in the function when we plug it in. We can then simplify the resulting expression.

Nested Functions

To take this concept a step farther, let's look at the idea of using the output from one function as the input for another function. Let's imagine that we have one function called $f(x)$, and another function we'll call $g(x)$. Function $f(x)$ will be equal to $x^2 + x + 2$, and function $g(x)$ will be equal to $\frac{x}{3} - 1$ in this example.

Example:

$f(x) = x^2 + x + 2$ **(definition of $f(x)$)**

$g(x) = \frac{x}{3} - 1$ **(definition of $g(x)$)**

We can evaluate an expression like $f(g(x))$ by plugging x into $g(x)$ first, and then taking the result and plugging it into $f(x)$.

Let's follow that process to find $f(g(9))$.

Example:

$$g(x) = \tfrac{x}{3} - 1 \qquad \text{(definition of } g(x)\text{)}$$

$$g(9) = \tfrac{(9)}{3} - 1 \qquad \text{(plug in 9 for } x \text{ in } g(x)\text{)}$$

$$g(9) = 2 \qquad \text{(simplify)}$$

So we see that $g(9) = 2$. Now we plug 2 into $f(x)$.

Example:

$$f(x) = x^2 + x + 2 \qquad \text{(definition of } f(x)\text{)}$$

$$f(2) = (2)^2 + (2) + 2 \qquad \text{(plug in 2 for } x \text{ in } f(x)\text{)}$$

$$f(2) = 8 \qquad \text{(simplify)}$$

So by plugging 9 into $g(x)$ and plugging the result of $g(9)$ into $f(x)$, we find that $f(g(9)) = 8$.

We can also find an expression equal to $f(g(x))$ by plugging $g(x)$ into $f(x)$, and then simplifying. This is essentially the same thing as plugging an algebraic expression into the function $f(x)$; the only minor difference is that the algebraic expression we're plugging in is the definition for another function.

Example:

$$f(x) = x^2 + x + 2 \qquad \text{(definition of } f(x)\text{)}$$

$$g(x) = \tfrac{x}{3} - 1 \qquad \text{(definition of } g(x)\text{)}$$

$$f(g(x)) = (\tfrac{x}{3} - 1)^2 + (\tfrac{x}{3} - 1) + 2 \qquad \text{(plug in the definition of } g(x) \text{ where } x \text{ appears in } f(x)\text{)}$$

Domain and Range

Every function has a "domain" and a "range," which are attributes of a function that allow us to describe the numbers that can be plugged into the function, and the numbers that can be generated by the function.

The domain of a function is the set of x-values that can be plugged into the function to produce a y-value that's a real number.

There are two ways to limit the domain of a function:

1. The definition of a function can include a note with an arbitrary limitation on the domain, such as "the function $t(x)$ is valid for all real numbers greater than 2," which would tell us that the domain of the function includes all real numbers greater than 2.

2. A function's domain cannot include x-values that would result in mathematically undefined outputs. For example, the function $g(x) = \tfrac{1}{x}$ has a domain that excludes $x = 0$, because an x-value of zero would make the denominator of the fraction in the function equal to 0, and the result of dividing any number by zero is mathematically undefined.

The range of a function is the set of outputs that can be produced by plugging in all the numbers from the domain. For example, in the function $f(x) = x + 3$, the range is all real numbers, because it's possible to produce any y-value by plugging in some x-value. But in the function $f(x) = x^2$, the range is from 0 to infinity, because it's possible to produce any number ranging from 0 to infinity by plugging in some x-value, but it isn't possible to produce a negative number, since the square of any real number must be either a positive number or 0.

Graphing Functions

We can graph functions on the xy-coordinate plane by plotting a series of points with (x, y) coordinates, where x is the number plugged into the function and y is the result.

Example:

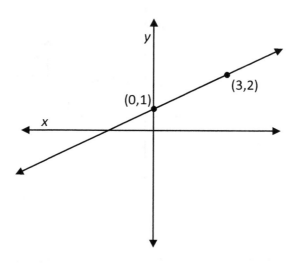

This graph represents the function $f(x) = \frac{x}{3} + 1$, with labels indicating two specific points on the graph, and a line indicating the set of all points with coordinates that satisfy the function.

The Slope Of A Function Graph

On the Math Level 2 Test, the slope of a graph is the measure of how slanted or tilted the line of a graph is. (It's possible to find the slope of a point in a curve, but the Math Level 2 Test doesn't ask us to do that, so we won't cover it in this Black Book.)

There are two general ways to determine the slope of a graph on the Math Level 2 Test:

1. We can look at the equation of the function that generated the graph.

2. We can find the slope using two points on the graph.

The slope is a fraction that expresses a measurement of how far "up" the line travels for a given distance that it travels from left to right:

- The number of units traveled "up" goes in the numerator of the slope fraction. (A negative number in the numerator indicates that the line travels "down" as it goes from left to right, and a zero in the numerator indicates that the line is horizontal.)

- The number of units traveled from left to right is the denominator of the slope fraction.

For this reason, the slope fraction is often described as "rise over run"—the number of units traveled up (the "rise"), divided by the number of units traveled from left to right (the "run").

Example:

> **If the slope of a line is $\frac{1}{3}$, then the line travels 1 unit up for every 3 units it travels from left to right, because the numerator, or "rise," is 1, and the denominator, or "run," is 3.**

This means we can calculate the slope between two points on a function graph by finding the vertical distance between them, and dividing it by the horizontal distance between them:

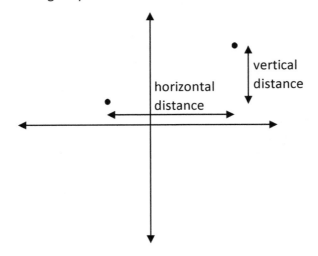

The vertical distance between the two points is the difference between the *y*-values of the points, and the horizontal distance between them is the difference between the *x*-values.

Example:

> **The slope between the points (5, 3) and (19, 8) is equal to $\frac{8-3}{19-5}$, or $\frac{5}{14}$.**

By convention, we take the values from the left-most point and subtract them from the values of the right-most point, but it doesn't actually matter which order you subtract in, as long as you use the same order for coordinates in the numerator and denominator, and you keep track of any minus signs.

Example:

> **If we switch the order of subtraction for the points from the previous example, we get $\frac{3-8}{5-19}$, or $\frac{-5}{-14}$, which is still equal to $\frac{5}{14}$.**

A line with positive slope is slanted upward as we read from left-to-right, and a line with a negative slope is slanted downward:

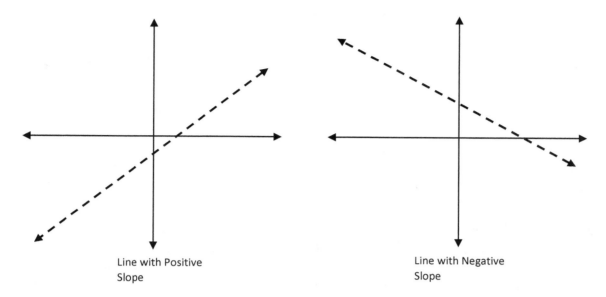

Line with Positive
Slope

Line with Negative
Slope

Slope-Intercept Format

We can also easily find the slope of a line when the function equation for the line is in something called "slope-intercept format," which looks like this:

$$y = mx + b$$

The variables in slope-intercept format represent the following aspects of the graph:

- y and x represent the values in an (x, y) coordinate pair of any point on the graph

- m represents the slope, often in fraction form

- b represents the y-intercept, which is the y-value of the function where $x = 0$, and is also the point on the y-axis where the function graph crosses the y-axis.

So when a line is in slope-intercept form, the coefficient of x is the slope of the line.

Example:

For the function $y = 4x - 7$, the slope of the line is 4, and the y-intercept is (0, -7).

For the function $y = \frac{x}{5} + 1$, the slope is $\frac{1}{5}$, and the y-intercept is (0,1). (Remember that $\frac{x}{5}$ is the same as $\frac{1}{5}x$.)

Graphing Functions On A Calculator

Your graphing calculator makes it easy to see how a function behaves in the xy-coordinate plane.

You should be familiar with the process for graphing a given function on your calculator (this process can vary slightly depending on the type of graphing calculator you use).

You should also know how to adjust aspects of your calculator's display, such as the following:

- the scale or zoom

- the number of units on each axis that are displayed in the window

- the units that are used in the display (such as radians, etc.)

You should be able to view the table of values for a given function. The table of values shows selected pairings of *x*- and *y*-values for a given function.

Finally, you should be able to use the trace feature on your calculator to identify specific (*x*, *y*) points on a graph of a function.

Some questions on the Math Level 2 Test will ask you about the behavior or features of the graph of a function. The fastest and easiest way to answer a question like this is often just to graph the function on your calculator and then refer to the graph when you choose your answer, instead of trying to answer the question by analyzing the equation for the function, as a math teacher would usually require.

Unique Output For Every Input

Part of the definition of a function is that any input number that we plug into the function can only result in one output number. For example, if the graph of a function contained the point (3, 7), then it could not also contain the point (3, 1), because then the input value of *x* = 3 would be linked with two outputs: 7 and 1.

Another way to think of this rule is to use the "vertical line test." If you can draw a vertical line on the graph of an equation and cross the graph in more than one place with the same vertical line, then the equation that generated the graph isn't a function.

Example:

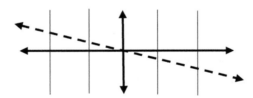

The dashed line in this diagram is the graph of a function. We can see that it's not possible to draw a vertical line in such a way that the vertical line crosses the function more than once.

Example:

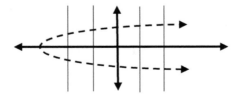

In this example, however, we can see that it's possible to draw a vertical line in such a way that it crosses the graph more than once. The graph in this example fails the vertical line test, so this isn't the graph of a function.

Inverse Functions

For any given function, the inverse of the function is a second function that reverses the inputs and outputs of the original function. So if f and g are inverse functions of one another, and $f(3) = 19$, then $g(19) = 3$.

The Math Level 2 Test sometimes asks us to find the inverse function of a particular function, or to evaluate a particular x-value in the inverse function of a given function.

Inverse function notation takes the form f^{-1}, where f is the original function. (For example, h^{-1} would indicate the function that's the inverse of function h.)

To find the inverse function of a specific value, we simply set the function equal to that value and solve for x. If we find $f^{-1}(5)$, then we're saying "what is the x-value that will give us an $f(x)$ equal to 5?"

Example:

Find $f^{-1}(5)$ for $f(x) = 2x - 3$

$5 = 2x - 3$	(plug in 5 for $f(x)$)
$8 = 2x$	(add 3 to both sides)
$4 = x$	(divide both sides by 2)

So we know that $x = 4$ gives us an $f(x)$ equal to 5, which means $f^{-1}(5) = 4$ for the function $f(x) = 2x - 3$.

To write the algebraic equation for an inverse function, we follow these steps (assuming that we're dealing with a function called f):

1. Change $f(x)$ into y (if $f(x)$ was used in the original function)

2. Change all instances of x from the original function into instances of y.

3. Change all instances of y from the original function into instances of x.

4. Re-solve the new version of the equation for y.

5. Change y to $f^{-1}(x)$ if you want. (This step isn't strictly necessary, but it may help you keep things straight.)

Example:

Find $f^{-1}(x)$ for $f(x) = 2x - 3$

$y = 2x - 3$	(change $f(x)$ to y)
$x = 2y - 3$	(change all instances of x to y, and all instances of y to x)
$y = \frac{x + 3}{2}$	(re-solve the new equation for y)
$f^{-1}(x) = \frac{x + 3}{2}$	(change y to $f^{-1}(x)$)

So $f(x) = \frac{x + 3}{2}$ is the inverse function of $f(x) = 2x - 3$. Another way to say this is that $f^{-1}(x) = \frac{x + 3}{2}$, given that $f(x) = 2x - 3$.

Triangles

Questions about triangles appear frequently on the Math Level 2 Test. Many of these questions involve trigonometry, which we'll discuss in the next section, but you'll need to know more fundamental concepts related to triangles as well. This information includes the following ideas, among others:

- notable properties

- area

- right triangles

- special triangles

- Pythagorean Theorem

Notable Properties Of Triangles

The measures of the three angles of a triangle must always add up to 180°.

In any triangle, the largest angle is across from the longest side, the smallest angle is across from the shortest side, and the angle that is neither largest nor smallest is across from the remaining side.

Example:

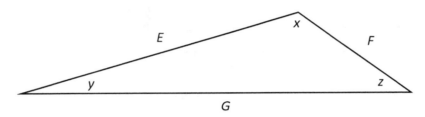

In the triangle above, G is the longest side, and it's opposite x, the largest angle. F is the shortest side, and it's opposite y, the smallest angle. E is the remaining side, and it's opposite z, the remaining angle.

The sides of a triangle follow a rule called "the triangle inequality." This rule says that the length of any side of a triangle must have the following attributes:

- It must be *larger* than the *difference* of the lengths of the other two sides.

- It must be *less* than the *sum* of the lengths of the other two sides.

Example:

The diagram below cannot be a triangle because the longest side is longer than the other two sides put together. As a result, the two shorter sides can't connect to close the shape.

Area Of A Triangle

The area of a triangle is equal to one half times the length of the base times the height, or $\frac{1}{2}bh$.

Any side of a triangle can be thought of as a base, although we normally see the bottom of a triangle labeled as its base, in diagrams where a triangle's bottom side is horizontal.

We can find the height of a triangle by starting at the vertex that is opposite the base, and then drawing a line segment perpendicular to the base, stopping when we hit the base. (For an obtuse triangle, the height is extended until it touches where the base would be if we extended the base far enough to touch the height (as in the example triangle on the right below.)

That might sound a little confusing, so here are a couple of examples of triangles with their heights and bases labeled.

Examples:

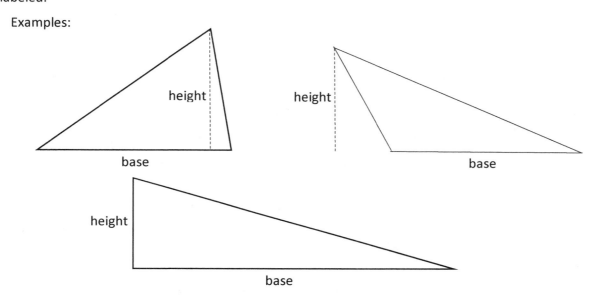

Now let's find the area of an example triangle.
Example:

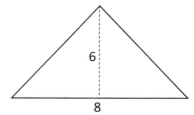

In the triangle above, the base is 8 and the height is 6.
So the area is $\frac{1}{2}(8)(6)$, or 24.

Right triangles

A right triangle is a triangle in which one of the three angles is a right angle.

In a right triangle, the longest side is called the hypotenuse, while the other two sides are called legs.

The square of the length of the hypotenuse is equal to the sum of the squares of the lengths of the legs. This relationship is called the Pythagorean Theorem, and it's written this way, where a and b are the lengths of the legs and c is the length of the hypotenuse:

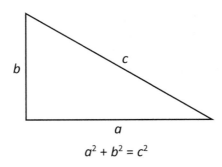

$$a^2 + b^2 = c^2$$

A Pythagorean triple is a set of three numbers that can be the lengths of the sides of a right triangle. There are four Pythagorean Triples that you'll want to be particularly familiar with, because they can sometimes be used to help answer questions on the Math Level 2 Test.

- **{3, 4, 5} is a Pythagorean triple because $3^2 + 4^2 = 5^2$.**

- **{5, 12, 13} is a Pythagorean triple because $5^2 + 12^2 = 13^2$**

- **{1, 1, $\sqrt{2}$} is a Pythagorean triple because $1^2 + 1^2 = \sqrt{2}^2$ (this is also the ratio of side lengths in an isosceles right triangle)**

- **{1, $\sqrt{3}$, 2} is a Pythagorean triple because $1^2 + \sqrt{3}^2 = 2^2$ (this is also the ratio of side lengths in a 30°-60°-90° triangle)**

Special Triangles

Some triangles have unique properties that can make them useful tools for answering questions on the Math Level 2 Test, including the following:

- equilateral triangles

- isosceles triangles

- certain right triangles

An equilateral triangle has three sides of the same length and three angles of the same measure. Each of the three angles of an equilateral triangle is 60°.

Example:

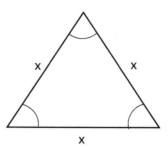

In the equilateral triangle above, all sides are of length x and each angle is 60°.

An isosceles triangle has 2 sides of the same length. The angles opposite the sides of the same length have the same degree measurements.

Example:

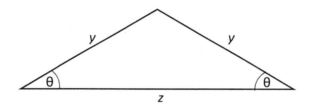

In the isosceles triangle above, two sides are the same length y, and the angles whose vertices are the ends of the third side both have measures of θ°.

The 45°-45°-90° triangle and the 30°-60°-90° right triangle are shown below, along with the ratios of their side lengths. You should be familiar with these triangles and their measurements.

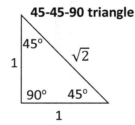

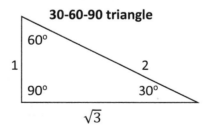

A triangle inscribed in a semi-circle (so that one side of the triangle is formed by the diameter of the semicircle and one point of the triangle is found on the circumference of the semi-circle) is always a right triangle.

Example

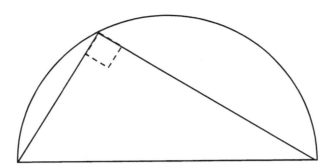

Trigonometry

For the purposes of preparing for the Math Level 2 Test, we can think of trigonometry as an area of math that relates triangle side lengths to their angle measurements.

Most of the trigonometry on the Math Level 2 Test is related to right triangles, but some isn't.

SOHCAHTOA And The Six Basic Trig Functions

There are three main trigonometric functions: sine, cosine, and tangent. These functions relate the lengths of the hypotenuse, adjacent side, and opposite side of a right triangle to one another.

We use the mnemonic device SOHCAHTOA to remember what these functions represent (we'll explain what "opposite" and "adjacent" mean in a moment):

Sine = **O**pposite/**H**ypotenuse

Cosine = **A**djacent/**H**ypotenuse

Tangent = **O**pposite/**A**djacent

When we look at an angle in a triangle, the "opposite" leg is the side across from the angle—the side that the angle isn't touching. The "adjacent" leg is the leg that the angle is touching.

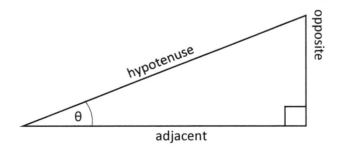

When we find the sine, cosine, or tangent of an angle, we use the values for the lengths of the appropriate sides to create the fraction dictated by SOHCAHTOA. For example, if we want to find the sine of an angle in a right triangle, we check SOHCAHTOA, which tells us that **S**ine = **O**pposite/**H**ypotenuse. So we create a fraction whose numerator is the length of the opposite leg, and whose denominator is the length of the hypotenuse. That fraction is equal to the sine of the given angle.

In addition to sine, cosine, and tangent, you also need to be familiar with cosecant, secant, and cotangent. These functions are the reciprocals of sine, cosine, and tangent, respectively:

$$\csc \theta = \frac{1}{\sin \theta} = \text{Hypotenuse/Opposite}$$

$$\sec \theta = \frac{1}{\cos \theta} = \text{Hypotenuse/Adjacent}$$

$$\cot \theta = \frac{1}{\tan \theta} = \text{Adjacent/Opposite}$$

Inverse Trig Functions

Finding the inverse of a given trig function is the opposite process from finding the trig function itself: instead of starting with an angle measurement and finding the value of the ratio for the trig function, we start with the value of the trig function and find an angle measurement that corresponds to it.

There are several ways to refer to the inverse of a trig function. For the sine function, the inverse can be written in any of the following ways:

- inverse sine

- arcsine

- $\sin^{-1}$

- arcsin

The inverses of the other trig functions have similar naming conventions. For example, the inverse tangent of a number can also be referred to as the arctan, $\tan^{-1}$, etc.

In general, we'll use a scientific or graphing calculator to find the value of an inverse trigonometric function. (This might not be the way a mathematician would find an inverse trigonometric function, but it's what we'll do on the Math Level 2 Test.)

Degrees and radians

Math Level 2 questions will use one of two different units to measure the size of an angle:

- Degrees

- Radians

When we use a calculator for anything related to trigonometry, we need to make sure it's in the proper mode—degree mode if the angle in the question is measured in degrees, or radian mode if the angle in the question is measured in radians.

(We'll talk about radians in more detail when we discuss the unit circle later in this section.)

If the question mentions angle measures in degrees (either with the word "degrees," or with a degree symbol), then the calculator needs to be in degree mode. If the question and/or answer choices mention angle measures without degree symbols, then the calculator needs to be in radian mode (angle measures in radians will often—but not always—include the symbol π).

If the calculator is in the wrong mode, it will give you a different value from the correct one, even if you do everything else right. So it's VERY important that you pay attention to what mode your calculator is in when you answer a trig question on test day.

Law Of Sines

The law of sines is a trigonometric formula that doesn't require a right triangle. The law tells us that in a specific triangle, the ratio of the sine of each angle to its opposite side is constant. In other words, for the following triangle, $\frac{a}{sinA} = \frac{b}{sinB} = \frac{c}{sinC}$:

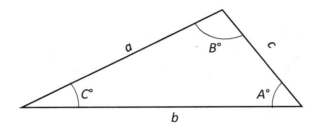

We can use this law to find the lengths of sides or the measures of angles when we know enough information about a given triangle to fill in the rest of the proportion. Notice that we don't need the lengths and angle measures of all the sides and angles to use the law of sines; we can do so as long as we have the side length and angle measure of one angle and its opposite side, and either the side length or angle measure of another part of the triangle.

There may be a question or two on test day that can be answered using the law of sines, but we can actually work around the law of sines to find the correct answer, if we prefer. For an example of working around the law of sines, see the explanation in this book for question 43 from page 138 of the MSTB.

Graphs Of Trig Functions

You should be familiar with the graphs of the trigonometric functions, which are shown below:

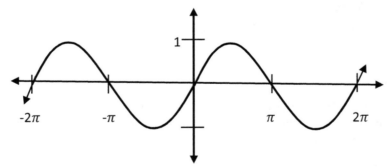

$$y = \sin x$$

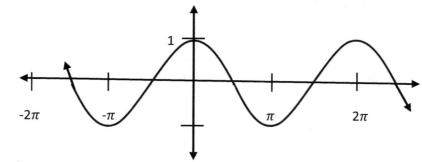

$y = \cos x$

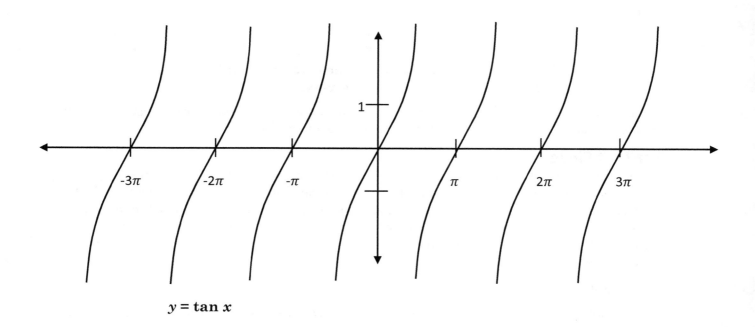

$y = \tan x$

The period of a graph is given by the smallest horizontal section of the graph that could be copied over and over again to recreate the graph.

Example:

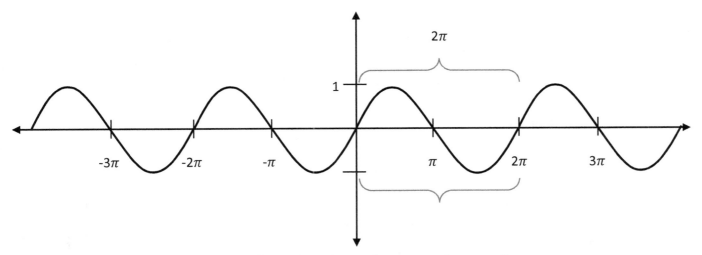

The period of $y = \sin x$ is 2π, because the graph repeats itself every 2π units along the x-axis.

It's good to be familiar with these graphs—but remember that you can graph these functions on your graphing calculator at any time if you need to refresh your memory.

The Unit Circle

The unit circle is a mathematical construct at the heart of trigonometry. It has many interesting applications in mathematical theory, but we're not concerned with most of those applications for the purposes of the Math Level 2 Test. In fact, questions on the Math Level 2 Test generally don't require us to know anything about the unit circle, although it sometimes happens that understanding the unit circle will allow us to answer a question more quickly. For these reasons, our discussion of the unit circle will be limited to the following:

1. giving a formal definition of the unit circle

2. explaining how the various trig functions can be evaluated for a given angle on the unit circle

3. explaining the difference between measuring angles in radians and degrees

Let's get started.

The unit circle is a circle drawn in the *xy*-coordinate plane with its center at (0, 0) and a radius of 1 unit. The unit circle therefore passes through the points (1, 0), (0, 1), (-1, 0), and (0, -1):

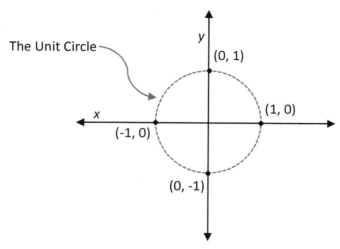

We can use the unit circle to determine the trig values for a given angle by taking the following steps:

1. Lay the angle over the unit circle in the following way:

    a. the vertex of the angle goes on the point (0, 0)

    b. one leg of the angle extends along the positive portion of the *x*-axis.

    c. the angle's other leg opens upward, counter-clockwise. If the angle is greater than 180°, then it opens past the point (-1, 0) and towards the point (0, -1).

2. Note the point where the leg from part (c) intercepts the unit circle:

    • The cosine of the angle is the *x*-coordinate of the point in Step 2.

    • The sine of the angle is the *y*-coordinate of the point in Step 2.

    • All other trig values for the angle can be calculated from the sine and cosine.

Example:

Let's find the trig values for a 60° angle. To do this, we start by imagining that we're placing the angle over the unit circle in the way we just described, which would look like this:

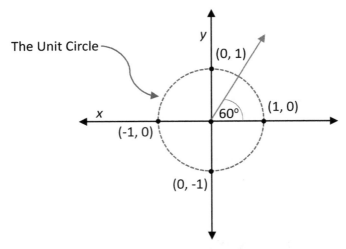

Next, we determine the coordinates of the point where the opening leg crosses the unit circle. (We'll use a calculator for this, because the goal here is to demonstrate how sine and cosine relate to the unit circle, not to determine the trig values of the angle for the first time ever. Remember that the rules and design features of the test make it impossible for the College Board to require you to write out a new proof of basic trig concepts from scratch.)

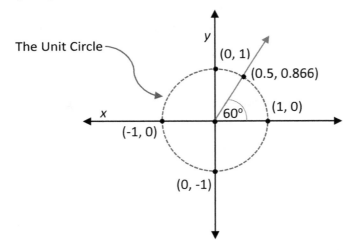

The *x*-coordinate of the point of intersection is the angle's cosine, and the *y*-coordinate of the point of intersection is the angle's sine. As we can see, the sine of a 60° angle is approximately 0.866, and the cosine is 0.5. These two values allow us to determine all the other trig values for the angle:

- Tangent 60° = (sine 60°/cosine 60°) $\approx \frac{0.866}{0.5} \approx 1.732$
- Secant 60° = 1/cosine 60° = $\frac{1}{0.5}$ = 2
- Cosecant 60° = 1/sine 60° $\approx \frac{1}{0.866} \approx 1.15$

- Cotangent 60° = 1/tangent 60° $\approx \dfrac{1}{1.732} \approx$ .577

Since the unit circle has a radius of 1, the circumference of the unit circle is 2π.

The relationship of sine and cosine to the unit circle helps us to see why it must always be true that $\sin^2\theta + \cos^2\theta = 1$, because we can form a right triangle using the following three elements:

- The sine of a given θ as the vertical leg of the right triangle

- The cosine of a given θ as the horizontal leg of the right triangle

- The one-unit radius of the unit circle as the hypotenuse of the right triangle

In addition to measuring angles in degrees, we can also measure angles with a unit called the "radian," which measures the portion of the unit circle marked off by a given angle when the angle is laid on the unit circle as described above. Since the full distance around the unit circle is 2π, an angle measure of 2π radians is equivalent to a measure of 360°. Similarly, an angle measurement of π radians is equivalent to 180°, and a measurement of $\dfrac{\pi}{2}$ radians is equivalent to 90°.

When you're working with angles or trigonometry on the Math Level 2 Test, it's important to make sure you notice whether the question is written in terms of degrees or radians—especially if you're using a calculator on the question, because you'll have to make sure you put your calculator in radian or degree mode to match the units in the question. As a rule, if a question on the test doesn't refer to degrees when specifying an angle's size, then the angle is being measured in radians.

Logarithms

A logarithm is kind of like the opposite, or inverse, of an exponential expression: it tells us the exponent to which a base must be raised in order to produce a particular result. (If that sounds confusing, just keep reading.)

Notation

A logarithm, or log, is written in this form:

$$\log_a b = c$$

In the logarithm above:

- a is the base in the exponential expression $a^c = b$

- b is the number whose logarithm we're finding for the given base

- c is the logarithm of b, given base a. In other words, c is the exponent we'd raise a to in order to get b: $a^c = b$

We would typically read $\log_a b = c$ aloud as "log base a of b is c." This statement tells us that we need to multiply a by itself c times to get b. In other words, if $\log_a b = c$, then $a^c = b$.

Example:

$$log_3\, 81 = 4, \text{ because } 3^4 = 81$$

In the previous example, the base is 3. But if you ever see "log" used without a base number, then the base is understood to be 10.

Example:

$$\log 100 = 2, \text{ because } 10^2 = 100$$

Properties Of Logs

For the purposes of the Math Level 2 Test, it will be useful to memorize the following properties of logs:

$\log_a(xy) = \log_a x + \log_a y$

Example:

$$\log_5 18 = \log_5 6 + \log_5 3, \text{ because } 6 \times 3 = 18$$

$\log_a(\frac{x}{y}) = \log_a x - \log_a y$

Example:

$$\log_5 3 = \log_5 18 - \log_5 6, \text{ because } \frac{18}{6} = 3$$

$\log_a x^y = y\log_a x$

Example:

$$\log_3 9^2 = 2\log_3 9$$

Natural Log

Another very important logarithm is the natural log. The natural log of x is written as ln(x), and it is equal to $\log_e x$.

The value of e is approximately 2.7183. (For the purposes of this test, we don't need to know how the value of e was originally determined.)

If $e^y = x$, then ln(x) = y.

One of the most important applications of the idea of natural log on the Math Level 2 Test is to help us isolate variables in exponents of the number e, because ln(e^x) = x.

Example:

$$5 = e^{2x}$$

$\ln(5) = 2x$ \qquad (take natural log of both sides)

$\frac{\ln(5)}{2} = x$ \qquad (divide both sides by 2)

To find the natural log of a number on the Math Level 2 Test, we use a calculator. The button for finding the natural log is usually labeled "ln." In the case of our example, the calculator tells us that $\frac{\ln(5)}{2}$ equals approximately 0.8047.

A specific application of the idea of e and the natural log is the growth/decay formula. This is a formula that can show up in problems related to things like money earning continuous interest, or radioactive materials decaying. These problems follow a basic formula that looks something like $A = Pe^{rt}$, where

- *A* is the final amount

- *P* is the initial amount

- *e* is the constant whose value is approximately 2.7183, as discussed above

- *r* is the rate of growth or decay with respect to time *t*

- *t* is the amount of time

Some people like to remember this formula by making the right side of the equation, Pe^{rt}, into the word "pert," so you may know it that way from school. (If you need to use this formula on the test, it will be provided in the question.)

You don't need to know anything special about this formula for the Math Level 2 Test. You don't even actually need to know the formula, because questions involving the formula always provide it and explain which variable represents which value from the question. As long as you understand the inverse relationship between *e* and the natural log, and you can do the kind of algebra used in other Math Level 2 questions, you should have no trouble with questions involving *e*. (Of course, you'll see my solutions for questions involving this formula in the walkthroughs later in this book.)

Exponents

When an expression is raised to an exponent, the exponent tells us to multiply the original expression by itself a certain number of times.

Example:

7^3 means we should multiply three 7s, giving us $7 \times 7 \times 7$, or 343. So $7^3 = 343$.

The number being raised to the exponent is called the "base."

Any number raised to an exponent of 1 is equal to itself, and any number raised to an exponent of 0 is equal to 1.

Example:

$5^1 = 5$

$17^0 = 1$

To find the value of a negative exponent, we create a fraction. The numerator of the fraction is the number 1. The denominator of the fraction is the original number raised to the absolute value of the exponent.

Example:

$3^{-6} = \dfrac{1}{3^6}$

Squares and Square Roots

Squaring a number is the process of multiplying that number by itself.

Example:

$$5^2 = 5 \times 5 = 25$$

Taking the square root of a value means finding the number that results in the original value when multiplied by itself. When we're given the symbol $\sqrt{\ }$ over a number, it represents the *positive* square root of that number. An expression with the $\sqrt{\ }$ symbol can also be called a radical expression.

Example:

$$\sqrt{25} = 5$$

When you square the square root of a number, you get the original number.

Example:

$$(\sqrt{25})^2 = 25$$

We can evaluate the square or the square root of any kind of value, or even of entire expressions:

Example:

$$(x + 14)^2$$

$$\sqrt{3x - 19}$$

We can multiply radical expressions together.

Example:

$$\sqrt{7} \times \sqrt{3} = \sqrt{21}$$

$$\sqrt{10} \times \sqrt{3} = \sqrt{30}$$

We can also factor radical expressions.

Example:

$$\sqrt{34} = \sqrt{17} \times \sqrt{2}$$

When a factor is a square, we can simplify the expression further by taking its square root.

Examples:

$$\sqrt{18} = (\sqrt{9})(\sqrt{2}) = 3\sqrt{2}$$

$$\sqrt{80} = (\sqrt{16})(\sqrt{5}) = 4\sqrt{5}$$

Cubes and Cube Roots

Cubing a number is the process of multiplying that number by itself twice.

Example:

$$4^3 = 4 \times 4 \times 4 = 64$$

Taking the cube root of a value means finding the number that results in the original value when multiplied by itself twice. When we see the symbol $\sqrt[3]{\ }$ over a number, it represents the cube root of that number.

Example:

$$\sqrt[3]{64} = 4$$

When you cube the cube root of a number, you get the original number.

Example:

$$(\sqrt[3]{64})^3 = 64$$

We can find the cube or the cube root of any kind of value, or even of entire expressions.

Example:

$$(x + 9)^3$$

$$\sqrt[3]{2x - 4}$$

We can multiply cube root expressions together.

Example:

$$\sqrt[3]{11} \times \sqrt[3]{4} = \sqrt[3]{44}$$

We can also factor cube root expressions.

Example:

$$\sqrt[3]{42} = \sqrt[3]{7} \times \sqrt[3]{6}$$

When the number in a factor is a cube, we can take the cube root of that factor to simplify the expression further.

Example:

$$\sqrt[3]{24} = \sqrt[3]{8 \times 3} = (\sqrt[3]{8})(\sqrt[3]{3}) = 2(\sqrt[3]{3})$$

Real Numbers

For our purposes, a "real number" is any number that is *not* an imaginary number, and therefore does *not* involve *i*. Real numbers can be positive or negative, whole or fractional, and rational or irrational.

Example:

Real numbers include 1, 0, -7.2, $\frac{1}{9}$, π, $\sqrt{5}$, 100, and others.

For more on imaginary numbers (that is, numbers that involve *i*), see the "Imaginary Numbers" section in Part II of this toolbox.

Absolute Value

A number's absolute value is its distance from zero on the number line.

Example:

-7 and 7 both have an absolute value of 7. We signify the absolute value of a number with vertical bars on either side of the number: |-7| = |7| = 7.

We can create equations using absolute values and one or more variables using the following steps:

1. If the absolute value expression is not isolated on one side of the equation, we isolate it on one side of the expression.

2. Once the absolute value expression is isolated on one side of the equation, we create two versions of the equation:

   - In one version of the equation, we simply remove the absolute value bars.

   - In the other version of the equation, we remove the absolute value bars and multiply the other side of the equation by -1.

3. We solve the two equations separately and come up with 2 values for the variable.

   Example:

$\|x\| = 4$	(given equation)
$x = 4$ or $x = -4$	(split the given equation into two versions)

   Example:

$\|3x + 2\| = 17$	(given equation)
$3x + 2 = 17$ or $3x + 2 = -17$	(split the given equation into two versions)
$3x = 15$ or $3x = -19$	(combine like terms)
$x = 3$ or $x = -\dfrac{19}{3}$	(divide by 3 to isolate x)

Factors

The factors of a number are the integers that can be multiplied together to produce that number.

   Example:

   The factors of 12 are 1, 2, 3, 4, 6, and 12, because $1 \times 12 = 12$, $2 \times 6 = 12$, and $3 \times 4 = 12$.

Common factors are factors that two numbers have in common.

   Example:

   The factors of 12 are 1, 2, 3, 4, 6, and 12. The factors of 9 are 1, 3, and 9. The common factors of 12 and 9 are 1 and 3, because 12 and 9 both have factors of 1 and 3.

Any factor of a number x is also a factor of all numbers for which x itself is a factor.

Example:

> 2 is a factor of 10, and 10 is a factor of 100; therefore, 2 must be a factor of 100.

Prime Numbers

A prime number has exactly two different factors: 1 and itself.

Example:

> 11 is a prime number because its only two factors are 1 and itself, 11.

> 34 is NOT a prime number, because 34 has factors other than 1 and itself. In addition to 1 and itself, 34 has factors of 2 and 17.

All prime numbers are positive.

The only even prime number is 2.

1 is NOT a prime number because 1 has only one factor (itself). Prime numbers must have exactly two unique factors.

Operations on Algebraic Expressions

Algebraic expressions include variables.

Basic Arithmetic Operations

Algebraic expressions can be added, subtracted, multiplied, and divided—just like the numbers they represent—but sometimes there are special rules we need to follow.

We can add or subtract two algebraic expressions when they involve the same variable expressions.

Example:

> We can add $2a$ and $7a$ to get $9a$, because the $2a$ and $7a$ both involve the same variable expression: a.

> We can subtract $10x^3y$ from $35x^3y$ and get $25x^3y$ because both terms involve the variable expression x^3y.

> But if we want to add $7a$ to $10x^3y$, we can't combine those two expressions any further algebraically because they have different variable components. So all we can do is write $7a + 10x^3y$ and leave it at that.

We can multiply two algebraic expressions by multiplying every term in the first expression by every term in the second expression.

Examples:

$$(9q)(2r) = 18qr$$

$$(2x + 7)(5y + 4) = 10xy + 8x + 35y + 28$$

We can divide any algebraic expression by another algebraic expression when both expressions have factors in common. (See the discussion on factoring algebraic expressions later in this Math Toolbox.)

Example:

$$\frac{72ab}{8b} = 9a$$

FOIL

When we multiply two binomial algebraic expressions, we can often use the "FOIL" technique. "FOIL" is an acronym that stands for "First, Outer, Inner, Last," and refers to the order in which the terms of the two expressions are multiplied together.

(You've probably used FOIL in your math classes, but don't worry if you used some other technique.)

Example:

We can use FOIL to multiply the expressions $(2x - 6)$ and $(3x + 5)$.

The "First" pair in the acronym is $2x$ and $3x$, because they're the first terms in each expression. We multiply these and get $6x^2$.

The "Outer" pair in the acronym is $2x$ and 5. We multiply these and get $10x$.

The "Inner" pair in the acronym is -6 and $3x$. We multiply these and get $-18x$.

The "Last" pair in the acronym is -6 and 5. We multiply these and get -30.

Now we just add up all those terms, which gives us the expression $6x^2 + 10x - 18x - 30$. We can simplify this further by combining the two x-terms, giving us the following:

$$6x^2 - 8x - 30$$

So $(2x - 6)(3x + 5) = 6x^2 - 8x - 30$

Don't worry if this seems a little complicated right now. It doesn't show up very often on the test anyway, but there are times when being familiar with the concept of FOIL can help you understand a question better.

Factoring Algebraic Expressions

For our purposes, factoring an algebraic expression means breaking that expression down into two other expressions that can be multiplied together to produce the original expression.

Example:

> **If we have an expression like (6y + 18), we can break that down into the factors 6 and (y + 3), because 6(y + 3) = 6y + 18.**

There are three main types of factoring situations you'll need to recognize:

1. factoring out common factors

2. doing "FOIL" in reverse

3. recognizing a difference of squares

When we factor using the first method above, we do it by observing that every term in a given expression has a common factor, and then we "divide through" by that term. (This is what we saw in the last example.)

Example:

> **In the expression (12ab^2 + 9b), both of the terms have the common factor 3b, so we can factor the expression like this: 3b(4ab + 3).**

Factoring polynomials usually involves doing the "FOIL" process in reverse. That might sound intimidating, but it's really not as hard as it sounds.

Examples:

$$2x^2 + 3x - 35 = (x + 5)(2x - 7)$$

$$3a^2 + 7a + 4 = (3a + 4)(a + 1)$$

When an algebraic expression is the difference of two terms that are both squares, we can find the following two factors of the expression:

- the sum of the square roots of the two squares

- the difference of the square roots of the two squares

Examples:

$$4x^2 - 81 = (2x + 9)(2x - 9)$$

$$16a^2 - 1 = (4a + 1)(4a - 1)$$

Polynomials

For our purposes, a polynomial is an expression that fits one or more of the following descriptions:

- Adding or subtracting terms with more than one variable or combination of variables

- Adding or subtracting terms that include expressions with the same variable raised to different exponents

In this context, the "degree" of a variable in a polynomial refers to the highest exponent to which that variable is raised in the expression. So $x^3 + 5x^2 - x - 7$ is a third-degree polynomial, because the highest exponent of an x-term in the polynomial is 3.

The Math Level 2 Test sometimes asks us about the "zeros" or "roots" of a polynomial. The term "zero of a polynomial" is interchangeable with the term "root of a polynomial," and they both refer to a value of a variable (usually x) that makes the polynomial expression equal to zero.

Example:

$x^2 + 2x - 3$

$(1)^2 + 2(1) - 3$ (plug in 1 for x)

$1 + 2 - 3$ (combine like terms)

0 ($x = 1$ is a zero, or root, of $x^2 + 2x - 3$)

When we plug $x = 1$ into $x^2 + 2x - 3$, we get zero. So $x = 1$ is a zero of the polynomial.

When we graph a function that involves setting y equal to the output of a polynomial expression, a root of the function appears in the graph as an x-value of any point where the graph touches or crosses the x-axis. For this reason, one of the easiest ways to find the roots of an expression on the Math Level 2 Test is to graph the expression on your calculator and find the x-values where the graph crosses or touches the x-axis.

Another way to find the zeros of a polynomial is to factor the polynomial, which involves breaking down the polynomial into separate expressions that can be multiplied together to produce the original polynomial.

Once we know the factors of a polynomial, we can set them equal to zero to find the zeros of the polynomial (because if any of the factors equals zero, then the whole expression must be equal to zero).

Example:

$x^2 + 2x - 3 = 0$ (original polynomial, set equal to zero)

$(x + 3)(x - 1) = 0$ (factor the expression)

$x + 3 = 0$ or $x - 1 = 0$ (identify the two separate possibilities to make the original expression equal zero)

$x = -3$ or $x = 1$ (solve to find the two roots of the original polynomial)

We've found that $x = -3$ and $x = 1$ are both zeros of the polynomial, because the factors are $(x + 3)$ and $(x - 1)$; if either of those factors is equal to zero, then the whole expression must equal zero.

In the explanation above, we found that $(x + 3)$ was a factor of the polynomial. When we set $(x + 3)$ equal to zero, we determined that a root or zero of the polynomial was -3. We can also work in the other direction—if we know that -3 is a root or zero of a polynomial, then we know that one factor of that polynomial is $(x - (-3))$, or $(x + 3)$.

Similarly, if we know that 1 is a root or zero of a polynomial, then we know that $(x - 1)$ is a factor of that polynomial.

Arithmetic Mean

You may see the concept of "mean" or "arithmetic mean" on the Math Level 2 Test. We find the arithmetic mean of a set of numbers by adding up all the numbers in the set, and then dividing the result by however many numbers are in the set. You've probably also heard this concept called the "average" of a set of numbers.

Example:

> To find the mean of 7, 15, 31, and 19, we first add the four numbers:
>
> 7 + 15 + 31 + 19 = 72
>
> Next, we divide 72 by the number of things we just added. The number of things we just added was four, so we divide 72 by 4.
>
> 72 ÷ 4 = 18
>
> So 18 is the arithmetic mean of 7, 15, 31, and 19.

Series, Sequences, and Progressions

Depending on the question, the Math Level 2 Test might describe the concept we'll discuss in this section as a series, sequence, or progression. For our purposes, in the context of this test, these terms all refer to the same thing: an ordered set of numbers that are generated according to some process or rule.

There are two main types of series you're likely to encounter on the Math Level 2 Test:

- arithmetic progressions
- geometric progressions

An arithmetic progression is a series of numbers where each term can be calculated by adding a constant amount to the previous term.

Example:

> 2, 5, 8, 11, 14, 17, 20

In the arithmetic progression above, each term is the result of adding 3 to the previous term. We could find the next term in the progression by adding 3 to 20 to get 23.

A geometric progression is a set of numbers where each term can be calculated by multiplying the previous term by a constant amount.

Example:

> 3, 18, 108, 648

In the geometric progression above, each term is the product of 6 and the previous term. We could find the next term in the progression above by multiplying 648 and 6 to get 3,888.

Recursive notation

Sometimes the rule to find the next term in a progression involves something other than multiplying or adding a consistent value. In this case, the rule that's used to find the next term in this type of progression is often provided by the question, or you may have to figure it out on your own. When the rule is explained, the explanation sometimes uses the following notation, which is called "recursive notation."

Example:

$$n_1, n_2, n_3, n_4, n_5, n_6, n_7, n_8 \ldots$$

Each n represents a term in the progression, and the subscript tells us the order of the terms— n_2 comes immediately before n_3 and immediately after n_1, and so on. There can also be terms that come before n_1, like this:

Example:

$$n_{-2}, n_{-1}, n_0, n_1 \ldots$$

Typically, the series is described with one or more abstract rules, which look something like this:

$$n_x = 2n_{x-1} + 9$$

where:

- n_x represents any particular term you want to find—the "xth" term
- n_{x-1} refers to the term that comes before the term you want to find

For example, if you want to find n_3, then the subscript x is equal to 3, and n_{x-1} is equal to the previous term, which is n_2, because n_2 is equal to n_{3-1}.

The easiest way to understand a rule like the one above is probably just to solve for a certain term in the progression. Let's imagine that we know n_2 is 5, and we're asked to find n_3. We'll need to take the values we have and plug them into the given rule:

$n_x = 2n_{x-1} + 9$	(given rule)
$n_3 = 2n_{3-1} + 9$	(plug in $x = 3$, because we're looking for the 3rd term and we know the 2nd term)
$n_3 = 2n_2 + 9$	(simplify subscript on right-hand side of the equation)
$n_3 = 2(5) + 9$	(plug in $n_2 = 5$ from the given information)
$n_3 = 10 + 9$	(multiply 2 and 5)
$n_3 = 19$	(add 10 and 9)

So if $n_2 = 5$, then $n_3 = 19$.

Of course, now that we know $n_3 = 19$, we can use the value for n_3 to find n_4, like this:

$$n_x = 2n_{x-1} + 9 \qquad \textbf{(given rule)}$$

$$n_4 = 2n_{4-1} + 9 \qquad \textbf{(plug in } x = 4 \textbf{, because we're looking for the 4th term and we know the 3rd term)}$$

$$n_4 = 2n_3 + 9 \qquad \textbf{(simplify subscript on right-hand side of the equation)}$$

$$n_4 = 2(19) + 9 \qquad \textbf{(plug in } n_3 = 19 \textbf{)}$$

$$n_4 = 38 + 9 \qquad \textbf{(multiply 2 and 19)}$$

$$n_4 = 47 \qquad \textbf{(add 38 and 9)}$$

We can also work backwards, using n_2 to find n_1. We just need to make sure that we plug our values in the right places. We can see that n_x represents a number whose subscript is one greater than the subscript of n_{x-1}. So n_x must represent n_2 in this case, and n_{x-1} must represent n_1, since n_2 has a subscript that's one greater than the subscript of n_1.

Let's find the value for n_1, using the value for n_2. Remember that we already know the value for n_2 is 5.

$$n_x = 2n_{x-1} + 9 \qquad \textbf{(given rule)}$$

$$n_2 = 2n_{2-1} + 9 \qquad \textbf{(plug in } x = 2 \textbf{, because we know the 2nd term and we're looking for the 1st term)}$$

$$n_2 = 2n_1 + 9 \qquad \textbf{(simplify subscript on right-hand side of the equation)}$$

$$5 = 2n_1 + 9 \qquad \textbf{(plug in } n_2 = 5 \textbf{ from the given information)}$$

$$-4 = 2n_1 \qquad \textbf{(subtract 9 from both sides)}$$

$$-2 = n_1 \qquad \textbf{(divide both sides by 2)}$$

So we can use a given rule for a progression to find the next term (or a previous term) in the progression, as long as we know the values for enough of the terms in the progression to be able to follow its rules. (In this case, we knew the value of n_2 and we were able to use that to find values before and after n_2 in the progression, because of the way the rule was written.)

But notice that recursive notation only makes it possible to find the value of a term if we know enough of the values of the other terms to be able to follow the rules of the notation—for example, if a series is described with recursive notation that requires us to multiply the three previous terms in order to find the next term, then we need to know at least three of the terms.

In general, if the Math Level 2 Test asks you a question about a series described with recursive notation, the best approach will be to use the information about a given term to keep finding successive terms in the series until you can answer the question. For example, if the question asks about the 5th term and only gives you information about the 2nd term, you may need to use the 2nd term to find the 3rd term, and then use the 3rd term to find the 4th term, and then finally use the 4th term to find the 5th term.

Inequalities

On the Math Level 2 Test, inequalities are statements that show how the sizes of two different expressions relate to one another by using one of these symbols:

- The symbol < means "is less than."

- The symbol > means "is greater than."

- The symbol ≤ means "is less than or equal to."

- The symbol ≥ means "is greater than or equal to."

You solve an inequality in the same way you solve an equation, with one difference: if solving for the variable involves multiplying both sides of the inequality by a negative number, then you have to switch the direction of the inequality.

Example:

$$2 - y \leq 18$$

$-y \leq 16$ (subtract 2 from both sides)

$y \geq -16$ (multiply both sides by -1 and change the direction of the inequality symbol)

Factorials

A factorial is the result when a number, such as n, is multiplied by $(n - 1)$, $(n - 2)$, $(n - 3)$, and so, on until the product is multiplied by 1. The notation for a factorial involves putting an exclamation point after the given number, as in 9!, which is pronounced "9 factorial."

Example:

$$9! = 9 \times 8 \times 7 \times 6 \times 5 \times 4 \times 3 \times 2 \times 1 = 362,880$$

We can find a factorial on a calculator by using the ! button.

Factorials are often used in counting problems, as we'll discuss in the next section.

"Counting Problems"

Counting problems (typically called permutations and combinations problems in math classes) involve figuring out how many different ways something can happen. For example, a question might involve figuring out something like the following:

- the number of different orders in which a group of students can be arranged to form a line

- how many different outfits a person can create from a certain number of shirts, pants, and hats

One general way to solve these problems is to figure out how many different ways each step in the process can happen, and then multiply the numbers of outcomes from each step.

Example:

Emily, Daniel, Jennifer, and Susan sit single-file on a bench. In how many different orders can they sit?

To solve this problem, we start by considering each position on the bench, one at a time. How many students are possible candidates to sit in the first position? There are 4 students, and any individual student can sit in the first position, so that means 4 different students can sit in the first position. How many can sit in the second position? Only 3, because one student is already sitting in the first seat, so there are only 3 other students for the next seat. How many can sit in the third position? Just 2, because there are already two students in the first two seats. Finally, there's only one student left to sit in the fourth seat.

In order to find the number of possible permutations, we multiply all the possibilities together. Four possible candidates could sit in the first position on the bench, and so the first number is 4. Once that position is assigned, there are three left for the second position, and so the next number to be multiplied is 3. The number to multiply after that is 2, because there are two possible people who could sit in the next position. Finally, we multiply by 1, because only one person is left to occupy the last seat. So the number of permutations in this case is 4 × 3 × 2 × 1, or 24. That means there are 24 different possible orders. (Notice that this calculation is equal to 4!, which is also 4 × 3 × 2 × 1.)

Let's look at one more example.

Example:

How many different 3-number addresses exist in which the first number isn't zero, but the other two numbers can be any digit?

Again, we think of one step at a time. The first number can be any digit but zero, so that leaves 9 digits available for the first position (1, 2, 3, 4, 5, 6, 7, 8, and 9). The second number can be any one of 10 digits (0, 1, 2, 3, 4, 5, 6, 7, 8, and 9), and the third number can also be any one of 10 digits (again, 0, 1, 2, 3, 4, 5, 6, 7, 8, and 9). That means the total number of possibilities in this situation is 9 × 10 × 10, or 900. (Note that this isn't a question that calls for a factorial, because we're not talking about a situation where the number of possibilities for any part of the process is affected by the choices made for any other part of the process.)

Counting problems don't come up too often on test day; when they do appear, they often don't require calculators. Still, the test occasionally asks a question that can best be answered with the help of the nCr or nPr functions on a calculator. See "Advanced Combinations and Permutations" in Part II of this toolbox for a discussion of those situations.

Probability

The probability of an event is a measurement of the likelihood that the event will happen, expressed as a fraction (remember that fractions can also be expressed as decimals, ratios, or percentages). If the probability that something will happen is 0.8, that's the same as saying it has an 80% chance of happening, which is the same as saying that, given 10 opportunities, a certain event is expected to happen 8 times out of the 10.

When expressed as a decimal, probability can range from 0 (which indicates something that will definitely not happen, or can never happen) to 1 (which indicates something that definitely will happen, or must always happen).

When expressed as a percentage, probability can range from 0% (will definitely not happen, or will never happen) to 100% (will definitely happen, or will always happen).

Some questions will tell you the probability that an event will happen, and then ask about the probability of the event NOT happening. In this case, we find the probability of the event NOT happening by subtracting the probability that the event WILL happen from 1.

Example:

> **If a test flight has a 0.12 probability of failure, then the probability that the flight will be successful is 0.88, because 1 – 0.12 is 0.88.**

Sometimes we have to calculate the probability of multiple separate events happening. This is called a compound probability. To find a compound probability, we simply multiply the probabilities of the separate events.

Example:

> **On any given night, the probability of a thunderstorm is 0.1, and the probability of a toaster fire is 0.05. The probability of having a thunderstorm and a toaster fire on the same night is 0.005, because 0.1 × 0.05 = 0.005.**

Invented Symbols

Sometimes a question on the Math Level 2 Test will use some kind of invented symbol or notation. Whenever this happens, the question will tell you *exactly* how to use that invented symbol or notation. Simply follow the instructions in the question.

Example:

> **"The expression a Җ b is equal to $2ab^2$. What is the value of 3 Җ 5?"**
>
> **We've probably never seen the symbol "Җ" before, but the question explains exactly what we should do with "Җ." In this example, the 3 corresponds to a and the 5 corresponds to b. So, according to the idea that a Җ $b = 2ab^2$, we know that 3 Җ 5 = $2(3)(5^2)$, or 150.**

Word Problems

Word problems on this test can describe either real-life situations or abstract concepts. First, we'll look at a word problem that describes a real-life situation.

Example:

> **"Aaron buys four hats for eight dollars each, and a pair of pants. Aaron gives the cashier fifty dollars and receives three dollars in change. How much did the pair of pants cost?"**

One way to answer this question is to use mathematical notation to transform it into a problem that we can solve with math. To do that, we take the following steps:

1. Note all the numbers given in the problem, and write them down on scratch paper.

2. Identify key phrases and translate them into mathematical symbols for operations and variables.

3. Use the operations and variables from step 2 to connect the numbers from step 1 in ways that reflect the wording of the original problem.

Example:

> In the phrase "four hats for eight dollars each," the word "each" means we have to multiply the four hats by the eight dollars in order to find out how much the four hats were in total: 4 × $8 = $32. So thirty-two dollars were spent on the four hats if they were eight dollars each.
>
> The phrase "Aaron gives the cashier fifty dollars and receives three dollars in change" tells us that the total cost of Aaron's purchase was $50 – $3, or $47.
>
> If we know that Aaron's total cost for the hats and the pants was $47, and we know the hats cost $32, then the pants must have cost $47 – $32, or $15.

Now let's look at a word problem about an abstract concept.

Example:

> "If y is the sum of two positive integers whose product is 31, how much is y?"

Now we transform the words into a math problem.

Example:

> The phrase "y is the sum of two positive integers" means that there are two positive integers that can be added together to equal y. We can make up any two variables to represent those two integers; we'll use a and b. So $a + b = y$.
>
> The phrase "two integers whose product is 31" means that two integers equal 31 when multiplied together. Notice that these are the same integers that equal y when added together, so we have to use the same variables as before. So now we know that $ab = 31$.
>
> Now we know that $a + b = y$ and $ab = 31$. We also know that a and b are integers.
>
> In a high school math class, we might try to do some algebra involving the equations $a + b = y$ and $ab = 31$, but on this test it's often more productive just to think about each equation for a moment. If we do that, we'll probably realize that the only two positive integers that can be multiplied together to equal 31 are 1 and 31. That means y is equal to 31 + 1, or 32.

As we can see, once we translate the word problem into numbers and symbols, we can solve it like any other problem on this test (see the SAT Math Path in this Black Book for more on that).

Math Toolbox Part II

The material in this section of the Math Toolbox tends to appear less frequently on the Math Level 2 Test than the material we just discussed in Part I of this Toolbox. Although you should read through this section so you'll be familiar with topics that may appear on the test, you shouldn't put much effort into studying these concepts until you're thoroughly familiar with the material in Part I of the Math Toolbox and with the strategic concepts in the rest of this Black Book, because the material in Part II of the Math Toolbox doesn't appear frequently enough to account for a meaningful portion of the points you're likely to score on test day.

The College Board probably includes this kind of material on the Math Level 2 Test to make untrained test-takers think the test is more advanced than it really is. Test-takers who prepare for the test often get so distracted by concepts like vectors and matrices that they don't realize those specific concepts, on average, appear less than once per test, while the majority of Math Level 2 questions involve simpler concepts.

The concepts we'll cover in Part II will probably only show up in a handful of questions on test day—it's not possible to predict the exact number of questions, but it will almost certainly be lower than 10, and probably closer to 5. Bear in mind that on most test days you can leave 6 or 7 questions blank and still score a "perfect" 800 on the test, as long as you answer the other questions correctly. That means it's nearly always possible to score an 800 on the test and never answer a single question on any of the topics in this part of the Toolbox.

This should remind us of two important things:

1. We need to master the topics in Part I of the toolbox before we worry about Part II, because the topics in Part I show up much more often on the test.

2. We shouldn't hesitate to leave questions blank on the Math Level 2 Test if they contain concepts we're not comfortable with (once we make sure that the question isn't really just a strange presentation of basic concepts, of course).

For more on skipping questions and scoring, refer back to the sections of this Black Book titled "Time Management On Test Day" and "Guessing On The Math Level 2 Test."

Transformations Of Functions

We can alter the graph of a quadratic function like $f(x) = x^2$ in a predictable way by modifying any or all of the following parts of the function equation:

- the coefficient of x

- the amount added to x before it's raised to an exponent

- the amount added to the x expression after it's raised to an exponent

Examples

- Changing the size of the coefficient of x will affect how steep the function is (its slope, effectively). A larger coefficient will result in a steeper graph. A smaller coefficient will result in a flatter graph. A negative coefficient will result in a graph that opens "down," while a positive coefficient will result in a graph that opens "up," as in the figures below. Take a few moments to reflect on these ideas, and then consider the figures below:

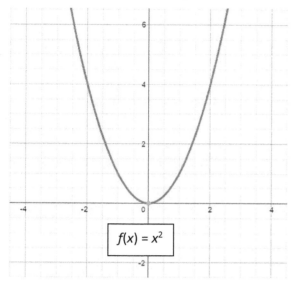

$$f(x) = x^2$$

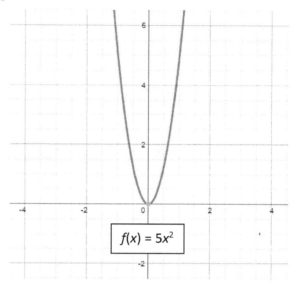

$$f(x) = 5x^2$$

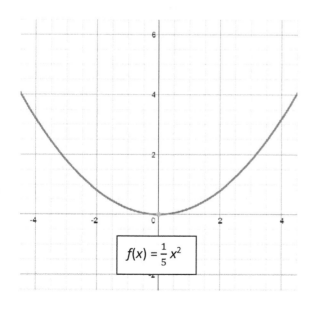

$$f(x) = \frac{1}{5}x^2$$

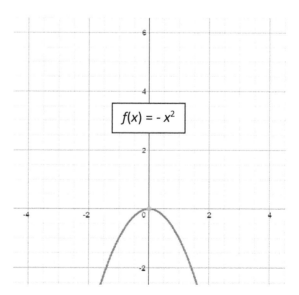

$$f(x) = -x^2$$

- Changing the amount added to x *before* it's raised to an exponent will shift the graph *horizontally*. Adding a value to x will shift the graph to the left; subtracting a value from x will shift the graph to the right.

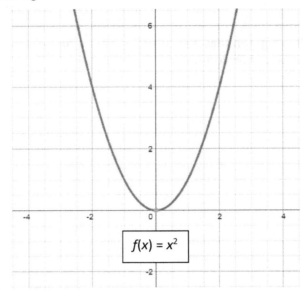

$$f(x) = x^2$$

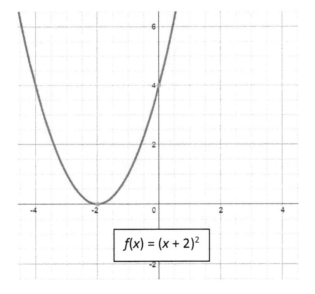

$$f(x) = (x + 2)^2$$

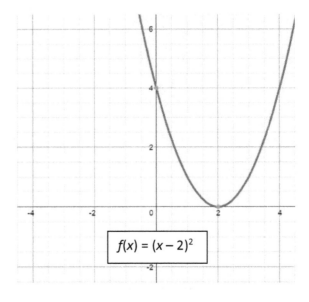

$$f(x) = (x - 2)^2$$

- Changing the amount added to the *x* expression *after* it's raised to an exponent will shift the graph *vertically*. Adding an amount will shift the graph up, while subtracting an amount will shift the graph down.

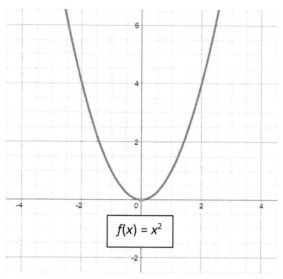

$f(x) = x^2$

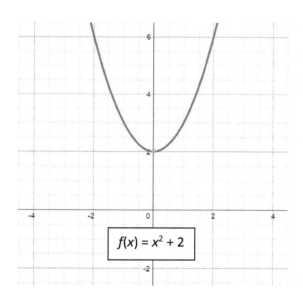

$f(x) = x^2 + 2$

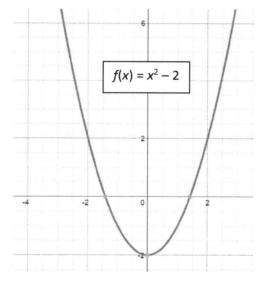

$f(x) = x^2 - 2$

3-D Geometry

Three-dimensional geometry, as the name implies, deals with three-dimensional objects like cubes, spheres, pyramids, and cones. Don't worry about memorizing formulas for these things, though: the first page of your test booklet contains the volume formulae for spheres, pyramids, and right circular cones, as well as the formula for the surface area of a sphere.

Beyond that, it's important to understand the concept of the *z*-axis, and of *xyz*-coordinate space.

As I'm sure you remember, the *x*-axis is the horizontal axis we commonly see in the coordinate plane, and the *y*-axis is the vertical axis we commonly see in the coordinate plane:

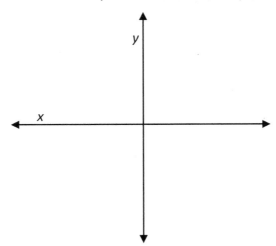

The *z*-axis is a third axis that comes "straight out off the page," so to speak, so that it's perpendicular to the *xy*-coordinate plane (it also goes "into" or "through" the page, of course, because its length is infinite, like the length of the other two axes). When we add the *z*-axis to the *xy*-coordinate plane to create the *xyz* space, we end up with something like this:

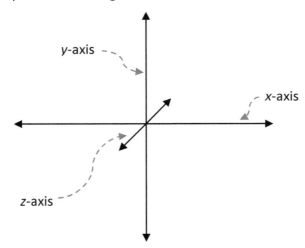

Just as we can have (*x*, *y*) coordinates in a two-dimensional plane, we can have (*x*, *y*, *z*) coordinates in a three-dimensional space.

(Of course, you'll never have to graph an (*x*, *y*, *z*) coordinate on the test, just like you'll never have to graph an (*x*, *y*) coordinate on the test—the multiple-choice format doesn't allow you to produce a graph of your own. Instead, you might have to pick an answer choice with a graph, or do something similar. But it's still helpful to understand three-dimensional coordinate space for some questions.)

Imaginary Numbers

An imaginary number is a number that involves *i*.

The number i is equal to the square root of -1:

$$i = \sqrt{-1}$$

To put that another way, i squared is equal to -1:

$$i^2 = -1$$

Some examples of imaginary numbers include i, -3i, 7i, and 415i.

Imaginary numbers can be added, subtracted, multiplied, and divided. We simply treat i like a variable, and every time we multiply an i by another i, the product is -1.

Examples:

$$6i + i = 7i$$
$$4i - 13i = -9i$$
$$i \times 5i = 5i^2 = (5)(-1) = -5$$
$$8i \div 9 = \frac{8i}{9}$$

Complex Numbers

A complex number is a quantity that involves two terms being added or subtracted:

1. One term is a real number, like 7 or -12 or 50.

2. The other term is an imaginary number, which is a number including i.

Complex numbers are written in this form, where a is a real number and b is the coefficient of i:

$$a + bi$$

Complex numbers can be graphed on their own special axes. When we graph complex numbers, the vertical axis represents the imaginary value, and the horizontal axis represents the real value.

Example of the graph of 2 + i:

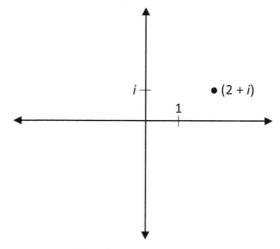

Complex numbers can be added, subtracted, multiplied, and divided. We simply manipulate the real elements and the imaginary elements separately, treating i like a variable; every time we multiply one i by another i, the product is -1. When the i is canceled out from multiplying imaginary terms in this way, the resulting product becomes part of the real term, because it no longer includes i.

Example of adding complex numbers:

$$(4 + 2i) + (5 + i) = 9 + 3i$$

Example of multiplying complex numbers:

$(4 + 2i)(5 + i)$	(expressions to be multiplied)
$20 + 4i + 10i + 2i^2$	(FOIL)
$20 + 4i + 10i + 2(-1)$	(substitute -1 for i^2)
$20 + 14i + -2$	(add $4i$ and $10i$)
$18 + 14i$	(add 20 and -2)

Matrices

A matrix is a group of numbers laid out in columns and rows.

Examples of matrices:

$$\begin{bmatrix} 3 & -2 & 7 \\ -5 & 11 & 8 \end{bmatrix} \qquad \begin{bmatrix} 1.6 \\ 9 \\ 20 \end{bmatrix} \qquad \begin{bmatrix} 19 & 76 & 33 \\ 74 & 38 & 70 \\ 45 & 54 & 56 \end{bmatrix}$$

We can describe the dimensions of a matrix using the convention $a \times b$, where a is the number of rows and b is the number of columns.

$$\begin{bmatrix} 1 & 37 \\ 7 & 6 \\ 34 & 19 \end{bmatrix}$$

This is a 3 × 2 matrix, since it has 3 rows and 2 columns.

When two matrices have the same number of columns and rows as each other, we can add them together. We do this by adding each value in one matrix to the corresponding value in the other matrix. The resulting matrix has the same number of rows and columns as each of the original matrices.

$$\begin{bmatrix} a_1 & b_1 & c_1 \\ d_1 & e_1 & f_1 \end{bmatrix} + \begin{bmatrix} a_2 & b_2 & c_2 \\ d_2 & e_2 & f_2 \end{bmatrix} = \begin{bmatrix} a_1 + a_2 & b_1 + b_2 & c_1 + c_2 \\ d_1 + d_2 & e_1 + e_2 & f_1 + f_2 \end{bmatrix}$$

Now let's look at an example of matrix addition using numbers instead of variables.

$$\begin{bmatrix} 3 & 7 & 0 \\ 0 & 5 & -1 \end{bmatrix} + \begin{bmatrix} 5 & -5 & 9 \\ 0 & 11 & 4 \end{bmatrix} = \begin{bmatrix} 8 & 2 & 9 \\ 0 & 16 & 3 \end{bmatrix}$$

If two matrices don't have the same number of columns and rows as each other, we can't add them.

To multiply an entire matrix by a number, we multiply each value in the matrix by that number:

$$a \times \begin{bmatrix} x & y & z \\ p & q & r \end{bmatrix} = \begin{bmatrix} ax & ay & az \\ ap & aq & ar \end{bmatrix}$$

Now let's look at an example using numbers instead of variables.

$$3 \times \begin{bmatrix} 5 & 8 & 4 \\ -2 & 0 & 7 \end{bmatrix} = \begin{bmatrix} 15 & 24 & 12 \\ -6 & 0 & 21 \end{bmatrix}$$

We can multiply one matrix by another matrix if the number of *columns* in the *first* matrix is equal to the number of *rows* in the *second* matrix. The resulting matrix will have the same number of rows as the first matrix and the same number of columns as the second matrix.

Matrix multiplication involves simple steps; the challenge is keeping the steps straight. I'll explain those steps in the abstract now, and then we'll look at a couple of examples.

To multiply one matrix by another, we multiply the terms in the *rows* of the first matrix by the terms in the *columns* of the second matrix. Each time we multiply a row by a column, we create one value in the matrix product. When we multiply the first row of the first matrix by *each* column of the second matrix, we create the first row of the matrix product. When we multiply the second row of the first matrix by *each* column of the second matrix, we create the second row of the matrix product, and so on.

When we multiply a row by a column, we generate one term in the matrix product. The first term is created by adding the product of the first term in the first row of the first matrix and the first term in the first column of the second matrix to the product of the second term in the first row of the first matrix and the second term in the first column of the second matrix, and also to the product of the third term in the first row of the first matrix and the third term in the first column of the second matrix, and so on until we've used all the terms in that row and column. The sum of those products will give us the first value in the first row of the matrix product.

Next we find the second term in the first row of the matrix product: we add the product of the first term in the first row of the first matrix and the first term in the second column of the second matrix to the product of the second term in the first row of the first matrix and the second term in the second column of the second matrix, and also to the product of the third term in the first row of the first matrix and the third term in the second column of the second matrix, and so on, until we've used all the terms in that row and column. The sum of those products is the second value in the first row of the matrix product.

We repeat these steps until we've multiplied the first row in the first matrix by each of the columns in the second matrix, which gives us the complete first row of the matrix product. Then we repeat the process to multiply the second row of the first matrix by each of the columns of the second matrix, which gives us the second row of the matrix product. We continue in this way until each row of the first matrix has been multiplied by each column of the second matrix, completing our matrix product.

Let's look at an example of a 3 × 2 matrix being multiplied by a 2 × 2 matrix:

$$\begin{bmatrix} a & d \\ b & e \\ c & f \end{bmatrix} \times \begin{bmatrix} w & x \\ y & z \end{bmatrix} = \begin{bmatrix} aw + dy & ax + dz \\ bw + ey & bx + ez \\ cw + fy & cx + fz \end{bmatrix}$$

Notice that we were able to multiple these two matrices because the number of columns in the first matrix (which was 2) matched the number of rows in the second matrix. Also notice that the resulting matrix has the same number of rows as the first matrix (3) and the same number of columns as the second matrix (2).

Now let's look at an example using numbers instead of variables:

$$\begin{bmatrix} 2 & 0 \\ 6 & 3 \\ 1 & 2 \end{bmatrix} \times \begin{bmatrix} 7 & 1 \\ 2 & 4 \end{bmatrix} = \begin{bmatrix} (2 \times 7) + (0 \times 2) & (2 \times 1) + (0 \times 4) \\ (6 \times 7) + (3 \times 2) & (6 \times 1) + (3 \times 4) \\ (1 \times 7) + (2 \times 2) & (1 \times 1) + (2 \times 4) \end{bmatrix} = \begin{bmatrix} 14 & 2 \\ 48 & 18 \\ 11 & 9 \end{bmatrix}$$

Working with matrices gets more complicated than the examples we've discussed in this section, but this section covers what you'll need to know for the Math Level 2 Test.

Asymptotes

Sometimes the graph of a function has one or more asymptotes. An asymptote is a line that's constantly approached by a function graph, but never actually reached by the graph, so that the distance between the asymptote and the graph constantly approaches zero.

Example:

This is the graph of $f(x) = \dfrac{150}{0.1x - 5} + 20$:

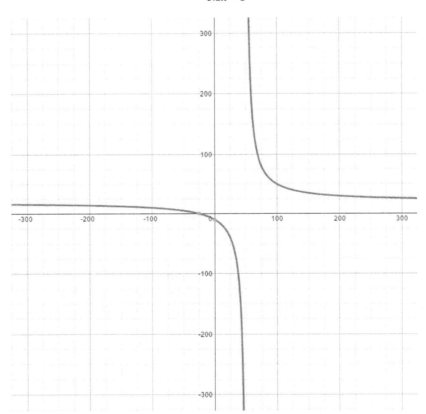

Notice that the curve of the graph constantly approaches the lines $x = 50$ and $y = 20$, but it can never actually touch either of them. The line $x = 50$ is the vertical asymptote of the graph, while the line $y = 20$ is the horizontal asymptote of the graph.

Because of its multiple-choice format, the Math Level 2 Test can never require you to come up with the equation for an asymptote on your own; you can only be asked to do things like identify the answer choice that contains the equation for an asymptote. For this reason, the fastest way to answer a question about an asymptote is usually just to graph a given function on your calculator and then refer to the graph.

Even so, it can be helpful to be aware of another property of *vertical* asymptotes in particular. Vertical asymptotes are possible when the value of a function is undefined for a particular *x*-value, which can happen when an *x*-value would cause the value of a denominator in a fraction to equal zero.

Example:

$$f(x) = \frac{1}{x-3}$$

In the function above, the denominator is $x - 3$. So when $x = 3$, the denominator of the fraction is zero, and the value of the function is undefined for $x = 3$. That means the function may have a vertical asymptote at $x = 3$. This function can't have a vertical asymptote anywhere else, because the function is only undefined at $x = 3$.

Notice that in the example above we just established where vertical asymptotes are *possible*, not necessarily where they appear. Simply knowing where vertical asymptotes can exist (and where they can't exist) can often help you rule out answer choices out and/or double-check the findings from your graphing calculator. For more on this aspect of vertical asymptotes, see the explanation for question 13 from page 126 of the MSTB in the walkthroughs of this book.

Vectors

A vector is a quantity that has both magnitude (or "size") and direction. When we draw a vector, it looks like an arrow. The length of the arrow indicates its size, and the direction it points in shows its direction. A vector is named with a bold letter, like **a** or **v**.

Vectors can be added and subtracted. When two vectors point in the same direction, the direction is unchanged and the magnitudes are added together.

Example:

For the vectors above, which have identical directions, if the magnitude (or length) of **a** is 5 and the magnitude (or length) of **b** is 8, then the sum of these two vectors would be a new vector with the same direction, and a magnitude of 13, because 5 + 8 = 13. We'll call the new vector **c**:

When two vectors that point in exactly opposite directions are added together, the resulting vector has the direction of the larger vector, and its magnitude is the difference between the two original vectors.

Example:

For the vectors above, which are pointing in exactly opposite directions, if the magnitude (or length) of **x** is 5 and the magnitude (or length) of **y** is 30, then the sum of these two vectors would be a vector pointing in the same direction as **y**, with a magnitude of 25. We'll call the new vector **z**:

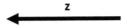

Subtracting a vector is like adding a vector with the same magnitude and opposite direction.

Example:

If we want to subtract vector **q** from vector **p**, that's the same as adding a vector with the same magnitude as **q** that's pointed in the opposite direction, like this:

Example:

The vector that would result from subtracting vector **q** from vector **p** would be the following vector, which we'll call vector **r**. Notice that **r** has the same direction as **p**, but its magnitude is equal to the difference of **p** and **q**, which is also equal to the sum of **p** and -**q**:

Example:

When adding two vectors whose directions are unknown, the largest possible magnitude of the resulting vector is the sum of the two vectors' magnitudes. This is the magnitude that would result if the two vectors were pointing in exactly the same direction. On the other hand, the smallest possible magnitude that can result from adding two vectors is the difference between the two vectors' magnitudes. This is the magnitude we would get if the vectors were pointing in exactly opposite directions.

It's also possible to add vectors together that are at angles to one another. First, we place the vectors head-to-tail. The vector that results from adding the two vectors will extend from the tail of the first vector to the head of the second vector when the two vectors are placed head-to-tail.

In order to add vectors **a** and **b** below, we put **a** and **b** head to tail. The vector that extends from the tail of **a** to the head of **b** is the sum of **a** and **b**, which we'll call **c**. It doesn't matter whether **a** is first or **b** is first when we place them head to tail; either orientation results in the same vector **c**.

Example:

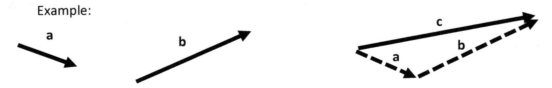

We can also find the direction and magnitude of **c**. To add the magnitudes of vectors in this way, we treat each vector like the hypotenuse of a right triangle. Then we use the angle and magnitude of each vector to find the lengths of the horizontal and vertical "legs." We add the horizontal components of each vector and the vertical components of each vector to get one horizontal value and one vertical value. Then we find the hypotenuse that corresponds to the new horizontal and vertical values, and the angle and magnitude of the new "hypotenuse" define the new vector.

Example:

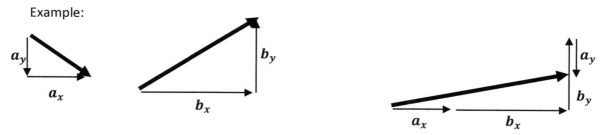

You don't need to know the details of this process on the Math Level 2 Test, but understanding the basic idea could help you answer a question on test day.

Proofs

A proof is a series of statements, based on given information, that lead to a logical conclusion. On the Math Level 2 Test, you're occasionally told which conclusion you're trying to prove, and then asked about statements that would help to prove the conclusion. You can't be asked to write a proof on your own, because the test is multiple-choice.

A direct proof proves the conclusion that is given.

An indirect proof begins by assuming a statement that's the *opposite* of its actual conclusion, and then proves that the assumed statement must be false, thereby showing that the original statement is true.

Conic sections

Parabola

A parabola is the set of (*x*, *y*) points such that each point on the curve is the same distance from the following two things:

1. a single fixed point in the *xy*-plane, called the "focus"

2. a fixed straight line in the *xy*-plane, called the "directrix"

(Note that in a parabola the actual distance from any point to the focus is the same as the distance from that point to the directrix, while in a hyperbola the *ratio* of one of those distances to the other is constant for all points on the hyperbola.

A parabola looks sort of like a mixture of a U and a V. The diagram of the parabola below shows the focus (represented by a point) and directrix (represented by a dashed horizontal line):

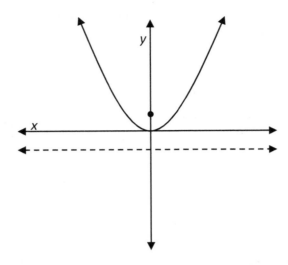

On the Math Level 2 test, the most basic equation for a parabola is the following:

$$y = x^2$$

The above equation is for a parabola that opens upward, with a vertex at the origin. The same parabola with a vertex not at the origin can be expressed with the following equation:

$$y = (x - h)^2 + k$$

The parabola described by the above equation will have a vertex at (h, k).

A parabola has an axis of symmetry that runs through the focus and perpendicular to the directrix.

The "vertex" of a parabola is the point where the parabola intersects the axis of symmetry.

In the diagram below, the point at the origin is the vertex, and the axis of symmetry runs along the y-axis.

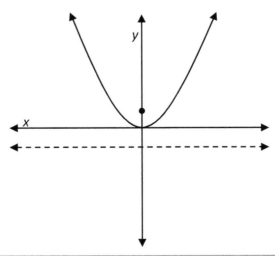

Go to www.Math2PrepVideos.com.

Hyperbola

The graph of a hyperbola is two separate, symmetrical curves. Each curve is composed of the set of (*x*, *y*) points such that the distances between the following elements are always in a constant ratio:

1. a single fixed point for each curve, called the "focus"

2. a fixed straight line for each curve, called the "directrix"

A hyperbola looks like two symmetrical curves opening away from each other. The diagram of the hyperbola below shows the foci (represented by two points) and directrices (represented by two dashed lines):

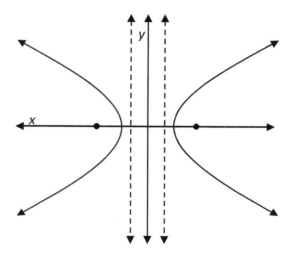

A hyperbola has an axis of symmetry, which is the line that runs through the two foci. On the diagram above, the axis of symmetry runs along the *x*-axis.

The standard equation of a hyperbola that's centered on the origin is the following:

$$\frac{x^2}{a^2} - \frac{y^2}{b^2} = 1$$

Using the generalized formula for a hyperbola above, one vertex is at (-*a*, 0) and the other is at (*a*, 0). The hyperbola also has two asymptotes that can be represented by $y = \frac{b}{a}x$ and $y = -\frac{b}{a}x$, respectively:

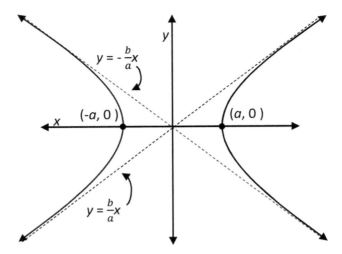

When a hyperbola opens "up" and "down" (vertically) instead of "left" and "right" (horizontally), the equation changes so that the numerators are switched, like so:

$$\frac{y^2}{a^2} - \frac{x^2}{b^2} = 1$$

The hyperbola equations we've looked at so far are for hyperbolas with centers at the origin. The same hyperbola with a center not at the origin can be expressed with one of the following equations:

$$\frac{(x-h)^2}{a^2} - \frac{(y-k)^2}{b^2} = 1 \qquad \text{(for horizontal hyperbolas)}$$

$$\frac{(y-k)^2}{a^2} - \frac{(x-h)^2}{b^2} = 1 \qquad \text{(for vertical hyperbolas)}$$

The hyperbolas described by either of the above equations will have a center at (h, k).

Circle

A circle is the set of (x, y) points such that each point is the same distance from a fixed point called the "center" of the circle. In the diagram below, the center of the circle is the point at the origin:

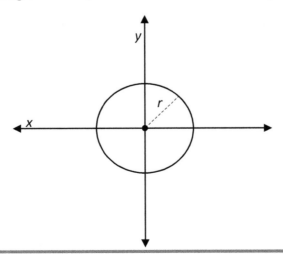

A "radius" of a circle is a line connecting any point on the circle to the center of that circle. On the diagram above, the radius is the dashed line labeled *r*.

The standard equation for a circle with a center at the origin and a radius of *r* is given below.

$$x^2 + y^2 = r^2$$

The above equation is for a circle with a center at the origin. The same circle with a center not at the origin can be expressed with the following equation:

$$(x - h)^2 + (y - k)^2 = r^2$$

The circle described by the above equation will have a center at (*h*, *k*).

A "diameter" of a circle is any line that starts on one side of the circle, passes through the center of that circle, and touches the other side of the circle. In the diagram below, the line labeled *d* is one example of a diameter for the given circle.

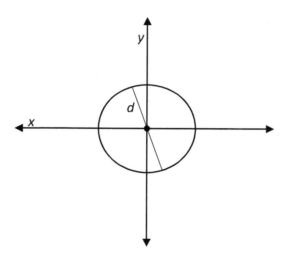

Ellipse

An ellipse is the set of (*x*, *y*) points such that the sum of the following three things is constant:

1. the distance between the two "foci" of the ellipse, which are analogous to a circle's center

2. the distance from the first focus to the point

3. the distance from the second focus to the point

An ellipse looks like a circle that has been flattened a little bit on two opposite sides. This flattened appearance occurs because the ellipse has two focal points, while a circle has only one focal point (the center of the circle). The diagram of the ellipse below has the foci indicated:

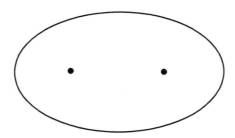

The following diagram shows an ellipse centered on the origin, followed by the standard equation for an ellipse centered on the origin:

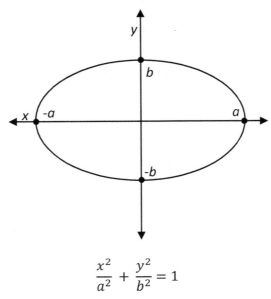

$$\frac{x^2}{a^2} + \frac{y^2}{b^2} = 1$$

When an ellipse is taller than it is wide, the equation changes so that the numerators are switched, like so:

$$\frac{y^2}{a^2} + \frac{x^2}{b^2} = 1$$

The ellipse equations we've looked at so far are for ellipses with centers at the origin. The same ellipse with a center not at the origin can be expressed with one of the following equations:

$$\frac{(x-h)^2}{a^2} + \frac{(y-k)^2}{b^2} = 1 \qquad \text{(for wide ellipses)}$$

$$\frac{(y-k)^2}{a^2} + \frac{(x-h)^2}{b^2} = 1 \qquad \text{(for tall ellipses)}$$

The ellipses described by either of the above equations will have a center at (h, k).

An ellipse has two axes: a minor axis, and a major axis. The minor axis is the shortest distance across the ellipse that passes through the center of the ellipse. In the following diagram, the dashed line is the minor axis of the ellipse:

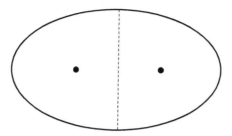

The major axis is the longest distance across the ellipse that passes through the center of the ellipse. In the following diagram, the dashed line is the major axis of the ellipse:

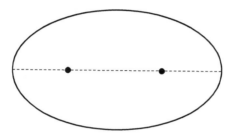

Using the generalized formula for an ellipse above, the length of the ellipse's axes are 2*a* and 2*b*. The longer of those two axes is the major axis, and the shorter of the two is the minor axis.

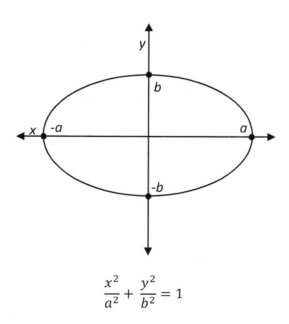

$$\frac{x^2}{a^2} + \frac{y^2}{b^2} = 1$$

In the ellipse pictured above, the horizontal axis is longer, so it's the major axis. Its length is $2a$. The length of the minor axis is $2b$.

Sum of an Infinite Geometric Series

It is possible to find the sum of an infinite geometric series when the common ratio for that series is between -1 and 1.

The formal notation for an infinite geometric series looks like this:

$$\sum_{n=1}^{\infty} (\frac{1}{3})^n$$

But you won't need to know this notation for the Math Level 2 Test. If you're asked about the sum of an infinite geometric series on the test, the series will be specifically described as an infinite geometric series, and instead of being expressed using the notation above, the series will be spelled out as a set of terms added together, like this:

Example:

$$1 + \frac{1}{3} + \frac{1}{9} + \frac{1}{27} + \frac{1}{81} + . . .$$

The formula for the sum of an infinite geometric series is $s = a_1/(1-r)$, where

- s is the sum of the series

- a_1 is the first term in the series

- r is the common ratio

To find a term in a geometric series, we multiply the previous term by the common ratio. In the example above, the common ratio is $\frac{1}{3}$, because we multiply 1 by $\frac{1}{3}$ to get $\frac{1}{3}$, and we multiply $\frac{1}{3}$ by $\frac{1}{3}$ to get $\frac{1}{9}$, and we multiply $\frac{1}{9}$ by $\frac{1}{3}$ to get $\frac{1}{27}$, and so on.

In the example above, a_1 is equal to 1, and r is equal to $\frac{1}{3}$. So the sum of the infinite geometric series is equal to $\frac{1}{1-\frac{1}{3}}$, or $\frac{1}{2/3}$, or $\frac{3}{2}$.

Advanced Combinations and Permutations

(The commands we're going to discuss in this section are typically labeled nCr and nPr on a calculator, but not every calculator is the same. If you've mastered Part I of the toolbox, *and* you're comfortable with all the other aspects of the Math Level 2 Test, *and* you're now in the process of mastering Part II of the toolbox, then be sure to investigate the permutation and combination commands on your particular calculator. For the rest of this discussion, I'll use nCr and nPr to refer to the calculator commands for combinations and permutations, respectively.)

In Part I of the toolbox we discussed "Counting Problems," or problems involving permutations and combinations. When these problems appear on the Math Level 2 Test, they often involve finding different ways to choose all the elements of a group.

But sometimes a question will involve choosing only some of the members of a group. For example, a question might ask how many different groups of 3 people we can make out of a group of 7 people. In this case, we can't rely on the approach we discussed in the "Counting Problems" portion of Part I of this toolbox. Instead, we need to use the nCr command on our graphing calculator.

Example:

How many different groups of 3 people can be selected from a group of 7 people?

To solve this problem, we enter 7 nCr 3 in our graphing calculator. We can think of this as "7 things taken 3 at a time" or, in this case, "7 people taken 3 at a time." When we hit enter, we'll get the answer—in this case, 35.

In the example above, we used the nCr command, because the question was about a combination of elements, as opposed to a permutation. Remember that in a combination the order of the things chosen isn't important, whereas in a permutation the order is important. For example, if we're counting combinations of letters, then ABC and ACB would be considered the same combination, because they involve the same elements—it doesn't matter that the order changes. If we were counting permutations, though, ABC and ACB would be two separate permutations, because they're ordered differently. In a question about permutations we would use the nPr command.

Example:

Find the number of permutations possible when selecting 2 letters from the following set: A, B, C, D, E, F, G, H.

Since there are 8 total letters in the set, and we're choosing 2 of the 8 letters, and we know that the order in which they're selected matters, we'll use the nPr command.

When we enter 8 nPr 2, we get 56.

That's not quite it . . .

That wraps up every math topic we'll cover in the Math Toolbox in this Black Book, but it's still possible that you could encounter one or two questions on test day that involve subject matter not discussed in this book.

The majority of questions on the Math Level 2 Test will deal with subject matter from Part I of this toolbox. Only a handful of questions will involve the more advanced material we just discussed in Part II of the Math Toolbox.

One of the College Board's tactics for making the test seem more challenging and less predictable is to include just a few questions on more obscure, more advanced topics, like the ones we covered in Part II of the Toolbox.

But don't worry! Remember that the scoring on this test is intentionally designed so that you can leave several questions blank and still get a perfect score. This is the College Board's tricky way of making it possible to include a few obscure, challenging concepts that make the test seem more intimidating to untrained test-takers without actually making it any more difficult to get a perfect score on the test.

Also remember that if you want a perfect or near-perfect score on the Math Level 2 Test, you need to be comfortable with all the topics in Part I of this Black Book's toolbox. Once you master Part I, and you feel comfortable with all the other ideas presented in this book, you should get comfortable with the topics in Part II. Beyond that, you *might* see a question or two on test day involving other topics, but as long as you're comfortable with everything in this Math Toolbox, one or two questions about other topics can't stop you from getting a perfect score.

Conclusion

We've just finished discussing all the math concepts you'll need to learn before test day; earlier, we already covered all the strategies and tactics you'll need to exploit the weaknesses in the test's design.

Now, it's time to combine everything and go through some real Math Level 2 questions from the College Board. In the next part of this Black Book, I'll give you detailed explanations of all of the Math Level 2 questions in the two official practice tests in the MSTB, so you can see how everything we've talked about up to this point can be effectively applied on test day.

Question Walkthroughs

In this section, we'll take all of the ideas we've covered so far and put them into action on real Math Level 2 Test questions from the MSTB. This is an important part of your training, because it gives you a model to emulate on test day, and because it allows you to validate the ideas from this Black Book with real questions from the College Board.

By the way, you may notice that some of the discussions in this section get a bit long— but that doesn't mean the process for answering these questions on test day needs to be long!

In each of these walkthroughs I typically cover at least 2 separate approaches to answering a question, and sometimes we'll cover even more than that. When I do this, I'm not just working out the solution in a couple of different ways; instead, I'm explaining the entire process of reading the question, thinking of a possible solution, and trying out that solution, and sometimes I'm going through that whole process 2 or even 3 or 4 times per question. This gives you a very complete picture of what's going on with each question, because I want you to draw the right lessons from each question and be on the lookout for the right things on test day. Remember that the College Board isn't going to give you questions on test day that look exactly like the ones in the MSTB! Instead, the College Board is going to give you questions that follow the same standards and demonstrate the same kinds of deeper relationships as the ones in the MSTB.

The solutions you come up with on test day will be much less involved than my walkthroughs here, because you only need to find one way to solve each question. I'm going into a lot of detail in these walkthroughs for the purpose of training you as thoroughly as possible.

Walkthroughs Of Questions From Practice Test 1 Of The MSTB

Page 122, Question 1

If we happened to glance at a question like this on a typical high school math test, we'd probably expect to be asked to solve the given equation for both x and k, or to express one variable in terms of the other. But this question asks us to solve for only one of the two variables in the equation—and the answer choices are all numbers, with no variables in them. This is the kind of thing that might confuse an untrained test-taker for a moment (or longer). But we trained test-takers know that we'll often see unusual questions on the Math Level 2 SAT Subject Test, and we know that we need to read carefully and think in relatively simple terms when we attempt to figure out what a question wants us to do.

So how can a math question present us with *two* variables in an equation, and then ask us to determine a numerical value for only *one* of the variables?

Well, when we read the question carefully, we notice the phrase "for all x." This phrase means that the value of k must remain unchanged no matter what x is. So instead of having to isolate x or solve for it or anything, we can just plug in any arbitrary value for x that we want, because the question tells us that k is the same no matter what x is.

Now, as trained test-takers, we know that it's a good habit to avoid plugging in numbers with special properties, such as -1, 0, 1, or any numbers that appear in a given question. As we discussed in the article on backsolving earlier in this Black Book, these kinds of numbers are generally more likely to result in false positives when we try out all of the answer choices, which means we'd just have to pick another number and plug that new number in all over again anyway. So I'll choose to plug in the number 5 for x, just because I know I should generally avoid picking numbers that appear in the question or have bizarre properties. (Actually, in this particular question, the test explicitly tells us that it doesn't matter what we choose to plug in for x, because the value of k is the same "for all x." But it's a good habit to avoid plugging in numbers that are generally more likely to result in false positives on most questions, so I'll plug in 5.)

When we plug 5 in for x and solve for k, we get this:

$$3x + 6 = \frac{k}{4}(x + 2) \qquad \text{(original expression)}$$

$$3(5) + 6 = \frac{k}{4}((5) + 2) \qquad \text{(plug in 5 for } x\text{)}$$

$$21 = \frac{k}{4}(7) \qquad \text{(combine like terms)}$$

$$3 = \frac{k}{4} \qquad \text{(divide both sides by 7)}$$

$$12 = k \qquad \text{(multiply both sides by 4)}$$

So the correct answer is (D), because $k = 12$.

Most of my students find that this is the easiest approach to this question. Of course, if you prefer, you can also solve the original equation for k as described in the explanation on page 147 of the MSTB.

As trained test-takers, we know that we're not done thinking about a question just because we're pretty sure we've solved it. We always want to check the rest of the answer choices to see if we can figure out what the College Board had in mind when it constructed the question. Let's do that now.

Notice that we multiplied 3 and 4 to arrive at 12 in the last step of our solution, and that both 3 and 4 are present as wrong answer choices. Also notice that one step of our solution involved the expression $\frac{k}{4}$, which is very similar to the $\frac{1}{4}$ we find in choice (A). Finally, notice that choice (E) is 24, which is two times the correct answer. These are all examples of some of the answer choice patterns we discussed earlier in this Black Book: (A), (B), and (C) are all examples of values we encountered on the way to finding the solution, while (E) is an example of a value that's twice as much as the answer we believe to be correct. We trained test-takers know that seeing these kinds of relationships among the answer choices helps us approach the question from another angle, and gives us added confidence that we haven't made a mistake on the question.

Speaking of mistakes, remember that a relatively simple question like this one counts just as much towards our score as a more challenging question does. That's why it's so important to make sure we answer this question with total confidence, working as quickly as we can without sacrificing accuracy. It would be a shame to miss a question like this just because we forgot to multiply by 4 at the end.

Page 123, Question 2

For most test-takers, the biggest challenge in a question like this is just making sure that we understand what the question is actually asking. Always remember that reading comprehension is the most important skill on any major standardized test—even on math tests!

The question asks us to express K in terms of F. We can confirm this both by reading the question carefully, and by noticing that all the answer choices provide different equations that define K in terms of F.

This is a good moment for me to remind you that it's always a good idea to be aware of the answer choices before we start working on a question, because the answer choices often indicate the important elements of the question. In this instance, some test-takers might have rushed into the question and started working on an equation that would have left F by itself on one side of the equation, which obviously wouldn't work with these answer choices. The answer choices clearly show that K should be alone on the left-hand side of the final equation, and the only variable on the right-hand side should be F, even though the wording of the prompt doesn't specify that.

The explanation for this question on page 147 of the MSTB actually gives us a pretty useful, straightforward solution, as far as it goes: since the question already gives us C in terms of F, we can just plug that given value in for C in the equation that relates C to K. Let's go through that approach quickly, and then talk about some other aspects of the question that a trained test-taker would notice.

The value we were given for C is $\frac{5}{9}(F - 32)$. When we plug that expression in for C in the equation $K = C + 273$, we get the following:

$$K = \frac{5}{9}(F - 32) + 273$$

This means the correct answer is choice (C), just as the solution on page 147 of the MSTB describes.

Now let's talk about the patterns we can find in the answer choices, in order to continue to build your awareness of the roles these patterns can play in the design of the test. We know that the College Board often likes to provide us with wrong answers that mimic elements of the correct answer, and that the correct answer often (but not always!) includes the most common characteristics from the other answer choices.

If we look at the answer choices for question 2, we notice that they all have the same beginning elements:

$$K = \frac{5}{9}(F$$

Obviously, the correct answer choice has to start this way, since all the answer choices start this way.

After that, we might notice the following:

- Three of the five choices involve 273, while only 2 don't. So we'd expect the correct answer will probably (but not definitely!) involve the number 273.

- Of the three choices that include 273, we can see that two of the three involve subtracting 32 (as opposed to adding 32).

- Of the three choices that include 273, we can see that two of the three involve adding 273 (as opposed to subtracting 273).

With all of that in mind, we'd expect that the correct answer choice *probably* includes the number 273, and *probably* involves subtracting 32 and adding 273. The only answer choice that includes all of these elements is the correct answer, (C).

Of course, as trained test-takers, we know that we can't depend solely on answer choice patterns when we choose the answer to a question, because the patterns aren't 100% reliable. But, as we discussed earlier in this Black Book, having an awareness of these patterns can give us another way to look at a question, which is always helpful, because guarding against small mistakes is one of the most critical parts of taking any multiple-choice standardized test. In this case, the set of answer choices is clearly signaling that we need to pay close attention to whether 32 and 273 should be positive or negative in the correct answer, because the choices give us multiple opportunities to make small mistakes on the signs of those two numbers.

Page 123, Question 3

This question gives us two points and then asks for the slope of the line connecting them. This is one of the many times on the SAT Math Level 2 Test when remembering the definition of a term comes in handy: the "slope" between two points is equal to the "rise" over the "run" between them. In other words, the slope of a line is what we get when we take the vertical distance between the two points and divide it by the horizontal distance between the two points. (If you don't feel comfortable with this concept, be sure to review slope in the Math Toolbox in this Black Book.)

(Notice that the answer choices are decimal expressions rather than fractions, even though most test-takers would expect to see a slope expressed as a fraction in a math class. But, as trained test-takers, we know that the test sometimes presents concepts in ways we might not expect. So it shouldn't surprise us to see slopes expressed as decimals here.)

Of course, there's a formula for determining the slope of a line in the *xy*-coordinate plane from two points on the line, and we could use that formula here if we wanted. It looks like this, where *m* is the slope:

$$m = \frac{y_2 - y_1}{x_2 - x_1}$$

But, whenever I have the option, I prefer to *understand a concept* rather than *memorize a formula*. The memorization approach can fall apart if we misapply what we've memorized, but we're much less likely to make those kinds of mistakes if we actually understand the fundamental concepts underlying a question. So, for purposes of our discussion, I'll rely on my conceptual understanding of slope as "rise over run," rather than on the dry formula I just mentioned. (If you prefer to use the formula to answer this question, and you're consistently able to find correct answers that way, then, by all means, go ahead—I'd just caution you to remember that many of the questions you'll see on test day will rely much more heavily on understanding concepts than on memorizing formulas—in fact, you'll see several questions on test day that don't involve memorized formulas at all, so it's important not to rely on formulas in general when taking the Math Level 2 Test.)

The numerator of the slope fraction represents the vertical separation between the two points, and the denominator of the slope fraction represents the horizontal separation between the two points. So we need to find these values in order to construct our slope fraction.

Well, the vertical separation between the two points must be the difference between their *y*-values. Since the *y*-values are 11 and 5, the difference between those values is 6. That means the numerator in our slope fraction is 6.

The horizontal separation between the two points must be the difference between their *x*-values. Since the *x*-values are 3 and -2, the difference between those values is 5. That means the denominator of our slope fraction is 5.

That gives us a slope fraction of $\frac{6}{5}$.

(In this case, all the answer choices were positive, so we didn't really need to worry about the slope being positive or negative, practically speaking. But remember that a line with a positive slope is angled upward as we move from left to right across the graph. Since the point on the left, (-2, 5), is lower than the point on the right, (3, 11), we know the slope has to be positive.)

As we mentioned above, four of the answer choices are decimals, and one is an integer, so we'll have to change our $\frac{6}{5}$ expression into a different format if we want to compare it to the answer choices. Dividing 6 by 5 gives us 1.2, so we know the correct answer is (D).

Now let's consider the set of answer choices. Do you notice anything interesting about them? You might not see it at first, but let's think about the kinds of mistakes that careless test-takers would be likely to make on a question like this. If the correct answer is equal to $\frac{6}{5}$, we might expect to see a wrong answer that's equal to $\frac{5}{6}$, because some test-takers will probably switch the numerator and denominator in the slope fraction. Sure enough, choice (B) gives us the decimal equivalent of $\frac{5}{6}$, for people who mistakenly think a slope fraction should have the "run" in the numerator and the "rise" in the denominator.

Another mistake that might lead to a wrong answer would be to find the differences between the points *in each coordinate pair*, instead of the differences between the *y*-values and the *x*-values of both points together. In other words, a test-taker might incorrectly find the difference between 3 and 11 from the first coordinate pair, and then divide that by the difference between -2 and 5 from the second coordinate pair. The result of that mistake would be $\frac{-8}{-7}$, which rounds to 1.14, which is choice (C).

We might also notice that choice (E) is simply the difference between the *y*-values in the two points, ignoring the *x*-values altogether.

Once more, we can see that the College Board deliberately goes out of its way to offer us wrong answers that reflect mistakes that untrained test-takers would be very likely to make, even if they understood the underlying concepts in the question. When we notice these relationships among the answer choices, we should feel comforted by the fact that we seem to be able to understand what the College Board had in mind for the question—but we also have to remember to confirm our answer, since we know how easy it would be to make a small calculation error and pick a wrong answer.

Page 123, Question 4

This is the sort of question that can actually be solved pretty quickly if we approach it in the most efficient way possible, even though some test-takers could easily end up wasting a lot of time and effort on it—and possibly getting it wrong, as well.

Most untrained test-takers will see this question and immediately jump to the conclusion that they have to solve for every variable in the question, because years of high school math and science classes have conditioned them to expect that every variable in a question must have a specific value. But this conclusion is wrong! If you want to do your best on this test, it's a good idea to get comfortable with the idea that you'll occasionally see variables on this test *and not have to solve for them!* (In fact, some questions will include variables that you literally can't solve for, because the question doesn't provide enough information to allow you to do that.)

So, as trained test-takers, we know a couple of things about the design of this question that most untrained test-takers won't know:

1. We know that we might not have to solve for x and z, because the question didn't ask us to solve for them, and because we know that the test likes to try to confuse us by introducing variables that can't be solved for.

2. We know that the Math Level 2 Test doesn't usually require us to go through long, complicated calculations with lots of steps, so there's probably some way to look at this question that makes the solution relatively fast and simple.

We'd also want to notice the answer choices, of course. It looks like the College Board definitely thinks the number 3 and 17 will play some role in the average test-taker's approach to the question, because those numbers appear multiple times throughout the answer choices.

Now, keeping all of that in mind, let's identify some ways to attack this question. I can think of two major ways:

1. If we prefer to try backsolving, we could take the numbers in each answer choice and plug them into the equations for y, to see if one of the answer choices results in a set of consistent values for all three variables.

2. If we're comfortable with algebra, we could treat this like a system of equations, and try adding and subtracting the equations together until we're left with y equal to a specific numerical value.

As I usually like to do in this Black Book, I'll start with the backsolving approach, because it's more concrete than the algebraic one. Then we'll discuss the more abstract, algebraic way to handle the question.

For (A), if we plug in -3 for y in the first equation, we get a value of 5 for x. If we plug in $y = -3$ for the second equation, we get a z-value of 8. Now we plug all of those values into the last equation and check to see if the last equation is valid: is it true that $5 + -3 + 8$ equals 10? We can see that, yes, it is true. So (A) is the correct answer—assuming we've done our substituting and our calculations correctly. Because we're trained test-takers and we understand the importance of avoiding unnecessary mistakes on the test, we're still going to check out all the other answer choices, of course.

Plugging in the values for y from all the other answer choices gives us these results:

(B)   For the equation with x:

$x + y = 2$	(original equation)
$x + (\frac{3}{17}) = 2$	(substitute $\frac{3}{17}$ for y)
$x = \frac{31}{17}$	(subtract $\frac{3}{17}$ from both sides)

So we can see that a y-value of $\frac{3}{17}$ results in an x-value of $\frac{31}{17}$ here.

For the equation with z:

$$y + z = 5 \qquad \text{(original equation)}$$

$$\left(\tfrac{3}{17}\right) + z = 5 \qquad \text{(substitute } \tfrac{3}{17} \text{ for } y\text{)}$$

$$z = \tfrac{82}{17} \qquad \text{(subtract } \tfrac{3}{17} \text{ from both sides)}$$

So z has a value of $\tfrac{82}{17}$ when y is $\tfrac{3}{17}$ in this equation.

Now we take the values we've just worked out for x and z, and plug them into the last equation, along with the value for y that appears in choice (B). We're looking to see if the equation is valid with those values substituted.

$$x + y + z = 10 \qquad \text{(original equation)}$$

$$\left(\tfrac{31}{17}\right) + \left(\tfrac{3}{17}\right) + \left(\tfrac{82}{17}\right) \neq 10 \qquad \text{(plug in } y = \tfrac{3}{17} \text{ from choice (B); } x = \tfrac{31}{17} \text{ and } z = \tfrac{82}{17} \text{ from above)}$$

When we take the values for x and z that result from a y-value of $\tfrac{3}{17}$ and then plug them into the equation that relates x, y, and z, we end up with an invalid equation. So (B) is wrong.

(C) For the equation with x:

$$x + y = 2 \qquad \text{(original equation)}$$

$$x + (1) = 2 \qquad \text{(substitute 1 for } y\text{)}$$

$$x = 1 \qquad \text{(subtract 1 from both sides)}$$

So a y-value of 1 results in x also being 1, at least in this equation.

For the equation with z:

$$y + z = 5 \qquad \text{(original equation)}$$

$$(1) + z = 5 \qquad \text{(substitute 1 for } y\text{)}$$

$$z = 4 \qquad \text{(subtract 1 from both sides)}$$

In this equation, a y-value of 1 gives us a z value of 4.

For the equation relating x, y, and z:

$$x + y + z = 10 \qquad \text{(original equation)}$$

$$(1) + (1) + (4) \neq 10 \qquad \text{(plug in } y = 1 \text{ from choice (C); } x = 1 \text{ and } z = 4 \text{ from above)}$$

So (C) is wrong, because the equation that relates all three variables is invalid when we plug in the values that result from a y-value of 1.

(D) For the equation with x:

$$x + y = 2 \qquad \text{(original equation)}$$

$$x + (3) = 2 \qquad \text{(substitute 3 for } y\text{)}$$

$$x = -1 \qquad \text{(subtract 3 from both sides)}$$

When y is 3, we see that this equation results in a value of -1 for x.

For the equation with z:

$y + z = 5$	(original equation)
$(3) + z = 5$	(substitute 3 for y)
$z = 2$	(subtract 3 from both sides)

So z in this equation is 2 when y is 3.

For the equation relating x, y, and z:

$x + y + z = 10$	(original equation)
$(-1) + (3) + (2) \neq 10$	(plug in $y = 3$ from choice (D); $x = -1$ and $z = 2$ from above)

As we can see, the equation from the prompt that relates the three variables to 10 is invalid when we plug in the values that result from a y-value of 3. So (D) is wrong.

(E)   For the equation with x:

$x + y = 2$	(original equation)
$x + (\frac{17}{3}) = 2$	(substitute $\frac{17}{3}$ for y)
$x = \frac{-11}{3}$	(subtract $\frac{17}{3}$ from both sides)

For the equation with z:

$y + z = 5$	(original equation)
$(\frac{17}{3}) + z = 5$	(substitute $\frac{17}{3}$ for y)
$z = \frac{-2}{3}$	(subtract $\frac{17}{3}$ from both sides)

For the equation relating x, y, and z:

$x + y + z = 10$	(original equation)
$(\frac{-11}{3}) + (\frac{17}{3}) + (\frac{-2}{3}) \neq 10$	(plug in $y = \frac{17}{3}$ from choice (E); $x = \frac{-11}{3}$ and $z = \frac{-2}{3}$ from above)

So (E) is also wrong, because the x- and z-values that result from a y-value of $\frac{17}{3}$ don't satisfy the equation from the prompt that relates all three variables to 10.

(As you can see, this backsolving approach could take some time, especially when it comes to adding and subtracting the fractions for choices (B) and (E). So if you were going to resort to this strategy on test day, you might want to skip this question at first and come back to it after you'd already gone through the test and tackled everything you could answer more quickly. Remember that we discussed going through the test in multiple passes in the section of this Black Book called "Time Management On Test Day.")

Now that we've discussed how to backsolve, let's talk about the faster way to approach the question, which is probably to notice that we can add the first two expressions together to create another equation that relates all three variables, like this:

$$x + y \quad\quad = 2$$
$$\underline{+ \quad\quad\quad\quad y + z = 5}$$
$$x + 2y + z = 7$$

So we can see that $x + 2y + z$ is equal to 7.

We can also see that this whole expression is actually 3 less than $x + y + z$, because the prompt tells us that $x + y + z$ is 10.

This means that adding a second y on the left-hand side of the equation had the effect of reducing the right-hand side of the equation by 3. In other words, adding y is the same thing as taking away 3. This means that y must equal -3, so we can see again that (A) is the correct answer.

This algebraic approach is essentially the College Board's solution on page 147 of the MSTB.

Let's look at one more way to approach this question. We can find the value of y quickly if we notice a few things. First, if $x + y$ is 2, and $x + y + z$ is 10, then we know that adding z increases the value of the expression $x + y$ from 2 to 10, which means that z equals $10 - 2$, or 8. Similarly, if $y + z$ is 5, and $x + y + z$ is 10, then we know that adding x increases the value of the expression $y + z$ from 5 to 10, which means that x equals $10 - 5$, or 5. When we know that $x = 5$ and $z = 8$, we can quickly find y by plugging the values we just found into any of the three equations in the question.

(Notice that the College Board could easily have written this question with equations that didn't make the values of x and z so obvious; instead, the provided equations make it possible for us to answer the question relatively quickly if we stop and think about them for a minute. Remember that the College Board often writes questions so they can be answered more quickly if we don't automatically jump to an approach that might be required in a classroom setting.)

Now let's talk about where some of the wrong answers might be coming from. Notice that choices (B) and (E) reflect what a test-taker might come up with if she added all three equations together *and* made an algebra mistake. To illustrate this, let's imagine that someone added up all three equations, like this:

$$x + y \quad\quad = 2$$
$$y + z = 5$$
$$\underline{+ \quad\quad x + y + z = 10}$$
$$2x + 3y + 2z = 17$$

If a test-taker then thought the $2x$ and $2y$ expressions cancelled each other out somehow, she could incorrectly set the $3y$ term equal to 17, and end up with this:

$$3y = 17$$
$$y = \frac{17}{3} \quad\quad \text{(divide both sides by 3)}$$

This is the incorrect answer choice (E), and its reciprocal is the incorrect answer choice (B).

Page 124, Question 5

There are two basic ways to approach this question. If we feel comfortable with the concepts of natural log and e, we can work out the solution pretty quickly on paper. If not, we can still find the right answer with a calculator.

Whether or not we use a calculator, we need to know that finding $f(g(5))$ involves working from the inside out, which means that we evaluate $g(5)$, and then we take that value and plug it into the f function. In other words, we follow these steps:

1. Plug 5 into $g(x)$.

2. Solve for $g(5)$.

3. Plug the resulting value from Step 2 into the f function.

(If you don't feel comfortable with these concepts, be sure to review the section on functions in this book's Math Toolbox.)

Let's see what happens when we follow the above steps.

$g(x) = e^x$ (definition of $g(x)$ from the prompt)

$g(5) = e^5$ (plug $x = 5$ into $g(x)$)

$3 \ln(e^5) - 1$ (take the $g(5)$ expression and plug it into the f function)

If we're familiar with the natural log and e, we know that they're inverses of each other—in other words, $\ln(e^x) = x$, which means that $\ln(e^5) = 5$. So evaluating $3 \ln(e^5) - 1$ gives us this:

$3 \ln(e^5) - 1$

$3 (5) - 1$ (simplify $\ln(e^5)$)

$15 - 1$ (multiply 3 by 5)

14 (subtract 1 from 15)

That means the correct answer is choice (C).

As I said earlier, the above solution is pretty simple if we know that ln and e are inverse concepts. But what if we don't know that, or we've forgotten it?

It turns out we can also use a calculator to answer this question, although the solution is a little more time-consuming. Again, remember that evaluating $f(g(5))$ requires us to work from the inside out, so we need to plug 5 into $g(x)$, and then plug that result into $f(x)$.

So we start by finding e^5. When we plug that into our calculator, we see that it's equal to 148.413159103. Now we need to plug this number into $f(x)$, which looks like this:

$f(x) = 3 \ln(x) - 1$ (definition of $f(x)$ from prompt)

$f(x) = 3 \ln(148.413159103) - 1$ (plug in 148.413159103 for x)

$f(x) = 3(5) - 1$ (use the calculator to take ln of 148.413159103)

$f(x) = 14$ (combine like terms)

Again, we find that the correct answer is 14, choice (C).

Even though this question might intimidate some test-takers, it actually only requires a little understanding of functions, along with either of the following:

- knowing that natural log and *e* are inverse concepts of one another, or

- careful calculator use

(If you don't feel comfortable with the natural log and *e*, make sure you review the section on logarithms in the Math Toolbox in this Black Book.)

Now, as always, let's try to put ourselves in the College Board's position, and see if we can figure out where some of these wrong answers might be coming from. What kinds of mistakes do you think untrained test-takers are likely to make on this question? Well, some people might plug 5 into *f(x)* first, and then plug the result into *g(x)*, instead of the other way around. Doing that would result in a wrong answer of 45.98, which is choice (D). Of course, as trained test-takers, noticing this should remind us to double-check that we've followed the steps in the correct order during our solution. Untrained test-takers might also accidentally forget the order of operations when they tried to evaluate 3(5) − 1, and accidentally get 3(5 − 1), which is 12, choice (B).

As I often remind you, being able to see where some of the wrong answer choices come from is a great way to check that we've probably understood what's going on in the question.

Page 124, Question 6

In this question, we're asked which shapes can be formed from the intersection of a cube and a plane. A lot of test-takers might see a question like this and worry that they've never been tested on this exact concept in class before. But, as trained test-takers, we know that it's normal for the College Board to combine basic ideas in strange ways to create challenging questions; when we run into a combination of concepts that we've never seen before, we keep calm, read carefully, and try to think in terms of the properties and definitions of the concepts in the question. So let's do that now.

The question asks whether a plane's intersection with a cube can be a square (I), a parallelogram (II), or a triangle (III), or if some combination of the three is possible. Let's consider each shape individually.

For the purposes of this discussion, it might be helpful to think of the plane and the cube in terms of everyday objects. Let's imagine that the plane is a perfectly flat sheet of paper, and that the cube is a throwing die. Is it possible for the sheet of paper to cut through the die so the cross-section of the die would be a square?

Yes, it is. If the sheet of paper slices evenly through the center of the die, and the front and back of the die are parallel to the paper, then the intersection will be a square, as demonstrated by the dashed line in the following diagram:

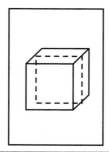

So we know that option I is possible.

Could the intersection be a parallelogram? There are two general ways we could choose to figure that out. One way would be to realize that a square is, by definition, a type of parallelogram—since we just worked out that the intersection could be a square, we already know it can be a parallelogram. But if we forget that aspect of the definitions of the term "square" and "parallelogram," we can still work out a scenario that allows the area of intersection to be a non-square parallelogram. Imagine that we change the arrangement of the original cube and plane by tilting the plane a little bit on its vertical axis, and then tilting it a little bit on its horizontal axis. If we did this, the opposite sides of the intersection would still be parallel, but the corners of the intersecting shape wouldn't be right angles, as demonstrated in the dashed lines below:

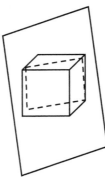

So we can see that the area of intersection can definitely be a parallelogram as well, for multiple reasons. This means option II is also valid.

Now, if we're completely confident that both I and II are possible, then we already know that (E) must be correct, because it's the only answer choice that includes both I and II. But I would still recommend that we take a look at III, because, as trained test-takers, we want to make sure that we always give ourselves every possible chance to discover any small mistakes. We know that even a small mistake can cost us a question.

If we imagine a sheet of paper that intersects with just the corner of a throwing die, that intersection would be a triangle, as indicated by the dashed line below:

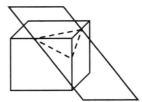

(Another way to visualize this is to imagine a knife cutting the corner off of a cube of cheese—the exposed portion of the block of cheese would be a triangle.) So we know that all three shapes are possible, which means that choice (E) is correct

From a training standpoint, it's important to realize that a lot of untrained test-takers might draw the wrong conclusion from the fact that this question appears in the College Board's book. It would be a mistake to think that you're likely to see another question on test day that discusses the ways a plane can intersect with a cube, and it would be a waste of time to try to memorize any of the details from this question in the hope that you might use them in the future. Instead, the lesson to learn from this question is that the College Board can always combine basic concepts into a question that looks unlike anything you've ever seen before on the surface, and that it's important to stay calm and remember your training when you run into those kinds of questions, just as we did here.

Page 124, Question 7

This question involves trigonometry, but it's pretty straightforward if we read carefully and remember our training. The solution we'll look at here is basically the same as the one you'll find on page 148 of the MSTB, and after that we'll discuss some answer choice patterns.

The question describes a rocket taking off vertically. When the rocket reaches a height of 12 km, its angle of elevation from point A is 84.1°, and its angle of elevation from point B is 62.7°. We're asked to find the distance from A to B. Let's go ahead and make a sketch of the information we have so far (note that this sketch is similar to the one on page 124 of the MSTB, with the addition of the 12 km height):

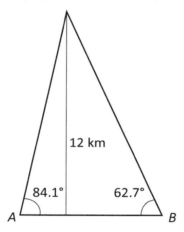

At this point, a lot of untrained test-takers might be trying to remember some semi-obscure trig formula to work out the length of a side of a triangle between two angles, given the measures of the angles and the height of the triangle as measured from the unknown. On the other hand, a trained test-taker knows that the College Board doesn't ask about obscure trig formulas on this test, which means that there must be some way to approach this question using nothing more than SOHCAHTOA. (If you're unfamiliar with the mnemonic device SOHCAHTOA, please look in the relevant portion of the Math Toolbox in this Black Book for an explanation.)

So how can we apply SOHCAHTOA in a situation that lacks a right triangle? Well, in this case, we can sub-divide the given triangle into two smaller right triangles, which will allow us to work with the hypotenuse values that are required in SOHCAHTOA.

Once we start thinking in terms of two right triangles that share a long leg of 12 km, we see that the distance from A to B is actually the sum of the lengths of the shorter legs of the triangles. I'll label those sides x and y, just for purposes of clarifying this explanation:

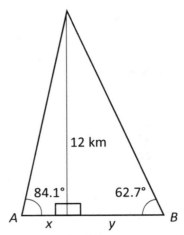

Now let's solve for the *x* and *y* distances individually, so we can add them together and answer the question. We'll look at *x* first.

For the triangle that includes the *x* leg, we have one angle measurement of 84.1°, and the measure of the side opposite that angle, which is 12 km. We want to find the length of the leg adjacent to point *A*. We know from SOHCAHTOA that the trigonometric ratio that relates an angle's opposite leg to its adjacent leg is the tangent ratio (from the "TOA" part of SOHCAHTOA, which tells us that **T**angent = **O**pposite/**A**djacent). So let's set up an equation that will allow us to find *x*:

$\tan A = \dfrac{\text{opposite}}{\text{adjacent}}$ (definition of tangent from SOHCAHTOA)

$\tan(84.1°) = \dfrac{12}{x}$ (plug in 84.1 for *A*, 12 for opposite, and *x* for adjacent)

$x \tan(84.1°) = 12$ (multiply both sides by *x*)

$x = \dfrac{12}{\tan(84.1°)}$ (divide both sides by tan(84.1°))

When we enter $\dfrac{12}{\tan(84.1°)}$ into a calculator (making sure the calculator is in degree mode, since the question is written in terms of degrees), we find that *x* is approximately 1.24. But we have to remember that 1.24 isn't the answer that we're ultimately looking for! The question asks us for the distance from *A* to *B*, but 1.24 only represents the length of *x* in the diagram above. (There's no answer choice with 1.24 as an option anyway, but we will often see wrong answer choices with numbers that we'd see in earlier steps of a correct solution, so we always have to be in the habit of keeping in mind exactly what the question is asking us for.)

Now that we know the length of *x* from the diagram above, let's find the length we called *y* so we can add the two lengths and find the answer to the question.

As was the case with *A*, we know the degree measure of *B* and the length of the leg opposite *B*, and we need to find the measure of the leg adjacent to *B*, so we'll use tangent again, just like we did to find the value of *x*:

$\tan B = \dfrac{\text{opposite}}{\text{adjacent}}$ (definition of tangent from SOHCAHTOA)

$\tan(62.7°) = \dfrac{12}{y}$ (plug in *B* = 62.7°, opposite = 12, and adjacent = *y*)

$y \tan(62.7°) = 12$ (multiply both sides by y)

$y = \dfrac{12}{\tan(62.7°)}$ (divide both sides by $\tan(62.7°)$)

When we enter $\dfrac{12}{\tan(62.7°)}$ into a calculator—again, making sure the calculator is still in degree mode—we find that $y = 6.19$. (Remember that 6.19 isn't the answer to the question. It's only a step on the way to the answer.)

To find the full distance from A to B, we need to add the two values we just found. That gives us 1.24 + 6.19, which is equal to 7.43, so (C) is correct.

Now that we've done the math, let's think about the other answer choices. We might expect that a common mistake many test-takers would make with trigonometric ratios would be to use the wrong ratios: to find sine or cosine instead of tangent, or to find cotangent instead of tangent. As the College Board notes in its explanation on page 148 of the MSTB, choice (D) is what we'd get if we used sine instead of tangent, and we plugged in 12 for the hypotenuse. Choice (E) is what we'd get if we switched 12 for the unknown side when we were setting up the problem. Doing so would give us tangents equal to $\dfrac{x}{12}$ instead of $\dfrac{12}{x}$, and $\dfrac{y}{12}$ instead of $\dfrac{12}{y}$. Choice (A) would be the result if we cross-multiplied incorrectly.

If we think carefully about the answer choices when we first address the question, we might notice that we can eliminate some of the answer choices right away. Let's look one more time at the big triangle in our diagram:

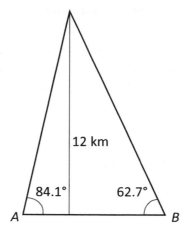

Since we know two of the three angles, we can fill in the measure of the remaining angle, because the angles of a triangle always add up to 180. We know that $180 - 84.1 - 62.7 = 33.2$, so the angle at the top of the triangle must equal 33.2°. Let's fill that in:

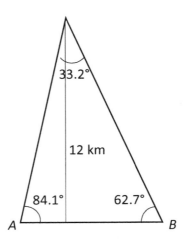

We can see that side AB must be the smallest side of the triangle, since it's opposite the smallest angle in the triangle. Even though this triangle isn't drawn exactly to scale, we can probably tell from the sizes of the different angles, and from the height of the triangle, that choice (E) is too large to be the correct answer for the length of AB. We can probably also tell that even choice (D) is too large. Along similar lines, we can see that choice (A) is too small. All of this information taken together serves to reinforce our confidence that (C) is the correct answer.

Of course, you can technically answer this question correctly without analyzing the answer choices in this way. But I'd strongly recommend that you learn to start looking out for these kinds of alternative approaches to test questions, because they can help you in a lot of ways—from helping you avoid possible mistakes all the way up to letting you answer questions with certainty using little or no calculation.

(As always, if you felt uncomfortable with the concepts in this solution, I'd recommend you review the relevant concepts in the Math Toolbox in this Black Book—in this case, the material related to basic trig.)

Page 125, Question 8

This is a good example of a question that's relatively simple, but that we can still mess up if we don't pay careful attention. It's also a pretty transparent example of some of the ways the College Board tries to fool us, so it will be good to discuss those now and keep them in mind for the future.

We're asked to find the value of x^2, given that $x = \sqrt{(15^2 - 12^2)}$. There are a few ways we could choose to approach this question. One common approach would be to find a numerical value for x, and then square that value—but most test-takers would only be doing this because they've been conditioned to try to solve for x reflexively, whenever they see x in a question.

But solving for x by itself doesn't really make much sense for this question, though, because the question never actually asks for the numerical value of x itself. Instead, a trained test-taker will realize that it's possible just to work out a numerical value for x^2 directly, which is what the question is actually asking us to do, without bothering to find x by itself first.

But how can we work out a numerical value for x^2? Well, we're told that x is equal to a particular numerical expression. When we square both sides of that equation, we'll have x^2 on one side of the equation, and whatever is on the other side will be the numerical value of x^2.

When we square both sides of the given equation, we see that x^2 is the same as $(\sqrt{15^2 - 12^2})^2$, and from there it's a matter of some simple math.

$x = (\sqrt{15^2 - 12^2})^2$ (original equation from the prompt)

$x^2 = 15^2 - 12^2$ (square both sides of the equation)

$x^2 = 225 - 144$ (square 15 and 12)

$x^2 = 81$ (subtract 144 from 225)

So the correct answer is (D), 81.

Remember that we were asked for the value of x^2, and not of x. But you'll notice that one of the wrong answers is 9, which could be the value of x itself, because $9^2 = 81$. It's easy to imagine that some test-takers might try to approach the question by solving for x itself, and then forget to square that value at the end. The College Board often likes to include wrong answers that reflect numbers we might encounter on the way to finding the right answer.

There's another common wrong answer pattern here, too. Notice that all five choices follow a series of sorts: from left to right, each answer choice is the square of the one before it. This tells us that the College Board thinks we'll make a mistake and square something, or take its square root, one too many times. When we notice that pattern, we realize that we need to be extra careful we didn't make this mistake, because the College Board is basically showing us that it would be a very easy mistake to make. Also notice that our answer choice isn't the first or last term in the series, which means it fits another one of the answer choice patterns we discussed earlier in this Black Book. As trained test-takers, we know this isn't enough to guarantee that an answer choice is right, but it's a good indicator that we're probably on the right track. If we re-check our work and our reasoning, we can be confident that (D) is the correct answer.

I realize that this question is relatively easy in the context of the Math Level 2 Test, and you may feel like you don't need to notice these patterns and relationships in order to answer the question correctly. That may be true, but I always want my students to appreciate these things on easier questions because doing so makes it easier to notice them on harder questions, where they can be more helpful to you.

Page 125, Question 9

This is a great example of a question that intimidates a lot of test-takers because it seems to involve concepts that don't usually come up in a normal high school class. But, as trained test-takers, we know not to panic, because we expect to encounter questions that combine basic ideas in strange ways. We know that we can figure out the answer to a strange question like this if we read carefully and approach things in terms of the properties and definitions of the concepts in the question. So let's do that.

We're told that the points in a coordinate plane are "transformed" in such a way that every point P at (x, y) becomes P' at $(2x, 2y)$.

We might not ever have heard the term "transformed" in math class, but we can work around the word because the question tells us exactly what happens to a point when it's transformed: the value of the *x*-coordinate is multiplied by 2, and the value of the *y*-coordinate is multiplied by 2.

Then the question tells us that the distance from the origin to a point is called *d*. The question asks what happens to *d* after the transformation.

There are two general ways to approach this question. One approach relies on applying the distance formula (which is basically the Pythagorean Theorem); this is essentially the approach from page 149 of the MSTB, but we'll go through it in a more concrete way below. The other approach is probably faster and easier if you're comfortable with it, but it's a bit more abstract, which might make some test-takers uncomfortable. I'll take you through this approach after we walk through the concrete approach below.

So let's get started with the more concrete approach. If we want to see what happens to *d* when a point is "transformed," we can just pick a random point and see what happens when we double the values of the point's *x*- and *y*-coordinates. When we pick values to try out, we know from the training in this Black Book that it's generally better to avoid -1, 0, 1, or any number from the prompt or answer choices, because we know those kinds of numbers are usually more likely to result in more than one answer choice seeming to be valid by coincidence. I'll just randomly choose the point (5, 5):

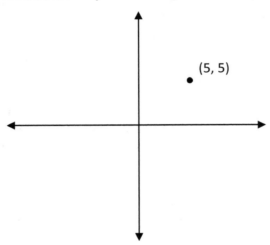

According to the question, the point (5, 5) would be "transformed" into the point (10, 10), since transforming in this context means doubling both the *x*-coordinate and the *y*-coordinate. So what happens to *d* when we do this? Let's take a look. To find *d* for (5, 5), we can construct a right triangle whose hypotenuse connects (5, 5) to the origin, and then use the Pythagorean Theorem (this process is basically the same thing as applying the distance formula). Here's what that might look like if we feel like diagramming it:

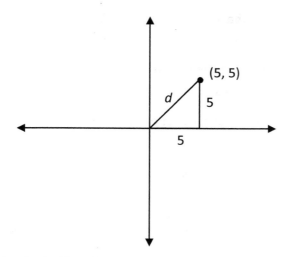

And here's what the calculation looks like when we apply the Pythagorean Theorem to find d:

$a^2 + b^2 = c^2$	(Pythagorean Theorem)
$5^2 + 5^2 = d^2$	(plug in 5 for the lengths of the legs and d for the hypotenuse)
$25 + 25 = d^2$	(square the leg lengths)
$50 = d^2$	(add the squared leg lengths)
$\sqrt{50} = d$	(take square root of both sides)
$\sqrt{25} * \sqrt{2} = d$	(express one root as the product of two other roots)
$5\sqrt{2} = d$	(simplify $\sqrt{25}$)

So for the point (5, 5), the value of d (the distance from the origin) is equal to $\sqrt{50}$, or $5\sqrt{2}$.

Now what happens to d when (5, 5) is "transformed" to (10, 10), as the question describes? Again, we can find out by graphing the new point, constructing a right triangle, and applying the Pythagorean Theorem:

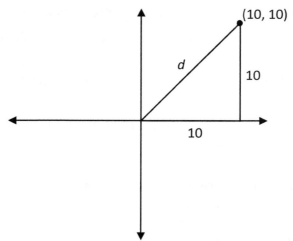

$a^2 + b^2 = c^2$ (Pythagorean Theorem)

$10^2 + 10^2 = d^2$ (plug in 10 for the lengths of the legs and d for the hypotenuse)

$100 + 100 = d^2$ (square the leg lengths)

$200 = d^2$ (add the squared leg lengths)

$\sqrt{200} = d$ (take square root of both sides)

$\sqrt{100} * \sqrt{2} = d$ (express one root as the product of two other square roots)

$10\sqrt{2} = d$ (simplify $\sqrt{100}$)

So the new value for d is $10\sqrt{2}$.

We can see that when we doubled the values of x and y, the value of d doubled as well, from $5\sqrt{2}$ to $10\sqrt{2}$. So the correct answer is (D), $2d$.

As I mentioned above, there's another way to approach this question that's quicker and a little more abstract. This approach requires us to realize that, for any point P with coordinate values (x, y), the d-value of that point must correspond to the hypotenuse of a right triangle with legs of length x and y, as we just demonstrated above. So if we transform the point by doubling its x- and y-coordinates, that's like doubling the lengths of the legs of a right triangle, which means the hypotenuse must double as well—in a sense, all that's happening is that we're scaling up all of the sides of the triangle by a factor of 2. Again, we see that the correct answer is $2d$.

Now that we've discussed how to approach the question from multiple perspectives, let's analyze the answer choices a little bit. If we understand what the question is asking, we know that any coordinate pair (besides (0, 0)) that gets "transformed" must end up farther away from the origin than before, since both the x- and y-values of the point are multiplied by 2. That means (A), (B), and (C) must be wrong, because none of them would necessarily result in an increase in d. Further, we can see that choice (E) could also result in values smaller than d when d is a number between 0 and 1, so (E) can't be right, either. (Choice (E) is probably included to trick test-takers who get confused when they try to apply the distance formula or Pythagorean Theorem, which would involve squaring values, as we saw above.)

Finally, an argument can be made that (D) follows the "wrong answers imitate right answers" pattern:

- Three of the five answer choices aren't fractions, which suggests that the correct answer is likely not to be a fraction

- Four of the five choices don't have exponents, which suggests that the correct answer is likely not to include an exponent.

- Three of the five answer choices involve the number 2, which suggests that the correct answer is likely to involve the number 2.

We see that only choice (D) agrees with all of these predictions, which makes it more likely to be the correct answer. (As always, we have to remember that we can't rely exclusively on these kinds of patterns when we choose an answer, because they aren't 100% reliable! Instead, we should use the pattern as an indicator of what's *likely* to be correct, and also let it give us another perspective on the question, which can give us more confidence that we've understood the question from the College Board's perspective and reasoned through it correctly.)

Page 125, Question 10

Many test-takers are intimidated by this question at first glance, because it seems to involve complicated functions—we see fractions with both squares and square roots above and below the fraction bars. In most math classes, a question with functions like this would require us to draw conclusions about the graphs of the functions, or to evaluate the functions at particular points, and so on. But as trained test-takers, we know not to be intimidated just because a question looks strange. As usual, we'll find the solution is actually pretty simple if we read carefully and approach the question in terms of properties and definitions. In this case, we'll find that the solution to the question depends on understanding basic function notation.

We're given the definitions of $f(x)$ and $f(g(x))$, and we're asked to figure out what $g(x)$ is. Let's start by thinking about what $f(g(x))$ means. If we're familiar with function notation, we know that $g(x)$ represents a function, and $f(g(x))$ means that $g(x)$ is being plugged into $f(x)$. So we should compare $f(x)$ to $f(g(x))$ and see if we can tell what was plugged into $f(x)$ to make $f(g(x))$—whatever that is will be $g(x)$.

When we do that, we can see that the difference between $f(x)$ and $f(g(x))$ is just that $f(g(x))$ has the expression $\sqrt{(x^2 + 1)}$ everywhere that $f(x)$ has x:

$$f(x) = \frac{2x - 1}{x + 1} \qquad f(g(x)) = \frac{2\sqrt{x^2 + 1} - 1}{\sqrt{x^2 + 1} + 1}$$

> Every x in the function definition on the left corresponds to $\sqrt{(x^2 + 1)}$ in the function definition on the right.

So $f(g(x))$ is $f(x)$ with $\sqrt{(x^2 + 1)}$ plugged in for x. That means $g(x)$ must be $\sqrt{(x^2 + 1)}$, which means that choice (B) is correct.

Notice that finding this answer didn't actually require us to calculate anything or do any real algebra. Instead, we just needed to pay careful attention and know how to understand function notation.

Now let's take a look at the other answer choices and see if we can figure out what the College Board might be trying to do with them. We see that choice (E) is similar to the correct answer, but ignores the radical sign, so we can probably imagine test-takers carelessly picking (E) if they don't notice the radical expression in $f(g(x))$. If we think of the "wrong answers imitate right answers" pattern on this question, we might be a little concerned that we think the correct answer choice includes a radical sign, since most of the answer choices don't include a radical sign. But we have to remember that we should never rely on these patterns completely—instead, we should let them remind us of key details in a question. In this case, when we look back over the prompt, we see clearly that $f(g(x))$ contains radical signs that don't appear in $f(x)$ at all, so it seems reasonable to conclude that the radical signs have to be present in $g(x)$, and we see again that (B) makes sense.

(If any of what we just discussed was unclear, you'll probably want to review the material on functions in the Math Toolbox in this Black Book.)

The other answer choices are things we might come up with if we don't read the functions carefully, especially if we think the "+ 1" expression in $g(x)$ is part of $f(x)$.

Page 126, Question 11

There are two primary ways we can answer this question:

1. We can take an abstract approach based on the unit circle.

2. We can take a concrete approach and use our calculators to figure out the value of A.

I normally prefer to begin discussing a question by going through the concrete approach if there is one. In this case, I'd rather start by discussing the abstract approach, because this is a rare situation where the concrete approach doesn't really help us understand the abstract one any better, and the abstract approach is faster. The abstract approach is also basically what the College Board relies on in its solution on page 149 of the MSTB.

As the College Board points out, every acute angle x has the property that $\sin x = \cos (90° - x)$. If we happen to remember that, then we know the answer is (E) right away.

But most test-takers won't remember that exact concept—in fact, they may never have learned it in math class, because it doesn't really have much application in high school math.

Still, if we understand the unit circle, it's possible to realize that (E) must be correct without having previously memorized anything about the relationship of sine and cosine in acute angles. Remember that sine is the value of the y-coordinate of the point where one leg of the angle would intercept the unit circle, and cosine is the value of the x-coordinate of the same point. With that in mind, we might visualize (or sketch out) an angle A in the unit circle that has a sine of 0.8, and then see what would happen if we also visualized an angle equal to $(90° - A)$. Let's do that now—here's a rough sketch of angle A in the unit circle (not to scale):

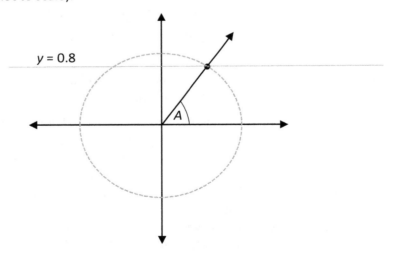

Now let's add in the angle that would correspond to (90° − A) and see what happens:

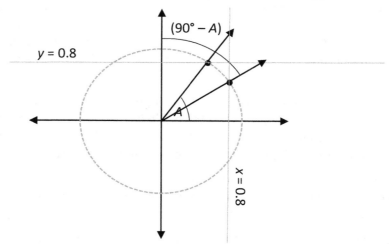

As the sketch shows, when we start from 90° and travel A degrees *back* towards the positive part of the x-axis, we end up intercepting the unit circle at a point with an x-coordinate of 0.8, just as angle A opens up from the x-axis and intercepts the unit circle at a point with a y-coordinate of 0.8.

Since the cosine of an angle can be defined as the x-coordinate of the point where the angle intercepts the unit circle, and since the angle indicated by (90° − A) intercepts the unit circle at a point with an x-coordinate of 0.8, we know that the cosine of (90° − A) would be 0.8.

But even if we weren't comfortable relying on the unit circle to approach this question, we could still use a calculator to answer the question relatively easily. If we use the calculator to identify the actual value of A, we can plug that value into the expression (90° − A) and use the calculator to evaluate that and tell us the answer to the question.

We're told that sin A = 0.8. So we just find the inverse sine (also written as arcsin, or sin⁻¹) of 0.8, and we see that it's approximately 53.13°, which means that A is approximately 53.13° (remember to put the calculator in degree mode for this, because the question is written in terms of degrees).

Now that we know the value of A, we can plug it into cos(90° − A). That gives us cos(90° − 53.13°), or cos(36.87°). When we use our calculators to evaluate cos(36.87°), we get 0.79999, which rounds to 0.8. (Remember that some rounding might be expected because we're dealing with decimal approximations of trig values.) So, again, (E) is the answer.

Notice that choice (D) would be the result if we accidentally switch sine and cosine and end up finding sin(36.87°) or cos(53.13°). It's easy to imagine untrained test-takers making a simple mistake like that and failing to correct it before choosing an answer.

We may notice that the answer choices (A), (B), (D), and (E) form a series, with each choice being .2 more than the choice before it (skipping choice (C)). As trained test-takers, we know that the College Board often avoids making the correct answer choice the first or last choice in a series, so we might be hesitant to choose (E) without re-checking all of our work. But when we do re-check, we see that (E) is, in fact, the right answer. Remember that the answer choice patterns we talk about in this Black Book are useful tools for evaluating a question from multiple perspectives—they aren't hard and fast rules for us to follow without thinking.

Page 126, Question 12

Most test-takers expect this question to require some kind of complicated calculation, or perhaps some advanced knowledge of algebra. As it turns out, though, we can actually answer this question pretty quickly in a few different ways, and two of them don't even involve picking up a pencil. I'll run through those solutions quickly, and then we can talk about how you might be able to reason your way through this question if you need to.

The fastest way to answer this question is to realize right away that $x^2 + y^2 + z^2 = 1$ is an example of a standard equation for a sphere centered on the origin in the xyz-coordinate space, just as $x^2 + y^2 = 1$ is an example of a standard equation for a circle centered on the origin in the xy-coordinate plane. This makes (C) the correct answer. This is basically the College Board's approach on page 149 of the MSTB.

Assuming we're familiar with points expressed in (x, y, z) notation, another fast way to answer this question is to realize that the set of prompt describes points in 3-dimensional space that can't be graphed on a 2-dimensional plane. Since only choice (C) is a 3-dimensional figure, it must be correct.

But those two approaches don't address the most common problem that test-takers have with this question: many test-takers don't understand the phrase "the set of points (x, y, z)" from the prompt, because they've only dealt with (x, y) coordinates in school, and aren't familiar with the idea of a coordinate point described in (x, y, z) notation. In order to discuss how a trained test-taker in that position might still be able to answer the question correctly with total confidence, we'll proceed for the rest of this discussion as though we don't know what (x, y, z) notation is when we first read the question.

As trained test-takers, we know it's critical not to panic when we see an unfamiliar concept on this test. We know that we need to read carefully and try to think in terms of the properties and definitions of the basic concepts that we do know, because there's a good chance that the question will give us enough information to be able to find the answer if we do that. So for this question in particular, there's a good chance that we'll eventually be able to understand the concept of an (x, y, z) point—or, at least, that we'll be able to understand it enough to answer the question.

We might start by trying to think of a few obvious points to satisfy the equation from the prompt, and see if that shows us anything. Well, some of the easiest points to think of would be points with a value of 1 for one of the three variables, and zeros everywhere else. That would work because $1^2 + 0^2 + 0^2 = 1$. These points would include the following:

- $(1, 0, 0)$
- $(0, 1, 0)$
- $(0, 0, 1)$

Of course, we could also do the same with -1 as a coordinate value and zeros everywhere else, because the square of -1 is also equal to 1. So that gives us the following additional points to satisfy the equation in the prompt:

- $(-1, 0, 0)$
- $(0, -1, 0)$
- $(0, 0, -1)$

This set of six points gives us something to compare to the answer choices, and see where things stand. (We wouldn't necessarily know what these points represented yet, if we weren't familiar with (x, y, z) notation, but looking through the answer choices could help us start putting things together. Remember that we should always keep the answer choices in mind as we try to answer a question!)

Choice (A) definitely seems to be wrong, because we've clearly shown that the set of points from the prompt isn't empty. We've identified six points that satisfy the equation in the prompt.

(B) also seems like it has to be wrong, because we've identified more than "a point" that satisfies the equation—again, we've identified six points so far.

(C) and (D) might be interesting, especially because we know that the College Board often likes to distract us from a correct answer choice by include a wrong answer that's similar to the correct answer, and we know that circles and spheres are similar concepts. Could our six points all fall on a sphere, or on a circle? Well, we know that four of the six points would fall on a circle—in fact, they would all fall on the unit circle in the *xy*-plane:

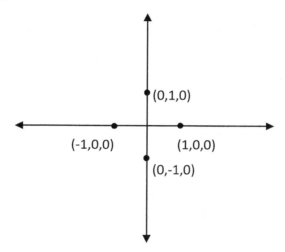

But what about the points with zero-values for *x* and *y*, but values of 1 and -1 for *z*? We know those don't fall on the unit circle, which means they don't fall on the same circle as the other four points we just thought of . . . so (D) definitely seems to be wrong, because we've discovered points that satisfy the equation in the prompt but that don't lie on the same circle with one another. It might be harder to think about (C) at this point, though (assuming for the sake of discussion that we've never seen an equation for a sphere before, which is the reason we'd have to go through this thought process in the first place). So let's take a look at the last answer choice while we keep (C) on the backburner.

(E) looks like it has to be wrong, too. We know that a plane extends infinitely in two dimensions, which means the plane would have to include points with coordinates like (999, 999)—points that wouldn't satisfy the $x^2 + y^2 + z^2 = 1$ equation in the prompt. So there's no way that the equation in the prompt describes all the points in a plane.

At this point in this approach, it looks like we've identified solid reasons why (A), (B), (D), and (E) must all be wrong, but we still don't feel like we understand (C). Many untrained test-takers would be happy to choose (C) without understanding the question any more than this—and, for this particular question, they'd get credit for choosing the right answer if they did that.

But as a trained test-taker, I know that it's critically important for me not to give up points by answering questions incorrectly. I also know that it's common for test-takers to be wrong when they think they've conclusively eliminated some of the answer choices in a College Board question, because the College Board is very good at writing questions that fool us into thinking we partially understand them. So before I mark (C), I want more evidence than just a strong feeling that the other four choices are probably *wrong*—I'd like to have a pretty solid idea of why (C) is *right*, too.

So I'd probably see if I could draw any connection between the idea of a sphere in choice (C) and the $x^2 + y^2 + z^2 = 1$ equation in the prompt. I might recall the roles of the (x, y) coordinates, and then think about how that concept might be extended to (x, y, z) coordinates. We know that the x-value tells us a point's horizontal separation from the origin, and that the y-value indicates the point's vertical separation from the origin. It makes sense that the z-value probably tells us something else—something the x-value and the y-value don't already tell us. Since the information provided by the x- and y-values accounts for any point that can appear in a two-dimensional plane (a flat surface, basically), we could reason that z must give us information about points that aren't limited to that plane. We might reason that it makes sense for the z-value to tell us about points that appear in three-dimensional space—points that would either "come up off" the page from a normal x and y coordinate grid, or that would "go down into" the page and come out the other side, so to speak. Ultimately, we'd want to realize that the z in (x, y, z) notation refers to a third axis that runs at a right angle to the xy-coordinate plane. Depicting this on a flat surface is challenging, but it would look something like this:

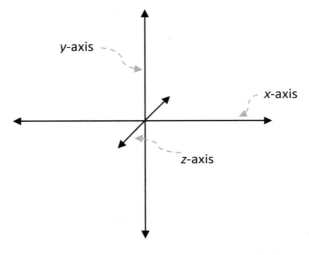

The points (0, 0, 1) and (0, 0, -1) could be plotted in this three-dimensional space like this:

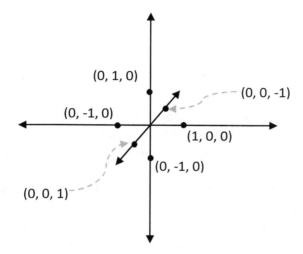

(Again, imagine that the diagonal line is the *z*-axis, which comes straight out of the page and goes straight down into the page.)

Now that we've graphed (or imagined) these six points, (C) starts to make more sense to us, and we can see how these points might all lie on a sphere. The sphere has its center at the origin and has a radius of 1 unit. I'll try to add it into the diagram for purposes of demonstration (of course you wouldn't need to do this in your own test booklet on test day):

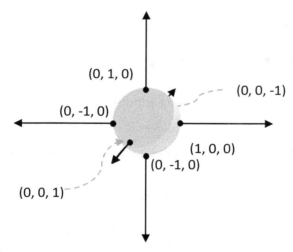

If we're not able to figure out what the *z* in the prompt represents, then we're going to have difficulty making progress on this question, and we may be better off skipping it for the moment and investing our time in other questions. But if we keep in mind what we know about *xy*-coordinate planes, circles, and the other concepts that are present in the question, then there's a good chance we can figure out that *z* relates to the third dimension by using a train of thought similar to the one detailed above.

Notice that the College Board could have made this question a lot more challenging by making the radius in the equation a non-square number, or even by centering the sphere on some other point besides the origin. In fact, the College Board could have chosen to give us an equation for a sphere that looked something like this:

$$(x - 17)^2 + (y + 3)^2 = 13 - (z - 13.22)^2$$

(That equation describes a sphere with a center at (17, -3, 13.22) and a radius of $\sqrt{13}$.)

But the College Board didn't try to confuse us in that way. Instead, the College Board gave us a relatively obvious equation for a sphere.

The question could probably also have been made more challenging with a different set of answer choices—for example, the answer choices could have included a cone, cylinder, or some other three-dimensional figure besides a sphere. Instead, the College Board decided to include only one three-dimensional figure in the answer choices, which makes the question easier to answer if a test-taker recognizes that the equation in the prompt describes a three-dimensional figure.

Now, you may think that we've thoroughly exhausted this question at this point, but there's one more idea that I want to drive home here, and it's probably the most important thing we can say about this question from a training perspective. A lot of test-takers will see this question and assume—incorrectly—that the College Board is going to focus on 3-dimensional coordinate systems on test day. But as trained test-takers, we should know that the subject-matter of questions on the Math Level 2 Test is much less important than the *style* of those questions, and learning to deal with the *style* is the most important thing you can do in your preparation. That's why this Black Book always breaks down test questions in terms of things like rules, patterns, basic math concepts, and other design principles. Keep this in mind as you continue to train.

Page 126, Question 13

Some test-takers will approach this question by factoring out the polynomial under the fraction bar and then finding the *x*-values that would result in a denominator of zero, which is basically the College Board's approach on page 149 of the MSTB. This approach is technically fine, of course, but it's more complicated than necessary.

There are at least two other ways we could approach the question:

1. We could backsolve from the answer choices if we know what a vertical asymptote is.

2. We could graph the equation on our calculator and probably figure out the answer even if we don't know what a vertical asymptote is.

For the backsolving approach, we see from the answer choices that the only numbers we need to worry about are 0, 4, and 5, since these are the only options we have. Let's test them by plugging them into the denominator to see which ones result in zero. (Remember that vertical asymptotes can only occur when the *denominator* of a function would equal zero, so we only need to worry about the denominator for this question.)

We'll start by testing $x = 0$:

$x^2 - 8x + 16$	(original denominator expression)
$(0)^2 - 8(0) + 16$	(plug in $x = 0$)
$0 - 0 + 16$	(combine like terms)

16   (combine like terms)

So plugging in 0 for x doesn't actually cause the denominator to be equal to 0, which means there can't be a vertical asymptote at $x = 0$. Now let's try $x = 4$:

$x^2 - 8x + 16$ (original denominator expression)

$(4)^2 - 8(4) + 16$ (plug in $x = 4$)

$16 - 32 + 16$ (combine like terms)

0   (combine like terms)

Plugging in $x = 4$ does result in a value of zero in the denominator, so there can be a vertical asymptote at $x = 4$. Let's try the last value, 5:

$x^2 - 8x + 16$ (original denominator expression)

$(5)^2 - 8(5) + 16$ (plug in $x = 5$)

$25 - 40 + 16$ (combine like terms)

1   (combine like terms)

When we plug in 5 as x, we don't get a value of 0 in the denominator, so there can't be a vertical asymptote at $x = 5$, either.

Since the answer choices only offer us three possible x-values, and since we only get a denominator of 0 when we plug in $x = 4$, we know that (B) must be correct. This approach allows us to answer the question without having to factor anything, which many test-takers don't like doing.

But the fastest, easiest way to answer the question is probably to use a graphing calculator. If we graph the given function, we get this:

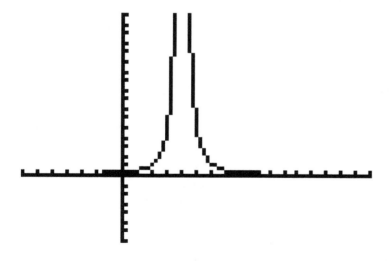

We can clearly see the asymptote at $x = 4$ this way, and all we have to do is make sure that we've entered the function into the calculator correctly. So, again, (B) is correct.

(By the way, even if we didn't know for sure what a vertical asymptote was before answering the question, we could still tell that (B) was right when we realized that the only vertical feature in the whole graph is centered on the line at $x = 4$.)

This question is a good reminder that the College Board doesn't care if you approach questions in a way that would satisfy most math teachers. As we just saw, the fastest, easiest, and most reliable way to approach a question may involve tactics like graphing a function or working backwards from the answer choices. If you want to maximize your performance on the Math Level 2 Test, you'll need to look out for these kinds of alternative solutions, which is why I explore them so thoroughly in this Black Book.

(By the way, if you're familiar with functions, you may know that having a zero in the denominator can also result in something called a "removable discontinuity." But we didn't have to worry about that here, because the answer choices tell us that there's a vertical asymptote on the graph for at least one x-value; since $x = 4$ is the only x-value that gives us a denominator of 0, we know that $x = 4$ has to be the location of the vertical asymptote. And if we graph the function on a calculator, it becomes clear again that $x = 4$ is the site of a vertical asymptote.)

Page 127, Question 14

Once more, we have a question that's actually much simpler than it appears, as long as we read carefully and remember the limitations of the multiple-choice testing format. As will often be the case, we'll find that there are at least two ways to approach this question. One relies on a calculator, and the other involves thinking in terms of abstract math principles. Let's take a look at both.

Most test-takers will be intimidated by this question at first, because most math teachers don't ask questions in class that require us to identify elements of a quadrinomial function from a graph. This is part of a larger issue that many test-takers face on the Math Level 2 Test. In a typical high school math class, students are conditioned to attempt specific pre-defined solutions in response to specific types of questions. When most test-takers see a function like the one in this question, they often assume they need to do something with x before they even finish reading the question. Then, if they do notice that the question is actually asking for something else, they usually panic, because they feel uncomfortable trying to do something for the first time during a test. So when we prepare for the Math Level 2 Test, we should train ourselves to look for different ways to find solutions *before* we plunge into an approach that would seem automatic in a classroom setting.

As trained test-takers, we know that real Math Level 2 practice questions often test concepts that are much more basic than they might appear to untrained test-takers. So we should try to look for ways to make this question simpler than it appears, instead of assuming that it's really as complicated as it might seem. Among other things, this means we need to read carefully and think about what's going on with the set of answer choices.

One approach would be to use your calculator to graph the function in the prompt five times, substituting each answer choice for c in the function. The correct answer choice will be the one that produces a graph identical to the one in the prompt. (If you use this approach, remember that the College Board has set the x-axis and the y-axis to different scales in the graph, so you'll have to do the same thing on your calculator if you want to recreate the appearance of the graph precisely!) When we do this, we see that (D) must be correct.

If we're more comfortable with the basic concepts relating to graphing functions, another approach might be to compare the answer choices to the graph and see if we notice anything. When we do that, we see that only two of the answer choices seem to have anything to do with the behavior of the graph that we can see. Choice (D) looks like it could correspond to the *y*-intercept of the graph, but none of the other answer choices seem immediately relevant to the graph at all. In fact, we can't even see what the graph is doing where *x* or *y* equals any other answer choice except (C), which is the opposite of (D)—and we know that the College Board often likes to include wrong answers that are the opposite of the correct answer in some way, which potentially makes (C) and (D) even more interesting.

So now we probably want to look at the question and see if there's any reason that *c* would have some connection to -72 or to 72, and whether it's relevant that -72 looks like it could be the *y*-intercept of the graph in the prompt.

When we look at the function, we notice that every term except *c* is multiplied by *x*. We might realize that the function would be simplified significantly, and *c* would be effectively isolated, if *x* were equal to 0. Then every term except *c* on the right side of the equation would equal 0, and we'd be left with $y = c$.

So when *x* is equal to 0, we know that *y* is equal to *c*. In other words, we see that the value of *c* must be the value of the *y*-intercept, because *c* is the value of *y* when $x = 0$. That makes (D) the only possible answer, because it's the only value that could be the *y*-intercept of the graph—the graph crosses the *y*-axis at a point near $y = -80$, and only choice (D) is anywhere near that value.

Page 127, Question 15

This question is pretty straightforward, and there are two basic ways to answer it. The most direct approach is probably just to know that secant is the reciprocal of cosine, which means sec *x* must be equal to $\frac{1}{0.4697}$, or 2.129. That means (A) is the correct answer. (This is basically the College Board's approach on page 149 of the MSTB.)

But if we've forgotten the definition of secant, we could always use a calculator to find the value of *x* itself, and then find sec *x*. We would do this by finding the inverse cosine (also called the arccosine, arccos, or $\cos^{-1}$) of 0.4697, which is roughly 61.99° if we're in degree mode, meaning that the *x* in the prompt has a value of roughly 61.99°. Then we just find sec *x* by evaluating the secant of 61.99° on our calculator, and we get a value of approximately 2.129, showing us, again, that (A) is correct. (Remember that it's okay for the decimal values to be slightly off if we use this approach, since we're working with decimal approximations of trig values.)

This question is another good example of how much the Math Level 2 Test relies on definitions and properties, rather than on tedious calculations.

When we look through the answer choices, we don't see much that seems to fit the College Board's normal patterns. It's true that (D) is two times 0.4697, instead of the reciprocal of 0.4697, and we can probably imagine an untrained test-taker multiplying 0.4697 by 2 for some reason. But it's difficult to see where the other wrong answers are coming from. This happens on some questions, and it shouldn't necessarily be a cause for alarm, but it's still a good reminder that we need to make sure we haven't made any errors, especially since the values of the answer choices are all so close together—it might be especially easy to make a small mistake and end up marking choice (B), for example.

Page 128, Question 16

The College Board's approach to this question, which appears on page 150 of the MSTB, is pretty good as far as it goes, but there are at least two other ways to approach the question as well.

While we're going to talk about three different ways to solve this question, it's important to remember that you don't always need to find multiple ways to answer a question on test day. We look at multiple solutions in training because different test-takers will prefer different approaches, and because thinking about different ways to answer the same question while you're training will give you a deeper understanding of how the College Board designs Math Level 2 questions, and how to adapt to different situations that you might encounter on test day.

Our discussion here will cover three general types of approaches:

1. A concrete, backsolving kind of approach (where we pick a number for *n*)

2. An abstract algebraic approach (which is basically the College Board's approach on page 150 of the MSTB)

3. An approach where we analyze the similarities and differences among the answer choices, relative to the prompt.

Again, you can use any one of these approaches on its own (and you might even be able to come up with your own approach that isn't discussed here, of course). Let's get started!

The first way that we'll approach this question involves backsolving by choosing a concrete number for *n*, and then working out the cost for each club member; then we'll plug our chosen *n*-value into each answer choice, and the choice that produces the correct cost will be the correct answer.

When we pick a value for *n*, we know that we should avoid -1, 0, 1, and any number that already appears in the question, to reduce the likelihood of picking a number with a unique property relative to the question. So let's say the *n*-value is 100—in other words, we're pretending there are 100 club members. Now we need to figure out the total cost of the trip, and then divide that total cost by the number of members.

So let's figure out the total cost of the trip for 100 club members. The question tells us there's an admission cost of $7 per person. If there are 100 club members going on the trip, then the total admission cost for them is $7 times 100 people, or $700. The question also says that the club members must share the $200 cost of the bus. That brings the total cost of the trip so far to $700 + $200, which is $900. Finally, the club members must also split the admission price for 2 chaperones. Since admission is $7 per person, admission for 2 chaperones is 2 times $7, or $14. When we add that to the $900 cost of the trip so far, we get $914.

We've figured out that the total cost of the trip is $914 for 100 members. To get the cost per member, we just divide $914 by 100. So the cost per member is $914 divided by 100, or $9.14.

This means that when *n* = 100, the cost per member should be $9.14. Now we go through each of the functions in the answer choices and see what we get when we plug in *n* = 100:

(A) $\quad c(n) = \dfrac{200 + 7n}{n}$ $\qquad$ (original function)

$\quad c(100) = \dfrac{200 + 7(100)}{100}$ $\qquad$ (plug in *n* = 100)

$\quad c(100) = \dfrac{900}{100}$ $\qquad$ (combine like terms)

$\quad c(100) = \$9.00$ $\qquad$ (simplify)

So choice (A) can't be right, because it would result in a per-member cost of $9, instead of $9.14. Now let's try choice (B).

(B) $c(n) = \dfrac{214 + 7n}{n}$ (original function)

$c(100) = \dfrac{214 + 7(100)}{100}$ (plug in n = 100)

$c(100) = \dfrac{914}{100}$ (combine like terms)

$c(100) = \$9.14$ (simplify)

We see that choice (B) results in a cost of $9.14 for each member, which was the result we were looking for. It looks like (B) could be correct so far, but we have to remember that this kind of concrete approach to a question can sometimes result in more than one answer choice seeming to be correct. This means we have to evaluate the rest of the answer choices before we can be sure we've found the right answer. So let's keep going and look at (C).

(C) $c(n) = \dfrac{200 + 7n}{n + 2}$ (original function)

$c(100) = \dfrac{200 + 7(100)}{100 + 2}$ (plug in n = 100)

$c(100) = \dfrac{900}{102}$ (combine like terms)

$c(100) = \$8.82$ (simplify)

Choice (C) would give us an average cost of $8.82, which means this isn't the correct answer. Let's try (D) now.

(D) $c(n) = \dfrac{200 + 7n}{n - 2}$ (original function)

$c(100) = \dfrac{200 + 7(100)}{100 - 2}$ (plug in n = 100)

$c(100) = \dfrac{900}{98}$ (combine like terms)

$c(100) = \$9.18$ (simplify)

This function gave us a result of $9.18. This is close to our target value of $9.14, but the closeness doesn't matter for our purposes: we're not working with decimal approximations of trig values or logs or anything like that in this question, so we need the correct answer choice to produce a value of exactly $9.14. So (D) is also wrong. Let's take a look at (E).

(E) $c(n) = \dfrac{214 + 7n}{n - 2}$ (original function)

$c(100) = \dfrac{214 + 7(100)}{100 - 2}$ (plug in n = 100)

$c(100) = \dfrac{914}{98}$ (combine like terms)

$c(100) = \$9.33$ (simplify)

(E) also results in an average cost that differs from $9.14, so we know it's wrong, too.

When we plug $n = 100$ into each answer choice, only choice (B) produces the same result we calculated for the per-member cost: $9.14. That means (B) is the correct answer.

A second way to approach the question would be to follow essentially the same process as the College Board's solution on page 150 of the MSTB, and use algebraic reasoning to construct an expression that describes the situation from the prompt. Let's go through the prompt sentence-by-sentence and see how this might be done.

The first sentence of the prompt mentions "an admission price of $7 per person." This suggests the idea of multiplying 7 by the number of people who will be on the trip, but this sentence doesn't tell us how to express the number of people on the trip yet. If we skim through the rest of the prompt, we see that the final sentence refers to "n, the number of club members going on the trip." So we might expect that we're going to end up multiplying 7 by n, which means $7n$ might be part of the final expression. Let's keep moving through the prompt and see what else we come up with.

The second sentence in the prompt says "the club members going on the trip must share the $200 cost of a bus and the admission price for 2 chaperones." So the shared cost is also going to include the sum of $200 and the admission for two more people. We know from the first sentence that admission costs $7 per person, so the admission cost for 2 people must be $14. That means this sentence is describing $214 in costs beyond the 7n costs we learned about in the first sentence.

So far, after the first two sentences, we've determined that the total amount being spent by the club members is $7n + 214$.

The final sentence asks us to express the cost "for each club member." In other words, we should take the cost of the trip and divide it by n, since n is the number of club members. When we do that, we end up with the expression $\frac{7n+214}{n}$, which is the same as $\frac{214 + 7n}{n}$, choice (B). So we see, again, that (B) is correct.

A third approach to this question depends on carefully noting the similarities and differences among the answer choices, and then thinking about how they relate to the prompt. Like the first approach we used on this question, this kind of solution is only possible because of the multiple-choice format, and, for that reason, it's exactly the kind of thing that most test-takers would never learn from their math teachers. Let's give it a shot.

When we compare the five answer choices, we should notice that each one is a fraction, with an algebraic expression in the numerator and another algebraic expression in the denominator. We'll obviously need to figure out which expressions should go in each part of the fraction. Let's start by thinking about the numerator. (We could also start with the denominator. I'm just picking the numerator first for no particular reason.)

Every answer choice has a numerator with the expression $7n$, so we know right away that $7n$ must be part of the correct answer, and we don't need to worry about that part of the expression further. (We may be interested in trying to figure out where it comes from anyway, in an effort to make sure we understand the question. We can see that $7 is the "admission price . . . per person" in the first sentence of the prompt, and we can see that n is the "number of club members" in the last sentence of the prompt, so it makes sense that a valid method of calculating the cost would end up including the expression $7n$, just as we've discussed above for other approaches to this question.)

As it turns out, the only difference among the numerators in the answer choices is that (A), (C), and (D) all have the number 200 in them, while (B) and (E) have 214 instead. So we clearly need to figure out whether the thing being added to $7n$ as part of the overall cost of the trip should be 200 or 214. If we look back at the prompt, we see that the overall cost includes the $200 for the bus, plus "admission . . . for 2 chaperones." When we remember that admission is $7 per person, we can see where the extra $14 comes from in the $214 price: it's the cost of admission for the two chaperones. Another way to realize that we need to add a number larger than $200 in the numerator is to realize that the expression $200 + 7n$ doesn't address the admission cost for the chaperones—notice that the prompt specifically states that n only refers to the club members, and that the chaperones are "accompany[ing]" the club members, which means that the chaperones aren't included in n.

So at this point, we've thought about both parts of the numerator and realized that $214 + 7n$ seems to be the correct option for what the numerator should contain. Now we look at the denominator and see what our options are there.

We see that there are three different choices for what goes in the denominator:

1. n

2. $n + 2$

3. $n - 2$

When we compare these choices, we see that the College Board clearly thinks we should be dividing the numerator by some kind of expression related to n, which we know is the number of club members; we also see that the College Board thinks it would be easy for a lot of test-takers to make some kind of mistake that would cause them to be off by 2 in one direction or another. This means that we want to figure out what should go in the denominator, of course, but we also want to try to figure out why the College Board thinks people are likely to be off by 2. If we can figure out both of these things, then we can have a reasonable expectation that we've understood the question correctly and chosen the correct answer.

When we look back at the prompt, we see that the number 2 is only mentioned once—it's the number of chaperones who are accompanying the club members, and the club members are represented by n. So the expression $n + 2$ would describe all the club members AND the chaperones. On the other hand, the expression $n - 2$ doesn't really seem to relate to anything in the prompt at all; $n - 2$ might seem like it was only included in the answer choices because it's kind of the "opposite" of $n + 2$, and we know the College Board likes to do that sort of thing sometimes. (There's actually another reason why $n - 2$ might have been included, but we'll talk about it when we're wrapping up our discussion of the entire question.)

Now we have to ask ourselves whether we should be dividing the cost by the number of club members (which is n), or by the sum of the club members and the chaperones (which is $n + 2$), or by the number of club members minus 2 for some reason. The prompt makes it clear that the cost is being shared by "each club member as a function of n," so the chaperones aren't paying anything. That means we want to divide by n, and not by $n + 2$.

We've now figured out that the proper denominator is n, and we already determined that the proper numerator was $214 + 7n$. The only answer choice that combines all of these elements is (B), and so we see, once more, that (B) is correct.

Now that we've discussed multiple ways to attack this question, I want to mention a pattern that we, as trained test-takers, might try to look for in the answer choices. As we've discussed earlier in this Black Book, the "wrong answers imitate right answers" pattern often applies in questions like this one, where the College Board has given us a set of highly similar answer choices that seem to mix-and-match minor variations of the same basic elements.

But if we try to follow that pattern here, we see that it wouldn't tend to point to the correct answer: more choices (three out of five) have 200 in the numerator than have 214, and the number of choices that have n in the denominator is equal to the number that have $n - 2$. This is an example of why we should never blindly trust answer choice patterns. Instead, we should view them as alternative ways to approach a question or to check our work. In cases like this question, where we see that (B) doesn't seem to fit the pattern we might have expected, we should be motivated to double-check our reading and our assumptions to make sure we haven't fallen for the kinds of small mistakes that the College Board likes.

There's one last thing I want to say about this question before we move on, and it actually has to do with reading comprehension. I've seen a lot of tutoring clients miss this question in their practice sessions—not because they don't understand the math, but because they misread the question and assume that the chaperones are members of the club, which means they think the cost should be divided by $n - 2$, so that the chaperones seem to be "removed" from the set of people indicated by n. This is a great example of the way that we can easily miss questions on the Math Level 2 Test for reasons that have nothing to do with math itself. Keep this kind of thing in mind during your training, and especially on test day.

Page 128, Question 17

Untrained test-takers usually aren't sure what to do when they see this question, because it doesn't really look like anything they've done in math class, and most people get uncomfortable when they have to do something for the first time on test day. But, as trained test-takers, we know that we're definitely going to run into questions on test day that ask us to do things we've never done before. We also know that the College Board likes to combine simple ideas in strange ways, so the best thing we can do in these situations is read carefully and think in terms of the properties and definitions of the concepts in the question, instead of trying to rely on obscure formulas.

As will often be the case on the Math Level 2 Test, there are several ways we could approach this question. The easiest way is probably just to graph each of the equations in the answer choices, and see which one consists of points that are equidistant from the two points in the prompt. So let's start there.

When we graph *x* = 2 from choice (A), we get this:

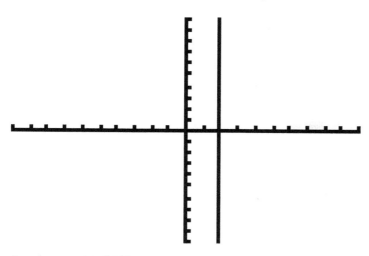

As we can see, this line contains points that aren't equidistant from (0, 0) and (0, 4). For example, (2, 0) is on the line, and we can see it's not the same distance from (0, 0) as it is from (0, 4). So (A) isn't right.

(B) gives us this when we graph it:

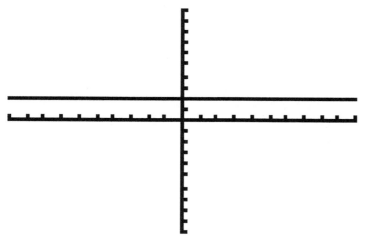

When we look at this graph, we see that every point on the line is the same distance from (0, 0) as it is from (0, 4). For example, the point (0, 2) is 2 units from both of those points. But we should still consider the rest of the answer choices, so we can make sure we've understood the question correctly.

When we graph (C), we get this:

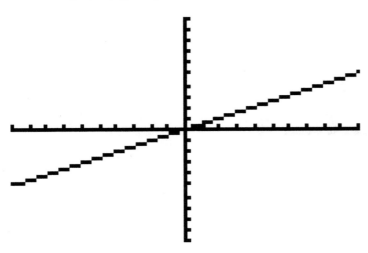

It's clear that this line contains points that aren't the same distance from (0, 0) as they are from (0, 4). In fact, one of the points on the line is (0, 0) itself, which is obviously zero units away from itself, but four units away from (0, 4).

Now let's take a look at (D):

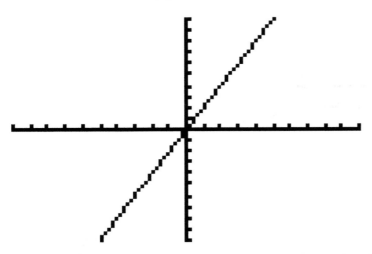

Just as we saw with (C), one of the points on this line is (0, 0) itself, and that point is obviously closer to itself than it is to any other point, so we know this line contains points that aren't equidistant from the points in the prompt.

Finally, let's check out choice (E):

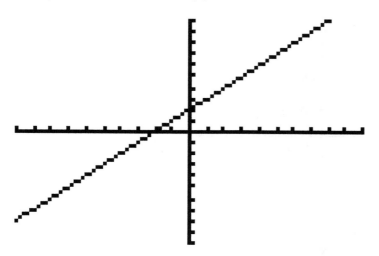

We can see that this line also contains points that aren't equidistant from the points in the prompt. For example, we might notice that every point below the x-axis is closer to (0, 0) than it is to (0, 4) . . .

. . . and once we realize that this is true of the line $y = x + 2$, we should also realize that it's true of every line that goes below *the* x-axis, actually: any portion of a line that's below the x-axis must be closer to (0, 0) than it is to (0, 4). That means any line that crosses the x-axis must contain points that aren't equidistant from the two points in the prompt. We can actually see this at work if we glance back through the graphs for choices (A), (C), (D), and (E).

At this point we might also realize that the only kind of line that would never cross the x-axis is a horizontal line, and that choice (B) is the only option we have that creates a horizontal line. This further cements our idea that (B) must be the correct answer.

But it might not occur to us that we can just graph the answer choices and see which one satisfies the prompt. In that case, another way to approach this question could be just to sketch out a coordinate plane, start drawing in some points, and see what happens. Let's walk through that approach now.

First we might start by sketching in the two points from the prompt, (0,0) and (0,4):

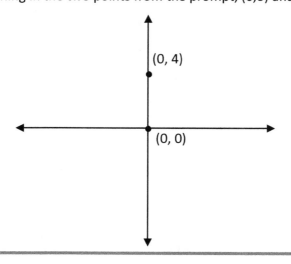

Now we can start drawing in points that are equidistant from these two points. Probably the most obvious one would be the point directly between them, at (0, 2):

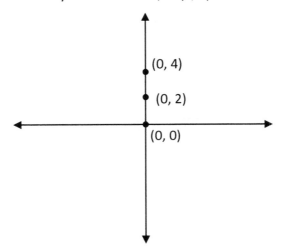

So (0, 2) is definitely equidistant from the two points. But none of the answer choices allows us to pick only the point (0, 2)—every choice is an equation that defines multiple points. That means there must be other points that are the same distance from (0, 0) and (0, 4). So where are they?

We can see that we can't move up or down from the point at (0, 2), because that would also move us closer to one of the original points than to the other, which isn't what we're looking for.

If we can't move up or down from (0, 2), then the only possibility is to move left or right. A point directly to the left of (0, 2) doesn't move any closer to either (0, 0) or (0, 4) than (0, 2) was. The same is true of any point directly to the right of (0, 2):

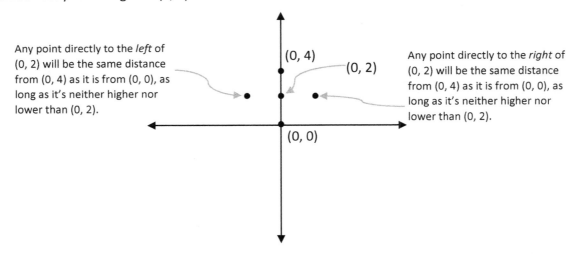

If we start adding more of these points, we'll see that they create a straight line from left to right, through the point (0, 2):

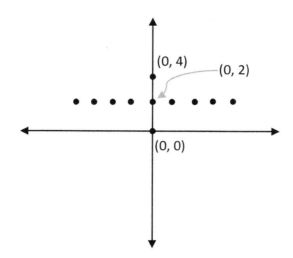

The line can't ever slant or curve up or down, because then it would be moving closer to one of the original two points and farther away from the other, and the question told us that the correct answer should only include points that are equidistant from the two original points. We can see that all of the points we've plotted have a *y*-value of 2, no matter what their *x*-values are, which means the points are described by the line *y* = 2. That means, again, that (B) is the correct answer.

The College Board takes a very different approach to the question on page 150 of the MSTB, by proposing an algebraic solution based on the distance formula. It's not an approach I would recommend to most people, because it seems unnecessarily complicated to me, but let's discuss it anyway—partly for the sake of completeness, and partly because the College Board's discussion of the approach skips over a few steps, making it even harder for most readers to follow. Again, I wouldn't recommend that you actually use this approach, because the approaches above are probably easier for most test-takers.

The College Board's approach basically involves the following steps (again, the text description on page 150 of the MSTB doesn't explicitly mention all of these steps, but it does assume them):

1. Use the coordinate pair (*x*, *y*) to refer to an unknown point that's equidistant from the points (0, 0) and (0, 4).

2. Write a distance expression to describe the distance from the point (0, 0) in the prompt to the point (*x*, *y*) from Step 1 (see below for the distance formula if necessary).

3. Write a distance expression to describe the distance from the point (0, 4) in the prompt to the point (*x*, *y*) from Step 1 (again, see below for the distance formula if necessary).

4. Take the distance expressions from Step 2 and Step 3, and set them equal to each other, to reflect the fact that we're looking for (*x*, *y*) values that are the same distance from (0, 0) as they are from (0, 4).

5. Solve the equation from Step 4.

Let's go through all of those steps. We'll start by writing our distance expressions—remember that the distance formula is based on the Pythagorean Theorem, and looks like the following, where *d* is the distance between two points, and those points have coordinates of (x_1, y_1) and (x_2, y_2):

$$d = \sqrt{(x_2 - x_1)^2 + (y_2 - y_1)^2}$$

To express the distance between (0, 0) and our unknown point (x, y), we can let (0, 0) be (x_1, y_1), and (x, y) be (x_2, y_2), which gives us this:

$$d = \sqrt{(x_2 - x_1)^2 + (y_2 - y_1)^2}$$ (distance formula)

$$d = \sqrt{(x - 0)^2 + (y - 0)^2}$$ (plug in (0, 0) for (x_1, y_1), and (x, y) for (x_2, y_2)))

$$d = \sqrt{x^2 + y^2}$$ (subtract 0 from x and from y)

Now, to express the distance between (0, 4) and our unknown point (x, y), we can make (0, 4) be (x_1, y_1), and (x, y) be (x_2, y_2), giving us this:

$$d = \sqrt{(x_2 - x_1)^2 + (y_2 - y_1)^2}$$ (distance formula)

$$d = \sqrt{(x - 0)^2 + (y - 4)^2}$$ (plug in (0, 4) for (x_1, y_1), and (x, y) for (x_2, y_2)))

$$d = \sqrt{x^2 + (y - 4)^2}$$ (subtract 0 from x)

Now that we have our two distance expressions, we set them equal to each other, to reflect the idea that (x, y) is the same distance from (0, 0) as from (0, 4):

$$\sqrt{x^2 + y^2} = \sqrt{x^2 + (y - 4)^2}$$ (set both distance expressions equal)

$$x^2 + y^2 = x^2 + (y - 4)^2$$ (square both sides)

$$y^2 = (y - 4)^2$$ (subtract x^2 from both sides)

$$y^2 = y^2 - 8y + 16$$ (square (y – 4))

$$0 = -8y + 16$$ (subtract y^2 from both sides)

$$8y = 16$$ (add 8y to both sides)

$$y = 2$$ (divide both sides by 8)

So we can see that $y = 2$ when a point (x, y) is the same distance from $(0, 0)$ and $(0, 4)$, just as the College Board describes. This means that the horizontal line $y = 2$ will contain all the points that are equidistant from both $(0, 0)$ and $(0, 4)$. But as I mentioned before, this algebraic approach is probably the slowest and most complicated way to answer this question, even though it's the approach suggested by the College Board on page 150 of the MSTB. You're probably better off trying something more like the first two approaches we looked at.

Now that we've examined three different ways you could choose to approach this question, let's take a look at the answer choices, and see if we can understand them from the College Board's perspective. We see that (A) looks like a fairly predictable mistake that an untrained test-taker might make if she accidentally thought that horizontal lines had unchanging x-values instead of unchanging y-values. For that matter, (D) and (E) also look like the kinds of mistakes that a test-taker could make in trying to construct a horizontal line through $(0, 2)$. We might also notice that the answer choices are very similar to one another, and try to apply the "wrong answers imitate right answers" pattern. If we do that, we could note the following:

1. Most of the answer choices (three out of five) begin with y rather than x.

2. Most of the answer choices (three out of five) don't involve multiplication.

3. Most of the answer choices (four out of five) don't involve addition.

This suggests that if there were an answer choice that began with y, didn't involve multiplication, and didn't involve addition, we might expect that choice to have a higher likelihood of being right—and, as it turns out, choice (B) has all of those attributes. But remember that this kind of pattern should never be the sole reason we pick an answer, because it's not always reliable! As trained test-takers, we know that we should only use patterns like this to give us new ways to approach a question or check our work. (By the way, another way we might analyze these answer choices would be to notice that three of the five answer choices have a variable on the right-hand side of the equation, which might suggest that (B) isn't the choice indicated by the "wrong answers imitate right answers" pattern. This is one more example of how these patterns are never enough by themselves for us to answer a question with complete certainty. Instead, they provide another lens for us to use when looking at the question.)

Page 128, Question 18

This is an example of a question that might actually appear in a traditional math class, which puts it in the minority for a Math Level 2 question, as we've discussed. For that reason, test-takers who approach this question will largely fall into two groups:

- those who remember the formula for summing an infinite geometric series

- those who don't remember it or never learned it (which is the majority, in my experience)

So we'll discuss two ways to approach this question. The first one is the approach you can take if you happen to remember the formula that would normally be used for a question like this in school, and the second is an approach from the point of view of someone who has forgotten the formula, or who never learned it. Let's get started.

The solution described on page 150 of the MSTB is basically the only formal way to approach this question. It relies on the formula for the sum of an infinite geometric series, which is $s = \frac{a}{1-r}$, where:

- s is the sum of the infinite geometric series

- a is the starting term of the infinite geometric series
- r is the common ratio (in other words, the ratio of any number in the series to the number before it)

In this question, the first term in the series is $\frac{1}{4}$, so a is $\frac{1}{4}$. Further, each number is half the previous number, so $r = \frac{1}{2}$. That gives us enough information to solve for the sum, s:

$$s = \frac{a}{1 - r}$$ (formula for the sum of an infinite geometric series)

$$s = \frac{1/4}{1 - (1/2)}$$ (plug in $a = \frac{1}{4}$ and $r = \frac{1}{2}$)

$$s = \frac{1/4}{1/2}$$ (combine like terms)

$$s = \frac{1}{2}$$ (simplify)

That shows us the answer is (A), $\frac{1}{2}$.

So that's how we find the answer if we remember the formula for the sum of an infinite geometric series. But what if we're like most test-takers, and we don't remember the formula? In fact, what if we've never even heard the term "infinite geometric series" before?

As trained test-takers, we have to remember that we shouldn't assume we can't answer a question just because it contains a term we don't understand. We can often work around these unknown terms through some combination of relying on our training and playing around with the concepts in the question that we do understand. Similarly, we may be able to work around the fact that we don't know a formula for this question by considering all the concepts in the prompt and in the answer choices, and seeing what we can come up with after that. We have to remember that the College Board often puts us in the position of being able to answer a question without recalling a formula for the question, so it's important to be flexible when we take this test. So let's play around with these ideas and see where we end up.

We may be able to figure something out by examining the meanings of the individual words in the phrase "infinite geometric series." The word "infinite" describes something that goes on forever. We probably think of the word "geometric" as describing something related to shapes. We might not see an immediate connection between this question and the idea of being related to shapes, so let's move on for now and look at the third word in the term. We know that a "series" is basically a set of numbers, often following a rule or pattern.

So after thinking about the meaning of each word in the term "infinite geometric series," we've determined that it describes a set of numbers that goes on forever, and that is somehow "geometric," whatever that means in this context.

When we look at the fractions that are added together in the prompt, and we see the ellipsis after the last plus sign in the prompt, we can make the connection that the "series" in the prompt is the series of fractions, and the ellipsis represents the idea that the series of fractions being added together goes on forever. In other words, we're not just adding $\frac{1}{4}, \frac{1}{8}, \frac{1}{16}$, and $\frac{1}{32}$. We're also adding other numbers that would come after the given fractions in the "infinite geometric series."

So it seems like we need to figure out what those other fractions in the series would be. Now we're in a position where we don't know the connection of the word "geometric" to the question, and we don't know how to figure out which other numbers will be part of this "infinite geometric series." Since we have one unknown word ("geometric"), and one unknown idea (how to figure out the missing numbers in the series), and since all the other words and ideas in the question are accounted for, we can conclude that the word "geometric" probably describes the rule that would tell us the other numbers in the series.

Now let's think about how we might figure out the other numbers. It seems pretty clear that there must be some pattern in the series—if the series were just composed of random numbers, it would be impossible to answer the question, because we'd be trying to add together an unpredictable series of numbers. When we look at the given fractions, we notice that the denominator in each fraction is twice the denominator of the fraction before it. This is the same as saying that each fraction is half of the fraction that comes before it.

This pattern holds for all four of the given fractions, so we can conclude that all the rest of the fractions in the "infinite geometric series" will follow this pattern as well. So the term after $\frac{1}{32}$ would be $\frac{1}{64}$, and then $\frac{1}{128}$, and then $\frac{1}{256}$, and so on, forever. That seems to make sense.

Now let's use what we think we've figured out to see if we can apply it to what the question is asking us for: "the sum of the infinite geometric series." So the question wants to know the result when we add up all the fractions in this infinite geometric series.

At first, we might automatically think that the sum of an infinite set of numbers must be infinitely large itself, because finding the sum would involve adding new values to our starting value forever. But if we look at the answer choices, we notice that the highest available number is $\frac{5}{2}$, and there's no answer choice that says anything about the sum being infinity itself. So there must be some way for our infinite set of smaller and smaller fractions to give us a sum with a finite value.

Let's try to think of how that might work with the numbers we're given. We start out with $\frac{1}{4}$. Then we add $\frac{1}{8}$, which is half of $\frac{1}{4}$. Then we add $\frac{1}{16}$, which is half of $\frac{1}{8}$, and so on.

Let's keep thinking. If we started with $\frac{1}{4}$ and added another $\frac{1}{4}$ and stopped, we'd get $\frac{1}{2}$. But instead, we add $\frac{1}{8}$, which is only half of $\frac{1}{4}$. Then we add $\frac{1}{16}$, which is only half of $\frac{1}{8}$. Then $\frac{1}{32}$, which is only half of $\frac{1}{16}$, and so on, forever. So we'll always be adding a fraction that represents half of the difference between the current sum and $\frac{1}{2}$.

At this point, there are two things we could realize, and both of them would lead us to the conclusion that (A) must be correct.

One thing we might realize is that the running sum of this series is constantly approaching $\frac{1}{2}$ by an amount that's equal to half of the difference between $\frac{1}{2}$ and the current sum, so that with every fraction in the series added to the sum, the distance between the sum and $\frac{1}{2}$ is always cut in half. If we're familiar with the concept of infinity, then we understand that the difference between the running sum and $\frac{1}{2}$ is infinitesimally small . . . which means it's effectively 0. In other words, there is no difference between the infinitely running sum and $\frac{1}{2}$, which means the running sum *is* $\frac{1}{2}$. But this is a little more abstract than many test-takers might be comfortable with.

The other thing we might realize is that there's no way the running sum could ever exceed $\frac{1}{2}$, because we see that each successive fraction added to the running sum results in a new sum that gets closer to $\frac{1}{2}$ by the same proportion with each new added fraction, without ever exceeding $\frac{1}{2}$. So even if we don't know the formula and we don't feel confident definitely saying that the sum of the infinite series is $\frac{1}{2}$, we can say with confidence that the sum won't reach 1. Since it won't reach 1, we can eliminate 1, and every answer choice higher than 1, which only leaves (A), the correct answer.

Again, that means the correct answer is choice (A).

Of course, if this were test day and you found yourself in the position of having gone through most of this thought process and still not feeling certain about the correct answer, then you should fall back on your training and skip the question for the moment—you can always come back later if you have the time and you want to reconsider it. As we've discussed earlier in this Black Book, the willingness to skip questions you don't understand (as opposed to answering them incorrectly and losing points on them) is a cornerstone of effective test-taking on tests with wrong-answer penalties.

Before we finish our discussion of this question, I'd like to point out that the College Board could have made this question much more challenging by including answer choices that were less than $\frac{1}{2}$, because that could have required us to understand the idea of an infinite series in more detail, so that we'd be able to determine whether the sum would reach an answer choice with a number like, say, $\frac{15}{32}$ or $\frac{31}{64}$ or something. Instead, the College Board gave us a selection of answer choices that made it possible for us to rule out all four of the wrong answer choices if we could just recognize that the sum would never exceed $\frac{1}{2}$, even if we didn't realize it could actually reach $\frac{1}{2}$ when we first read the question.

Some untrained test-takers might react to this question by memorizing the formula for summing an infinite series. That's an understandable reaction to a certain extent, because untrained test-takers expect that the Math Level 2 Test will function in basically the same way as a math test does in school. They expect that this concept will be tested in the same way on future tests. But as trained test-takers, we know that's pretty unlikely—not necessarily impossible, but unlikely. For that reason, I wouldn't necessarily recommend that you devote a lot of your mental energy to memorizing the formula from this question, or expecting to use it on test day. Of course, knowing this formula on test day won't hurt you or anything, but it's not very likely to help, either. It would be much more helpful to continue to develop your instincts for reading carefully, reasoning through strange situations, analyzing the answer choices, and so on. If your prep time is limited, I'd recommend that you prioritize those kinds of skills over memorizing lots of formulas.

Page 129, Question 19

The problem with this question is that any algebraic inequality has an infinite number of equivalent statements, so untrained test-takers can get frustrated if they try to come up with their own equivalent version of the given inequality and then can't find it in the answer choices. The College Board's approach to the question, which appears on page 150 of the MSTB, correctly states that one of the answer choices is equivalent to the statement in the prompt, but the College Board doesn't really explain *how* you could figure that out if you didn't realize it right away. So let's talk a little bit about the specific things you might notice in this question that could lead you to the correct answer.

As trained test-takers, we know that we always need to consider the answer choices as part of a question, because the relationships among the answer choices can often indicate the important elements of the prompt.

In this case, we might notice that each answer choice has only one term on either side of the inequality sign. That means it must be possible to get rid of at least one term on either side of the original inequality. So let's think about how we could get rid of a term on each side of our inequality.

We might notice that there's a p on either side of the inequality. If we subtract p from both sides, we'll be able to get rid of that term:

$p + s > p - s$ (original inequality)

$s > -s$ (subtract p from both sides)

At this point, we've gotten rid of the p, and we're down to one term on each side. In that sense, our inequality is similar to all of the answer choices. But when we look at the answer choices, we see that none of them contains our current expression.

So we still need to modify our version of the inequality until it matches one of the answer choices. What do most of the answer choices have in common that's still missing from our inequality? One thing we could realize is that every answer choice with an s on one side has either a p or 0 on the other side. We've already gotten rid of the p in our version of the inequality, so let's see if we can end up with 0 in the inequality somehow:

$s > -s$ (inequality from our last step)

$s + s > -s + s$ (add s to both sides)

$2s > 0$ (simplify both sides)

$s > 0$ (divide both sides by 2)

Now we've modified the inequality so that s appears on one side and 0 appears on the other—and it turns out that we've arrived at exactly what choice (D) says, so (D) is correct.

We can also think about this question a bit more abstractly if we want, and find the answer without picking up a pencil. Take a look at the original inequality. It says that "p plus s" is greater than "p minus s." What does that mean? Well, if we start from a particular value (p), and we see that adding s to that value results in a bigger number than subtracting s gives us, then we know that s must be positive—if adding a number results in a larger value, then we know that the number we added is positive.

Saying that s is positive is the same thing as saying $s > 0$, which, again, corresponds to choice (D).

Let's also look at some patterns in the answer choices. We see that (E) is there to trap test-takers who make a mistake with a negative sign, or who misread the direction of the inequality symbol in the prompt. As trained test-takers, we know that seeing the opposite of our answer as another answer choice is generally a good indication that we've probably understood the question correctly.

This set of answer choices also follows the "wrong answers imitate right answers" pattern that we discussed earlier in this Black Book:

- Most of the answer choices (three out of five) begin with *s*, and so does the correct answer.

- Most of the answer choices (four out of five) have the > symbol, and so does the correct answer.

- Most of the answer choices (three out of five) end with 0, and so does the correct answer.

As always, we have to remember that answer choice patterns like this are never enough on their own to justify picking a particular answer—instead, these patterns can help give us another way to view the question, and possibly reassure us that we've probably understood the question from the College Board's perspective.

Page 129, Question 20

At first glance, this question looks like it requires us to know some obscure property of functions. But, as usual on this test, we'll find that close and careful reading shows us the question isn't as challenging as it first appears.

Most untrained test-takers would try to figure out something about the *f* function described in the prompt, but the prompt doesn't really give us a lot of information about that function. For all we know, *f* could be a linear function, or it could be a parabola, or it could have asymptotes, and so on. As trained test-takers, we know that the specific nature of *f* must not be important, because the College Board didn't give us any details about the function. But untrained test-takers usually aren't good at noticing these kinds of clues in the way a question is constructed, so they're likely to get nervous from not knowing much about *f*.

Untrained test-takers would also be unlikely to pay close attention to the answer choices when they first thought about this question, but trained test-takers like us would always be ready to analyze the answer choices before we attacked a question. In this case, when we analyze the answer choices, we see something interesting, before we really even start thinking about the concepts in the prompt: the answer can only be (A), (D), or (E), because (B) and (C) are both "contained" in (D).

Here's what I mean by that. As trained test-takers, we know that exactly one answer choice can be correct on each question. We also know that if *a* is less than *b* or *a* is greater than *b*, then it must also be true that *a* and *b* aren't the same number—in other words, if either (B) or (C) is true, then (D) must also be true. This means that (B) and (C) must both be wrong, because if either one is a true statement, then (D) is also a true statement; on the other hand, (D) can still be the right answer, because (D) can always be true without specifying whether *a* is larger than *b* in a particular instance, or the other way around.

So we can see that a willingness to pay attention to the answer choices has helped us simplify the point of the question in our minds. We're really just down to three options:

- Choice (A), which says that at least one of the variables has to have a value of zero

- Choice (D), which says that the variables must have different values

- Choice (E), which says that the variables must have the same value

So let's focus on those options and see what we can figure out.

We're told that plugging *a* into the function gives us a lower value than the one we get when we plug in *b*. Now, with reference to the three possibilities we just identified above, we might ask ourselves three questions about the fact that $f(a)$ is less than $f(b)$:

- Does this fact indicate that *a* and/or *b* has to be zero? If so, then (A) must be right.

- Does this fact indicate that the variables must have different values? If so, then (D) is right.

- Does this fact indicate that the variables must be equal? If so, then (E) must be right.

When we try to answer the first question, we see that there's no reason to think the concept of zero is particularly relevant to the prompt, since we don't know any details of function *f*, and since we know from experience that functions can frequently have domains and ranges with numbers that are greater than, less than, or equal to zero. So there's no reason to think (A) is correct.

But let's think about the idea of the two variables being necessarily different or necessarily identical (since these ideas are different sides of the same coin in a sense, it's hard to think about one without thinking about the other). We know that a function, by definition, can't have more than one $f(x)$ value for any individual *x*-value. (This is a fundamental aspect of a main concept from the prompt, not an advanced concept or formula.)

Since we're told that $f(a)$ and $f(b)$ are different numbers, we know that *a* and *b* themselves must not be the same number—if they were the same number, then $f(a)$ and $f(b)$ would have to be the same number, too, since a function can only have one output for every input. Since *a* and *b* must be different numbers, we know (D) is correct.

Before we move on to the next question, I'd like to point out a couple of important aspects of the way this question is designed. The first thing I'd like to mention is the importance of the word "must" in the prompt, which tells us it's not enough to find an answer choice that "can" be true—if it were, then any choice besides (E) would be possible, given the information in the prompt. Some untrained test-takers won't pay attention to the wording of the prompt, and won't consider all the answer choices before moving on; they'll just pick the first choice that "can" be true, and they'll lose points on this question, even though they might have been able to figure out the correct answer if they had been paying attention. This is one more example of the critical importance of reading comprehension skills on this test, even though most people think of it as a pure math test. Keep this in mind on test day!

I'd also like to call your attention to some ways that the answer choices fit into patterns that we've seen in other questions, even though they don't really involve numbers. For example, note that (E) is the "opposite" of the correct answer. This is a common relationship to observe on the Math Level 2 Test, but it normally takes the form of two numbers being opposite each other on a number line, or being reciprocals of one another, or being complements of one another within the context of the question, and so on. Here, though, we see the College Board continuing to follow the pattern even when the answer choices aren't numbers. Similarly, we could argue that the choices fit the "wrong answers imitate right answers" pattern if we notice things like the following:

- Three out of the five choices indicate that *a* and *b* aren't equal in some way.

- Four out of the five choices are presented only in terms of *a* and *b*, without referring to other values.

Again, these are the kinds of relationships we often observe in answer choices that feature numbers. But we see here that the College Board can incorporate them in other ways, too. Make sure you look out for these kinds of things on test day!

Page 129, Question 21

Before we get into the solution, let's talk about an issue in this question that can be challenging for some test-takers: the prompt mentions values like "75 percent" and "40 percent," but all the answer choices are decimal values.

It's important for us to understand that decimals, percentages, and fractions are just different ways to represent the same kinds of numbers. To convert a percentage to a decimal, we just divide the percentage by 100. So 75 percent is the same as $\frac{75}{100}$, or 0.75. Similarly, 40 percent is the same as $\frac{40}{100}$, or 0.4. With that in mind, let's try to solve the question.

If 75 percent of the population lives within 10 miles of a city, and 40 percent of those people live in single-family houses, then we just need to find 40% of 75% to get the percentage of people who live in a single-family home within ten miles of the biggest city. That means we multiply 0.75 by 0.4, which gives us 0.3. So choice (C) is correct.

As trained test-takers, we'll find that the wrong answers reflect the kinds of simple mistakes that test-takers might easily make if they're not paying careful attention. We notice that choice (D) would be the result if we *subtract* 0.4 from 0.75, instead of multiplying them together. Somewhat similarly, choice (E) is what we get if we *divide* 0.4 by 0.75. Further, choice (A) is sort of the complement of the correct answer, because it represents the result of multiplying 0.25 by 0.4, instead of multiplying 0.75 by 0.4; this choice might be present as a trap for people who badly misread the question. Finally, we can see that choice (B) is half of the correct answer, which follows another common wrong answer pattern. When we see these kinds of answer choices and reflect on how they relate to the concepts in the prompt, it makes us more confident that we've correctly multiplied 0.4 and 0.75, and that those two numbers were the correct numbers to work with.

By the way, this is about as complicated as compound probability questions will get on the Math Level 2 Test. Even so, there are several test prep companies that publish fake practice tests with probability questions that are significantly more complicated than this one was. This is one of the reasons I always recommend that my students only work with real practice questions from the College Board. If you're preparing for the Math Level 2 Test, there's very little benefit to studying advanced probability concepts that won't appear on the actual test.

(Of course, if you had trouble with this question, be sure to review the section on probability in the Math Toolbox.)

Page 129, Question 22

This is a pretty straightforward trigonometry question, and the College Board's explanation on page 151 of the MSTB is also pretty straightforward. Let's start out with our own look at the formal solution, and then we'll discuss some interesting aspects of the answer choices.

This question describes a triangle, but it doesn't provide a picture of the triangle. I'll draw the triangle here in agreement with the description in the prompt, because that might help make the solution more apparent:

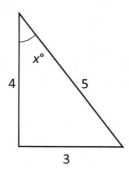

(Notice that the longest side of a right triangle must be the hypotenuse, by definition.)

Often in questions about the lengths of the sides of triangles, we're only given two side-lengths of the triangle, which means we have to use the trigonometric function that relates the two given sides. For example, if we only had the lengths of the opposite leg and the hypotenuse, we'd have to use sine, because sine is the ratio of the lengths of the opposite leg and the hypotenuse.

But in this question, we're given all the side lengths, so we can pick any trigonometric function we want. I'll pick tangent, for no particular reason—I just like the way it sounds.

Remember that we wanted the measure of the smallest angle, which is the angle opposite the smallest leg by definition. In my diagram above, the smallest angle is the one at the top of the triangle, and the smallest leg is the horizontal leg.

We know from SOHCAHTOA that **T**angent = **O**pposite/**A**djacent. So we set up the equation, where x is the unknown angle, and then we solve (remember to put your calculator in degree mode, because the question refers to degrees):

$$\text{Tangent} = \frac{\text{Opposite}}{\text{Adjacent}}$$ (Definition of Tangent from SOHCAHTOA)

$$\tan x = \frac{3}{4}$$ (substitute leg lengths: opposite = 3, and adjacent = 4)

$$x = \tan^{-1}\frac{3}{4}$$ (take inverse tangent (also called arctan, or $\tan^{-1}$) of both sides)

$$x \approx 36.87°$$ (evaluate $\tan^{-1}\frac{3}{4}$ with a calculator in degree mode)

The question asks for the angle measure "to the nearest degree," so we round to 37°. That means (C) is correct.

As trained test-takers, we should be comfortable with this level of trigonometry, but we could also answer this question using another approach. This second approach is going to get a little abstract, but try to stick with it, and you'll see an interesting way to think about Math Level 2 problems.

The prompt tells us that a triangle with sides of 3, 4, and 5 is a right triangle. That means one of the angles is 90°. If one of the angles is 90°, the other two angles together must add up to 90°, because the sum of the three angle measures of any triangle is 180°.

So the other two angles must add up to 90°. The question asks us to find the "smallest angle," so we know one of the two angles is smaller than the other. Since half of 90° is 45°, we know that the smaller angle has to be less than 45°, right? If it were larger than 45°, then both of the unknown angles would have to add up to more than 90°, which is impossible here. So the smallest angle in the triangle must be less than 45°. That means (D) and (E) must be wrong.

Now let's look at the remaining answer choices. We might not conclude anything about (A) or (C) right away, but let's think about choice (B), 30°. If the smaller angle were 30°, then the other angle would have to be 60° (because, as we just discussed, we know the triangle has a 90° angle, and we know the sum of the three angles must be 180°).

So if the smaller angle were 30°, then we'd be dealing with a 30°-60°-90° triangle, which is a triangle with common side-ratios we should recognize. (If you don't recognize this type of triangle, be sure to review the Triangles section of the Math Toolbox in this Black Book.) In a 30°-60°-90° triangle, the ratio of the sides is $1:\sqrt{3}:2$.

If the triangle in this question were a 30°-60°-90° triangle, then the ratio of its sides would also have to be $1:\sqrt{3}:2$. But $1:\sqrt{3}:2$ isn't the same as 3:4:5, which means choice (B) must be wrong.

Now let's think—does this tell us anything about the remaining choices, (A) and (C)? It does, actually. Choice (A) is the only choice that's less than (B), and choice (C) is the only choice between 30° and 45°. As it turns out, our analysis can tell us whether the smallest angle in our 3:4:5 triangle is bigger or smaller than 30°.

A 30°-60°-90° triangle has a side ratio of $1:\sqrt{3}:2$. In the triangle from the prompt, which we sketched out above, the small leg is 3, but the largest side is only 5; on the other hand, if we were dealing with a 30°-60°-90° and the smallest leg were 3, then the longest leg would be 6, because 6 is twice as large as 3. That means the shortest leg of our triangle is proportionally longer, relative to the hypotenuse, than the shortest leg of a 30°-60°-90° triangle.

Since the smallest *leg* of a 3-4-5 triangle must be proportionally larger than the smallest *leg* of a 30°-60°-90° triangle, we know that the smallest *angle* of a 3-4-5 triangle must also be proportionally larger than the smallest *angle* of a 30°-60°-90° triangle. In other words, the smallest angle of our triangle must be larger than 30°. Since (C) is the only answer choice that's larger than 30° but less than 45°, we know (C) has to be correct.

Now, you might be wondering why I bothered to discuss the second approach to this question, since the first approach is more orthodox, and probably a lot easier for most people to understand. I gave you the second approach for two important reasons. First, I want to keep exposing you to the idea that most of the questions on this test can be approached in multiple ways, because it's important to keep that in mind when you run into dead-ends on test day. Second, and more importantly, I want to use this question to point out, once again, that the College Board seems to be deliberately making these kinds of alternative approaches possible. The College Board knows that most test-takers are familiar with the idea of a 30°-60°-90° triangle having side ratios of $1:\sqrt{3}:2$, and I would argue that the decision to include only one answer choice with a value between 30° and 45° was deliberate—in fact, the inclusion of 30° as an answer choice is probably also deliberate, possibly intended to help alert test-takers realize there was another way to approach the question, or at least to check their results. In other words, the College Board could have picked answer choices like 36°, 37°, 38°, 39°, and 40°; instead, it gave us answer choices we could analyze and figure out. (On a relatively straightforward question like this one, you might be wondering why any of this matters—but thinking about these things on easier questions will make it easier for you to notice them on harder questions, where you're more likely to need the help.)

By the way, there's still one more thing we want to notice here. The question asks us for the smaller of the unknown angles in the 3-4-5 triangle. As trained test-takers, we could guess that a common mistake for untrained test-takers would be to come up with the *larger* of the two angles instead, so we might expect to see the larger angle appear as a wrong answer. Since we know that the sum of the angles in a triangle equals 180 degrees, and we know that one angle in this triangle is 90 degrees, the remaining two angles—the smaller angle value we're looking for, and the larger angle value we aren't looking for— must add up to 90 degrees. Sure enough, choices (C) and (E) are the only pair of answer choices that adds up to 90°, and the lesser of the two is the correct answer. Remember that this kind of analysis isn't enough on its own to justify picking an answer, but it can often point you in the right direction, and it can also help you to confirm that you've probably understood the question correctly.

(If you were unfamiliar with any of the topics we discussed in this walkthrough, be sure to review the sections on trigonometry and triangles in the Math Toolbox in this book.)

Page 130, Question 23

The College Board's approach to this question on page 151 of the MSTB is, as usual, technically correct, but arguably incomplete. If we remember that perpendicular lines in the *xy*-coordinate plane have slopes with negative reciprocals by definition, and if we remember that the slope of a line is the coefficient of *x* in slope-intercept format (or "*y* = *mx* + *b*" format), then we know the correct answer has to be (C), because the slope of the equation in the prompt is -2, and choice (C) is the only one with a slope of $\frac{1}{2}$. This is essentially the College Board's approach.

But if we've forgotten that perpendicular lines have negative reciprocal slopes, or if we've forgotten how to read slopes in *y* = *mx* + *b* format, we can still answer this question with total confidence. The easiest way to do that would probably be to graph the line from the prompt on a calculator, and then graph each of the lines in the answer choices. The graph of the equation from the answer choices that crosses the original graph at 90° will be the correct answer.

When we do that, we'll find that only the graph of the equation in choice (C) crosses the graph of the original equation at 90°. Again, that means choice (C) is correct.

The College Board has made this question easier than it could have been by putting all the equations in slope-intercept format (except (E), but even that one has *y* isolated so that we can compare it easily to the equation in the prompt). This makes it easier to tell the slopes of the lines at a glance, because the coefficient of *x* is automatically the slope. Slope-intercept format is also the easiest format to use for graphing the lines with a calculator. But it's still possible to make small mistakes on the question and end up missing it, and we always have to be on the lookout for those kinds of things on test day! Notice that most of the slopes in the answer choices are set up to trick people who mis-remember the "negative reciprocals" idea:

- (B) uses the opposite of the original slope, instead of the negative reciprocal.

- (D) uses the reciprocal of the original slope, instead of the negative reciprocal.

- (E) uses the reciprocal of the entire right-hand side of the original equation.

And, on top of that, (A) reflects a different kind of "opposite" idea, because it switches the *b* and *m* values from the line in the prompt.

This question is another very good example of the ways the College Board can still manage to fool unsuspecting test-takers with answer choices that are deliberately designed to take advantage of small, easily overlooked mistakes.

Page 130, Question 24

As trained test-takers, we know that answering most questions on this test boils down to knowing the definitions and attributes of relatively basic math concepts. In order to answer this question, we must understand the term "range" with respect to functions: the "range" of a function is the possible set of *y*-values that can be produced by plugging in all possible *x*-values. (If you don't feel comfortable with this concept, be sure to review the Functions section of the Math Toolbox in this book.)

The College Board's approach, on page 151 of the MSTB, is exactly the kind of approach your math teacher would recommend. But for most test-takers, the quickest and simplest way to answer this question will be to graph the given function on a calculator, and then look at the minimum and maximum *y*-values of the graph. This approach doesn't require us to remember anything much about the graph of the sine function or how to transform that graph, which means it's less likely to result in mistakes for most people.

When we use the calculator to graph $f(x) = -4 + 3 \sin(2x + 5\pi)$, we get this:

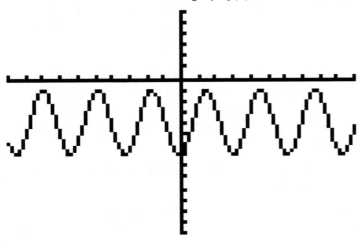

As we can see, the lowest points on the graph occur at $y = -7$, and the highest points on the graph occur at $y = -1$, with no break in continuity, so the range is from $y = -7$ to $y = -1$, which is what (B) says. So (B) is right.

If you don't feel comfortable with that approach for some reason, or if you'd just like another way to solve the question, we can also find the solution without a graphing calculator.

The classic way to figure out the range of a function that contains a trig expression is to think about how the numerical values in the function would affect the range of the basic trig function. In this case, the basic trig function in the expression is sine, and we know sine has a range from -1 to 1, because it's based on the *y*-coordinates of points on the unit circle, which has a radius of 1. The expression $(2x + 5\pi)$ doesn't affect the range of the function, because it only shifts the graph left or right—it only modifies *x* *before* the sine part of the function happens. The two numbers that modify the function *after* the sine is taken are 3 and -4. The 3 changes the amplitude of the range, because it's multiplied by the result of the sine. We know that sine can have values from -1 to 1, and the effect of multiplying those by 3 is to stretch the range from -3 to 3. The -4, on the other hand, is added to the sine value after we multiply by 3, which is why the final range of the function in the prompt is -7 to -1, and (B) is correct.

We can see that the other answer choices use elements of the ranges we arrived at on our way to the final range. (E) is the range of sine itself, while (C) is the range of 3*sine. (A) and (D) represent the result if we remember to add -4 to one end of the range of 3*sine, but not the other. In this way, all of these answer choices can be said to follow the "on the way" pattern we discussed earlier in this Black Book. When we realize this, it can simultaneously reassure us that we thought about the right things on the way to our answer, and also remind us to make sure that we've actually provided the result that the question was asking for, instead of taking things a step too far, or not far enough. Once again, we see how a strong familiarity with the test's design can help us avoid the kinds of small mistakes that can lower an untrained test-taker's score all too easily.

Page 130, Question 25

When untrained test-takers see a term like "standard deviation," they often worry that they'll have to remember some complex formula or concept from statistics and probability. But as we've seen repeatedly in these walkthroughs, we only really need to have a basic understanding of the concepts in most questions to be able to answer them. In this case, an awareness of the answer choices makes it much easier to answer the question, but a familiarity with your calculator can also help.

We'll discuss the calculator-based approach first, and then we'll discuss the approach for people who aren't familiar with the concept of standard deviation before they see this question.

You can use your calculator's standard deviation function to calculate the standard deviations for each answer choice, and then pick the answer with the smallest standard deviation. When you do that, you'll get these results:

(A) Standard deviation: 4

(B) Standard deviation: 2.52

(C) Standard deviation: 2.08

(D) Standard deviation: 1

(E) Standard deviation: 0

(I'm not sure which type of calculator you have, so I can't tell you how to find standard deviation with your calculator, but you can find instructions if you need them by searching online for your calculator model and the phrase "standard deviation," as we discussed in the section of this Black Book called "Your Calculator For The Math Level 2 Test.")

This makes it clear that (E) must be the correct answer, because it has the smallest standard deviation.

But what if we don't know the term "standard deviation," and may not even be aware that our calculators can find the standard deviation of a set of numbers? Let's discuss how we could still approach the question from that standpoint.

When we see an unfamiliar term like "standard deviation," it's always important to keep from panicking, and not just assume that we have to give up on the question and move on. As trained test-takers, we have to remember that the College Board often intentionally writes Math Level 2 questions in such a way that we can still find a solution even if we don't immediately recognize every concept in the question. Instead, we should read carefully, think about the meanings of the individual words in the terms we don't recognize, and consider the information in the rest of the question, including the answer choices. When we do that, we often find that we can understand the question well enough to find the answer.

So let's start by thinking about each of the words in the term "standard deviation." "Standard" means something like "regular" or "normal." What about "deviation?" Well, "to deviate" from something means "to be different" from the thing, or "to move away" from the thing. This suggests that "deviation" must mean something like "the state of being different from something."

So it seems that "standard deviation" means something like "the regular or normal state of being different from."

(Of course, if you know the term "standard deviation," you can tell that this definition isn't exactly precise, and might not be very helpful in a typical math classroom. But we'll see how this kind of definition can be useful on this question, and how this general type of thinking can be helpful on the rest of the test.)

Now let's think about the answer choices. It seems that we need to pick a set of numbers with the "smallest standard deviation." What could we do to each set of numbers that would seem like finding the smallest "regular or normal state of being different from something?"

If we're looking at a list of numbers, and we're trying to apply the idea of being "different from something" as little as possible, then the only thing that the numbers in a set can be different from is each other. Being "different" requires some kind of comparison, and the question doesn't give us anything else to compare the numbers in the answer choices to, besides each other.

So we want to find the set of numbers with the smallest differences from one another. That would have to be the answer choice whose numbers are all the same, which is choice (E). The numbers in (E) have no difference from each other at all, so that must be the smallest difference.

Understanding this question can really help us to see how the College Board designs questions. In this case, the College Board gave us an answer choice with no difference at all from number to number, so we were able to find the correct answer if we had only the slightest understanding of what "standard deviation" meant.

If the test-makers actually wanted us to calculate any standard deviations, they wouldn't have included choice (E). They could have made this question much more challenging, and they could have written it so that finding the answer would require a much more sophisticated understanding of "standard deviation." But that's not how questions on the Math Level 2 Test generally work. Questions on this test tend to reward an understanding of basic concepts, and a willingness to read carefully and to think a little creatively when faced with unfamiliar material or unfamiliar presentations of basic ideas.

Page 131, Question 26

This question involves raising e to an exponent which means we know its solution is probably going to involve the natural log. (If you're not sure why that is, you should review the section on logarithms in the Math Toolbox of this Black Book.) Let's keep that in mind as we take a look.

We're given the formula $A = Pe^{0.08t}$. Then we're told that A is equal to the worth of a savings account after the initial investment (called P) is in the account for t years. We're asked how long it will take for an initial investment of $1,000 to become $5,000 in this kind of savings account.

After we've carefully read through the prompt and the answer choices and started to think about the different approaches we can take, we'll probably decide that the easiest approach is to take the values from the prompt and plug them into the formula from the prompt. The question tells us that P is the initial investment, and that the initial investment is $1,000. So we know we can plug in $1,000 for P.

The prompt also tells us that A is the amount that an investment will be worth after t years. After a certain number of years, the initial investment will be worth $5,000, according to the prompt. So we can plug in $5,000 for A.

Let's plug those numbers into the given formula and see what happens:

$A = Pe^{0.08t}$ (given formula from the prompt)

$5,000 = 1,000e^{0.08t}$ (plug in A = 5,000 and P = 1,000)

Now we need to solve for t, because the question asks us "how many years" something will take, and t represents the number of years in the original formula. So we'll divide both sides by 1,000, as a step towards isolating the expression with t on one side:

$5 = e^{0.08t}$ (divide both sides by 1,000)

We need to isolate t to find the time that the question asked for, but t is still part of the exponent above e. To get rid of e and get the t out of the exponent, we need to take the natural log of both sides:

$\ln 5 = 0.08t$ (take the natural log of both sides)

Now it's just a simple matter of dividing both sides by 0.08 to isolate t:

$\frac{\ln 5}{0.08} = t$ (divide both sides by 0.08)

When we divide $\ln 5$ by 0.08, we get approximately 20.118, which rounds to 20.1. That means the correct answer is (D).

Choice (E) is an example of an incorrect answer choice placed here by the College Board to catch someone who makes a likely algebra mistake, because you can arrive at choice (E) if you make the mistake of dividing 5 by $0.08e$, instead of taking the natural log of both sides and then solving for t.

Notice that this question just required some simple algebra combined with a basic understanding of e and the natural log. Again, if you're unfamiliar with these concepts, be sure to review the sections on Natural Log and Logarithms in the Math Toolbox of this Black Book. It's not often that the College Board gives us a question like this one, which is very similar to the kinds of things that a math teacher might ask us in school. When we do see a question like this, it's very important to make sure we don't make any small mistakes that could cause us to throw points away for no reason!

Page 131, Question 27

The College Board's solution to this question appears on page 152 of the MSTB. That solution is okay, as far as it goes, but I'd like to expand on it a little bit, especially because the College Board makes it sound like we should have memorized the signs of the different trig functions in different quadrants, instead of just memorizing the definitions of the trig functions, and then working out the signs of those functions from that basic knowledge.

We're told that $\sin \theta > 0$. This means that $\sin \theta$ is positive, since anything greater than 0 is positive by definition.

Then we're told that the product of sin θ and cos θ is less than zero. Let's think about what that tells us. We know that if the product of any two numbers is negative, then exactly one of those two numbers is negative, and we know that exactly one of the numbers must be positive. Since we were just told that sin θ is positive, we now know that cos θ must be negative.

Now that we know the sine of θ is positive and the cosine of θ is negative, we have to figure out what that tells us about the quadrant that must contain θ. In other words, we need to figure out which quadrant in the diagram corresponds to a point with a *positive* sine and a *negative* cosine.

If we're familiar with the unit circle, we know that the sine of an angle, by definition, is the same as the y-coordinate of the point where that angle intercepts the unit circle. The cosine of an angle, by definition, is the x-coordinate of the point where the angle intercepts the unit circle.

Since we know our cosine value is negative and our sine value is positive, we know that our angle would intercept the unit circle at a point with a negative x-coordinate and a positive y-coordinate. That would place the point of intersection in the second quadrant, so choice (B) is correct.

We could also approach this question in a more concrete way by taking an angle from each quadrant and evaluating its sine and cosine, to see which angle has a positive sine and a negative cosine. For example, we might take the following angles, one of which is in each quadrant:

- 45°
- 135°
- 225°
- 315°

When we evaluate sine and cosine for each one, we get the following results (I'll use decimal approximations here, because I'm assuming that we'd use a calculator to find the values, but you may have already memorized the values for class, which is fine, too):

- 45°: cosine = 0.71, sine = 0.71
- 135°: cosine = - 0.71, sine = 0.71
- 225°: cosine = - 0.71, sine = - 0.71
- 315°: cosine = 0.71, sine = - 0.71

When we look at these results, we see that the angle with a positive sine and negative cosine is the 135° angle, which, again, is in the second quadrant. So we see that (B) is correct once more.

Notice that we never had to figure out the actual value of θ from the prompt—in fact, there isn't enough information in the question to determine a precise value of θ even if we wanted to. Instead, the question focused on the properties and definitions of concepts like positivity, negativity, multiplication, sine, and cosine. As we've seen so far, and as we'll continue to see, this is a normal way for the College Board to design questions, and it's exactly the kind of thing we should expect to see on test day.

Page 132, Question 28

Untrained test-takers are often bothered by the way this question never actually tells us what the *f* function is, because they think they need to know the equation for the function in order to know which points are on the graph of the function.

But, as trained test-takers, we know that there must be enough information for us to reach a definitive answer, because there's no answer choice indicating that the question doesn't provide enough information to answer the question. So if the prompt doesn't tell us more about f, then we don't need to know any more about f than what's already in the prompt.

What we *do* need is to be familiar with the properties of functions themselves, and with $f(x)$ notation.

The question starts out by telling us that $f(x)$ is equal to $f(-x)$, when x is any real number.

Let's think about what that means. We know that $f(x)$ is a bit of notation that means "the result of the f function when x is plugged into the f function." When the prompt tells us that $f(x)$ is equal to $f(-x)$, that's the same thing as saying, "the result of the f function with x plugged in is equal to the result of the f function when the opposite of x is plugged in." (Remember that the expression $-x$ doesn't mean that we're necessarily plugging in a negative number! It just means we're plugging in the *opposite* of whatever the original x would be. So if the original x is 7, then $-x$ is -7; on the other hand, if the original x is -7, then $-x$ is 7.)

The prompt tells us that the point (3, 8) is on the graph of the function. In other words, plugging 3 into f gives us a value of 8 for $f(x)$. The prompt asks us which other point must also exist on the graph of the function.

Well, if we know that plugging in 3 for x gives us 8 for $f(x)$, then we know that $f(3) = 8$, by definition.

If $f(3) = 8$ and $f(x)$ must always be equal to $f(-x)$, then $f(3)$ must be equal to $f(-3)$, which means that $f(-3) = 8$. Another way to express the same ideas would be this:

If $x = 3$, then $f(x) = f(-x) = f(3) = f(-3) = 8$

Since $f(-3) = 8$, the point (-3, 8) must exist on the graph of function f. So (C) is correct.

All the other answer choices represent mistakes you could make if you misread the question, got mixed up on the relationship between x and $f(x)$, or had trouble with the negative sign.

As trained test-takers, when we see very similar answer choices like these, we know the College Board is trying to set us up to make some small error—like misreading the question, or misplacing a negative sign. We also know that avoiding a mistake involving a negative sign is probably particularly important for this question, because a lot of the values in the answer choices are opposites of one another.

Incidentally, the "wrong answers imitate right answers" pattern in the answer choices would suggest that the first value in the correct answer should be -3 (since -3 is the most common first value in the answer choices), and that the second value should be -8 (since -8 is the most common second value in the answer choices). We just saw that the correct answer is actually (-3, 8), which reminds us that these patterns can be very helpful in allowing us to approach questions from multiple directions, but they should never be the sole reason that we commit to an answer choice. In this case, an awareness of the patterns should prompt us to do one more check on our negative signs, to make sure that we haven't accidentally messed them up.

In the end, the key to this question is just understanding what a function is, and knowing how to read $f(x)$ notation. This is a great example of a challenging question that would never appear on the average high school math test. It's also a great example of a challenging "math" question that doesn't actually involve any calculations—in fact, we never even needed to know what the f function actually was. Remember that the Math Level 2 Test isn't written like a typical high school math test. If you want to improve on the Math Level 2 Test, it's more important to focus on understanding the test's design than to focus on memorizing formulas. (I keep repeating that . . . hmmm. It must be important :))

Page 132, Question 29

Some untrained test-takers will assume that they need to have studied formal logic to answer a question like this one. But, as we keep seeing, simply reading carefully and paying attention to small details will allow us to arrive at the correct answer.

There are two ways to approach this question. The first way is a bit slower and more complicated, and it's the one the College Board recommends on page 152 of the MSTB. The second way relies on a keen understanding of the test's design; we'll discuss it after we address the College Board's approach below. So let's get started.

The question begins with the following statement:

If $x = y$, then $x^2 = y^2$

Then we're asked which answer choice can't be inferred from the given statement.

(Even though the word "CANNOT" is in all caps in this question, untrained test-takers overlook words like NOT and FALSE and CANNOT all the time, and then get a question wrong without realizing why. This kind of thing is just one more reason why we always read ALL the answer choices when we answer a question. In this case, for example, if we accidentally ignore the word "CANNOT," we'll think that (A) is a valid answer to the question; if we're in the bad habit of moving on to the next question as soon as we find an answer choice that seems correct, then we'll miss the question. But if we read through the other answer choices before moving on to the next question, then we'll realize that (B), (C), and (D) also all seem to be correct if we've overlooked the word "CANNOT." This would show us that we had misread or misunderstood the question, because only one answer choice can be correct.)

This question is a great example of how the Math Level 2 Test often focuses on our understanding of definitions and properties, rather than on memorized formulas or tedious calculations. The key concepts in this question are indicated by words like "infer," "sufficient," "necessary," and "imply." We also have to understand what it means to square something.

With all of that in mind, let's look at each answer choice in turn.

Choice (A) says that in order for x^2 to be equal to y^2, it is sufficient that x be equal to y. What does "sufficient" mean? It's essentially the same as the word "enough." So the answer choice is saying that in order for us to know that x^2 equals y^2, it's enough to know that x equals y. Well, the given statement tells us that if x and y are equal, then their squares are equal. This is basically a direct restatement of the sentence in this answer choice, so the statement in choice (A) can be inferred from the given statement . . . which means this is NOT the answer choice we want to pick, because the question asked us to find the choice that CANNOT be inferred from the original statement! So let's look at the next choice.

Choice (B) says that in order for x to equal y, it must be the case that x^2 equals y^2. The given statement says that if x equals y, then x^2 equals y^2. So the statement in choice (B) can be inferred from the given statement—again, the two sentences are practically restatements of each other, which means this choice is also wrong, just like (A) was.

Choice (C) can also be inferred from the original statement—again, it says basically the same thing that the original statement said. That means choice (C) is also incorrect.

Choice (D) says that if the squares of two numbers are not equal, then the two numbers cannot be equal either. The given statement tells us that when two numbers are equal, their squares are equal. So it would make sense to conclude that two numbers can't be equal if their squares aren't equal. This means (D) can be inferred from the given statement, so this choice isn't correct, either.

Finally, (E) says that if x^2 is equal to y^2, then x must be equal to y. The given statement doesn't actually imply that this is the case. The sentence in (E) reverses the relationship between the "if" and "then" parts of the sentence in the prompt, which means (E) doesn't follow from the sentence in the prompt, because the sentence in the prompt doesn't say anything about what must be true if x^2 is equal to y^2. That means the statement in (E) CANNOT be inferred from the given statement, which makes it the correct answer for this question.

What we've gone through so far has been an expanded discussion of the College Board's approach on page 152 of the MSTB. As I noted above, that approach is okay, but it's a bit more complicated than necessary. As trained test-takers, we would expect that the College Board has actually left open a sort of shortcut in approaching this question, as it often does—and, as it turns out, we'd be right.

To see the shortcut, we need to realize that the original statement in the sentence is *true*, and that everything that follows from a true statement is also, necessarily, true. In other words, if a sentence is true, then that true sentence can't lead to a false conclusion—if the sentence led to a false conclusion, then the sentence would be false itself. I realize that you've probably never explicitly thought about this kind of thing in math class, but that doesn't mean you can't think about it now :). As trained test-takers, we know that this test often requires us to think carefully about basic concepts in ways we might never have done before, so this kind of thought process should really come as no surprise at this point.

Now, as it turns out, only one of the answer choices in the question contains a false statement, and that choice is (E). We see that (E) is false because it ignores the fact that squaring a negative number results in a positive number—for example, 9 is the square of both 3 and -3, but 3 isn't equal to -3. Since (E) is false, we know for sure that it can't be inferred from a true statement like the statement in the prompt. This means (E) is the correct answer.

This second approach allows us to move through the answer choices and consider only whether each choice contains a true statement. If any choice contains a false statement, then we know right away that the statement can't be inferred from the true statement in the prompt. This approach keeps us from having to figure out whether a given true statement can be inferred from the prompt (for example, a statement like "square numbers can't be prime" is true, but it's not inferred by the prompt).

The College Board could have made this question significantly more difficult by giving us five answer choices that were all true statements, and forcing us to pick out the true statement that wasn't logically implied by the statement in the prompt. Instead, we were given four true statements that followed logically from the prompt, and one statement that wasn't true, and therefore couldn't possibly follow from the true statement in the prompt. Once more, we see that the College Board has set up a question so it offers a faster solution to test-takers who make a small effort to stand back from a question for a moment and consider its design.

Page 132, Question 30

This question is actually fairly similar to the kind of thing we'd see on a math test in school. If we're familiar with permutation questions like this one, we'll know that the answer is equal to 9!, which is the same as 9 × 8 × 7 × 6 × 5 × 4 × 3 × 2 × 1, or 362,880. So the answer is (D), 362,880. This solution is basically the same as the one the College Board describes on page 152 of the MSTB.

But what if we didn't know right away that 9! should be the answer to the question? We could still figure out the answer, but we'd need to read and think carefully.

We might start to approach the situation described in the question by focusing on one position at a time. This is a good place to start if we don't know what else to do, because it allows us to focus on a specific aspect of the question, which might help us avoid getting overwhelmed.

How many different students can be the first one in line? Well, there are nine different students, and the first position can be occupied by any one of them. So there are 9 people who could occupy the first position.

What about the second position? A lot of test-takers might think that 9 students could occupy the second position too, but that's actually not the case. If one person already occupies the first position, then that person can't also occupy the second position—one person can't be in two positions. So the number of people who can occupy the second position is 8, since one of the original 9 is already in the first position.

What about the third position? There are already 2 people in the first and second position, so that leaves 7 people who could occupy the third position.

You may be starting to see the pattern here. I'll list out the remaining positions:

- The 4th position could have 6 possible students.

- The 5th position could have 5 possible students.

- The 6th position could have 4 possible students.

- The 7th position could have 3 possible students.

- The 8th position could have 2 possible students.

- The 9th position could have 1 possible student.

Let's try to think about what these numbers mean. Again, let's focus on one position at a time. We know that 9 people can occupy the first position. So that's nine different ways for the line to start. We also know that 8 people can occupy the second position, since there will be 8 people left to choose from after one person takes the first position. If there are 9 people who can occupy the first position, and 8 who can occupy the second position, then so far there are 72 different ways that the first two positions can play out: 9 different people in the first position, times 8 different people in the second position. Since 9 times 8 is 72, there are 72 different permutations possible for the first two people in the line.

We determined that there are 7 people who can occupy the third position. So how many different permutations are there for the first three positions? We've found that there are 72 permutations for the first two positions. Well, each one of those 72 permutations can go with 7 different possible people in the third position. That means the number of different possible permutations of people in the first three positions is given by 72 × 7, or 504.

Do you see the pattern? To account for each new position in the line, we just multiply the number of people that can possibly occupy each new position, resulting in the following calculation:

$$9 \times 8 \times 7 \times 6 \times 5 \times 4 \times 3 \times 2 \times 1 = 362{,}880$$

So, again, the correct answer is choice (D).

We can see that untrained test-takers might get confused and end up picking 9^2, which is choice (B), or even just 9 itself, which is (A). Also, if a test-taker forgot that each new position has one fewer possible person than the previous one, he might end up multiplying 9 nines together, which would result in choice (E). Finally, notice that choice (C) is half of the correct answer, which means (C) is following a common wrong answer pattern on the Math Level 2 Test. Because we're trained test-takers, noticing this relationship will help reassure us that we've probably approached the question correctly when we choose (D).

Page 133, Question 31

There are two basic ways to approach this question, and they both involve calculators. The easiest approach is to use a calculator to view the graph of $y = \dfrac{\ln x}{x-1}$ around $x = 1$. When we graph that function, we'll see something like the following on our screens, depending on our window settings:

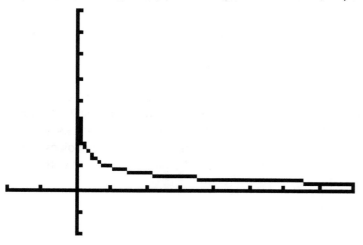

When we look at the area around $x = 1$, we see that the graph approaches 1 from both sides, and we know that (C) is correct.

(Again, this is, by far, the easiest solution to this question. Whenever we encounter Math Level 2 Test questions about the behavior of a graph, we should see if it might be possible to find the solution just by graphing the function on a calculator and looking at the graph.)

The other way to solve this problem is to pick two different numbers for x, and then evaluate them in the expression in the prompt. One number should be a little less than 1, and the other should be a little more than 1. We'll plug these numbers into $\dfrac{\ln x}{x-1}$ and see what the resulting values are close to. Let's start by trying $x = 0.99$:

$\dfrac{\ln x}{x-1}$	(original expression)
$\dfrac{\ln 0.99}{0.99-1}$	(plug in $x = 0.99$)
1.005	(resolve expression with a calculator)

We can see that the value of $\frac{\ln 0.99}{0.99-1}$ is very close to 1. Now let's try an x-value that's a little *more* than 1, so we can see if the expression approaches the same value from both sides—we especially need to do this because choice (E) leaves open the possibility that the function might approach two different values from different sides. So we'll use 1.01 this time:

$\frac{\ln x}{x-1}$ (original expression)

$\frac{\ln 1.01}{1.01-1}$ (plug in $x = 1.01$)

0.995   (resolve expression with a calculator)

We can see that the value of the expression is very close to 1 on either side of $x = 1$, so we can conclude that the value of the expression approaches 1 as x approaches 1. That means the correct answer is (C).

Notice that if the answer choices had been much closer to 1, this question would have been harder to answer using the second approach. What if there had been answer choices like 1.0012, or 0.9989? These numbers are so close to 1 that we wouldn't be able to tell which choice the function was approaching, just from plugging in numbers. But the College Board didn't include answers that were extremely close to 1, so we were able to plug in some x-values and find the right answer. This shows, once again, that the College Board often writes questions so they'll be easier to attack in unorthodox ways.

Page 133, Question 32

This question is a great example of the importance of reading the answer choices before we start to work on a question! If we don't read the answer choices, we might think we should just plug 2 into the given function, find the resulting value, and be done. But if we take a look at the answer choices, we can see that our goal isn't just to find the value of $f(x)$ when $x = 2$, because none of the answer choices are simple numbers. Instead, our goal is to figure out which other x-value can be plugged into $f(x)$ with a result that will equal $f(2)$.

There are three major ways to approach this question:

- graphing the function on a calculator

- backsolving

- using algebra

We'll tackle the approaches in that order. (Remember that we're not discussing multiple approaches for each question because you actually need to solve each question more than once—we're only discussing multiple approaches because I want to drive home the fact that questions can be approached in a variety of ways, so that you'll be trained to identify the best possible solution for you on test day.)

First, we can plug this function into our graphing calculator and look at the graph. If we do that, we can see the value of the function at $x = 2$, and we can also see which other x-value produces a value equal to $f(2)$. This is by far the quickest and easiest approach for most students.

When we graph the function, we get something like this:

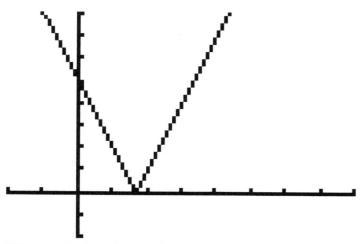

When we look at the graph, we can see that $y = 1$ when $x = 2$. This is the same as saying that $f(2) = 1$. Now we need to know which other x-value will result in a y-value of 1 when plugged into this function. We can see on the graph that y also equals one for some x-value between 1 and 1.5. The only answer choice in that range is (D), so (D) must be right. (Of course, if we want to, we can use the zoom or trace features on our calculator and identify a specific x-value where y is 1. That might look like the following:

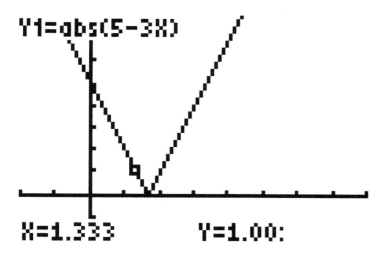

Since we know that 1.333 is a decimal approximation of $\frac{4}{3}$, we see, again, that (D) is correct.)

The backsolving approach to this question would be to figure out the value of $f(2)$, and then find the value of each of the answer choices, and see which one is equal to $f(2)$.

We've already shown that $f(2) = 1$. Let's see which answer choice also resolves to 1:

To evaluate choice (A), we need to find the value of $f(-2)$:

$f(x) = |5 - 3(x)|$ (original expression)

$f(-2) = |5 - 3(-2)|$ (plug in $x = -2$)

$f(-2) = |11|$ (combine like terms)

$f(-2) = 11$ (take absolute value)

11 isn't equal to 1, so choice (A) isn't correct.

To evaluate choice (B), we plug in $x = -1$:

$f(x) = |5 - 3(x)|$ (original expression)

$f(-1) = |5 - 3(-1)|$ (plug in $x = -1$)

$f(-1) = |8|$ (combine like terms)

$f(-1) = 8$ (take absolute value)

We see that (B) is also wrong.

To evaluate choice (C), we need to find the value of $f(1)$.

$f(x) = |5 - 3(x)|$ (original expression)

$f(1) = |5 - 3(1)|$ (plug in $x = 1$)

$f(1) = |2|$ (combine like terms)

$f(1) = 2$ (take absolute value)

2 isn't equal to 1 either, (C) is also wrong.

To evaluate choice (D), we find the value of $f(\frac{4}{3})$:

$f(x) = |5 - 3(x)|$ (original expression)

$f(\frac{4}{3}) = |5 - 3(\frac{4}{3})|$ (plug in $x = \frac{4}{3}$)

$f(\frac{4}{3}) = |1|$ (combine like terms)

$f(\frac{4}{3}) = 1$ (take absolute value)

This shows us that $f(\frac{4}{3})$ and $f(2)$ are both equal to 1, so (D) is correct, assuming our analysis and calculations are correct so far.

Of course, as trained test-takers, we know that we still need to evaluate choice (E), to help reassure ourselves that we haven't made a mistake. When we find the value of $f(\frac{7}{3})$, we get the following:

$f(x) = |5 - 3(x)|$ (original expression)

$f(\frac{7}{3}) = |5 - 3(\frac{7}{3})|$ (plug in $x = \frac{7}{3}$)

$f(\frac{7}{3}) = |-2|$ (combine like terms)

$f(\frac{7}{3}) = 2$ (take absolute value)

So (E) isn't correct, because 2 isn't equal to 1.

Once again, we can see that (D) is the correct answer, because (D) is the only answer choice that has the same value as $f(2)$.

Finally, let's look at the algebraic approach. This is probably the most difficult approach for most test-takers, because most test-takers don't enjoy working with absolute values in algebra. This is also essentially the College Board's approach on page 152 of the MSTB.

Since the question tells us to find another value for x that will produce the same $f(x)$ as $x = 2$, we can start this approach by seeing what $f(2)$ actually is:

$f(x) = |5 - 3x|$ (given function)

$f(2) = |5 - 3(2)|$ (plug in $x = 2$)

$f(2) = |-1|$ (combine like terms)

$f(2) = 1$ (take absolute value)

Now, we set our original function equal to 1, and use algebra to find all the x-values that could result in $f(x) = 1$:

$|5 - 3x| = 1$ (set $f(x) = 1$)

$5 - 3x = 1$ or $5 - 3x = -1$ (account for absolute value)

$-3x = -4$ or $-3x = -6$ (subtract 5 from both sides)

$x = \dfrac{4}{3}$ or $x = 2$ (divide both sides by -3)

So we can see that the two possible values of x where $f(x) = 1$ are $x = \dfrac{4}{3}$ and $x = 2$. That means $f(2) = f(\frac{4}{3})$, so choice (D) is, once more, the correct answer.

As usual, we see the College Board has positioned wrong answer choices to trap test-takers who make small, predictable mistakes. For example, choice (A) would be the result if you incorrectly assumed that $f(2)$ and $f(-2)$ must be the same because $f(x)$ involves absolute value notation, and (B) has an x-value equal to $f(2)$. Seeing these kinds of tricky, but predictable, answer choices should remind us once again how important it is to pay attention to small details on test day! (Note, by the way, that the calculator approach at the beginning of this discussion is also the approach that's least likely to result in accidentally choosing a wrong answer—even if we made a mistake with the calculator, it probably wouldn't lead us to any of the answer choices, which would show us that we needed to fix a mistake somewhere.)

Page 133, Question 33

There are two basic ways that most test-takers could approach this question: we can use a graphing calculator, or we can rely more on our knowledge of trigonometry. (Remember that using a graphing calculator is typically the fastest and simplest option when a question on this test asks about the behavior of a function—it's also usually the option that's least likely to lead you to a wrong answer choice if you make a mistake.)

First, if we understand the meaning of the term "period" in the context of a trigonometric function, we can just graph the function on our calculator and see what the period is. (The period of a graph is the smallest space along the x-axis in which the graph repeats itself once. If you're unclear on this concept, review the section on trigonometry in the Math Toolbox of this Black Book.)

In this case, when we graph the function, we get this:

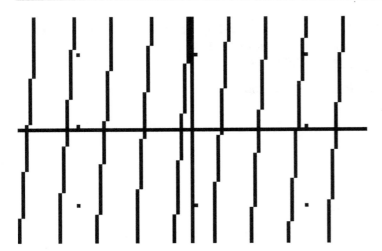

It might be a little hard to read the period from this graph at first, because it doesn't go through any integer coordinates on the x-axis. But if we compare the graph to the answer choices, it becomes pretty clear that $\frac{1}{3}$ is the correct answer, so (D) is right. We can tell this because we see that the graph of the function intercepts the x-axis three times in a space that corresponds to one horizontal unit—it's just that the first of these x-intercepts is shifted a little bit to the left of (0, 0), and the last one is a little to the left of (1, 0):

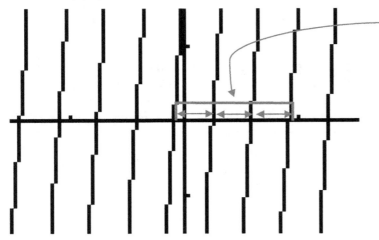

One-unit horizontal distance on the x-axis, with three repetitions of the graph $y = 2 \tan(3\pi x + 4)$, indicating a period of 1/3.

The other answer choices are all much larger than $\frac{1}{3}$, so we can tell that only (D) can be correct once we notice that the graph repeats itself three times in a space that seems to be about one unit across. (Remember that π is a little more than 3, so $\frac{\pi}{3}$ would be more than 1, and it's clear from the graph that the period is significantly less than 1.)

Another way to find the period is to know that the period of $y = \tan kx$ is always equal to $\frac{\pi}{k}$, where k is the coefficient of x. In this case, the coefficient of x is 3π, so the period of the graph would be $\frac{\pi}{3\pi}$, or $\frac{1}{3}$. Again, we can see that choice (D) is correct. (Just for reference, the 2 in the original function changes the amplitude of the graph, and the 4 shifts the graph horizontally. Neither of these two factors changes the period of the graph.) This is essentially the approach the College Board gives us on page 153 of the

MSTB, but, as I said above, I'd recommend that most test-takers use the calculator approach, because it's easier and more reliable for most people.

When we look at the answer choices, we'll see that they reflect the kinds of mistakes that we know the College Board expects untrained test-takers to make. Choice (B) is double the correct answer, which fits the College Board's common pattern of including an incorrect answer choice that's twice as much or half as much as the correct answer. Choice (E) is the result we'd get if we thought the coefficient of x was just 3, instead of 3π, and choice (A) is twice as much as choice (E). Choice (C) seems to be set up for test-takers who assume that the period of a tangent graph is the same as the coefficient of tangent in the function. Notice, again, that it's harder to fall for any of these careless errors if you just solve the question by graphing the function on your calculator, instead of relying on a memorized formula to find the period of the graph.

Page 134, Question 34

The College Board's solution to this question, which appears on page 153 of the MSTB, is actually pretty thorough, and even includes a good breakdown of the wrong answer choices. Still, the College Board's approach is a little more formulaic than I'd probably recommend, and it does leave out one other thing I'd like to point out about the answer choices, so we'll go through the question again here.

We're told that two vehicles are on two perpendicular, intersecting roads. One vehicle is broken down at point A, which is 20 miles from the intersection, and the other, a tow truck, is at point B. Points A and B are 50 miles apart. The tow truck is traveling on the roads at 45 miles per hour, and we need to figure out how long it will take the tow truck to reach the broken-down car by traveling along the two perpendicular roads.

It might seem strange to be given a question dealing with sides of a triangle and then have to come up with an answer that's expressed in minutes, but, as always, we should avoid panicking, and just think about the information we're given, and about what the question is asking us. If we know how fast the tow truck is traveling, and we're asked how much time it spends traveling, then the first thing we need to figure out is the distance the truck will travel, right? Once we know how far the truck is traveling, we can combine that with the truck's speed to figure out how much time it must have taken to cover that distance.

The distance that the tow truck travels will be from point B, to the intersection of the two roads, to point A. We already know that the distance from the intersection to point A is 20 miles, because that's labeled on the diagram. So the next step is to find out the distance from point B to the intersection.

We can form a right triangle by diagramming the distance between the two roads and the distance between the two cars. We know the lengths of the hypotenuse and the short leg, and we're looking for the length of the long leg:

To find the remaining side length, we just apply the Pythagorean Theorem:

$a^2 + b^2 = c^2$ (Pythagorean Theorem)

$a^2 + 20^2 = 50^2$ (plug in known side lengths)

$a^2 + 400 = 2500$ (square the numbers)

$a^2 = 2100$ (subtract 400 from both sides)

$a \approx 45.83$ (take the square root of both sides)

So the longer leg of the triangle, which is the distance from point B to the intersection, is about 45.83 miles long. When we add that to the 20 mile length of the short leg, we see that the tow truck has to travel approximately 65.83 miles to get from B to A while traveling on the two roads. But we still haven't quite answered the question yet, because the question asks how much time it will take the tow truck to cover that distance.

If the tow truck is covering 65.83 miles at 45 miles per hour, then we can find the travel time by dividing the traveling distance by the traveling speed, like this:

$$\frac{65.83 \text{ miles}}{45 \text{ miles per hour}} = 1.46 \text{ hours}$$

Be careful! A lot of untrained test-takers would just choose (E) at this point, because they wouldn't realize that "1.46 hours" is NOT the same thing as "1 hour and 46 minutes." This is another example of the way the College Board tries to anticipate the mistakes that test-takers are most likely to make, and it's one more reminder that we always need to be vigilant, even when we think we've done all the hard parts of a question.

To find out how many hours and minutes would be the equivalent of 1.46 hours, we need to convert 0.46 hours into minutes. There are 60 minutes in an hour, and 60 times 0.46 gives us 27.6 minutes. Since all the answer choices are given in whole minutes, we need to round 27.6 minutes to the nearest minute, which gives us 28 minutes.

There we go—the correct answer is choice (C), 1 hour and 28 minutes.

(Notice that we didn't really need to calculate 1.46 hours if we notice that 1.46 is just a little less than 1.5, and only one answer choice is just a little less than an hour and a half, or one hour and thirty minutes.)

As I mentioned above, the College Board's solution for this question on page 153 of the MSTB actually goes through all the wrong answer choices, which isn't too common for the College Board to do. As you can see, all of the wrong answer choices reflect mistakes that a test-taker might make if he were confused or in a hurry:

- Choice (A) is the time it takes to travel the length of the small leg in the right triangle we drew above (which is the distance along East Road in the College Board's diagram).

- Choice (B) is the time it would take to travel across the hypotenuse of our diagram above, straight from point B to point A, instead of following the two roads that make up the legs of the triangle, as the question specifies.

- Choice (D) is the time it would take to travel the 50 mile straight-line distance, *plus* the 20 mile distance of the shorter leg. We can probably imagine that a confused test-taker might accidentally add those two values, and then not know to check her work for small mistakes like this.

- Choice (E), as we've discussed, reflects the mistake of thinking that 1.46 hours is the same thing as 1 hour and 46 minutes.

Page 135, Question 35

This is another example of a type of question that's unlike what we would normally see on a classroom test in high school. High school math tests rarely give you a list of values for x and $f(x)$, and then ask you to figure out what $f(x)$ could be equal to. Further, even if a high school math teacher did present you with a question like this, that question would be unlikely to use the multiple-choice format.

So we might not know where to start when we see this question. In these situations, it's especially important to remember the "Math Path" from earlier in this Black Book. Using it will allow us to gather a lot of information about the concepts and relationships in the question without panicking like the average test-taker would.

You'll remember that the first three steps in the Math Path are to read the prompt carefully, read the answer choices carefully, and look at any diagrams carefully, while thinking about the concepts and relationships that we find—and we do all of this *without* trying to focus on answering the question yet! We're just trying to get our bearings at this point. So let's see what we come up with.

First, we see that the prompt refers to "a polynomial of degree 3." We may not remember exactly what that expression means, but when we see that the answer choices all involve multiplying three expressions that include x, we should remember that a third-degree polynomial is what you'd get if you multiplied three different expressions that each involved the sum of x and some number. This has to be why all five of the answer choices show three x-expressions being multiplied, right?

The next thing we might notice is that the prompt tells us that four pairs of (x, y) values for f are shown in the table. (Remember that $f(x)$ is another way to refer to the y-value that corresponds to a given x-value in a function named f). When we look at the table, we should notice that all of the pairs include either a 0 or a 1, which may be important for the question, since we know that the numbers 0 and 1 often have special properties in a wide variety of scenarios.

Finally, the prompt asks us which answer choice could be a way to express f. When we look at the answer choices, we see that they mostly involve positive and negative versions of the numbers from the table of four values that we just looked at! The only number that appears in the answer choices but not in the table is $\frac{1}{2}$ . . . and, somewhat interestingly, $\frac{1}{2}$ appears in the majority of the answer choices.

In fact, as trained test-takers, we might look at these answer choices and think of the "wrong answers imitate right answers" pattern, because the choices seem to mix and match a small set of elements; the fact that $\frac{1}{2}$ appears in three of the five choices would tend to suggest that it might be part of the correct answer . . . IF the "wrong answers imitate right answers" pattern applies to this question.

For that matter, if we try to apply the "wrong answers imitate right answers" pattern, we'd end up noticing the following:

- $\frac{1}{2}$ appears in three of the five answer choices; in two of those three appearances, it's negative.

- 1 appears in all five choices, including twice in (C); in four of those six appearances, it's positive.

- 2 appears in all five choices, including twice in (E); it's negative in three of those appearances, and positive in the other three.

Based purely on these observations, the "wrong answers imitate right answers" pattern would suggest that choice (B) is correct, because (B) is the only choice that incorporates both $-\frac{1}{2}$ and 1 (we can basically disregard the 2 in this analysis, because every answer choice incorporates 2, and the negative and positive versions of 2 appear equally throughout the answer choices). Of course, as trained test-takers, we know that we shouldn't just pick (B) right away because it seems to fit a pattern; instead, we should just note that the pattern seems to suggest (B) is most likely to be correct, and we should pay attention to the issues that our analysis has raised:

- The numbers $\frac{1}{2}$, 1, and 2 are clearly important, since they're the only numbers in the answer choices.

- Answering the question will require us to figure out whether $\frac{1}{2}$, 1, and 2 should be positive or negative in the correct answer choice.

At this point, we're starting to realize which elements of the question we should be focusing on as we try to determine which answer choice contains an expression that corresponds to the table of values we see in the question. (By now, we may have remembered the concept of the "roots" or "zeros" of a function, and noticed that the table shows two of the roots directly, and enough information to determine the third root—but not every student will notice this, in my experience, so I'll continue to discuss ways the question could be attacked even if we haven't noticed it, in addition to the approaches that become possible if we do realize that roots are relevant.)

The next step in the Math Path is to look for the easiest possible way to approach the question, keeping in mind that the ideal approach might include things like backsolving, analyzing the answer choices, or using a calculator. Then we'll execute our solution and check our work.

There are three basic ways I've often seen students approach this question, and none of them matches the approach that the College Board provides on page 153 of the MSTB. So we'll explore the three common approaches first, and then I'll explain what the College Board's discussion is trying to express.

Here are the three common approaches, ranked from fastest to slowest for most test-takers:

1. Use a calculator to graph each answer choice as a function, and then compare the graph to the values in the table. The correct answer choice will be the only one that creates a graph that passes through all the points in the table.

2. If we realize that the table gives us information about the roots of the function, then we can see which answer choices reflect that information correctly. From there, we can work back and forth between the choices and the table to determine which choice fits the table completely.

3. We can try each of the x-values from the table in each of the answer choices to see which answer choice produces the correct $f(x)$ for each x, according to the table.

Any one of these solutions, all by itself, can be an effective way to approach the question. I'll discuss them all here, in addition to the College Board's approach from page 153 of the MSTB, because I want to keep driving home the idea that test questions can be attacked in a variety of ways, so you can develop a flexible mindset for test day. So let's tackle these solutions in the order that I listed them above.

When we graph the expression from choice (A), we get the following:

We can see that this graph doesn't go through all of the points from the table—the easiest missing point to notice right away is probably (1, -1), because this graph doesn't even go into the fourth quadrant, where that point lies.

When we graph (B), we get this:

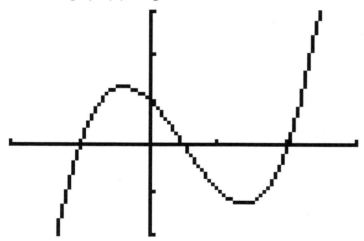

Looking at this graph, we see that it does go through all four points from the table in the prompt. That means (B) must be the correct answer, assuming that we've read the question correctly and entered everything into the calculator accurately. Of course, as trained test-takers, we know that we always need to go through every answer choice when we approach a question in this kind of way, so we're not done yet.

Graphing (C) gives us this:

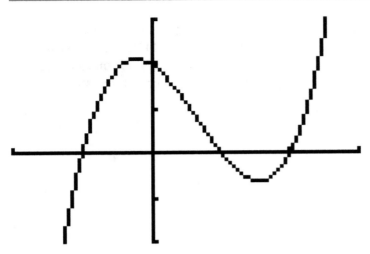

This graph clearly doesn't match the pairs of values in the table. (0, 1) and (1, -1) are probably the easiest places where we can observe this.

Choice (D) gives us this when we graph it:

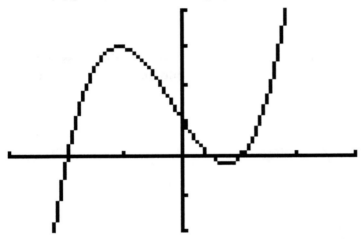

We can see that this graph doesn't match the points from the table, either.

Finally, choice (E) results in the following graph:

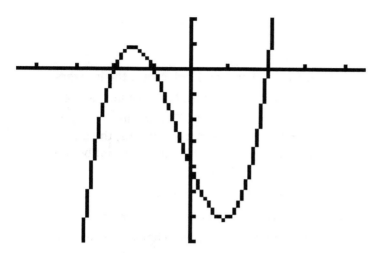

We can see that (E) also doesn't match all the points from the table. The easiest point where we can observe the discrepancy is probably (0, 1).

After all this graphing, we can see that (B) is the only choice that goes through all the points in the table, so we know (B) must be correct. (Remember that we've already seen that (B) fits the "wrong answers imitate right answers" pattern, which further suggests—but doesn't prove!—that we've accurately understood the question from the College Board's point of view, and approached it correctly.)

Now let's try the second-fastest approach, which relies on noticing that the table includes information about two of the three roots that f must have.

(Again, this approach is for test-takers who remember that the roots of a function, also called the "zeros" of a function, are the points where the graph of the function touches the x-axis. In other words, these are the points on the function where the $f(x)$ value is 0. If you don't remember the idea of roots or zeros from math class, then this approach may not make a lot of sense to you.)

The table of values shows that f has a zero at x = -1, because $f(-1)$ = 0. So one of the factors of the expression must be ($x + 1$), because plugging -1 into ($x + 1$) would make that factor equal to zero, which would cause the entire expression to have a value of zero.

The next zero in the table is at x = 2, since the table shows us that $f(2)$ = 0. That means another factor of f must be ($x − 2$), because plugging 2 into ($x − 2$) makes that factor equal to zero, which would make the whole expression equal to zero.

So that takes care of two of the roots that we needed to find. But what about the third root?

As trained test-takers, we know the question must provide all the necessary information to allow us to answer it with total certainty, because there's no answer choice that says anything like "this question cannot be answered using the given information." But we can also see that there are only two x-values listed in the table with $f(x)$ values of 0, and we've already identified them. There must be a third x-value that would also result in 0 when plugged into f, because the question tells us f is a third-degree expression.

At this point in this approach, we might remember that we still haven't really accounted for why $\frac{1}{2}$ might be appearing in a majority of the answer choices. When we look at the table, we see that it doesn't include an x-value of $\frac{1}{2}$ . . . so why does the College Board think test-takers would be interested in the idea of $\frac{1}{2}$ when they choose an answer?

If we look at the table, we see that it does list $f(x)$-values for $x = 0$ and $x = 1$, which are the integers immediately before and after $x = \frac{1}{2}$. And if we look at the $f(x)$ values for those two x-values, we see something interesting: one of the $f(x)$-values is positive, and one is negative. That means the graph must cross from a positive $f(x)$-value at $x = 0$, to a negative $f(x)$-value at $x = 1$—in other words, the graph crosses the x-axis between those two x-values . . . which means there must be another root between $x = 0$ and $x = 1$.

When we look at the answer choices, we see that the only value between 0 and 1 that appears in the answer choices is $\frac{1}{2}$, which is added to x in one factor from choice (A), and subtracted from x in choices (B) and (D). We know that it should be subtracted from x in the correct answer choice, because that means an x-value of $\frac{1}{2}$ would produce a value of 0 for that factor, resulting in an overall value of zero for the entire f expression. It looks like we've found our third root.

So we now know that the correct answer should include the following factors:

- $(x + 1)$
- $(x - 2)$
- $(x - \frac{1}{2})$

The only answer choice that incorporates all of those factors is (B), so we know (B) is correct.

A third way to approach this question would be to take the x-values from the table and plug them into each answer choice, and see which answer choice produces the appropriate $f(x)$-values to match the table. As I noted above, this approach will give us the correct answer, but it's probably the most labor- and time-intensive way we could choose to attack the question. On the other hand, it's an approach that doesn't require us to remember or understand what roots or zeros of functions are, so it might be attractive to some test-takers for that reason.

We'll work out each answer choice until we reach a point where it turns out to be invalid—that is, where it doesn't produce the appropriate $f(x)$-value for a given x-value in the table. Let's get started.

For choice (A), we'd get this:

$(x + \frac{1}{2})(x + 1)(x + 2)$ (expression from choice (A))

$(-1 + \frac{1}{2})(-1 + 1)(-1 + 2)$ (plug in $x = -1$ to test the first x-value in the table)

$(-\frac{1}{2})(0)(1)$ (add and subtract as indicated in each set of parentheses)

0   (multiply terms)

So we can see that choice (A) would produce an $f(x)$-value of 0 where $x = -1$. This is what the table calls for, so (A) looks good so far. Now we test out the next value in the table, which is $x = 0$, against choice (A):

$(x + \frac{1}{2})(x + 1)(x + 2)$ (expression from choice (A))

$(0 + \frac{1}{2})(0 + 1)(0 + 2)$ (plug in $x = 0$ to test the second x-value in the table)

$(\frac{1}{2})(1)(2)$ (add and subtract as indicated in each set of parentheses)

1 (multiply terms)

Again, choice (A) produces the correct result for one of the pairs of values from the table, because the table shows that $f(0) = 1$, which matches with (A). So we test the next value in the table against (A):

$(x + \frac{1}{2})(x + 1)(x + 2)$ (expression from choice (A))

$(1 + \frac{1}{2})(1 + 1)(1 + 2)$ (plug in $x = 1$ to test the third x-value in the table)

$(\frac{3}{2})(2)(3)$ (add and subtract as indicated in each set of parentheses)

9 (multiply terms)

Now we've run into a place where (A) fails to match the table, because the table shows that we should get a result of -1 when we plug in $x = 1$, but we've ended up with 9 instead. So we can see that choice (A) can't be correct, assuming that we've understood everything correctly and done our math accurately.

Now we test choice (B). As before, we'll start by plugging the first x-value from the table into the expression from (B):

$(x + 1)(x - 2)(x - \frac{1}{2})$ (expression from choice (B))

$(-1 + 1)(-1 - 2)(-1 - \frac{1}{2})$ (plug in $x = -1$ to test the first x-value in the table)

$(0)(-3)(-\frac{3}{2})$ (add and subtract as indicated in each set of parentheses)

0 (multiply terms)

We can see that the expression in (B) correctly generates a result of 0 when we plug in $x = -1$, just as the table calls for. Now we test the next pair of values from the table by plugging in $x = 0$:

$(x + 1)(x - 2)(x - \frac{1}{2})$ (expression from choice (B))

$(0 + 1)(0 - 2)(0 - \frac{1}{2})$ (plug in $x = 0$ to test the second x-value in the table)

$(1)(-2)(-\frac{1}{2})$ (add and subtract as indicated in each set of parentheses)

1 (multiply terms)

Choice (B) produces an $f(x)$ of 1 where $x = 0$, exactly as the table indicates. So we keep testing (B) by plugging in the next x-value from the table, which is 1:

$(x + 1)(x - 2)(x - \frac{1}{2})$ (expression from choice (B))

$(1 + 1)(1 - 2)(1 - \frac{1}{2})$ (plug in $x = 1$ to test the third x-value in the table)

$(2)(-1)(\frac{1}{2})$ (add and subtract as indicated in each set of parentheses)

-1 (multiply terms)

The table shows that $f(1) = -1$, and we've just seen that this holds true for choice (B), as well. So now we test $x = 2$, which is the last x-value from the table:

$(x + 1)(x - 2)(x - \frac{1}{2})$ (expression from choice (B))

$(2 + 1)(2 - 2)(2 - \frac{1}{2})$ (plug in $x = 2$ to test the last x-value in the table)

$(3)(0)(\frac{3}{2})$ (add and subtract as indicated in each set of parentheses)

0 (multiply terms)

Now that we've tested all four of the x-values from the table against the expression in (B), we can see that all of them produce the correct $f(x)$ values according to the table. This means that (B) is the correct answer, assuming we haven't made any mistakes in our calculations. As trained test-takers, we know that we still need to test the other answer choices, to make sure we haven't misunderstood the question. (We always have to keep in mind that one of the College Board's most effective weapons against us is our own carelessness, which can always cost us a question, even if we understand everything the question is asking us to do!)

So we'll go on and test (C) now, starting with $x = -1$, just as we have with the other answer choices:

$(x + 1)(x - 2)(x - 1)$ (expression from choice (C))

$(-1 + 1)(-1 - 2)(-1 - 1)$ (plug in $x = -1$ to test the first x-value in the table)

$(0)(-3)(-2)$ (add and subtract as indicated in each set of parentheses)

0 (multiply terms)

Just like (A) and (B), choice (C) works for the first x-value in the table, which is -1, because it generates an $f(x)$-value of 0. So now we test the second x-value from the table against the expression in (C):

$(x + 1)(x - 2)(x - 1)$ (expression from choice (C))

$(0 + 1)(0 - 2)(0 - 1)$ (plug in $x = 0$ to test the second x-value in the table)

$(1)(-2)(-1)$ (add and subtract as indicated in each set of parentheses)

2 (multiply terms)

We can see that choice (C) generates an $f(x)$ value of 2 where x is 0, but this doesn't agree with the table—according to the table, $f(0)$ is 1. So (C) doesn't work with the table, which means it's not the right answer (assuming, of course, that we've done our calculations correctly, without accidentally overlooking a minus sign or something).

Now let's test out (D):

$(x + 2)(x - \frac{1}{2})(x - 1)$ (expression from choice (D))

$(-1 + 2)(-1 - \frac{1}{2})(-1 - 1)$ (plug in $x = -1$ to test the first x-value in the table)

$(1)(-\frac{3}{2})(-2)$ (add and subtract as indicated in each set of parentheses)

3   (multiply terms)

The table indicates that $f(-1) = 0$, but plugging -1 into the expression from (D) gives us 3. So we can see that (D) isn't correct, assuming that we've executed the calculations correctly.

Finally, we test choice (E):

$(x + 2)(x + 1)(x - 2)$ (expression from choice (E))

$(-1 + 2)(-1 + 1)(-1 - 2)$ (plug in x = -1 to test the first x-value in the table)

$(1)(0)(-3)$ (add and subtract as indicated in each set of parentheses)

0   (multiply terms)

Choice (E) gives us a value of zero when we plug in -1, just as the table requires. So far, so good—now we plug in the second value from the table:

$(x + 2)(x + 1)(x - 2)$ (expression from choice (E))

$(0 + 2)(0 + 1)(0 - 2)$ (plug in x = 0 to test the second x-value in the table)

$(2)(1)(-2)$ (add and subtract as indicated in each set of parentheses)

-4   (multiply terms)

We see that (E) doesn't match up with the table when x is 0, because the table shows that $f(0) = 1$, but (E) would give us an $f(0)$ equal to -4.

So we see, once more, that only (B) matches up with the table completely when we test the x-values from the table against the expressions in each answer choice. This means (B) is correct.

At this point, we've discussed three separate ways to handle this question successfully. As I mentioned above, these are the ways that I've seen students attack the question in the past, with the first two (the calculator approach and the roots approach) accounting for the vast majority of students' approaches.

But the College Board's approach (on page 153 of the MSTB) is more formulaic, and probably more similar to something that an algebra teacher would suggest. It doesn't involve a calculator, and it doesn't take the answer choices into consideration, so it ends up being a lot slower and more complicated than it needs to be. I still want to discuss it, because I've had students ask me about it in the past—the wording can be a little confusing, especially with the variable a, which seems to come out of nowhere for a lot of people.

The College Board's approach is based on noticing that the table gives us a lot of information about points that involve a coordinate of zero. (Remember that zero has unique properties in a wide range of situations that we'll encounter on this test.) We've already talked about noticing that f must have roots at x = -1 and x = 2 because those both have $f(x)$ values of zero, and the College Board's approach also starts out by noting that $(x + 1)$ and $(x - 2)$ must both be factors of f because -1 and 2 are roots of f. So far, so good.

But then the College Board introduces the idea of $(x - a)$, and this is where a lot of readers seem to get lost—where is this a suddenly coming from?

All the College Board is trying to say is that there must be a third factor of *f*, because we're told that *f* is a third-degree polynomial, and that this factor must also involve an expression in parentheses where we subtract a number from *x*, just like the first two factors do. Since we don't know what the third factor is yet, we have to use some kind of variable if we want to refer to it, and the College Board has chosen to use $(x - a)$. So $(x - a)$ is just a way to refer to the third factor, and *a* by itself would be the third *x*-coordinate where the graph crosses the *x*-axis, just like -1 and 2 are also *x*-coordinates where the graph crosses the *x*-axis.

The College Board's approach requires us to give a name to the third factor because the College Board has decided to use a purely algebraic solution, instead of using calculators or looking at the answer choices as we did above. In other words, we needed to be able to refer to $(x - a)$ because we're about to set up an algebraic equation that will let us solve for *a*.

So how will we set up the equation for this approach? We've already used the information from the table to figure out that $(x + 1)$ and $(x - 2)$ are both factors of *f*, and we've decided to call the third factor $(x - a)$, but that's not enough to create an equation. Let's go back to the table for more information.

When we look at the table, we should remember that 0 has unique properties, especially when it comes to identifying variables. In our situation, if we plugged in 0 for *x* in expressions like $(x - a)$, we might be able to isolate *a*. That's what the College Board does next in its solution: after naming the third factor $(x - a)$, the College Board sets up an equation where the three factors of $f(x)$ are set equal to $f(x)$, and then it plugs in $x = 0$ and $f(x) = 1$ because that pair of values appears in the table. The problem for a lot of readers is that the College Board doesn't really explain it's doing this, and it skips the step of writing out the equation without any values plugged in. So let's spell all of that stuff out here:

$(x + 1)(x - 2)(x - a) = f(x)$	(factorization of $f(x)$, with $(x - a)$ as the unknown third factor)
$(0 + 1)(0 - 2)(0 - a) = 1$	(set $x = 0$ and $f(x) = 1$, from the second set of values in the table)
$(1)(-2)(-a) = 1$	(add and subtract as indicated in the parentheses)
$2a = 1$	(multiply values on the left-hand side of the equation)
$a = \frac{1}{2}$	(divide both sides by 2)

Once we know that $a = \frac{1}{2}$, we know that the remaining factor could be $(x - \frac{1}{2})$, meaning the entire factorization of *f* could be $(x + 1)(x - 2)(x - \frac{1}{2})$, which means (B) is correct.

Of course, as trained test-takers, we want to make sure that we consider the set of answer choices before committing to an answer and moving on. As we discussed earlier, we can see that the answer choices all make use of a relatively small set of numbers, and we can see that the issue of whether we should add or subtract certain numbers is also very important, because we see that the only differences among some answer choices are whether the same numbers are being added or subtracted. We would also see that the "wrong answers imitate right answers" pattern suggests that (B) is likely to be correct. (Again, for further details on all of these points, see the earlier discussion on the answer choices that we went through before discussing each of the four approaches to the question.)

Discussing this question allowed us to consider a lot of important points that you should definitely make an effort to remember on test day. First, we saw a real-life application of the Math Path against a question that seems pretty odd to most test-takers, and we saw how analyzing the answer choices *before* attempting a solution can help us understand what the question might be focused on, and which small errors we might need to look out for. We also saw another example of how a graphing calculator can be used to make a solution much faster, and how much slower and more complicated a formal solution can be when compared to the kinds of solutions that a trained test-taker would use. I realize that this discussion was pretty lengthy, and you obviously wouldn't need to think about all of these things on test day, because you only need to find one solution for each question on test day; at the same time, I always want to make sure I give you a full explanation of what's actually going on in each question, and sometimes there's a lot to say.

Page 135, Question 36

As trained test-takers, we know that the College Board likes to test our awareness of basic concepts more than most people might expect. This question is a good example of that principle. The College Board seems to be testing whether we understand the concept of prime factorization in general. Specifically, the question requires us to know the following ideas:

- If y is a factor of z, then all the factors of y are also factors of z.

- The definition of the term "prime number."

If we know those ideas, and if we read carefully, then we should be able to answer this question without too much difficulty.

(Notice that I said—once again—that we need to read carefully. In this case, that includes making sure we catch the word "NOT." I know it's in capital letters, but test-takers overlook capitalized words all the time on this test, and often miss questions because of it. In this case, if we ignore the word "NOT," and if we forget to consider all of the answer choices before moving on to the next question, then we could easily make the mistake of picking the first choice that could be a factor of n. This is why we always remember to read carefully, and to look at every answer choice before moving on to the next question!)

Let's take a look at each answer choice and see if we can figure out any reasons that any of them might or might not be factors of n.

For (A), we should be able to figure out that the factors of 10 are 1, 2, 5, and 10. The only prime numbers in that set are 2 and 5, which are both factors of n, so we know that 10 *could* be a factor of n. That means (A) isn't the correct answer, so let's try (B).

The factors of 20 are 1, 2, 4, 5, 10, and 20. Just as in (A), the only prime numbers in this list are 2 and 5, which are both factors of n, so 20 could be a factor of n, too. Choice (B) must also be wrong, then.

When we consider (C), we see that the factors of 25 are 1, 5, and 25. Again, we know that 5 is a factor of n, so choice (C) isn't correct, because it also doesn't have any prime factors that aren't also prime factors of n.

The factors of choice (D) are 1, 2, 3, 5, 6, 10, 15, and 30. The prime numbers in that list are 2, 3, and 5 . . . but 3 must not be a factor of n, because we're told that the only prime factors of n are 2, 5, 7, and 17. (Remember that if 30 were a factor of n, then every factor of 30 would also have to be a factor of n.) So (D) must be correct, assuming we've read carefully and haven't made any mistakes. Of course, as trained test-takers, we know that we also need to check choice (E) before we can be satisfied that we've found the correct answer.

For (E), the factors of 34 are 1, 2, 17, and 34. The only prime numbers in that list are 2 and 17, which are also both prime factors of *n*, so we can see that (E) is also wrong.

(I want to mention two things here that you might be wondering about. First, it's important to remember that 1 isn't a prime number, which is why we never paid much attention to 1 in this explanation. Second, I didn't do a prime factorization of the numbers in the answer choices because that's basically what the College Board did, and I wanted to give you as many different ways to look at the question as possible. If you'd like to see those prime factorizations, you can find them on page 153 of the MSTB, or even do them yourself, but they aren't strictly necessary for answering the question.)

When we look back over the answer choices, it seems pretty clear that 30 would have a factor of 3, which is prime, and that 3 isn't in the list of factors for *n*. If we think about it, this is actually another telling clue about the way the College Board designs questions for this test: once we understand the basic concepts involved, the College Board often doesn't make us do challenging calculations to find the answer. The College Board could have made this question a lot more time-consuming by doing any of the following:

1. Making the list of prime factors longer, which would have made it harder to check to see if an answer choice had a prime factor that wasn't in the list.

2. Making the prime factor of the correct answer (that wasn't a factor of *n*) be a more difficult prime to recognize, like 19 or 53.

3. Making the numbers in the answer choices larger, which would have required more effort for factoring.

Instead, we were given a fairly short list of factors for *n*, and a set of relatively low numbers in the answer choices, including a correct answer that pretty obviously has a factor of 3.

Keep this in mind on test day—if you find yourself thinking that several questions will require convoluted calculations, you're probably not approaching them in the most efficient ways possible, because the College Board generally likes to make it possible to answer these questions with minimal calculation.

Page 135, Question 37
Before we get into actual approaches for this question, let's address the fact that we're being asked to find a number between 0 and $\frac{\pi}{2}$, but all the answer choices are expressed as decimals, not as fractions of π. If we want a fast way to estimate which answer choices are likely to fall in the proper range of values, we could just estimate that π is a little more than 3, so half of π is a little more than half of 3, which is 1.5. When we look at the answer choices, we see they're all between 0 and 1.5, so we don't need to worry about satisfying the condition of being between 0 and $\frac{\pi}{2}$, because all the choices do that.

With that out of the way, let's think about the different ways we could figure out which answer choice reflects a value for *x* so that sin *x* is equal to 3cos *x*.

We'll look at three different ways to approach this question:

1. We can take a concrete, backsolving-oriented approach, and just plug each answer choice into the equation from the prompt to see which one makes a true statement. This is going to be the simplest and most reliable approach for some test-takers.

2. We can take a more abstract approach and use a little trigonometry and algebra to find the answer (this is basically the College Board's approach on page 153 of the MSTB).

3. We can use a graphing calculator to find a point of intersection of the two given functions.

Note that all of these approaches will require a calculator, because they all require us to work with decimal approximations of trig functions that we haven't memorized beforehand. We want the calculator to be in radian mode, because the question is written in terms of π.

Let's get started with the backsolving approach. We'll take each answer choice and plug it into the equation from the prompt, and the correct answer will be the one that makes a true statement (remember that there may be a small amount of rounding involved, because we're dealing with approximations of actual trig values).

We evaluate choice (A) by plugging in $x = 0.322$:

$\sin x = 3\cos x$	(original equation)
$\sin (0.322) = 3\cos (0.322)$	(plug in $x = 0.322$)
$0.316 = 2.846$	(use a calculator in radian mode to simplify each side)

These values aren't equal, so choice (A) is wrong.

Now we try choice (B) by plugging in $x = 0.333$:

$\sin x = 3\cos x$	(original equation)
$\sin (0.333) = 3\cos (0.333)$	(plug in $x = 0.333$)
$0.327 = 2.835$	(use a calculator in radian mode to simplify each side)

These values aren't equal either, so choice (B) is also wrong.

For (C), we plug in $x = 0.340$:

$\sin x = 3\cos x$	(original equation)
$\sin (0.340) = 3\cos (0.340)$	(plug in $x = 0.340$)
$0.333 = 2.828$	(use a calculator in radian mode to simplify each side)

Again, the values are clearly not equal, so (C) isn't correct.

Now we test (D) by plugging in $x = 1.231$:

$\sin x = 3\cos x$	(original equation)
$\sin (1.231) = 3\cos (1.231)$	(plug in $x = 1.231$)
$0.943 = 1.000$	(use a calculator in radian mode to simplify each side)

These values are closer to each other than anything we've seen so far, but they're still not close enough for us to round them off to the same value. So choice (D) is wrong, too.

At this point, lots of untrained test-takers would assume that they could just choose (E) without actually testing it, because they know that one of the five choices must be correct, and the four choices they've tested so far are all wrong. In this particular case, (E) actually *is* the correct answer, as we'll see in a moment—but I still wouldn't choose (E) without testing it out! As I keep repeating, we always have to remember that it's very easy to make a mistake and give points away, even when we understand a question. For this reason, I make a point of going through all the answer choices when I use a concrete approach like this, because it's one of the best ways to find out if we've made a mistake somewhere—if we end up thinking more than one choice is correct, or no choices are correct, then we know for sure that we've misread the question or miscalculated something, or both. It will only take us a few seconds to check out (E) the same way we checked out the other four choices, and we would be foolish to risk missing the question just to save those few seconds. You might argue that you're sure (E) must be right in this case, but that's the problem: we can't know when we're mistaken about being right unless we test things out. So we still have to evaluate (E) by plugging in $x = 1.249$:

$\sin x = 3\cos x$ (original equation)

$\sin (1.249) = 3\cos (1.249)$ (plug in $x = 1.249$)

$0.9487 \approx 0.9488$ (use a calculator in radian mode to simplify each side)

These values are very close to being equal—they would both round off to 0.949. We know that the College Board sometimes gives us answer choices that have been rounded off, especially in questions involving trigonometry. With that in mind, we can be confident that choice (E) is the correct answer.

(If you don't feel comfortable with this discussion of rounding, go back and read the special article on rounding in this Black Book.)

Now let's take a look at the second approach, where we'll solve the question in a more abstract way, using algebra and trigonometry, more or less the same way the College Board does it on page 153 of the MSTB.

What can we do with the equation $\sin x = 3\cos x$? Well, we know that we need to find a value for x, so we should try to get all the terms that involve x on one side of the equation, and all the other terms on the other side of the equation. One way to move in this direction is to divide both sides by $\cos x$:

$\sin x = 3\cos x$ (original equation)

$\dfrac{\sin x}{\cos x} = 3$ (divide both sides by $\cos x$)

We should recognize the expression $\dfrac{\sin x}{\cos x}$ as one of the definitions of $\tan x$, which means we can now say this:

$\tan x = 3$ (substitute $\tan x$ for $\dfrac{\sin x}{\cos x}$)

Now we just put our calculator in radian mode and find the inverse tangent (or arctan, or $\tan^{-1}$, depending on your calculator) of both sides:

$x = \arctan 3$ (take arctan of both sides)

$x \approx 1.249$ (use a calculator in radian mode to approximate arctan of 3)

So, again, the answer is (E).

A third way to answer this question is to put your calculator in radian mode and use the graphing feature to find a point between $x = 0$ and $x = \dfrac{\pi}{2}$ where these two graphs intersect:

- the graph of $y = \sin x$
- the graph of $y = 3\cos x$

When we graph those two functions and trace the point where they intersect, we get something like this:

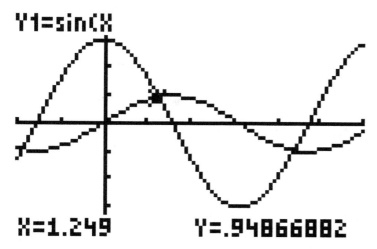

Y1=sin(X

X=1.249   Y=.94866882

We can see that the *x*-coordinate of the point of intersection is listed as 1.249, which means that sin *x* and 3cos *x* are equal to each other at some *x*-value very close to 1.249 (remember that 1.249 is an approximation of the actual value, which is probably a non-terminating decimal).

(This graphing approach isn't one that a lot of test-takers would use, but I wanted to go through it with you because you may find it useful for other questions on test day. It's important to remember that nearly every question on the Math Level 2 Test can be approached in more than one way, and some approaches will seem much easier and faster to you than other approaches.)

Now let's consider the answer choices before we move on to the next question, and see if we can figure out how the College Board may have been trying to fool us with some of them.

Notice that (A) is the arctan of $\frac{1}{3}$, while (B) is $\frac{1}{3}$ itself, (C) is the arcsin of $\frac{1}{3}$, and (D) is arccos of $\frac{1}{3}$. We can probably imagine how untrained test-takers could mess up the algebra in this question and arrive at any of those choices, especially (A) or (B). (As is often the case, the concrete approach and the graphing approach that we used would make it harder to arrive at those wrong answers—keep this in mind on test day, when you're deciding whether to use a more abstract, algebraic approach to a question. I'm not saying you should never approach questions that way, because sometimes those approaches are best; I'm just saying it's important to remember that a lot of wrong answer choices are based on algebraic mistakes, so you should make sure you're paying attention when you work through an algebraic solution.)

Page 136, Question 38

Answering this question comes down to knowing what an inverse function is, and recognizing the notation for one, which looks like this: $f^{-1}(x)$, where f is the original function.

This question is basically asking us to find the *x*-value that would produce an *f*(*x*) equal to 10 in the original function. (That might sound confusing if you've never heard it before, but it will probably make more sense once you see the concept applied.)

There are at least four ways we could approach this question:

- We could use a concrete approach, and backsolve by plugging each answer choice in as *x* in the original function to see which one gives us a value of 10.

- We could graph *f*(*x*) and see what the *x*-coordinate is for the point where *y* = 10.

- We could use algebra to set *f*(*x*) equal to 10, and then solve for *x*.

- We could use algebra to write the inverse function of *f*(*x*), and then evaluate that function where *x* = 10.

So let's get started with the concrete approach.

When we use a calculator to evaluate *f*(0.04) for choice (A), we get this:

$f(x) = 5\sqrt{2x}$	(original $f(x)$)
$f(0.04) = 5\sqrt{2(0.04)}$	(substitute $x = 0.04$)
$f(0.04) = 5\sqrt{0.08}$	(multiply 2 by 0.04)
$f(0.04) \approx 1.41$	(use a calculator to evaluate $5\sqrt{0.08}$)

Since (A) didn't give us a result of 10, we know that (A) is wrong. Now we try (B):

$f(x) = 5\sqrt{2x}$	(original $f(x)$)
$f(0.89) = 5\sqrt{2(0.89)}$	(substitute $x = 0.89$)
$f(0.89) = 5\sqrt{1.78}$	(multiply 2 by 0.89)
$f(0.89) \approx 6.67$	(use a calculator to evaluate $5\sqrt{1.78}$)

6.67 isn't equal to 10, so (B) must also be wrong.

When we try (C), we get this:

$f(x) = 5\sqrt{2x}$	(original $f(x)$)
$f(2.00) = 5\sqrt{2(2.00)}$	(substitute $x = 2.00$)
$f(2.00) = 5\sqrt{4}$	(multiply 2 by 2.00)
$f(2.00) = 5(2)$	(take the square root of 4)
$f(2.00) = 10$	(multiply 5 and 2)

Since *f*(2) = 10, we know that (C) reflects the value that produces an output of 10 when plugged into *f*(*x*), which is what the question asked for. So (C) must be correct, assuming we've understood the question and done our calculations correctly. Of course, as trained test-takers, we know that we always need to check all the answer choices when we backsolve like this, to help minimize the chance that we've made a mistake.

When we test (D), we get the following:

$f(x) = 5\sqrt{2x}$ (original $f(x)$)

$f(2.23) = 5\sqrt{2(2.23)}$ (substitute $x = 2.23$)

$f(2.23) = 5\sqrt{4.46}$ (multiply 2 by 2.23)

$f(2.23) \approx 10.56$ (use a calculator to evaluate $5\sqrt{4.46}$)

Just like (A) and (B), (D) gives us an $f(x)$ value that's not 10, so (D) is wrong. Finally, we test (E):

$f(x) = 5\sqrt{2x}$ (original $f(x)$)

$f(22.36) = 5\sqrt{2(22.36)}$ (substitute $x = 22.36$)

$f(22.36) = 5\sqrt{44.72}$ (multiply 2 by 22.36)

$f(22.36) \approx 33.44$ (use a calculator to evaluate $5\sqrt{44.72}$)

(E) doesn't give us a value of 10, either. So we know (C) must be the correct answer.

Another way to approach the question is to use your calculator to graph $f(x) = 5\sqrt{2x}$, and then find the point on the graph with a y-coordinate of 10 by using the trace feature. The x-coordinate of that point will be the correct answer to the question.

When we do that, we get something like this:

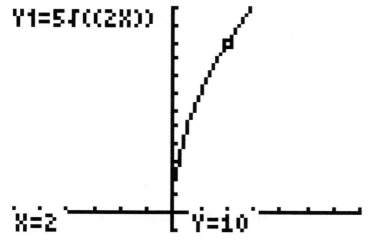

So we see, yet again, that 2 is the x-value that will generate a y-value of 10 in the original f function.

A third approach could be to use algebra without rewriting the original function. To do that, we'd just set the original function equal to 10, and solve for x. This is basically what the College Board does in its explanation on page 154 of the MSTB, but I'll provide the calculation in a little more detail here:

$10 = 5\sqrt{2x}$ (set function equal to 10)

$2 = \sqrt{2x}$ (divide both sides by 5)

$4 = 2x$ (square both sides)

$2 = x$ (divide both sides by 2)

Again, the correct answer is (C).

The last solution we'll look at here would be the one that most math teachers today would advocate: to use algebra to generate the inverse function of the original $f(x)$, and then evaluate that inverse function where $x = 10$. (As will often be the case, we'll find that the traditional approach to this question is probably the most complicated and time-consuming of all the approaches, which is why trained test-takers often opt for other approaches.)

The classic way to generate the inverse function for a given function is, in the words of my own math teacher, to "swap x and y, then re-solve for y." When we do that with the function in the prompt, we get this:

$y = 5\sqrt{2x}$ (original function)

$x = 5\sqrt{2y}$ ("swap x and y . . .")

$\frac{x}{5} = \sqrt{2y}$ (divide both sides by 5 as part of re-solving for y)

$(x^2)/25 = 2y$ (square both sides as part of re-solving for y)

$(x^2)/50 = y$ (divide both sides by 2 as part of re-solving for y)

Now that we've written out the inverse function of the original $f(x)$ from the prompt, all we have to do is evaluate it where $x = 10$:

$f^{-1}(x) = (x^2)/50$ (inverse function of the $f(x)$ in the prompt)

$f^{-1}(10) = (10^2)/50$ (substitute $x = 10$)

$f^{-1}(10) = (100)/50$ (square 10)

$f^{-1}(10) = 2$ (divide 100 by 50)

And we see, again, that (C) is the correct answer to the question.

(By the way, if you still don't feel comfortable with inverse functions after reading these approaches, be sure to take a look at the section on Inverse Functions in this book's Math Toolbox.)

Let's take a look at the answer choices and see if we can figure out what the College Board might have been thinking with them. For one thing, choice (E) is the result we'd get if we just plugged 10 into $f(x)$, instead of plugging it into $f^{-1}(x)$, or if we found the y-value when $x = 10$ for the graphing calculator solution, instead of finding the x-value when $y = 10$. Choice (D) is the answer from (E) divided by 10, for some reason. And (A) is the inverse of the value from (E) (that is $\frac{1}{22.36}$). As always, being able to see where some of these wrong answers come from will help us to be more certain that we've approached the question correctly.

Notice that the faster and more direct solutions to this question (in other words, the first three solutions) all relied on knowing what $f^{-1}(x)$ notation *actually means*. In other words, if all we know is that $f^{-1}(x)$ means "inverse function," without really understanding what an inverse function is, then we're left having to use an approach like the fourth one we just went through—something formulaic and slow, and more prone to small errors. But if we understand that $f^{-1}(10)$ really means "find the x-value that can be plugged into $f(x)$ to generate a result of 10," then we can take advantage of a wider variety of approaches that wouldn't normally be taught in math class. Once more, we see that understanding the definitions of basic concepts is more helpful than responding in a knee-jerk, formulaic way. This, again, is why it's so important to be aware of the weaknesses of the design of this test, and to train yourself to exploit those weaknesses, which is what we're doing in this Black Book.

Page 136, Question 39

This question gives us a definition for the Fibonacci sequence, and then it asks us for the 10th term in that sequence.

There are a few elements of this question that some test-takers may find strange. One of them is that we may be unfamiliar with the terms "Fibonacci sequence" and "recursively." But as trained test-takers, we know that Math Level 2 questions often provide enough information to allow us to work around unknown terms. Let's see what we can figure out if we read carefully.

We see the phrase "the Fibonacci sequence can be defined recursively as," and then we see some algebraic notation. Even if we don't know the word "recursively," we should know that the phrase "can be defined as" is going to introduce something that defines the Fibonacci sequence. So to understand what the Fibonacci sequence is, we need to understand the notation that comes after the word "as."

We might also be intimidated by the word "recursively." Even if we don't know this word, again, we can tell that it describes the way the Fibonacci sequence is being defined. So the notation after the word "as" must be a way of "recursively" defining something. We still don't know what "recursively" really means, but we're starting to see that we know where to look for the definition of the Fibonacci sequence, which seems to be the important thing for finding the answer to the question; we've realized that we need to figure out the meaning of the notation after the word "as."

Well, first we see that $a_1 = 1$, and also that $a_2 = 1$. The question tells us that we're looking at a "sequence." We know that a sequence is some set of numbers that has an order. Further, the question asks us for the 10th term in the sequence; if there's a 10th term, then there must be a first term, second term, third term, and so on. It makes sense that to find the tenth term, we might need to figure out the 9 terms leading up to the 10th term. With all of this in mind, we can probably figure out that a_1 and a_2 represent the first two terms in the sequence called a. It may seem strange that both the first and second terms are 1, but let's try to work around that for the moment, and see if it makes sense later.

So it looks like we've been given the first two terms in the sequence. What does the next line tell us—the one that describes a_n? What could that mean?

Again, let's think about it. We've already seen notation for a_1 and a_2. Now we're looking at another a, but with a subscript of n instead of a number, and we're told that this information about a_n is only valid when n is 3 or more. So it starts to make sense that this last line of information might be telling us how to find the 3rd, 4th, 5th terms in the sequence, and so on—the terms where the numbered position of the term in the sequence is 3 or more. This could mean that a_n is a general way to refer to the "nth" term in the sequence, as long as we're talking about the 3rd term or later.

And if a_n refers to the "nth" term, then a_{n-1} must refer to the term that comes *before* the nth term. For example, if we're talking about the third term, then n would be 3, and $n - 1$ would be 2. The expression a_2 would refer to the term before the third term—in this case, the term before the nth term.

By similar logic, a_{n-2} must refer to the term that comes *two terms before* the nth term. So if n were 3, then a_n would be the third term, and a_{n-2} would be the first term.

This interpretation of the meanings of a_{n-1} and a_{n-2} helps us understand why the definition in terms of n can only apply when n is 3 or more:

- When n is 3, then we have defined values for the a_{n-2} and a_{n-1} terms, which would be a_1 and a_2, or the 1st and 2nd terms of the sequence, respectively.

- If n were 4, then a_n would be the 4th term, and a_{n-1} would be the third term, with a_{n-2} being the second term. The prompt already tells us that the second term is 1, and we could figure out the 3rd term as described in the previous bulleted item. And once we had the 4th term, we could use the 3rd and 4th terms to generate the 5th; we could use the 4th and 5th to generate the 6th, and so on.

- But if n could be 2, then a_n would be the 2nd term, and a_{n-1} would be the 1st term . . . making a_{n-2} have to be the "zeroth" term. But the question didn't provide any information about a term like a_0, so we wouldn't be able to proceed if n could be 2. For that matter, we also wouldn't be able to proceed if n were another number below 3, like 1 or 0, because we don't have any information about terms like a_{-1} or a_{-2}.

So it looks like we've figured out the notation in the prompt, and why the rule for generating a_n could only be given where n is at least 3. That's good, but we still haven't answered the actual question yet!

We've been asked to find the 10th term. That means n will be 10 in the term that we're looking for—in other words, we need to determine a_{10}. So let's plug 10 in for n and see where that gets us:

$a_n = a_{n-1} + a_{n-2}$ (given equation for finding a_n)

$a_{10} = a_{10-1} + a_{10-2}$ (plug in $n = 10$)

$a_{10} = a_9 + a_8$ (simplify subscripts)

So it looks like we add together a_9 and a_8 to find a_{10} . . . but how do we find a_9 and a_8?

Well, if we're looking for a_9, then n is 9, and we go back to our given equation for finding a_n:

$a_n = a_{n-1} + a_{n-2}$ (given equation for finding a_n)

$a_9 = a_{9-1} + a_{9-2}$ (plug in $n = 9$)

$a_9 = a_8 + a_7$ (simplify subscripts)

This means that finding a_9 will require us to know a_8 and a_7 . . . but, again, how do we find a_8 and a_7?

You're probably starting to notice a pattern here.

Every term is defined as the sum of the two terms before it:

- To find the 10th term, we'd have to add the 8th and 9th terms.

- To find the 9th term, we'd have to add the 7th and 8th terms.

- To find the 8th term, we'd have to add the 6th and 7th terms.

- To find the 7th term, we'd have to add the 5th and 6th terms.

- To find the 6th term, we'd have to add the 4th and 5th terms.

- To find the 5th term, we'd have to add the 3rd and 4th terms.

- To find the 4th term, we'd have to add the 2nd and 3rd terms.

- To find the 3rd term, we'd have to add the 1st and 2nd terms.

So the easiest way to proceed is probably to start with the 1st and 2nd terms, since they were given to us in the prompt, and use them to generate the 3rd term. Then we can use the 2nd and 3rd terms together to generate the 4th term, and so on.

When we generate the 3rd term, we get this:

$a_n = a_{n-1} + a_{n-2}$ (given equation for finding the nth term of sequence a)

$a_3 = a_{3-1} + a_{3-2}$ (plug in $n = 3$)

$a_3 = a_2 + a_1$ (simplify subscripts)

Now we put in the given values for a_1 and a_2, from the prompt:

$a_3 = 1 + 1$ (plug in $a_1 = 1$ and $a_2 = 1$)

$a_3 = 2$ (add 1 and 1)

Now that we have a_3, we can find a_4 by adding a_3 and a_2:

$a_n = a_{n-1} + a_{n-2}$ (given equation for finding the nth term of sequence a)

$a_4 = a_{4-1} + a_{4-2}$ (plug in $n = 4$)

$a_4 = a_3 + a_2$ (simplify subscripts)

$a_4 = 2 + 1$ (plug in values for a_3 and a_2)

$a_4 = 3$ (add 2 and 1)

So the 4th term in the sequence is 3.

From here, we can proceed to find each of the terms leading up to the 10th term, by adding the two terms before any given term. Let's make a chart of the terms we find:

1st: 1

2nd: 1

3rd: 2 (because it's 1 + 1)

4th: 3 (because it's 2 + 1)

5th: 5 (because it's 3 + 2)

6th: 8 (because it's 5 + 3)

7th: 13 (because it's 8 + 5)

8th: 21 (because it's 13 + 8)

9th: 34 (because it's 21 + 13)

10th: 55 (because it's 34 + 21)

We can see that the tenth term is 55, so (C) is correct.

Now let's think about the other answer choices. If you were in the College Board's position, what kinds of mistakes would you expect test-takers to make on this question, and how could you try to exploit those mistakes? You might make the wrong answers be the terms in the sequence that come before and after the 10th term, because it's easy to imagine that an untrained test-taker might mis-count the terms and end up thinking the 9th term was the 10th one, for example.

Sure enough, the five answer choices are the 8th, 9th, 10th, 11th, and 12th terms in the sequence, in that order. As we discussed in the section of this Black Book that dealt with answer choice patterns, the College Board often likes to present us with some kind of numerical series in the set of answer choices. When this happens, we know the correct answer is generally less likely to be a number at the beginning or the end of the series in the answer choices, because the College Board wants to give us the chance to make a mistake in both directions, and pick a number that's either too early in the series or too late.

In fact, as trained test-takers, we could probably have predicted that at least some of the wrong answer choices would be other numbers in the series, before we even looked at the answer choices. Remember that answer choice patterns on their own are never enough to justify picking any particular answer, but they can often point us in the right direction with our solution.

So, in the end, this question is a great example of several aspects of our training for this test. First, we were able to work around notation that might have been unfamiliar. We did this by reading carefully, thinking in terms of basic concepts, and being willing to try a few things before giving up. Second, we saw that executing the solution to this question actually involved nothing more difficult than adding one- and two-digit numbers. And third, we saw that the College Board is following one of its common patterns in the set of answer choices, and that our awareness of that pattern helped us double-check our conclusion, reassuring us that we've successfully thought about this question from the College Board's perspective.

Most untrained test-takers who come across this question will assume they need to learn about the Fibonacci sequence before test day. But, as trained test-takers, we understand that it's unlikely we'll see another question about this exact sequence on test day; instead, we focus on developing the skills and instincts that will allow us to attack any question we see on test day, even if it seems strange at first.

(Remember that our solution assumed we were unfamiliar with recursive notation. Of course, if we are familiar with recursive notation, then we wouldn't need to go through the process of figuring out how to read that notation.)

Page 136, Question 40
As trained test-takers, we know that the easiest way to approach questions that ask about the behavior of a graph is to use a graphing calculator. (This is also what the College Board recommends in the solution on page 154 of the MSTB, though we know by now that the College Board doesn't always tell us when a calculator could be a useful part of an approach.) When we graph the function from the prompt on our calculator, we see this curve:

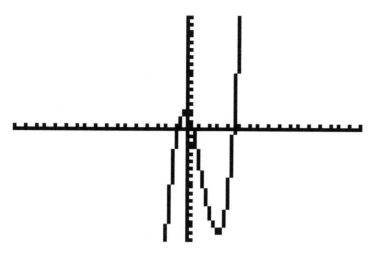

Now let's consider each statement in turn.

Statement I says the value of the function is increasing where $x \geq 3$. We can see that's true. If we start from where $x = 3$ and then move from left to right, we see that the curve of the function continues to go up from then on:

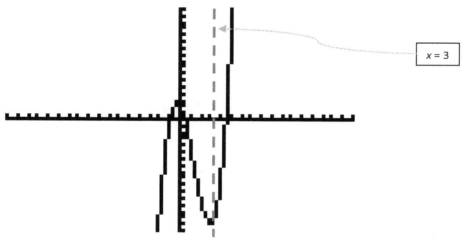

So Statement I is true.

Let's take a look at Statement II.

We know that when $f(x) = 0$, the graph of the function must touch or cross the x-axis. This is true because any point with a y-value of 0 must lie on the x-axis. We can see that the graph of the function crosses the x-axis three times, which means the equation $f(x) = 0$ has three real solutions—one for each time the graph crosses the x-axis:

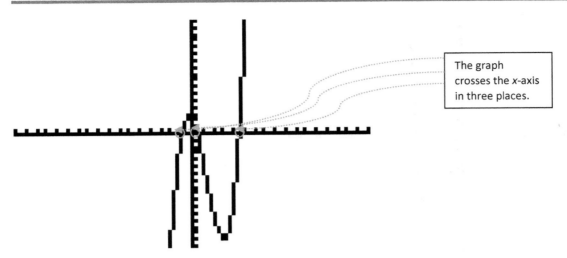

The graph crosses the x-axis in three places.

We know that the function in this question involves a third-degree polynomial because we can see that the highest exponent of x is 3, and we know that a third-degree function can have up to three solutions where $f(x) = 0$. We can see on the graph that all three solutions are real numbers, because the graph crosses the x-axis in three places, and all the numbers on the x-axis are real. This means there can't be any nonreal solutions to $f(x)$, so Statement II is false.

Finally, Statement III says that the value of the function is always at least -16 when x isn't negative. We can see on the graph that this is true:

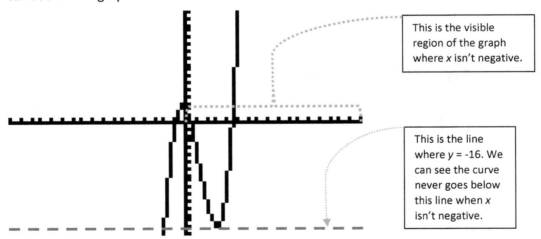

This is the visible region of the graph where x isn't negative.

This is the line where $y = -16$. We can see the curve never goes below this line when x isn't negative.

This means that statements I and III are true, while statement II is false, making (D) the right answer.

If we look carefully at the answer choices, we might notice that II appears in the answer choices more often than III does. This might make us doubt our conclusion, because we know that the College Board often likes to repeat elements of the correct answer in as many wrong answers as possible. But when we double-check our answer, we see pretty clearly that I and III must both be right, because the graph increases from the point where $x = 3$, and it never goes below $y = -16$.

Also note, once again, how important it is to read this question carefully. If we misread any of the inequalities or numbers in the statements with roman numerals, we could easily miss the question—not because we didn't understand the math concepts, but because we made a small reading mistake. Keep this in mind on test day.

Page 137, Question 41

For most test-takers, the difficult in this question lies in the fact that they've never seen notation like *fg* before. But the College Board's explanation for this question seems to assume that readers will know what that notation means (you can find that solution on page 154 of the MSTB).

So let's approach the question from the standpoint of someone who doesn't recognize the expression *fg*, and think about how we might work out the answer anyway.

One thing we might notice pretty quickly is that the question never tells us an actual formula or definition for *f* or *g* individually—instead, it only gives us a graph of both function curves over a limited area (from -1 to 1 on both axes). That means we don't have any equations to work with, so there's nothing we can plug values into, or anything like that. Most untrained test-takers panic when they realize this, because they expect to work with equations and calculations. But, as trained test-takers, we know that the question must contain enough information for us to be able to answer it, because there's no answer choice that says otherwise. So we stay calm, and keep trying to figure out whatever we can.

So what could *fg* mean? We might think that it refers to the idea of taking the output from one function and plugging it into the other function. But there are two problems with that idea:

1. There's already a different type of notation for that idea, and it looks like this: $f(g(x))$.

2. We don't have any equations to plug numbers into anyway, which makes it pretty unlikely that plugging something into an equation is part of the solution, unless there's a part of the question we're accidentally overlooking.

So it's unlikely that *fg* indicates a way to plug *f* and *g* into each other somehow.

There's another interesting thing we might notice: a certain symmetry to the combination of *f* and *g* in the original diagram. To the left of the *y*-axis, *g* is positive and *f* is negative, while the reverse is true to the right of the *y*-axis. This kind of suggests that *fg* should also have a sort of symmetry relative to the *y*-axis, because it seems to be some kind of combination of *f* and *g*. We see that only (A) and (B) are symmetrical about the *y*-axis.

Paying closer attention to (A) and (B) might lead us to notice that one difference between them is that (A) goes through the origin, while (B) doesn't. (Remember that it often helps to pay attention to zeros when they appear in strange questions, because zero has unique properties.) Does it make sense that *fg* would go through the origin? Well, even if we don't know what *fg* means, we can see that *f* and *g* in the diagram each go through the origin, which means that *f*(0) and *g*(0) are both 0. So, no matter what *fg* means, it's difficult to imagine any scenario where *fg* shouldn't also go through the origin, because any way that we can probably think of to combine 0 and 0 will either result in a value of 0 or an undefined value:

- $0 + 0 = 0$

- $0 - 0 = 0$

- $0(0) = 0$

- $0/0$ is undefined

This makes (A) look like a better option than (B), especially when we consider that (B) would show *fg* going through a value of approximately -0.8 at the *y*-axis, and it's hard to imagine any operation or function we could use on two zeros that would result in a value of -0.8.

So it's looking like (A) might be our answer at this point: it's symmetrical, and it goes through the origin, which both seem like attributes that would exist in a combination of *f* and *g*, according to the diagram.

But I still wouldn't be ready to mark an answer choice unless I were certain that I knew what the *fg* notation actually indicated.

At this point, though, we may have enough information to feel confident that we actually do know what *fg* means, and that (A) must be correct. For the reasons we mentioned above, it doesn't seem like *fg* would mean the same thing as *f*(*g*(*x*)) or *g*(*f*(*x*)). And where the result of both *f* and *g* is zero, the result of *fg* is zero, too, if (A) is correct. We also see that in the places where either *f* or *g* is negative, *fg* is negative if (A) is correct. Finally, there's the fact that *fg* looks a bit like another type of notation: the algebraic notation for multiplying two variables. From all of this, we can conclude that *fg* indicates we multiply *f*(*x*) by *g*(*x*), and that (A) is correct.

Now that I have a solid explanation of what *fg* seems to mean, and I can see that it makes sense for (A) to be correct, I would go ahead and mark (A) with full confidence. (Of course, you could also mark (A) with full confidence right away if you were familiar with this kind of notation before you read the question, but most test-takers have never seen it before, in my experience. This may also help explain why the College Board's chart on page 143 of the MSTB indicates that less than half of test-takers answered the question correctly.)

On the other hand, if you never do figure out what *fg* means, I'd advise you to skip this question rather than risk losing points by marking a wrong answer. (If you'd like a refresher on the reasons why skipping a question is preferable to making a guess, please see the section on guessing earlier in this Black Book.)

Whether you decide to answer this question or not, it's important to remember that no part of our discussion here involved an actual calculation or formula. This is one more example of the way the College Board can create a challenging question without actually requiring us to pick up a pencil and work with numbers in the way we'd usually expect to see in a math class. Keep this in mind as you continue your preparation.

Page 138, Question 42

This is another example of a question that challenges a lot of untrained test-takers, even though the solution doesn't have to involve a single calculation. In fact, it's possible to find the right answer to this question just by reading carefully and thinking about properties and definitions of basic math concepts like negativity and square roots—but the College Board's chart on page 143 of the MSTB shows us that only one-third of test-takers answered this question correctly.

In my experience, most test-takers who have trouble with this question are confused about the expression -*x* in the right-hand side of the equation in the prompt.

One of the most important aspects of answering this question is remembering that the notation -*x* may not be referring to a negative number! Instead, -*x* simply indicates "the opposite of *x*," no matter what *x* is: if *x* is positive, then -*x* will be a negative number . . . but if *x* is negative, then -*x* will be a positive number.

So if we restated the equation in the prompt in plain English, we might get something like this: "If you square a certain number and then take the square-root of that amount, the result is the opposite of the number you started with."

With that in mind, let's think carefully.

We know that squaring any number gives a positive result, and we know that the radical sign in this expression indicates the positive square root of the quantity under the radical. (If you were unaware that an expression like $\sqrt{x}$ indicates a positive square root of x if x is a positive number, you should probably review the section of the Math Toolbox on squares and square roots.) So we know that the right-hand side of the equation must be describing a positive number; in other words, the expression $-x$ must indicate a positive number. As we just discussed, that means x itself must not be positive.

At this point, we could try on our own to figure out what the set of all real numbers is that makes this statement true. But it would probably be faster and easier just to go through the answer choices and see what our options are.

Choice (A) says "zero only." Zero isn't positive, so that seems to fit with what we just discussed. Let's plug zero into the equation from the prompt and see what we get.

$\sqrt{x^2} = -x$	(original equation)
$\sqrt{0^2} = -0$	(plug in $x = 0$)
$\sqrt{0} = -0$	(square 0)
$0 = 0$	(take the square root of zero)

So when we plug in 0 for x, the resulting statement is true: zero is equal to zero. But that isn't enough for us to be able to say that (A) is correct! Choice (A) says "zero *only*" (emphasis mine), and we don't know yet if other numbers will work—all we've seen is that zero is one number that works. We still need to check the possibilities from the other answer choices.

Choice (B) says that only nonpositive real numbers make the statement true. The phrase "nonpositive numbers" means just what it sounds like: the set of numbers that aren't positive. That set includes negative numbers and 0.

We just showed that plugging in 0 makes the equation in the prompt true, so we don't need to do that again. But what about nonpositive numbers other than 0? To test those out, we should try a negative number. I'll pick -3.

(Remember that we generally avoid 1, -1, 0, and numbers from the question when we pick random numbers to plug into an expression on this test. We do this because those kinds of numbers sometimes have unique properties that might cause more than one answer choice to seem to be correct, as we discussed in the section of this Black Book on backsolving.)

$\sqrt{x^2} = -x$	(original equation)
$\sqrt{(-3)^2} = -(-3)$	(plug in $x = -3$)
$\sqrt{(9)} = 3$	(square -3)
$3 = 3$	(take the square root of 9)

So we when we plug in -3, the resulting statement is true: 3 is equal to 3. This makes sense, because the square root of a squared negative number will always be the positive version of that negative number, and the opposite of a negative number will also always be the positive version of that negative number.

But this isn't enough for us to choose (B) yet! We've shown that nonpositive numbers satisfy the given equation, but, for all we know at this point, it's possible that other kinds of numbers might satisfy the given equation as well. Choice (B) says "nonpositive real numbers only," and we don't know yet whether "only" nonpositive real numbers will make the equation true, because we haven't tested anything else.

(As trained test-takers, we also know that we always need to consider all the answer choices anyway, because it's one of the best ways to make sure we haven't made a small mistake somewhere. So let's take a look at the next answer choice.)

Choice (C) says that *only* positive real numbers make the equation true. But we just saw that nonpositive numbers make the equation true, so we know that (C) must be wrong. For the sake of illustration, though, I'll plug a positive number into the given equation, so you can see what happens. I'll choose to plug in 4:

$$\sqrt{x^2} = -x \qquad \text{(original equation)}$$

$$\sqrt{(4)^2} = -(4) \qquad \text{(plug in } x = 4\text{)}$$

$$\sqrt{(16)} = -4 \qquad \text{(square 4)}$$

$$4 \neq -4 \qquad \text{(take the square root of 16)}$$

We can see that plugging in a positive number like 4 doesn't result in a true statement. Now we can see that the square root of a positive number squared will always be the original positive number, and the opposite of a positive number will always be the negative version of the original positive number. A positive number isn't equal to its opposite, so we know that (C) is wrong.

Choice (D) says all real numbers will satisfy the equation, but we just saw that positive numbers don't satisfy the equation, so (D) must be wrong, because the set of real numbers contains the set of positive numbers.

Choice (E) says no real numbers satisfy the equation, but we saw earlier that nonpositive numbers do satisfy it, so (E) must also be wrong.

Now that we've gone through all the choices, we can see that choice (B) is definitely correct, because only nonpositive real numbers make the statement true. We can also see that (A) would have been an attractive wrong answer for test-takers who only tested out zero and then stopped reading the other answer choices. Choice (E), on the other hand, would attract people who didn't understand what -x meant, and thought that it must be referring to a negative number. Once more, we see that careful reading and thinking about basic ideas are the keys to answering a challenging question on this test. This is why I always remind you to focus on developing your test-taking instincts and skills, rather than on memorizing formulas or doing complicated calculations.

Page 138, Question 43

The College Board's explanation for this question makes use of the law of sines. You can find that explanation on page 154 of the MSTB.

Of course, there's nothing wrong with using the law of sines to answer this question. But it would be a mistake to read the College Board's solution and conclude that the College Board is particularly interested in the law of sines when it comes to the Math Level 2 Test; I'd argue that the construction of this question actually shows us that the College Board doesn't really seem to care about the law of sines very much, for reasons I'll explain below. Unfortunately, most untrained test-takers who come across this question during their preparation will miss most of what's really going on in this question, and won't recognize the question's deeper design principles when they encounter them in other questions on test day that aren't related to the law of sines. (For that matter, I'd be surprised if you see a question on test day that actually requires you to know the law of sines—this question doesn't require you to know it, either, as we'll see below.)

So let's see what's really going on here, and make sure we draw the proper lessons from this question.

The basic issue in this question is that we're asked for the sine of a, but we don't quite have enough information to find sine by using SOHCAHTOA, because we'd need to know the value of a hypotenuse in order to use Sine = Opposite/Hypotenuse.

Some untrained test-takers will leap to the wrong conclusion that the triangle is a 3-4-5 right triangle, which would make the unlabeled side of the triangle into a hypotenuse with a length of 5. If that were the case, then the answer would be (E), because the "opposite" of a would be 4, and the "hypotenuse" would be 5. But (E) is wrong, because the triangle isn't a 3-4-5 right triangle.

How do we know this isn't a right triangle? There are two ways to tell. Perhaps the most obvious way is that the angle at the top of the triangle clearly isn't a 90°-angle if we look carefully at it, and we weren't told that the diagram is out of scale, which means it must be to scale, according to the College Board's rules. On a more subtle level, we could notice that the angle on the right is a 30° angle, which means this would have to be a 30°-60°-90° triangle if it were a right triangle. But the lengths of the two short sides don't fit the ratio of the sides of a 30°-60°-90° triangle (which is $1{:}\sqrt{3}{:}2$) because 4 isn't equal to $3\sqrt{3}$.

So, again, we're in the position of needing to determine sine a without having an obvious way to refer to SOHCAHTOA, the unit circle, or anything else like that. This is the point where some people would reach for the law of sines, because their math classes have conditioned them to look for solutions that involve formulas without considering any alternatives. But a trained test-taker would notice two things in this question that suggest the law of sines isn't necessary:

- We're told that one of the angles is 30°, and we know that 30°-angles have unique properties when it comes to certain trig situations.

- We see that the answer choices are all nice, neat fractions, rather than non-terminating decimals. This suggests that there really is a way to use SOHCAHTOA on this question, because SOHCAHTOA can also generate nice, neat fractions.

All of this suggests that we may be able to answer this question by using SOHCAHTOA after all. Of course, if we're going to do that, we'll need to create at least one right triangle somewhere, because SOHCAHTOA only works when we're dealing with a right triangle. And, as trained test-takers, we know that all the questions on this test are written so that they can be answered relatively quickly by test-takers who know what they're doing, so we can have a pretty solid expectation that constructing a right triangle won't take a lot of time on this question, if it really is what we're supposed to do.

We'd also expect that the right triangle we create would be related to both the 30°-angle we were given, and to a, because we know that the College Board sets these solutions up so that they'll be quick and easy if we can see them—the whole point is that these alternative solutions are efficient.

With all of that in mind, we can realize that it's possible to divide the triangle we were given into two right triangles, by drawing a vertical line from the top angle straight down to the base:

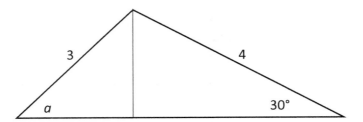

Now let's see if that gets us anywhere.

We know that the labeled angle is 30°, and we know that we drew our line so it would hit the base at a 90°-angle. So the remaining angle in the right-hand triangle must be 60°. Let's add those values in:

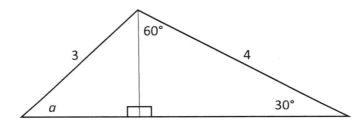

We should also recognize that a 30°-60°-90° triangle has sides with lengths in the ratio $1:\sqrt{3}:2$, where 1 corresponds to the short leg, $\sqrt{3}$ corresponds to the long leg, and 2 corresponds to the hypotenuse.

With this in mind, we know that the shortest leg of the triangle on the right must be half the length of its hypotenuse. That means the vertical line that we added to the diagram must be 2 units long, because it's half the hypotenuse, which is 4. Similarly, the longer leg must be $2\sqrt{3}$. Let's add those values to the diagram as well:

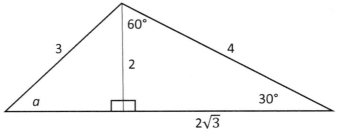

And if we're paying attention, we should realize that we now have a lot of information about the left-hand triangle.

Angle *a* is now part of a smaller right triangle whose opposite side and hypotenuse are labeled, and that's all we need to know in order to use SOHCAHTOA to find sine *a*. The opposite leg of the triangle from *a* is the line segment we drew in, with a length of 2; the hypotenuse of the triangle is the side with length 3. SOHCAHTOA tells us that the sine of *a* is equal to the ratio of the opposite leg to the hypotenuse, which is $\frac{2}{3}$. So choice (C) is correct.

Before we discuss the deeper significance of the way this question is designed, let's run through the more traditional way to approach it, which is to apply the law of sines, as the College Board does on page 154 of the MSTB. The law of sines tells us that every angle in a given triangle has a consistent ratio between its sine and the length of its opposite side. We can use this principle to find sine *a* by setting up something like this:

$$\frac{\sin a}{4} = \frac{\sin 30°}{3}$$

Now we just do some algebra to solve for *a*:

$$\frac{\sin a}{4} = \frac{\sin 30°}{3}$$

$\sin a = 4\frac{\sin 30°}{3}$ (multiply both sides by 4)

$\sin a = 4\frac{1/2}{3}$ (find sin 30°)

$\sin a = \frac{2}{3}$ (multiply the fraction by 4)

So, again, the correct answer is $\frac{2}{3}$, choice (C).

We can see that the wrong answers seem to come from a combination of simple arithmetic and trigonometry mistakes. Choices (A) and (D) would come from making a mistake in multiplying 4 by $\frac{1}{2}$ and dividing by 3. Choice (B) is the sine of 30° itself. And, as we discussed above, choice (E) reflects the mistake of thinking the original triangle is a 3-4-5 right triangle, and trying to apply SOHCAHTOA.

Now that we've got all of that sorted out, let's take a moment and think about what this question demonstrates about the College Board's method of designing test questions.

As I mentioned above, the College Board isn't actually trying to test our knowledge of the law of sines with this question. If that were the case, the question would have been designed so that the law of sines would be the only way to find the answer; on top of that, the question would probably feature angle measurements that would have required us to use our calculators. Instead, as we saw, the question and the answer choices are arranged in such a way that we can rely on basic trig to find the answer, which is a simple fraction instead of a non-terminating decimal.

So this question is actually rewarding our ability to pay careful attention to the way the College Board presents us with a set of information. If we don't really pay attention, and we try to rush right in with a formula, then we'll often fail, or at least have to do more work than necessary. On the other hand, if we develop the ability to look for clues about what the College Board is really testing, we'll often find we can answer questions quickly and easily, perhaps without having to rely on formulas or calculations. Remember this on test day when you run into a question that seems strange or difficult at first.

(Of course, if you'd prefer to use the law of sines to attack this question, there's nothing wrong with that! I only wanted to point out that the College Board has posed this question in a way that doesn't require us to use the law of sines if we don't want to or can't remember it, and it's important to keep this kind of thing in mind if you run into a question on test day that seems to require you to use a relatively obscure formula you've forgotten—there may very well be an easy way around the formula if you read carefully and remember your training.)

Page 138, Question 44

There are two key components to answering this question. First, we have to make sure we understand exactly which distance we're being asked to find. Second, we need to use the proper math to find it. My approach will be similar to the College Board's approach on page 155 of the MSTB, but we'll go into a little more detail here, to help make it clear why the Pythagorean theorem needs to be applied twice.

To make sure we know what we're even trying to do, we should probably sketch the rectangular solid the question is asking about. It would look something like this:

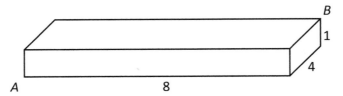

As you can see, the length, width, and height are all labeled. I added in points *A* and *B* to show the distance we need to find. The question asks for the length of the "the longest line segment whose end points are two vertices," and it's important to realize that those vertices will NOT be on the same face of the solid. In other words, the line that passes between the two points will also go through the center of the solid itself, instead of passing through the center of one of the faces.

The dashed line from *A* to *B* below indicates what I mean:

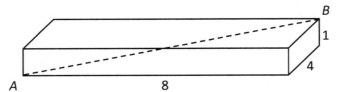

Now, how do we find the length from *A* to *B*?

If we're not sure where to start, we might take a closer look at the answer choices. Notice that two of them involve radicals. As trained test-takers, we know this suggests that finding the solution could involve taking the square root of something. When we think of taking square roots, and we look at the distance we need to find—which looks kind of like a hypotenuse in a right triangle—we might guess that we'll need to use the Pythagorean theorem somehow.

But we can't do that without constructing a right triangle that has AB as its hypotenuse. How can we do that?

In order to make a right triangle with *AB* as a hypotenuse, we'd need to know the distance from point *A* to the back bottom right corner—the one under point B—as pictured in this diagram:

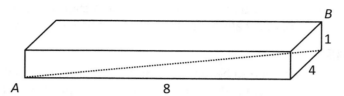

We don't know that length yet, but we can figure it out by using the Pythagorean theorem, because that distance is the hypotenuse of a right triangle with legs of 8 and 4—in other words, that distance is the diagonal across one of the large faces of the solid:

$a^2 + b^2 = c^2$ (Pythagorean theorem)

$8^2 + 4^2 = c^2$ (plug in leg lengths)

$64 + 16 = c^2$ (square 8 and 4)

$80 = c^2$ (add 64 and 16)

$\sqrt{80} = c$ (take square root of both sides)

$\sqrt{16 \times 5} = c$ (factor the radical expression)

$4\sqrt{5} = c$ (take square root of 16)

So the dashed line in the previous diagram has a length of $4\sqrt{5}$ . . . but this isn't the answer to the question yet! This is just the length of a diagonal of the largest face of the solid; it's not the length of the longest line segment connecting two vertices of the solid. Instead, $4\sqrt{5}$ is the length of the line segment that we'll use to help us construct a *second* right triangle with AB as a hypotenuse:

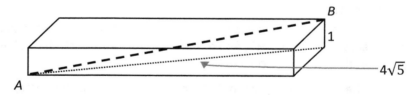

Now we can use the Pythagorean theorem to find the length of AB:

$a^2 + b^2 = c^2$ (Pythagorean theorem)

$(4\sqrt{5})^2 + 1^2 = c^2$ (plug in $4\sqrt{5}$ as one side length and 1 as the other)

$80 + 1 = c^2$ (square $4\sqrt{5}$ and 1)

$81 = c^2$ (add 80 and 1)

$9 = c$ (take square root of both sides)

This shows that the distance from *A* to *B* is 9, so the correct answer is (B).

As trained test-takers, we should notice that choice (A) is an example of the College Board's "on the way" pattern, because $4\sqrt{5}$ is a value that we found as part of executing the correct solution. This is a good sign that we've probably thought about the question correctly, because we can tell that the

College Board is hoping a lot of untrained test-takers will be likely to choose (A) after applying the Pythagorean theorem one time, without realizing that they haven't finished answering the question yet.

Page 139, Question 45

In order to answer this question, we need to be familiar with a basic property of logarithms. So if you're not familiar with the concepts we discuss for this question, make sure you review the section on Logarithms in the Math Toolbox of this Black Book.

Some untrained test-takers will rush through reading the prompt and assume the answer will be a numerical value. But this question doesn't provide enough information for us to determine a numerical value; if we didn't notice that when we read the prompt, we should notice it when we look at the answer choices and see that they're all expressed in terms of x and y.

To answer this question, we need to know that the logarithm of a number is equal to the sum of the logarithms of the factors of that number (assuming the bases of all the logarithms are the same, of course). In other words, $\log_a(xy) = \log_a x + \log_a y$.

We also need to notice that it's possible to multiply a certain number of 3's and 5's to arrive at a product of 45. Once we see that $45 = 3 \times 3 \times 5$, we know that $\log_a 45$ is equal to $\log_a 3 + \log_a 3 + \log_a 5$, using the "factor-adding" idea we discussed in the previous paragraph.

Since we know $\log_a 3$ is equal to x, and $\log_a 5$ is equal to y, we know that $\log_a 45$ is equal to $x + x + y$, which is the same thing as $2x + y$. So choice (A) is correct.

The other answer choices are all mistakes that could be made by someone who forgets the properties of logarithms, and/or mixes up some exponents and coefficients. For example, (C) is what we'd get if we thought that we should *multiply* the logs of the factors, rather than add them.

Page 139, Question 46

As we'll often see on the Math Level 2 Test, there are at least two different ways to address this question: a concrete backsolving approach, and a more abstract approach that relies on understanding the properties and definitions of basic concepts.

As usual, we'll address the concrete approach first, and then show how the abstract approach could be used.

If we want to backsolve on this question, we'll need to pick a value for θ from the interval described in the question, and then use our θ-value to find $\sin \theta$ and $\tan \theta$ in our calculators. We'll set t equal to the value of $\sin \theta$, and then we'll plug t into all the expressions from the answer choices and see which one matches the value we found for $\tan \theta$, which is what the question is asking for.

As trained test-takers, we should notice that four of the five answer choices are pretty similar to each other, and involve some combination of a fraction bar, a radical sign, and a squared variable. This relatively high level of complexity and similarity suggests that it would be easy for a careless test-taker to make a mistake when entering the necessary expressions in his calculator. At the very least, such a mistake could lead to frustration and lost time; at the worst, it could cause him to miss the question. So we'll make sure to proceed especially carefully.

I'll choose to make θ be equal to $\frac{\pi}{3}$ for my backsolving attempt, just because I need a number that's less than $\frac{\pi}{2}$, and I know that increasing the denominator in the fraction by 1 will result in a smaller fraction.

Using my calculator, I see that $\sin\frac{\pi}{3}$ is approximately 0.866, and $\tan\frac{\pi}{3}$ is approximately 1.732. (I put my calculator in radians mode to find those values, because the question doesn't mention degrees.) This means my value for t will be 0.866, and I'm trying to find the answer choice that's equal to roughly 1.732 when I plug in that t value.

Now it's time to use my calculator to evaluate the expressions in the answer choices:

For (A), my calculator gives me a value of roughly 1.999 when $t = 0.866$. This isn't very close to my target value of 1.732, so (A) is wrong, assuming I haven't made a mistake so far.

(B) works out to approximately 1.732 when $t = 0.866$. This is the rounded value I found above as $\tan\frac{\pi}{3}$, so it looks like (B) is correct. But as a trained test-taker, I know that I need to evaluate all the answer choices whenever I backsolve, to maximize my chances of discovering any mistakes I might have made. So let's keep going through the other choices.

(C) has a value of roughly 3.999 when $t = 0.866$, so it seems to be wrong.

(D) works out to approximately 3.46 when $t = 0.866$. This doesn't match 1.732, so it also seems wrong.

(E) is just the integer 1, so we can see that it doesn't match our value for $\tan\frac{\pi}{3}$ either.

So we can see that (B) is correct, since it's the only expression that works out to the same approximate value as $\tan\theta$ when θ is $\frac{\pi}{3}$.

Now we'll go through a more abstract approach to the question, focusing on the properties and definitions of the concepts in the question.

This question asks us to express $\tan\theta$, and we see that four of the five answer choices involve fractions. This should immediately call to mind the idea that $\tan\theta$ is equal to $\frac{\sin\theta}{\cos\theta}$ by definition.

Since we already know that $\sin\theta = t$, we might reasonably expect that t will be the numerator of the correct answer, because $\sin\theta$ is the numerator of the tangent fraction. (At this point, the only way we would expect the numerator to be something besides t would be if constructing the proper fraction involved adding or subtracting fractions, which might require us to restate one or more of the fractions with a different numerator. But we haven't seen any evidence that we'll need to do that, so t is probably going to be our numerator.)

If t is the numerator, what will the denominator be?

We know the denominator should correspond to $\cos\theta$. Across the five answer choices, our options are the following:

- $\sqrt{1 - t^2}$, in choices (A) and (B)

- $1 - t^2$, in choices (C) and (D)

- t, in choice (E) (I realize that choice (E) is just the number 1, but if our numerator is going to be t, then the denominator would also have to be t in order for the value of the entire expression to be 1.)

So it looks like the expression $1 - t^2$ could be important to this question, since the College Board devoted four answer choices to some version of it. Why would the idea of $1 - t^2$ be relevant to the cosine in the tangent fraction?

When we remember that t is the same thing as $\sin \theta$ in this question, we realize that $1 - t^2$ is the same thing as $1 - \sin^2 \theta$, which should remind us of the idea that $\sin^2 \theta + \cos^2 \theta = 1$.

It's looking like we have enough pieces of information to figure out how to express cosine in terms of t:

$\sin^2 \theta + \cos^2 \theta = 1$	(trig identity relating sine, cosine, and 1)
$t^2 + \cos^2 \theta = 1$	(plug in t for $\sin \theta$)
$\cos^2 \theta = 1 - t^2$	(subtract t^2 from both sides)
$\cos \theta = \sqrt{1 - t^2}$	(take the square root of both sides)

Now that we've worked out that cosine can be expressed as $\sqrt{1 - t^2}$, we can build our tangent fraction:

$\tan \theta = \dfrac{\sin \theta}{\cos \theta}$	(definition of tangent)
$\tan \theta = \dfrac{t}{\cos \theta}$	(substitute t for $\sin \theta$, according to the prompt)
$\tan \theta = \dfrac{t}{\sqrt{1 - t^2}}$	(substitute $\sqrt{1 - t^2}$ for $\cos \theta$)

So we can see that (B) is the correct answer.

When we look at the other answer choices, we can see that the College Board clearly seems to be trying to bait untrained test-takers into making small mistakes in their reading, algebra, or trigonometry. When we see this, we should be reminded that we need to re-check our answer to make sure that we haven't made a small mistake ourselves. Remember that a lot of untrained test-takers lose a lot of points on questions they actually understand, just because they aren't willing to pay attention and catch their mistakes. Don't be like that :)

Page 139, Question 47

Once again, there are basically two ways we could try to answer this question: we can take a concrete approach that would involve using a calculator to see which answer choice accurately describes the shift in the prompt, or we can take a more abstract approach that relies on algebra. As I usually do in this Black Book, I'll use the concrete approach first, and then I'll walk you through the abstract approach. (The College Board's solution on page 155 of the MSTB follows the abstract approach, by the way.)

Since the prompt asks which of the answer choices would produce the same shift of the original graph as we would find in the equation $y = x^2 - 2x + k$, the concrete approach would just be to choose a number for k, plug it into the prompt and the answer choices, and see which answer choice results in the same graph we generated from the prompt. Of course, as trained test-takers, we know that we have to pick a value for k that satisfies the requirement in the prompt, which says that k is greater than 2; we also know that it's generally a good idea to avoid picking any numbers that already appear in the question (not that that's a huge issue here, since 2 is the biggest number in the question anyway). So I'll pick $k = 5$, and graph the two equations from the prompt on my calculator:

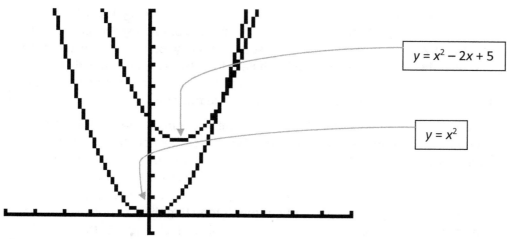

The prompt tells us clearly that the graph of $y = x^2 - 2x + k$ can be described as the result of shifting the graph of $y = x^2$, so how can we try to figure out what kind of shift we see between the graphs of $y = x^2$ and $y = x^2 - 2x + 5$ in our example? The easiest way to identify the shift is probably to compare the positions of two corresponding points on the graphs, and the easiest points to compare in this case are probably the lowest points of each graph (that is, the vertex of each parabola, which is the lowest point on each curve).

When we do that, we see that the lowest point on $y = x^2$ is at (0, 0), while the lowest point on $y = x^2 - 2x + 5$ is at (1, 4). So the graph of $y = x^2 - 2x + 5$ is the result when we take the graph of $y = x^2$ and shift it right 1 unit, and up 4 units.

Now we look at the answer choices to see which one describes that shift—remember that we've already set k equal to 5:

> (A) is wrong because it describes a shift to the left in the horizontal dimension, but we can see that the correct answer should describe a shift to the right.
>
> (B) is wrong because it also describes a shift to the left, just like (A) did.
>
> (C) is wrong because it describes a vertical shift of 6 units (since we're using $k = 5$, and $5 + 1 = 6$).
>
> (D) is wrong because it describes a shift to the left.
>
> (E) is correct because it describes a shift of 1 unit to the right and 4 units up (because $5 - 1 = 4$).

Now that we've seen how the question could be approached concretely, let's tackle it in a more abstract way.

As the College Board mentions in its solution on page 155 of the MSTB, the formal algebraic way to approach this question is by a process called "completing the square." If you're already familiar with the idea of completing the square from your math classes, then the College Board's explanation probably makes perfect sense to you. But my experience with clients suggests that a large number of math teachers never cover the concept of completing the square, so let's talk about how we could unravel the question even if we'd never heard of completing the square. (I should also note that the College Board doesn't seem to cover this topic too frequently on the Math Level 2 Test, so the odds of you running into it on test day are probably minimal. This is why I haven't included the idea of completing the square in the Math Toolbox in this Black Book—it's possible to answer this question without knowing that specific technique, and you won't see the technique come up often enough to make learning it worthwhile for this test. If I used this question as an opportunity to teach you the idea of completing the square, then I'd be focusing on a concept that you almost definitely won't see on test day; on the other hand, if I take this as an opportunity to model the process of using the Math Path to answer a question with a strange setup, then I'll be continuing to help you develop skills and instincts you'll definitely need on test day, even if you won't be using them on questions that look like exactly like this one.)

As trained test-takers, we'd notice a few interesting things about the structure of the question. For one thing, the prompt talks about one function representing a shift of another function, but one of the functions only has an x^2 term, while the other has both an x^2 term and an x term. (This is interesting because we know that shifting a graph usually involves adding or subtracting a constant numerical value to affect the domain or the range of the graph, instead of adding an x term, which is what the second function in the prompt seems to be doing at first glance.) Another interesting thing to note is that the answer choices refer to the horizontal shift being either 1 unit or 2 units, which suggests the idea of adding or subtracting 1 or 2 to the x term in $y = x^2$ before squaring it. We should also note that the vertical shifts in the answer choices are described in terms of k units, usually with 1 added to or subtracted from k, which is interesting because we've probably seen a lot of questions in math class that involve a vertical shift of exactly k units being signified by a k term at the end of a function expression.

When we take all of this into consideration, we begin to get a solid idea of what the question wants from us. We see that the function with k represents a shift of the function $y = x^2$ in a way that maintains the shape of the original function—otherwise, the prompt couldn't use the word "shift." So the function with k must still represent the idea of squaring an expression with x, just like $y = x^2$ does. We also see that the number 1 seems likely to be heavily involved in the question, since four of the answer choices include it twice each.

With all of that in mind, we could arrive at the key realization that the function $y = x^2 - 2x + k$ includes the expression $x^2 - 2x$, which looks like the beginning of what we'd get if we used FOIL to expand $(x - 1)^2$, because $(x - 1)^2 = (x - 1)(x - 1) = x^2 - 2x + 1$.

Now we can start to see more clearly why the number 1 appears so many times in the answer choices! We know that the equation $y = (x - 1)^2$ indicates a horizontal shift (or a domain shift) of one unit to the right from the equation $y = x^2$, which is reflected in some of the answer choices, so it looks like we might be on the right track. But what about k?

Well, when we look at the answer choices, we see that a lot of them reflect the idea of adding 1 to k, or subtracting 1 from k. We know that adding a constant number like k by itself to the end of a function expression will result in a vertical shift of k units . . . so why do so many of the answer choices involve a shift that differs from k by one unit? Now that we've realized that expanding $(x - 1)^2$ gives us $x^2 - 2x + 1$, we start to realize what's going on, which is that the k in this expression must be the sum of two quantities: the 1 that resulted from expanding $(x - 1)^2$, and the amount of the vertical shift of the second function. This is why the correct answer involves a shift of $k - 1$ units.

Now that we've pieced together the algebra to recognize that we're shifting the original function one unit to the right and $k - 1$ units up, we see again that (E) is correct.

If this second approach feels a little strange to you, remember that you could still decide to use a graphing calculator to answer the question, as we discussed above. Also remember that you're unlikely to see a question exactly like this one on test day, which is why we approached the question in a more generalized way that will equip you to approach other test questions in the future, rather than following the lead of the College Board's solution in the MSTB, which focuses on the one-off formal solution of completing the square.

Notice that the College Board could have made this question much more difficult from a calculation standpoint by altering a few key details in the prompt, but it decided not to do that—this demonstrates, once again, that the College Board's primary goal in designing the Math Level 2 Test is to challenge our ability to think creatively while dealing with relatively basic concepts, rather than to force us to write out a page full of formal math on the way to finding an answer. Instead of using more complicated functions, the College Board chose to use the basic equation for a parabola; instead of forcing us to write out a FOIL multiplication process, the College Board only required us to square -1, which we can do in our heads. In fact, the College Board even used the variable k to indicate a constant for the change in the range of the function, which might help to remind test-takers of a vertical translation of a function, since k is the variable commonly used in textbooks to represent a constant in that situation.

As I mentioned above, the most important thing to take away from this question isn't the idea of completing the square, because you almost definitely won't see that exact idea come up on test day. The much more important lessons from this question have to do with the idea of reading carefully and noting the key aspects of the way the College Board designed the question, so we can find the answer as easily as possible—which could mean using a calculator, noticing concepts in the answer choices, and so on. These are the skills that will definitely help you on test day, which is why this Black Book focuses on them so intently.

Page 140, Question 48

As we'll often see on the SAT Math Level 2 Test, there are two general ways to approach this question. We can use a strict formulaic approach, which is what the College Board advocates on page 155 of the MSTB, or we can do something a bit faster and easier by thinking about how the answer choices relate to the concepts in the question.

(By the way, don't forget that the College Board provides the formulas for the volumes of several 3-dimensional figures near the beginning of the test booklet. If we flip back to page 121 of the MSTB, we'll see that the formula for the volume of a right circular cone with radius r and height h is $V = \frac{1}{3}\pi r^2 h$, in case you'd forgotten it.)

We won't bother to go through the algebraic approach here, because the College Board's explanation of that is actually pretty thorough. The basic idea is that we modify the original volume expression to reflect that the new height is only 92% of the original height, and that the new volume is only 85% of the original volume, and then we solve for the new radius as a percentage of the original radius. If you'd like to see it, consult page 155 of the MSTB.

But a trained test-taker will recognize that the formulaic approach is probably a bit more complicated than most solutions we use on this test, and she'll invest a few seconds in trying to find an alternative approach. One alternative approach, which we'll talk about now, involves carefully reading the entire question, thinking about the formula for the volume of a cone, and considering how the answer choices relate to all of those concepts.

Let's think about each piece of information that we've been given, one at a time.

First, the height of the right circular cone is decreased by 8%. What impact does decreasing the height (*h*) by 8% have on the volume? Let's look at the formula.

$$V = \frac{1}{3}\pi r^2 h$$

Decreasing something by 8% is the same as multiplying it by 92%, or 0.92. If we were to multiply *h* in the volume formula by 0.92, it would be the same as multiplying the whole expression by 0.92. So when the height of the cone is reduced by 8%, the volume of the cone is also reduced by exactly 8%.

The question tells us that the height of the cone is reduced by 8% *and* the radius of the base is decreased by some amount, and the result is that the volume of the cone is reduced by 15%. Well, we've determined that the reduction in the height, taken by itself, would account for an 8% decrease in the volume. That means that factoring in the reduction in the radius must account for a further 7% reduction in volume, because 15% - 8% = 7%.

Now let's think about how the size of the radius (*r*) fits into the volume formula. We see that the formula involves squaring *r*, which is different from how the formula treated *h*: whatever changes we make to *h* will affect *V* in exactly the same way they affect *h*, but changes to *r* will be squared before they affect *V*.

On top of that, we have to remember that the percentage reduction we apply to the radius will, in turn, be multiplied by the reduced height.

So what would happen if an untrained test-taker accidentally decided to decrease the radius by 7%, thinking that the decrease in the radius must account for a further 7% of the reduction in volume, since the decrease in height already accounts for a decrease of 8%? After all, 7% is one of the answer choices, and it might seem to make sense that a 7% reduction in radius would lead to a further decrease in volume of 7%, for a total decrease of 15%, just as the question asked. But, again, all changes to *r* will be *squared* and then *multiplied* by the change in height before they impact *V*. That means decreasing the radius by 7% will have an impact on the volume that's greater than 7%!

But factoring in the decrease in the radius only needs to result in a further 7% decrease in volume to satisfy the question. More than that would be too much.

In other words, at this point, we've figured out that 7% is too big of a reduction in radius to satisfy the question. The correct answer has to be an amount smaller than 7%.

As it turns out, there's only one answer choice that's less than 7%, and it's choice (A). So we can see that (A) must be correct . . . and we never had to go through all the calculations in the College Board's approach to figure this out. (By the way, (A) is an approximation of the actual amount we'd need to reduce the radius, in case you try to check the math for yourself. The actual amount is closer to 3.9%, but that's also an approximation.) Instead of working through lines of calculation, all we had to do was pay attention to all of the information in the question, including the answer choices, and think about the properties of the volume formula we were given. If we do those things, it's literally possible to answer this question with total certainty without ever even picking up a pencil.

Notice, though, that the approach above is only possible *because the College Board deliberately makes it possible.* If the College Board had given us more than one answer choice lower than 7%, then this approach wouldn't have worked, because it would have been impossible to figure out which of those answer choices was correct without actually doing the calculation. Instead, the question includes one answer choice that's exactly 7%, which almost seems like an invitation to consider whether 7% could be correct; once we realize it's too large, the question only includes one answer choice that's smaller, and must be right.

As I keep repeating, the best way to improve your performance on this test is to continue to build the instincts and awareness that will allow you to identify these kinds of solutions. (Of course, coming up with easier solutions isn't the only benefit you'll experience—you'll also be able to cut down on small mistakes, figure out how to address questions that don't involve formulas, and do all of the other things we've discussed in this Black Book.) It would be silly to respond to this question by drilling yourself on questions that ask about decreasing volume by decreasing components of that volume, because you almost certainly won't see anything like that again on test day. But you WILL see other questions that are constructed to allow trained test-takers to find easier approaches than untrained test-takers will have to use.

Page 140, Question 49

This question asks about matrices in the ways that we might expect a question on this test to do that: it doesn't require us to do any actual calculations, but it discusses two matrices in an abstract way, and then asks whether they can be multiplied together. In other words, it's a question about a basic property of matrices.

We'll look at two different ways to approach this question:

1. If we understand the rules for multiplying matrices, we can read the prompt and the numbered statements and figure out which statements must be true.

2. If we don't remember the rules for multiplying matrices (or we just don't want to use the first approach), we can use our calculators to make up arbitrary matrices and then check which statements are true for those matrices.

First, we'll look at the approach that requires us to remember the rules for multiplying matrices. Let's think through each statement in turn.

Statement I says that the product *BA* doesn't exist. Well, we know that you can multiply two matrices together if the number of *columns* in the first matrix equals the number of *rows* in the second matrix. But Matrix *B* has *p* columns and matrix *A* has *m* rows, and the prompt tells us that *p* and *m* are distinct from each other, so it isn't possible to multiply Matrix *B* by Matrix *A*. That means statement I is true.

Statement II says that product *AB* exists, and has dimensions *m* × *p*. We just discussed the idea that it's possible to multiply two matrices if the number of *columns* in the first matrix equals the number of *rows* in the second matrix. In this case, matrix *A* has *n* columns, and matrix *B* has *n* rows, so it's possible to find the product *AB*. To test the rest of this statement, we need to think about the dimensions of the resulting matrix. When we multiply two matrices, the product matrix has the same number of rows as the first matrix and the same number of columns as the second matrix. In this case, that means the resulting matrix has dimensions *m* × *p*. So statement II is correct.

At this point, we've seen that statements I and II are correct, and the only answer choice that says Statements I and II are correct is choice (D), so we're pretty confident (D) is correct. But, as trained test-takers, we know that we should consider all of our options, in order to give ourselves the best possible chance of catching any small mistakes we might have made earlier. So let's take a look at statement III.

Statement III says the product AB exists, which we know is true from our discussion of statement II. But statement III also says the dimensions of product AB are $n \times n$. We know from our discussion of statement II that the dimensions of product AB are $m \times p$, and we know from the prompt that m, n, and p all refer to different numbers. So we can see that statement III must be false.

After reviewing all three statements, we can be confident that choice (D) is correct. (Of course, if you were unclear on any of the concepts we just discussed, be sure to review Matrices in the Math Toolbox in this Black Book.)

But what if we don't remember the rules for multiplying matrices? After all, a lot of math teachers pay very little attention to matrices in their classes.

Fortunately, there's another way that we could approach this question if we need to, but it won't be as fast as relying on a knowledge of the basic attributes of matrices. If our graphing calculator can do matrix multiplication, then we can make up our own sample matrices that satisfy the requirements given in the question, and then we can see what conditions allow the matrices to be multiplied, because the calculator should give us an error message if we try to multiply matrices that can't be multiplied. We'll walk through that approach now.

The prompt says matrix A has dimensions $m \times n$, and matrix B has dimensions $n \times p$. Then we're told that m, n, and p are distinct positive integers. So let's make up values for m, n, and p. As trained test-takers, we know not to use 1 when we choose a random value to test an idea, because 1 has special properties that might cause problems in our solution. So let's pick the following values:

- $m = 2$
- $n = 3$
- $p = 4$

When we plug those numbers into the dimensions from the prompt, matrix A is a 2×3 matrix, and matrix B has dimensions 3×4.

At this stage, I would use my calculator to create two matrices with randomly chosen numbers in them. One matrix will be a 2×3 matrix, and will represent matrix A from the prompt. The other matrix will be a 3×4 matrix to represent matrix B. I'll use these stored matrices to test the statements in the question. (The numbers that go into the matrices don't really matter, because the point is just to see whether matrices of different sizes can be multiplied, and we don't really care what numbers are in their products—we only care what the dimensions of those products might be. Still, I would avoid picking numbers like 0 and 1, because we're proceeding under the assumption that we don't know much about matrices, and there's no point in risking the possibility that those numbers might have strange properties that could throw off our results.)

Statement I says that the product BA doesn't exist. Well, we could test this by telling the calculator to multiply the 3×4 matrix by the 2×3 matrix. If we try that, the calculator will tell us we can't do it, which means the product of the two matrices doesn't exist, so statement I is true.

Statement II says that product AB exists, and has dimensions $m \times p$. So we'd test this statement by telling the calculator to multiply the stored 2×3 matrix by the stored 3×4 matrix. The calculator shows us that the product of the two matrices does exist, and is a matrix with dimensions of 2×4. Since 2 is the value we picked for m, and 4 is the value we picked for p, we know the product AB has dimensions of $m \times p$. So statement II is true.

Finally, statement III says the product AB exists, which we just saw was true in our discussion of statement II. Statement III also says the dimensions of product AB are $n \times n$, but the dimensions of product AB were 2 × 4 when we just tested them, which was equal to $m \times p$. So the product AB has dimensions $m \times p$, which means statement III is false.

So we see again that choice (D) is correct.

A big lesson to learn from this question is that it's often possible to use a calculator to work around a gap in your knowledge if you're willing to be a little flexible. Keep this in mind on test day! You probably won't see a question on the dimensions of a product matrix on test day, but you'll definitely see other questions that might be constructed in ways that allow work-arounds like this one.

Page 141, Question 50

In my experience, this question is pretty challenging for most test-takers, because they haven't seen a graph of complex numbers before—even if they know what complex numbers are, and how to graph other kinds of values. And some test-takers aren't sure what a complex number is in the first place. For the sake of this discussion, we'll assume that we know that i is the square root of -1, but that we don't know what a complex number is, or how to graph one. (If you already do know how to graph a complex number, then a lot of this explanation will be pretty straightforward for you. I still recommend that you read it, because it demonstrates the kind of thought process we should follow when the test confronts us with something we're not used to. I also want to remind you that the idea of graphing complex numbers is unlikely to appear on any given test day, so the most important thing to take away from this explanation is the general approach, and not the specific mathematical rules for graphing complex numbers).

As trained test-takers, our first instinct should always be to stay calm, read carefully, and think about all the information in the question, without worrying if we feel like we can't solve the question right away.

When we look at the figure, we can see that there are two axes—but, if we pay attention, we realize that they aren't the normal axes we see in a graph. The horizontal axis has a location labeled with a 1. But if we look at the y-axis, we see it has a location labeled with the lower-case letter i, not the number 1.

So it looks like values on the x-axis are labeled in terms of real numbers, while values on the y-axis are labeled in terms of imaginary numbers—numbers with i in them, such as i, $2i$, and so on.

That probably seems abnormal to us. Let's keep thinking about the question and see if it's relevant to anything important.

When we take another look at the question prompt, we might notice that the question refers to w as a "complex number." We can see that w is in the upper left quadrant of the graph. Well, in order for a number to be graphed on a coordinate plane, it must have two elements. On the coordinate planes we're used to seeing, those two elements would be an x-coordinate and a y-coordinate, and both would be real numbers. But in this case, the x-axis seems to measure real numbers, and the y-axis seems to measure numbers involving i. So w would have two attributes associated with it: a real value corresponding to its coordinate on the x-axis, and an imaginary value indicated by its coordinate on the y-axis. This is starting to feel like it's making a little more sense.

At this point, we've figured out that *w* is a number with two elements: one real, and one that involves *i*. We also know that *w* can be plotted on the graph we were given, and that the *x*-axis gives us information about real numbers, while the *y*-axis gives us information about numbers involving *i*.

The question asks us which points could be *-iw*. In other words, we're asked which point on the graph corresponds to the result when *−i* is multiplied by *w*.

To answer that, we need to think of what we know about *w*. It's on the left side of the *y*-axis, so the real number component must be negative. It's also above the *x*-axis, so its component involving *i* must be positive.

So let's think about what would happen if we multiplied each component of *w* by *-i*. First we'll consider the real number component. The real number component is negative. So if we multiplied a negative real number by *-i*, the result would be a positive number involving *i*. For example, if we multiplied -3 by *-i*, we'd get 3*i*. So when we multiply the real number component of *w* by *-i*, we get a positive number involving *i*.

What about the component of *w* that involves *i*? Let's think about this: we know that *i* times *i* is -1. Well, *i* times *-i* is like multiplying *i* times *i* times -1, which is the same as -1 times -1, or 1. So multiplying a positive number involving *i* by *-i* would give us positive real number.

(If that doesn't make sense right away, go back and read it through one more time.)

Now we've figured out that multiplying *w* by *-i* would give us a positive number involving *i*, and a positive real number. If we look at the points on the graph in the figure, we'll notice that only point *A* is in the top right quadrant, so *A* is the only point with two positive components. That means choice (A) is correct.

Remember that the previous solution assumes that we don't know what a complex number is, or how to graph one. It may help you to grasp this concept better if you read through the following explanation as well—this explanation assumes an understanding of complex numbers.

A complex number involves two terms added together, where one term is a real number and the other term is a real number times *i* (the square root of negative 1). Since *w* is a complex number, we know it must involve a real number added to a real number times *i*.

Let's look at the graph of *w*. When we graph a complex number, the *x*-axis shows the value of the real term, and the *y*-axis shows the value of the term involving *i*. We can see this in this figure, since the *x*-axis has a label that says "1" and the *y*-axis has a label that says "*i*."

In this case, *w* has a negative *x*-value and a positive *y*-value. That means *w* can be expressed by *-a + bi*, where *-a* represents the real term and *bi* represents a real term times *i*.

(Again, we know this because the position of *w* on the graph tells us that the real term is negative and the term involving *i* is positive.)

The question asks us which point could represent *-iw*. So what happens if we multiply *-a + bi* by *-i*?

$-i(-a + bi)$	(write the expression for multiplying *-i* and *-a + bi*)
$ai - bi^2$	(distribute *-i*)
$ai - b(-1)$	(square *i*)

$ai + b$ (combine like terms)

The result is $ai + b$. Which point could represent $ai + b$? Well, both components of the complex number are positive, so the graph of this point would need to be in the top right quadrant. That means only point (A) could represent $-iw$. So again, choice (A) is correct.

(If anything we discussed in this walkthrough was unfamiliar to you, be sure to review Imaginary Numbers in the Math Toolbox.)

Walkthroughs Of Questions From Practice Test 2 Of The MSTB

Page 160, Question 1

This question might seem pretty straightforward at first. We're asked for the value of an expression involving x, and we're given an equation involving x, so one approach to the question might be to use algebra to find x, and then plug it into the expression $1 - \frac{1}{x}$. Let's do that now:

$1 - \frac{1}{x} = 3 - \frac{3}{x}$ (original expression)

$x - 1 = 3x - 3$ (multiply both sides by x)

$x + 2 = 3x$ (add 3 to both sides)

$2 = 2x$ (subtract x from both sides)

$1 = x$ (divide both sides by 2)

Now we know that x is equal to 1 . . . but the question didn't ask for the value of x. Instead, it asked for the value of the expression $1 - \frac{1}{x}$. To find that value, we have to plug in 1 for x, since we just determined that 1 is the value of x. That gives us $1 - \frac{1}{1}$, or 1 - 1, or 0. So the correct answer is (B).

The College Board's explanation of this question (on page 182 of the MSTB) takes a different algebraic approach, although that approach arguably isn't explained very well. Here's a step-by-step version of the College Board's solution:

$1 - \frac{1}{x} = 3 - \frac{3}{x}$ (original expression)

$1 + \frac{2}{x} = 3$ (add $\frac{3}{x}$ to both sides)

$\frac{2}{x} = 2$ (subtract 1 from both sides)

$2 = 2x$ (multiply both sides by x)

$1 = x$ (divide both sides by 2)

As before, once we know that $x = 1$, we plug that value into $1 - \frac{1}{x}$, which gives us $1 - \frac{1}{1}$, or 1 - 1, or 0. Again, the correct answer is (B).

If we look at the chart on page 178 of the MSTB, we see that this question was correctly answered by 79% of test-takers when the test was originally given, which means that the question was apparently relatively easy for that set of test-takers. Some people might think that the question was apparently easier because it's a relatively simple algebra question, but I think there's another factor involved, too.

Notice that the answer choices for this question don't really contain likely mistakes to the same extent they usually do on College Board math questions. For example, we might have expected one of the wrong answers to be the value of x itself, to trap test-takers who didn't read the question carefully.

So on this question, test-takers who make careless errors (like finding x instead of $1 - \frac{1}{x}$) are much less likely to find a wrong answer that matches their mistake than they normally would be on other questions. This means those test-takers would be more likely to realize their mistakes and eventually answer the question correctly.

Let this be an important reminder of the way that the set of answer choices can influence the overall process of answering a question! As we see repeatedly in this Black Book, trained test-takers always need to consider the answer choices as part of their approach to a given question.

Page 160, Question 2

As often happens on the Math Level 2 Test, there are a variety of ways we could choose to approach this question. I'll start out by discussing the approach your math teacher would probably endorse, which is similar to what the College Board recommends on page 182 of the MSTB. After that, I'll discuss how we might approach the question in a way that avoids algebra and relies more on backsolving with a calculator. Let's get started.

Our first impulse after reading this question is probably just to distribute the a to both $\frac{1}{b}$ and $\frac{1}{c}$, which would give us $\frac{a}{b} + \frac{a}{c}$. Unfortunately, the expression $\frac{a}{b} + \frac{a}{c}$ isn't one of the answer choices. If we think about what the answer choices have in common with each other that distinguishes them from $\frac{a}{b} + \frac{a}{c}$, we see that all the answer choices have only *one* fraction, with *one* denominator. This means that we *must* figure out some kind of way to turn the expression $\frac{a}{b} + \frac{a}{c}$ into a term with only one denominator. (This is one more example of why we always need to be aware of what's going on in the answer choices!)

Since our $\frac{a}{b} + \frac{a}{c}$ expression involves addition, one obvious way that we might think of to combine that into one fraction would be to add $\frac{a}{b}$ and $\frac{a}{c}$.

Now, how do we add two fractions with different denominators? First, we have to find the common denominator of the two fractions, and then we express both fractions in terms of that denominator. Then we add the numerators and write them over the common denominator.

We know that our common denominator will be the product of the factors of the original denominators. Since the original denominators are just two different variables, we'll simply multiply them by each other in order to find the common denominator. That means our common denominator is bc.

Now we need to express both of the given fractions with bc as the denominator. We'll start with $\frac{a}{b}$. To express $\frac{a}{b}$ with bc as the denominator, we'll need to multiply both the numerator and denominator by c (remember that we can't change the actual value of $\frac{a}{b}$ when we convert it, so we have to multiply by $\frac{c}{c}$, which is the same thing as multiplying by 1). Multiplying $\frac{a}{b}$ by $\frac{c}{c}$ gives us $\frac{ac}{bc}$ as the result.

Now let's convert $\frac{a}{c}$. In this case, we'll need to multiply by $\frac{b}{b}$ in order to arrive at a result with a denominator of bc. (Remember that multiplying by $\frac{b}{b}$ is the same as multiplying by one, because $\frac{b}{b}$ is equal to one. We aren't changing the value of the fraction—we're just changing the way the fraction is expressed.) When we multiply $\frac{a}{c}$ by $\frac{b}{b}$, we get $\frac{ab}{bc}$.

Now that both fractions have the same denominator, we can add them together: our new numerator will be the sum of the two numerators, and our denominator will be the common denominator from those converted fractions. The result is $\frac{ab+ac}{bc}$, which matches what (D) says. So (D) is correct.

The incorrect answer choices represent the various mistakes a test-taker could make if he didn't remember the proper way to find a common denominator and add the resulting fractions. For example, if we incorrectly thought that $\frac{1}{b} + \frac{1}{c}$ was equal to $\frac{1}{b+c}$, then we'd choose (B) ; if we incorrectly thought that $\frac{1}{b} + \frac{1}{c}$ was equal to $\frac{2}{b+c}$, then we'd choose choice (C).

Now let's talk about a way to use backsolving on this question—an approach that would rely more on a calculator than on remembering the algebraic rules for adding fractions with variable expressions. For this approach, we'd assign unique, arbitrary values to a, b, and c, and then use a calculator to evaluate the expressions in the prompt and in the answer choices; the correct answer will be the one that results in the same numerical value as the prompt, showing that the two expressions are equivalent.

When we take this kind of backsolving approach, we want to make sure we choose arbitrary values for the variables that aren't likely to have unique properties relative to the question, because we want to avoid a situation where more than one answer choice coincidentally arrives at the same numerical value. That generally means we avoid using -1, 0, 1, or numbers that appear in the question. So I'll pick the following values:

- $a = 3$

- $b = 5$

- $c = 7$

Now we plug in our arbitrary values and use our calculator to evaluate all the expressions in the question, and note the results so we can compare them. (Of course, when we do this, it's absolutely critical that we key things into the calculator accurately! A mistake here could easily cost us the question.)

Prompt: $a(\frac{1}{b} + \frac{1}{c}) = 3(\frac{1}{5} + \frac{1}{7}) = 1.0285714286$

Choice (A): $\frac{a}{bc} = \frac{3}{5(7)} = 0.0857142857$

Choice (B): $\frac{a}{b+c} = \frac{3}{5+7} = 0.25$

Choice (C): $\frac{2a}{b+c} = \frac{2(3)}{5+7} = 0.5$

Choice (D): $\frac{ab+ac}{bc} = \frac{3(5)+3(7)}{5(7)} = 1.0285714286$

Choice (E): $\frac{1}{ab+ac} = \frac{1}{3(5)+3(7)} = 0.2777777778$

After this analysis, we can see that choice (D) has the same numerical value as the prompt does once we plug in our values. This shows us that the expression in (D) is equivalent to the expression in the prompt, so we see again that (D) is the right answer.

I'm not suggesting that this calculator-based approach is the best one for this question; instead, I wanted to show you how a calculator could be used here because I want you to keep the tactic in mind for future questions. It's often easier to understand these kinds of things when you see them demonstrated on easier questions.

Page 161, Question 3

This question is really just testing some relatively basic knowledge about the graph of $y = \sin x$. The College Board's explanation on page 182 of the MSTB is pretty decent, but I'd like to discuss a few approaches to the question that are slightly different, because they don't require us to have memorized so much about the graph of $\sin x$. There's nothing wrong with the College Board's approach, of course, but I want to show that it's still possible to answer this question by combining very basic trig knowledge with the information provided in the question. I'm taking the time to do this because you'll probably find that these kinds of alternative approaches are also helpful on more complicated questions, and sometimes it's easier to learn how to do them on relatively simple questions. So let's get started.

We're told that that the minimum value of the graph occurs at point P, and we're asked for the coordinates of that point. Well, the question tells us that Figure 1 shows "one cycle of the graph of the function $y = \sin x$." We should know that the possible values of $\sin x$ range from -1 to 1; if the Figure shows one full cycle of the graph, then it must show the y-values from -1 to 1.

That means P, the minimum value of the cycle, must have a y-coordinate of -1.

Only choices (B) and (D) have y-values of -1, so (A), (C), and (E) all look like wrong answers at this point.

Now we need to figure out the x-coordinate of point P.

We should probably already know that the period of the sine function is 2π. But if we didn't know that, or if we'd forgotten it, we could still figure it out from the prompt, which tells us that "one cycle" of the graph goes from 0 to 2π on the x-axis. We see that point P occurs halfway through the *second half* of the graph; in other words, P occurs $\frac{3}{4}$ of the way through the cycle in the graph. We know the cycle takes up 2π units on the x-axis, so P must have an x-coordinate equal to three-fourths of 2π, which is $\frac{3}{4} \times 2\pi$, or $\frac{6\pi}{4}$, or $\frac{3\pi}{2}$.

So the x-coordinate for point P is $\frac{3\pi}{2}$, and the y-coordinate is -1, which means the correct answer is choice (D).

But there's a very different approach to the question that relies less on previous trig knowledge. For this approach, we really just have to know how to use our calculators to do three things:

1.   Find decimal approximations of $\frac{4\pi}{3}$ and $\frac{3\pi}{2}$.

2.   Graph $\sin x$

3.   Use the "trace" feature to find the coordinates for a point on our graph that corresponds to P in Figure 1.

For step 1, we can find the decimal approximation of $\frac{4\pi}{3}$ by entering the following expression into a calculator:

$(4\pi)/3$

The calculator will tell us the value of that expression is approximately 4.1887902048, so we know that $\frac{4\pi}{3}$ is approximately 4.19.

Similarly, we can find the decimal approximation of $\frac{3\pi}{2}$ by using a calculator to evaluate the expression $(3\pi)/2$, which shows us that $\frac{3\pi}{2}$ is approximately 4.71.

Now, let's graph the function $y = \sin x$ and use the trace feature of the calculator to find the coordinates of a point as close as possible to where point P appears in Figure 1. When we do that, our calculator screen will look something like this:

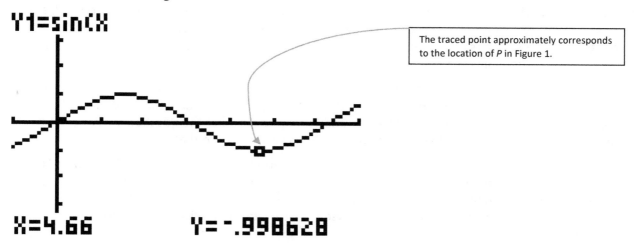

The traced point approximately corresponds to the location of P in Figure 1.

So the calculator shows us that the coordinates of point P are approximately (4.66, -0.999). Don't worry that your values will be slightly different when you trace the sine curve on your own calculator! You'll naturally end up selecting a point that's not *precisely* the same as the point I selected above. The important thing is that you trace as closely as possible to the point on your calculator that corresponds to P in Figure 1. When you do this, you'll see that the coordinates of the point you've traced are very close to (4.7, -1).

So the x-coordinate of the point we've traced on the curve of sin x is very close to 4.71, which is the decimal approximation we found for $\frac{3\pi}{2}$. We also see that the y-coordinate of the point we've traced is very close to -1. Given the answer choices in the question, this means that the precise coordinates of point P from Figure 1 must be the ones found in choice (D), so (D) is correct.

As I mentioned above, I went through this calculator-based approach to the question because I wanted to show you that the College Board often makes it possible to attack a question in ways that have little to do with the apparent subject matter of the question—in this case, it's possible to use a calculator to find the correct answer without really knowing much about the sine function. I'm not suggesting that this calculator-based approach is the best way for every test-taker to handle this question. I just wanted to show you how this kind of thing could work on a relatively simple test item, so you can start looking for opportunities to employ a similar approach on questions that might seem more challenging in the future.

Finally, notice that the answer choices look like they might be following the "wrong answers imitate right answers" pattern. We see that $\frac{3\pi}{2}$ is the most common x-value in the answer choices, and that the most common y-value is a tie between -π and -1. To a trained test-taker, this would suggest that either (C) or (D) is likely to be the correct answer, which should tend to reassure us that we've probably thought about the question correctly. And if we know that the possible values of sine range from -1 to 1, we know that y can't equal -π, so choices (A) and (C) can't be right.

Page 161, Question 4

This question really unsettles a lot of untrained test-takers, because it's a classic example of several of the ways the College Board likes to confuse people who expect this test to be similar to a high school math test. For one thing, the question relies heavily on reading comprehension—there's not a number or a diagram anywhere in it. For another thing, the question occurs pretty early in the test overall, so most test-takers expect it to be easy before they read it. Finally, all of the concepts in the question are things that most test-takers understand, but the question combines these basic concepts in ways that no test-taker has probably ever seen before.

But as trained test-takers, none of these things should surprise us. We know that the College Board likes to ask unusual questions that rely on an understanding of the properties and definitions of abstract concepts, and we know that if we read carefully and think through what the question is asking, we'll probably be able to figure out what's going on. So let's stay calm, and do that.

We see that the question mentions "points" and a "plane," and the answer choices include terms like "one side of a line," "interior of a square," and "interior of a circle." So it sounds like we're dealing with 2-dimensional geometry, because all of these terms are related to that. In fact, it might be helpful to try to sketch out what the question is describing, to see if we can start to realize anything about the question that way.

We can draw points P and Q on our paper to create the situation described in the question:

The question asks about "the set of all points in this plane that are closer to P than to Q." But we've probably never heard of any specific formula or theorem related to identifying points that are closer to one point than another, because this isn't really a common concept to encounter in high school math. So, since I can't think of anything else to try, I'll just add in some points that are closer to P than they are to Q, and see what happens:

The points I just added are basically on the line segment from P to Q, just because that's where it occurred to me put them. But if I think about it, there are also a lot of points above and below P and Q that are also closer to P than to Q. I'll add some of those in, too:

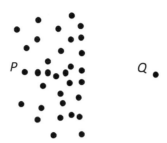

At this point, we can start to see that all the points that are closer to P than to Q, taken together, actually do make up a region on one side of a line. In my diagram, the line would be a vertical line between points P and Q, and every point on the vertical line would be equidistant from both P and Q; all the points to the left of this line, in my diagram, would have to be closer to P than to Q. I'll indicate part of this line in my diagram with a dashed line segment:

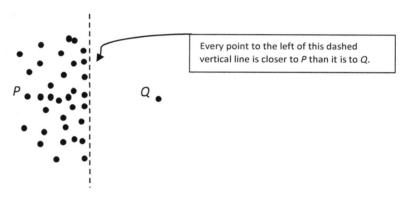

Every point to the left of this dashed vertical line is closer to P than it is to Q.

So we can actually see now that choice (A) is correct.

This is a great example of the way we sometimes have to be willing to just try things when we attack a strange question. If we're aware of the properties and definitions of the concepts in the question, and we keep looking for ways to combine them that are relevant to the set of answer choices, we'll eventually hit on the solution. The important thing is not to get frustrated by a question just because it's asking you to do something you've never actually done before.

In fact, that's the most important thing to remember about this question, in my opinion. There's probably no need to remember the idea that a straight line is the boundary of the region of a plane that contains points closer to one point than to another, because it's very unlikely that you'll ever use that particular concept again on this test (or for anything else, really). Instead, the important thing to take away is that you'll definitely encounter other strange questions on test day, but you can figure out how to solve them if you pay careful attention and remember your training.

Page 161, Question 5

This question involves relatively simple algebra, but it's still going to be very important for us to work carefully and pay attention. As trained test-takers, we always have to remember that every question ultimately has the same impact on our final score, which means that it's very important not to waste relatively easy questions like this one. So, after reading the question and taking a look at the answer choices, let's walk through the algebra quickly but carefully:

$$\sqrt{6y} = 4.73 \qquad \text{(original expression)}$$

$$6y = 22.3729 \qquad \text{(square both sides)}$$

$$y \approx 3.73 \qquad \text{(divide both sides by 6)}$$

So the correct answer is choice (C).

Another way to solve this question would be to plug in each answer choice for y and see which one made the statement true. The algebra in this question is pretty straightforward, though, so it's probably easiest for most test-takers just to use algebra.

We'll need to use a calculator no matter how we choose to approach this question. Remember to be especially careful when doing that—we don't want to give away points because of a careless calculator error! For example, if you accidentally divide by 6 twice at the end (by pressing the ENTER button twice, for example), you'll end up with choice (A), which is the correct answer divided by 6.

Page 162, Question 6

One of the first things a trained test-taker should notice in this question is that the answer choices are all variables. This means we'll have to come up with a variable expression as our answer, rather than an actual number. A lot of untrained test-takers will just read the prompt, look at the figure, and then start trying to use trigonometry to come up with a numerical answer somehow, because they're used to having to find numerical values for the cosine of a given angle in math class. But finding a numerical answer isn't possible here, because the question doesn't include any numbers in the first place. Many test-takers will get very frustrated if they don't pay attention to how the question is actually constructed. This is one example of why we always have to remember to read the answer choices before we start trying to solve a Math Level 2 question!

Since the question involves the cosine of θ, we need to think about the concept of cosine, and how it might be relevant in this question. One definition of cosine is that it's the x-coordinate of the point where a given angle intersects with the unit circle in the xy-coordinate plane, but that doesn't really seem relevant here, since there's no indication we're dealing with the unit circle in this case—nothing is being measured in radians, and we don't know if line segment OP is one unit long. But another definition of cosine is found in the mnemonic device "SOHCAHTOA," which tells us that **C**osine = **A**djacent/**H**ypotenuse. That could be relevant here, because we do have labeled sides for the given triangle, and we can see that the variables in the answer choices also appear on the labels of the sides. So let's pursue that and see where it gets us.

If **C**osine = **A**djacent/**H**ypotenuse, then that means cos θ in Figure 2 is equal to $\frac{x}{r}$, since x is the length of the side adjacent to θ, and r is the length of the hypotenuse.

But the question didn't ask us to find cos θ. It asked us to find r cos θ. So we can take our expression for cos θ, which is $\frac{x}{r}$, and then multiply it by r. That would give us the expression $r\left(\frac{x}{r}\right)$, which is the same thing as x. So the correct answer is (A).

Notice that we might have chosen (B) if we confused sine and cosine, which would be easy to do if we're not paying strict attention to this question. We always have to remember that the College Board likes to punish us for careless errors by including choices like this, so it's very important to keep track of small details on the test.

Page 162, Question 7

The College Board's explanation for this question (on page 183 of the MSTB) is pretty good in terms of finding the answer itself, but, as usual, the explanation leaves out a lot of things that I want you to understand for future questions. I'll walk through the basics of that explanation first, and then review a couple of important things that I want to make sure we remember on these kinds of questions, as trained test-takers.

This question tests our understanding of function notation, and what it means when we talk about $f(x)$ and $g(x)$. We've been given one equation for $f(x)$ and one for $g(x)$, and we're asked for the value of $g(f(10))$.

As trained test-takers, we know that we evaluate an expression like $g(f(10))$ by working from the inside out, so the first thing we'll need to do is determine the value of $f(10)$. Once we know the value of $f(10)$, we'll know what to plug in to the g function to find $g(f(10))$.

So first, we find $f(10)$:

$f(x) = \sqrt{(0.3x^2 - x)}$	(given definition of $f(x)$)
$f(10) = \sqrt{(0.3(10)^2 - 10)}$	(plug in 10 for x)
$f(10) = \sqrt{(0.3(100) - 10)}$	(square 10)
$f(10) = \sqrt{(30 - 10)}$	(multiply .3 and 100)
$f(10) = \sqrt{(20)}$	(subtract 10 from 30)

Since the answer choices involve decimal expressions and not radicals, we'll have to use a calculator to approximate the value of $\sqrt{(20)}$, which is roughly 4.47.

Now we know $f(10)$ is approximately 4.47 . . . but that doesn't make (D) the correct answer, even though 4.47 rounds off to 4.5! Remember that the question didn't ask for $f(10)$. Instead, it asked for $g(f(10))$, so we need to take the value we just determined for $f(10)$, and plug it into the $g(x)$ function:

$g(x) = \frac{x+1}{x-1}$	(given definition of $g(x)$)
$g(4.47) = \frac{4.47+1}{4.47-1}$	(plug in 4.47 for x)
$g(4.47) = \frac{5.47}{3.47}$	(combine like terms)
$g(4.47) \approx 1.6$	(divide and round off)

So the correct answer is (C), 1.6.

As trained test-takers, we shouldn't be surprised to realize that some of the wrong answers are designed to anticipate small mistakes in reading or calculation. For example, we might notice that choice (B) is equal to $g(10)$, instead of $g(f(10))$. We can imagine that some test-takers might misread the question, find $g(10)$ by accident, notice choice (B), and then choose it without realizing that the question is actually asking for something else. And we've already seen that (D) corresponds to $f(10)$.

As we can see, if we want to maximize our performance on this test, we have to stay constantly on guard against the kinds of small mistakes that can lead to wrong answers like (A) and (D). Remember that every question on the test has the same impact on your final score—correctly answering a question like this is just as important as correctly answering a question that might seem more difficult. That's why it's such a shame to see untrained test-takers throw away points by not paying careful enough attention to every single question. Keep that in mind on test day.

Page 162, Question 8

Like a lot of Math Level 2 questions, this one is really just testing our understanding of a mathematical definition or property in an unusual way. We're asked to find the value of n in this equation:

$$n^4p^7t^9 = (4n^3p^7)/t^{-9}$$

If we're familiar with negative exponents, we know that t^{-9} is the same thing as $1/(t^9)$. By similar logic, $1/(t^{-9})$ is the same thing as t^9.

That means the original expression of $(4n^3p^7)/t^{-9}$ on the right-hand side of the equals sign is actually the same as $(4n^3p^7)(t^9)$, which is ultimately the same thing as $4n^3p^7t^9$. So now we have this equation:

$$n^4p^7t^9 = 4n^3p^7t^9$$

We can divide both sides by p^7t^9 and get the following:

$$n^4 = 4n^3$$

From there, we can divide both sides by n^3 and arrive at this:

$$n = 4$$

(Of course, you can also combine two of the steps above by realizing that both sides of the equation can be divided by $n^3p^7t^9$, but I broke this down into two steps because I've seen that a lot of students realize that p^7t^9 appears in both expressions before they realize that both sides can also be divided by n^3.)

So the correct answer is (C).

If we look at the answer choices, we see the kinds of patterns and relationships that we might expect, as trained test-takers. For one thing, we see that (A) is the inverse of the answer we think is correct; it makes sense that the College Board might try to fool us in this way, because the question involves negative exponents. We might also realize that this question seems to follow the "wrong answers imitate right answers" pattern:

- four of the five answer choices include the numeral 4

- three of the five answer choices are non-fractions

- three of the five answer choices have no variables in them

Given those attributes, the "wrong answers imitate right answers" pattern would suggest that the correct answer choice would include the numeral 4 while avoiding fractions and variables. Only choice (C) meets those requirements. As always, we have to keep in mind that we shouldn't choose (C) just because it fits the "wrong answers imitate right answers" pattern—instead, seeing that (C) fits this pattern should help reassure us that we probably thought about the question correctly when we used basic algebra to determine that (C) was correct in the first place. As trained test-takers, we know that it's important to give ourselves as many opportunities as possible to realize any small mistakes we might have made, and an awareness of the College Board's answer choice patterns can help us with that.

Page 162, Question 9

Since this question asks us about the slope of segment *AB*, let's start by thinking about what we know about the concept of slope. The slope between any two points is the vertical distance between the two points divided by the horizontal distance between the two points—this is also called the "rise" over the "run." So in order to find the slope between any two points, we need to know both the horizontal and vertical separation between those two points, because the slope is the ratio of those two distances.

But in this question, we don't actually know the location of point *A*—all we know is that *A* is midway between *O* and *B*, because we know that *OA* is the same length as *OB*. But *OA* and *OB* could each be any length, as long as they're the same length as one another. We don't know if they're both 10 units long, or 3 units long, or 100,000 units long, because the question doesn't tell us.

For example, without violating the conditions in the question, we could make triangle *OAB* look something like this:

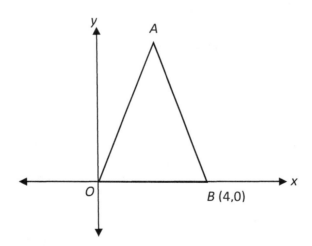

Or it could look something like this:

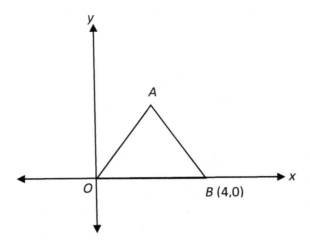

In each of those two examples, we've followed all the constraints of the question—the lengths of sides *OA* and *AB* are still equal to each other, and the base is still 4. But the slope of *AB* is different in each diagram.

The fact that we can theoretically change the slope of *AB* while keeping all the information in the problem constant means that we don't have enough information in the question to determine the slope. So (E) is correct.

As trained test-takers, we might notice that the other answer choices seem focused on the idea of $\sqrt{2}$. When we see $\sqrt{2}$ in a question about triangles, we might be tempted to think of isosceles right triangles, because they have sides in the ratio $1:1:\sqrt{2}$. That might seem even more relevant when we realize that this question is talking about an isosceles triangle as well, since *OA* and *AB* are the same length. But we have to realize that the triangle in this question isn't a right triangle—and even if we subdivided it into right triangles, there's no reason to think that we could know anything about the lengths of those triangles' hypotenuses, since point *A* could still be at any height from the *x*-axis as far as we know.

Page 163, Question 10

At first glance, a lot of untrained test-takers will expect this question to be related to the kind of trig formulas that math teachers often make us memorize for school. But we always have to remember that the College Board likes to play games with our expectations. It's important to read carefully and avoid leaping to conclusions about what a question wants us to do.

It turns out that answering this question only requires us to think carefully and to know the definition of cosecant. If we know that $\csc x$ is equal to $\frac{1}{\sin x}$ by definition, then we can tell that $\csc(2\theta)\sin(2\theta)$ is exactly the same thing as $(\frac{1}{\sin(2\theta)})(\sin(2\theta))$, or $\frac{\sin(2\theta)}{\sin(2\theta)}$, or 1. So the correct answer is choice (A).

If you don't feel like answering the question in this way, another approach would be to choose a random value for θ, plug it into the expressions from the prompt and the two answer choices with variables, and then evaluate those expressions with your calculator so you can compare the values from the answer choices to the value of the prompt.

For example, if we decide to see what happens when θ is 30°, then we could enter the following into our calculator to evaluate the expression in the prompt:

csc(2(30°)) sin(2(30°))

If we do that, we see again that the result is 1, which matches choice (A). But we'd also need to evaluate (D) and (E) with our value for θ, to see if we've chosen a θ value that coincidentally generates a false positive for choice (A). When we evaluate (D) where θ = 30°, we get this:

2csc(4θ)	(original expression from choice (D))
2csc(4(30°))	(plug in θ = 30°)
2csc120°	(multiply 4 by 30°)
2.31	(use a calculator to evaluate 2csc120°)

Since 2.31 doesn't match the value that we got when we plugged 30 into the expression from the prompt as θ, we know that (D) is wrong.

And when we evaluate (E) where θ = 30°, we get this:

2sec(4θ)	(original expression from choice (E))
2sec(4(30°))	(plug in θ = 30°)
2sec120°	(multiply 4 by 30°)
-4	(use a calculator to evaluate 2sec120°)

-4 doesn't match the value we found for the expression in the prompt when θ = 30°, so (E) is wrong, too.

This analysis allows us to see once more that (A) is correct.

Notice that there's a series in the answer choices here: choices (A), (B), and (C) are -1, 0, and 1. As trained test-takers, we know that when the set of answer choices contains a series, it's more likely that the correct answer will be part of that series, because that's something the College Board often likes to do for some reason. It's also more likely that the correct answer won't be the first or last number in that series; in this case, however, the correct answer is the last number in the series, 1. This is a good example of how an awareness of answer choice patterns can help us evaluate a question from multiple perspectives, but should never serve as the sole basis for choosing or avoiding a particular answer.

There's another answer choice pattern in this question, too. When a number and its opposite are in the answer choices, it's generally more likely that one of the numbers in the pair of opposites will be the correct answer. In this case, both -1 and 1 are in the answer choices, which a trained test-taker should recognize as a common type of answer choice pattern on this test.

This question is a great example of the way that Math Level 2 questions often reward us for having a solid understanding of properties and definitions. In this case, knowing the definition of cosecant allows us to answer the question quickly and confidently, possibly without even picking up a pencil. This kind of relatively quick, simple solution allows us to save time that we can invest in other questions that we might find more challenging.

Page 163, Question 11
The College Board's explanation for this question appears on page 183 of the MSTB. That explanation is technically correct, of course, but it's probably not very easy for the average reader to understand, unless that reader already knows how to answer the question in the first place, in which case the explanation would be unnecessary. So I'd like to explain the question in a slightly different way, and then discuss some of the issues that are likely to confuse some test-takers, and what we can learn from them.

Many untrained test-takers will spend unnecessary time trying to figure out what kind of function actually appears in Figure 4, because their math classes over the years have trained them to expect that a question with a function graph will require them to figure out something about the function itself. These untrained test-takers might even get a little nervous when they realize that Figure 4 doesn't include any numerical labeling, which might be useful information if we had to figure out something specific about the function. But if we think carefully, we realize that the question never actually asks us to identify or explain anything about $f(x)$ itself, which means we don't have to spend any time trying to figure out what kind of function it might be. Instead, the question is just telling us that there's some kind of function called $f(x)$, that it looks like the thing in Figure 4, and that it's our job to imagine how the diagram would change if we were only talking about the absolute value of $f(x)$, instead of $f(x)$ itself.

As trained test-takers, we should be pretty comfortable with the idea of absolute value, and with the idea of graphing a function. We should also know that if we understand all the concepts related to a question, then there's no reason we can't figure out the answer to the question.

If we understand the concept of absolute value, then we know that every point on the graph of $y = |f(x)|$ must have a y-value that isn't negative, because the y-value will be the absolute value of $f(x)$, and, by definition, it's impossible for an absolute value to be negative.

So we can tell right away that any answer choice with negative y-values must be wrong. That means (C) and (D) must be wrong, since they both have intervals where y is negative.

Now let's think a little more about what we see in the other answer choices, and how those answer choices relate back to the original drawing in Figure 4. Let's see if we can figure out which choice represents the absolute value of $f(x)$.

(A) doesn't have any values to the left of the y-axis, even though the graph in Figure 4 does show values to the left of the y-axis. But there's no reason that the correct answer should omit those values, because finding the absolute value of a number can't result in something like erasing the number or causing it not to exist. So (A) isn't correct.

(B) is just like the original $f(x)$, except that it omits the negative y-values from $f(x)$. But, as we just discussed when talking about choice (A), there's no reason that taking the absolute value of a number should result in deleting that number somehow, so (B) can't be the graph of $|f(x)|$, because no part of the graph in (B) corresponds to the negative y-values in Figure 4.

(E) looks like it could contain the graph of the absolute value of the function from Figure 4: the parts of Figure 4 where y was already positive are preserved in (E), and the part of Figure 4 where y was negative has been "flipped" into the region above the x-axis where y-values are positive. This makes sense—if we took the absolute value of $f(x)$, then every negative y-value would be replaced by a positive version of that same y-value. So we can tell that (E) is the correct answer.

Now that we've identified the correct answer, let's review how the College Board seems to be trying to trick us in the other answer choices.

For one thing, we might notice that choice (D) is the graph of $y = -f(x)$, rather than $y = |f(x)|$, which is why the graph of (D) shows every part of $f(x)$ rotated about the x-axis, instead of just the parts that originally had negative values. One other thing we might notice is that we can actually look for a "most like the other" pattern on this question, even though the answer choices are graphs. Let's say that the graph in Figure 4 can be divided into three regions: the "bump" to the left of the y-axis, the "bump" to the right of the y-axis, and the nearly vertical "stick" all the way to the right side of the graph. We can compare the answer choices in terms of how they handle each of these three regions to see which choice is the most like the others:

- For the left-hand "bump," three choices show the bump appearing, and two choices show nothing. Of the three that show it appearing, two show it pointing up, and one shows it pointing down. So if the pattern is being followed here, we'd expect the correct answer to include the bump, and to show it pointing up.

- For the right-hand "bump," three choices show the bump pointing up, one choice shows it pointing down, and one choice shows nothing. So we'd expect the correct answer to show this bump pointing up if the pattern is being followed.

- For the nearly vertical "stick," four choices show the stick above the x-axis, and one shows it below. So if this question follows the pattern, then the correct answer choice should show the stick above the x-axis.

When we combine all of these elements, we see that the "wrong answers imitate right answers" pattern would suggest that (E) is correct, because it contains all three of the most common features for each of the three regions of the graph we've identified:

1. It includes the left-hand bump and shows the bump pointing up.

2. It includes the right-hand bump and shows the bump pointing up.

3. It shows the stick above the x-axis.

As we always say when talking about patterns in this Black Book, it's important to remember that we shouldn't just blindly choose (E) because it seems to follow the pattern; we have to remember that the patterns are just additional tools for thinking about a test question from multiple perspectives. Still, the fact that this question seems to follow the "wrong answers imitate right answers" pattern is a reassuring sign that we've probably thought about the question correctly.

Page 164, Question 12

In order to answer this question, we have to understand what "zeros" of a function are, and we have to understand a little bit about how factors of a polynomial work, because both concepts are used in the prompt with no further explanation. So let's review them briefly.

A zero of a function is an x-value that can be plugged into the function to produce an output of zero—in other words, for this question, a zero of the function $p(x)$ would be an x-value such that $p(x) = 0$. These kinds of x-values are also called "roots" of functions. A root or a zero of a function is also a number that can be used to determine a factor of that function, in the following way: if 10 is a root of $f(x)$, then $(x - 10)$ is a factor of $f(x)$, because setting $(x - 10)$ equal to 0 gives us an x-value of 10. Finally, we need to remember that if two numbers are factors of a third number, then the product of those two numbers is also a factor of the third number. For example, 5 and 2 are both factors of 100, so 10 (which is the product of 5 and 2) is also a factor of 100.

(If you're not familiar with these concepts, be sure to review the sections on polynomials and factors in the Math Toolbox in this Black Book.)

With all of that in mind, there are probably three ways that we can figure out the answer to this question:

1. We can take a more concrete approach and backsolve from the answer choices.

2. We can take a more abstract approach and do some algebra.

3. We can use a calculator to graph the answer choices and see which one behaves correctly.

As usual, we'll look at the concrete approach first, so you'll start by seeing a specific example of the general concepts we'll discuss when we look at the algebraic approach. Finally, we'll discuss the calculator approach, which may be the fastest one for test-takers who feel confident using it.

The concrete way to backsolve this question would be to realize that the correct answer must be an expression that's relevant to the idea of both 3 and -2 being zeros of $p(x)$, because that's all the information we've been given about $p(x)$. If 3 and -2 are both zeros of $p(x)$, then they must both be zeros of the polynomial in the correct answer choice. So if we plug 3 and -2 into each answer choice as x, we'll see which choice results in a $p(x)$ value of zero for *both* of those x-values. So let's do that:

(A)	$x^2 - 6 = ?$	(expression in the answer choice)
	$(3)^2 - 6 = ?$	(plug in $x = 3$)
	$9 - 6 = 3$	(combine like terms)

We see that plugging in 3 for x gives us a $p(x)$ value of 3, not 0, so we already know that (A) can't be correct. We don't need to bother plugging in -2, because the question requires us to find an answer choice where *both* 3 *and* -2 make $p(x)$ come out equal to 0.

(B)	$x^2 - x - 6 = ?$	(expression in the answer choice)
	$(3)^2 - 3 - 6 = ?$	(plug in $x = 3$)
	$9 - 3 - 6 = 0$	(combine like terms)

Plugging in 3 for x gives us a $p(x)$ of 0, which is part of what we're looking for in the correct answer. Now let's try an x-value of -2, because both 3 and -2 have to generate a $p(x)$ of 0 in order for the answer choice to be correct:

	$x^2 - x - 6 = ?$	(expression in the answer choice)
	$(-2)^2 - -2 - 6 = ?$	(plug in $x = -2$)
	$4 + 2 - 6 = 0$	(combine like terms)

We see that plugging in -2 for x also gives us a $p(x)$ value of 0, so that means 3 and -2 are, in fact, zeros of the function $p(x)$. This looks like it's going to be the correct answer. Of course, as trained test-takers, we know that we have to try out every answer choice whenever we backsolve, so we can do our best to make sure we haven't made a mistake somewhere.

(C)	$x^2 + 6 = ?$	(expression in the answer choice)
	$(3)^2 + 6 = ?$	(plug in $x = 3$)
	$9 + 6 = 15$	(combine like terms)

When $x = 3$, (C) gives us a $p(x)$ value of 15, so (C) can't be correct.

(D)	$x^2 + x - 6 = ?$	(expression in the answer choice)
	$(3)^2 + (3) - 6 = ?$	(plug in $x = 3$)
	$9 + 3 - 6 = 6$	(combine like terms)

Plugging in 3 for x gives us a $p(x)$ of 6, so (D) is wrong too. Let's try the last choice:

(E)	$x^2 + x + 6 = ?$	(expression in the answer choice)

$$(3)^2 + (3) + 6 = ?$$ (plug in $x = 3$)

$$9 + 3 + 6 = 18$$ (combine like terms)

Plugging in 3 here gives us a $p(x)$ of 18, not zero, so we know (E) is wrong, too.

Since we've tried every answer choice, we can be sure that (B) is correct, because it's the only option with a $p(x)$ of zero for both $x = 3$ and $x = -2$, which is what the question asked us to find.

Now let's try a more abstract, algebraic approach. As we discussed above, if we know that 3 and -2 are *zeros* of $p(x)$, then, by definition, we know that $(x - 3)$ and $(x + 2)$ are *factors* of $p(x)$.

But no answer choice mentions just $(x - 3)$ or $(x + 2)$, either. So now what?

Well, if $(x - 3)$ and $(x + 2)$ are both factors, then we know that the product of $(x - 3)$ and $(x + 2)$ must be a factor too. We know this because, as we mentioned above, if two numbers are both factors of another number, then the product of those two numbers is a factor as well.

But we don't see $(x - 3)(x + 2)$ in the answer choices either! Instead, we see a bunch of expressions that all include some combination of the positive and negative versions of x^2, x, and 6. Since we know that two of the zeros for $p(x)$ are 3 and -2, we might realize that the expressions in the answer choice probably have something to do with the idea of multiplying 3 and 2 in some way, which accounts for the 6 that appears in each answer choice . . .

. . . in fact, going further through the same thought process, we can probably tell that the answer choices look similar to the polynomial we would get when we multiply the factors $(x - 3)$ and $(x + 2)$.

At this point, we probably realize that multiplying the two factors is likely to result in the expression from one of the answer choices, which makes sense—the College Board has simply found an equivalent way to state that $(x - 3)(x + 2)$ is the answer to the question, by making the correct answer contain the final product when the two factors are multiplied. So we can probably use FOIL to multiply these factors together, and then compare the result to the answer choices. Let's do that:

$$(x - 3)(x + 2)$$ (the factors that we determined from the information in the prompt)

$$x^2 + 2x - 3x - 6$$ (multiply First, Outer, Inner, Last, remembering plus and minus signs)

$$x^2 - x - 6$$ (combine like terms)

So we can see, again, that the correct answer is (B).

Finally, to approach this question with a calculator, all we would need to do is to graph each of the expressions from the answer choices, and look to see which answer choice creates a graph that crosses the x-axis at the two points that are described as zeros in the prompt:

- $x = 3$
- $x = -2$

Only choice (B) creates a graph that crosses the x-axis in those two places, so (B) must be correct.

As trained test-takers, we might expect the answer choices in this question to follow the "wrong answers imitate right answers" pattern that we discussed earlier in this Black Book, in which the College Board makes the incorrect answer choices share a lot of features with the correct answer choice. We know that this pattern *often* applies, but not *always*; in the case of this question, the pattern would lead us to think that choice (D) is probably correct, which turns out not to be true. But when we see that the pattern tends to suggest (D) would probably be right, we should be reminded that the answer choices are very clearly set up to take advantage of the average test-taker's sloppiness when it comes to details like positive and negative numbers. This, in turn, should lead us to double-check our own work to make sure we haven't made a small mistake like that.

It's also worth noting that the calculator-based approach is probably the one that makes it easiest to avoid small mistakes in doing our own calculations, provided we remember to pay close attention to details when we read the question and when we enter each of the answer choices into the calculator.

Page 164, Question 13

This question asks us how high a kite is off the ground, given the angle at which the kite is flown and the length of string leading to the kite.

There are two basic ways to find the answer to this question. The first approach I'll discuss below is basically the same as what the College Board advocates on page 184 of the MSTB; the second approach, which is probably a little faster if you're comfortable with it, involves using the answer choices in a way that most untrained test-takers wouldn't think of.

When a question describes anything involving shapes, lines, angles, or other geometric figures—but doesn't provide a diagram—it's often helpful to make our own diagram. My diagram appears below.

(You don't need to label your own diagram as thoroughly as I've labeled mine—I just did it this way to make it as clear to you as possible.)

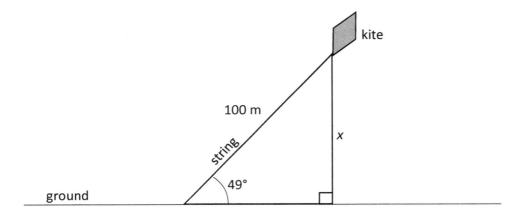

As you can see, I've included an x for the height we need to figure out, just because x is a common variable for these kinds of situations.

We know that the line segment corresponding to the height of the kite must hit the ground at a right angle, because we're told that the ground is level. That means the ground, the string, and the height of the kite combine to form a right triangle, with one angle of 49° and a hypotenuse of 100 m. We need to figure out the length of leg x in my diagram above, which is the leg opposite the angle of 49°.

We know from SOHCAHTOA that **S**ine = **O**pposite/**H**ypotenuse. In this case, we have an angle whose sine we can find with our calculator, and we have the length of the hypotenuse; what we're looking for is the length of the opposite leg.

So let's plug in the values we know, and set up the relationship that will let us solve for x:

$\sin\theta = \dfrac{\text{opposite}}{\text{hypotenuse}}$ (definition of sine from SOHCAHTOA)

$\sin 49° = \dfrac{x}{100}$ (plug in 49° for θ, 100 for the hypotenuse, and x for the "opposite")

Now we solve for x.

$\sin 49° = \dfrac{x}{100}$

$100 \sin 49° = x$ (multiply both sides by 100)

$75.47 \approx x$ (use a calculator to find 100sin49—remember to use degree mode!)

That means the height of the kite off the ground is approximately 75 meters. So the correct answer is choice (C). (Remember that the test sometimes rounds off numbers in the answer choices, especially when trigonometry is involved in a question, as it is here.)

Incidentally, choice (D) is what you'd get if you accidentally used the *cosine* of 49° instead of the sine, and choice (B) is what you'd get if you used *tangent* of 49° instead of the sine. As trained test-takers, we know that the College Board often likes to offer us wrong answers that rely on making small mental errors like this, which is why it's always so important for us to pay attention to small details on this test.

There's also a way that we could solve this problem without really using any trigonometry at all, if we take advantage of the answer choices. If you look at the triangle in the diagram, you can see that it has angles of 90° and 49°. That means the other angle must be 41°, because the sum of the angles of a triangle must always equal 180°, and 180° − 90° − 49° = 41°.

So the measures of the angles are 49°, 41°, and 90°. That's pretty close to a 45°-45°-90° triangle. We should know that the ratio of the sides of a 45°-45°-90° triangle is 1:1:$\sqrt{2}$, where the $\sqrt{2}$ side is the hypotenuse and the other two sides are the legs. If this were a 45°-45°-90° triangle with a hypotenuse of 100, the legs would be equal to $\dfrac{100}{\sqrt{2}}$, or approximately 70.7.

Of course, the triangle in the question is NOT a 45°-45°-90° triangle. Instead, it's a "49°-41°-90°" triangle. The slightly larger angle must be opposite the slightly longer leg, so the longer leg must be a little more than 70.7 meters long, which is how long it would be if it were opposite an angle of 45°. Since the x-value we want to find represents the longer of the two legs of the triangle, x must be a little more than 70.7. The only answer choice that fits this description is choice (C), the correct answer.

Of course, you don't need to use this kind of stripped-down approach to get the question right. But it's good to be aware that many real Math Level 2 questions from the College Board have relatively simple solutions if we're willing to pay attention to the answer choices and remember our training. Looking out for these kinds of solutions can often help us to find shortcuts, and to make sure we've understood a question correctly without making a mistake.

Page 164, Question 14

There are a few ways we could choose to approach this question, which should come as no surprise to a trained test-taker. The College Board's approach, which appears on page 184 of the MSTB, is definitely a good one, and I'll go through it in more detail below. But first, I'd like to discuss the way I would choose to approach the question. This is one of the rare times when my preferred approach actually involves a bit *more* algebra than what the College Board recommends. Remember that there's nothing inherently good or bad about using or ignoring any particular approach to a question on this test—we should always be willing to take whichever approach seems to be the easiest and most direct.

In this case, the approach that seems fastest to me is to plug in $g(1)$ wherever x appears in the given definition of $f(x)$, because the question tells us that $f(g(1)) = 11$. Here's what we get when we do that:

$f(x) = 3x + 5$	(given definition of $f(x)$ from the prompt)
$f(g(1)) = 3(g(1)) + 5 = 11$	(plug in $x = g(1)$, and set $f(g(1)) = 11$)

Now that we know that $3(g(1)) + 5 = 11$, we can solve for $g(1)$:

$3(g(1)) + 5 = 11$	
$3(g(1)) \quad = 6$	(subtract 5 from both sides)
$(g(1)) \quad = 2$	(divide both sides by 3)

At this point, we know that $g(1)$ has to be some kind of expression that results in a value of 2. But, if we think about it, we realize there are literally an infinite number of possible functions that could convert 1 into 2—we might multiply it by 2, or add 1 to it, or multiply it by a million and then divide by 500,000, and so on. That means this is a situation where it's *impossible* to answer the question before looking at the answer choices, since there's no way for us to know beforehand which particular expression the College Board is going to choose as the one that converts 1 into 2. So let's look through the answer choices and plug 1 into x for each of them, and see which one results in a $g(1)$ equal to 2:

(A) $7(1) - 5 = 2$

(B) $5(1) + 7 = 12$

(C) $5(1) - 7 = -2$

(D) $5(1) + 3 = 8$

(E) $-5(1) + 3 = -2$

At this point, we can see that only (A) provides us with an expression that allows for $g(1)$ to be 2, which means (A) is correct.

Another approach is to realize that $g(1)$ must be equal to whatever x-value results in $f(x) = 11$, because the question tells us that $f(g(1))$ also equals 11. Once we know that x-value for $f(x)$, we could check the answer choices to see which one gave us the correct value when we plugged 1 into it.

So in order to answer the question in this way, we'd need to do take two major steps:

1. Figure out which x-value results in an $f(x)$ value of 11.

2. Figure out which answer choice produces the value from Step 1 when we plug 1 into $g(x)$.

First, we set $f(x)$ equal to 11 and solve for (x):

$f(x) = 3x + 5$	(given definition of $f(x)$ from the prompt)
$11 = 3x + 5$	(plug in $f(x) = 11$)
$6 = 3x$	(subtract 5 from both sides)
$2 = x$	(divide both sides by 3)

So when $x = 2$, we know that $f(x) = 11$.

The question tells us that $g(1)$ produces a value of 11 when plugged into $f(x)$, and we now know that $f(2)$ also produces a value of 11. This means that $g(1)$ must be equal to 2, just as we determined in our other approach above.

Now we need to figure out which expression in the answer choices produces a value of 2 when $x = 1$. Again, the only real way to do this is just to plug 1 into each answer choice and see which expression ends up being equal to 2, as we did in the other approach:

(A) $7(1) - 5 = 2$

(B) $5(1) + 7 = 12$

(C) $5(1) - 7 = -2$

(D) $5(1) + 3 = 8$

(E) $-5(1) + 3 = -2$

Once more we see that only choice (A) gives us a result of 2 when we plug in 1 for x. So choice (A) is the only one that can be $g(x)$, because we know that $g(1) = 2$, and only choice (A) allows for that outcome. That means (A) is correct.

Now let's take a look at the wrong answers. Notice that most of them involve the numbers 7 and 5, which is a good sign that we're on the right track, since our answer also involves 7 and 5. But if we try to apply the "wrong answers imitate right answers" pattern to these answer choices, we'd guess that either (B) or (D) was correct, which means we may want to double-check ourselves. Remember that the answer choice patterns we discuss in this Black Book should never be the only basis for picking an answer choice, because they don't always lead to the correct answer, as we can see here.

Finally, note that if you misunderstood the question and thought that $g(1)$ needed to equal $f(1)$, you might have chosen (D). As always, we need to make sure we read each question carefully in order to avoid exactly this kind of mistake!

Page 165, Question 15

You may find this hard to believe, but there's a way to approach this question that will get you the answer in about 5 seconds, and you won't even have to pick up a pencil. But, before we get to that, let's recap the more traditional way to approach this question, which is basically what the College Board book uses on page 184 of the MSTB.

In order to answer this question in the traditional way, we'd need some way to figure out the lengths of the sides of ABCD. We'd probably settle on using the Pythagorean Theorem to find the length of any one side of ABCD as a hypotenuse of a right triangle, like the right triangle with the following corners:

- Point D

- Point C

- The unlabeled corner of the cube at the right-most and bottom-most point of the diagram.

Below is a diagram of the front face of the cube, showing points D and C and the line segment between them. (Notice that we know the smaller leg of the triangle is 1.5 cm long, since we're told C is a midpoint of one edge of the cube, and we're told that every edge of the cube is 3 cm long.)

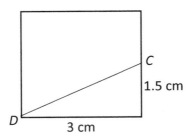

As you can see, line segment *CD* can be viewed as the hypotenuse of a right triangle with one leg of 3cm and another leg of 1.5cm.

To find the length of *CD*, then, we simply apply the Pythagorean Theorem:

$a^2 + b^2 = c^2$	(Pythagorean Theorem, where *c* is the hypotenuse and *a* and *b* are legs)
$3^2 + 1.5^2 = c^2$	(plug in lengths of the legs)
$9 + 2.25 = c^2$	(square the lengths of the legs)
$11.25 = c^2$	(combine like terms)
$3.354 \approx c$	(take square root of both sides)

We now know the length of one side of *ABCD*, but we have to add the lengths of all four sides to find the perimeter, which is what the question asked for. If we look at the diagram, we can tell that each of the four sides will be the same length, because each side is the hypotenuse of a triangle whose legs are 3cm long and 1.5cm long. So we can find the perimeter if we just multiply 3.354 by 4, since there are four sides to *ABCD*. The result is approximately 13.42, so we know that choice (C) is the correct answer (remember that the test often rounds when roots are involved).

Notice that (B) is the square of the length of a side of ABCD. A test-taker might arrive at this wrong answer by assuming that ABCD is a square, and then accidentally finding the *area* of that supposed square instead of its *perimeter*. Also notice that (D) is twice as much as (B), and (E) is twice as much as (D). On top of that, we see that (A) is half of the correct answer. All of these patterns and interrelationships are the types of things that trained test-takers like us are used to noticing in real College Board math questions. When we encounter them in this question, they can help us be sure that we've understood the question correctly.

But that's not the only way that a trained test-taker could exploit this set of answer choices! As I said at the beginning of this explanation, there's a way to solve this problem in a few seconds without even picking up your pencil, and it doesn't require us to use the Pythagorean Theorem. To approach the question in this way, we just need to notice two things:

1. Each of the four sides of *ABCD* must be a little *longer* than an edge of the cube, which is 3 cm.

2. (C) is the only answer choice that's a little larger than 4 × 3 cm.

If you notice those two things, then you can realize that the correct answer must be (C).

We know that (D) must be too large, because it would require each side of ABCD to be longer than 5cm, and there's no way a straight line drawn inside a 3cm × 3cm square could be that long. We can see this by looking at the diagram and remembering that all diagrams on the Math Level 2 Test are drawn to scale unless the question says otherwise—there's no way one side of ABCD could be 5 cm long if each side of the cube is 3 cm long, because we can see in the diagram that each side of ABCD is only a little longer than a side of the cube. By similar logic, we know that (E) must be too large, since it's even larger than (D). Further, we can see that (A) and (B) must be too small to be correct, because they're both less than 12 cm—we determined that each of the 4 sides of ABCD must be longer than 3 cm, which means the perimeter of ABCD must be more than 4 × 3 cm, or more than 12 cm.

Once more, we see that the College Board could have made a question much more difficult by supplying different answer choices. In this case, if more than one answer choice had a value that was a little bit larger than 12, we probably would have had to do a more complicated calculation to figure out which answer choice was correct. But the College Board seems to have deliberately included only one answer choice that was close to our estimated value of "a little bit more than 12," which made it easy to identify the answer to this question—again, provided we remember that the College Board often gives us the opportunity to use these kinds of shortcuts if we look out for them, and that we need to consider the answer choices when we figure out how to solve a problem!

We won't find shortcuts like this on every question on the test, of course. But we'll find them more often than the average person might expect. Remember that every second you can save (without sacrificing accuracy) is an extra second you can invest somewhere else.

Page 165, Question 16

The most important thing to remember when approaching this question is that the equation for the line needs to work for all points on the line, not just for the one labeled point at (0,2).

There are a couple of ways that we can approach this question. If you're pretty comfortable with lines and graphs, you probably know that a horizontal line passing through (0,2) is the graph of the function $y = 2$, because every point on the line has a y-value of 2, no matter what x is. (We know the line must be horizontal because it hits the y-axis at a right angle.) That means (B) is the correct answer. This is basically the College Board's approach on page 184 of the MSTB.

Another approach would be to look at each answer choice and see which one matches up with the points on the graph in the figure.

Choice (A) is $x = 2$. But we know this can't be right, since the one point that's labeled on the graph has an x-value of 0, not 2. So (A) is wrong.

Choice (B) is $y = 2$. This works for the labeled point in the figure, because the y-value of that point is 2. We can also imagine that any other point to the left or right, regardless of the x-value, will have a y-value of 2 as well, because the line is perfectly horizontal. Choice (B) will be the correct answer, but let's look at the other choices as well—as trained test-takers, we know that we always need to consider all the answer choices before moving on to the next question.

Choice (C) is $x = 0$. This works for the labeled point of (0,2), because the x-value of that point is 0. But we can see that there are points to the left and right of the labeled point that must have x-values other than 0, so we know that (C) can't be right.

Choice (D) is $y = x + 2$. This is written in $y = mx + b$ format, and we know that the coefficient of x in the equation of a line written in that format is the slope of the line. So the graph of $y = x + 2$ will have a slope of 1. But the line in the figure is flat, which means it has a slope of 0. So (D) can't be correct, either.

We can rewrite choice (E) as $y = -x + 2$. Using the same logic from our analysis of choice (D), we can tell this line would have a slope of -1, while the line in the figure has a slope of 0. That means (E) can't be right.

One other approach would be to take every function from the answer choices and graph it on your calculator, and look to see which graph matches the diagram. Again, you'd see that only (B) does.

Notice that some test-takers might have accidentally chosen (B) if they thought that the equation for a horizontal line would include an *x* instead of a *y*. Also notice that the most common expression in the answer choices on the left side of the equals sign is *x* or *y*, and the most common expression on the right side of the equals sign is a 2. So the "wrong answers imitate right answers" pattern would suggest that either (A) or (B) is more likely to be correct. As trained test-takers, we know that we can use our knowledge of these kinds of patterns to help reassure us that we've probably thought about the question correctly.

This may seem like a pretty easy question for the Math Level 2 SAT Subject Test, but that's exactly why we need to make absolutely sure we answer it correctly! It would be a shame to give away points on a relatively easy question like this one because of a careless mistake.

Page 165, Question 17

As will often happen on this test, we can choose to approach this question in two ways:

1. We can take a more concrete, "backsolving" kind of approach and work through each answer choice, re-averaging the weights of the classmates, and see which answer choice leads to an average weight of 111 pounds.

2. Alternatively, we can take a more abstract approach, and set up an equation with a variable to represent the weight of the new student.

Either approach will work equally well if you do it correctly, but I'll discuss the concrete approach first, as I usually do. Then we'll talk about the algebraic approach, which is basically what the College Board recommends on page 184 of the MSTB. Finally, I'll mention another approach that's probably the most efficient one, but that might seem strange to some test-takers.

In order to backsolve this question, we can just recalculate the average weight that would result from each answer choice; whichever choice gives us a new average of 111 pounds must be the correct answer.

We would find the average weight of the students by adding up the total weight of all the students, including the new student, and then dividing by the number of students—again, including the new student. Since the group of 19 students has an average weight of 112 pounds, we know that the total weight of those 19 students must be 19 × 112 pounds, which is 2,128 pounds. (We know this because the average of a set of values is found by dividing the sum of the values by the number of values in the set; this means that multiplying the average by the number of values in the set must give us the sum of all the values.)

If we add the weight of all 19 students to the weight of the new student, we get the total weight of all 20 students. We can then divide this total weight by 20 to get the average weight of the set of 19 students plus the new student.

To check choice (A), we would add 2,128 and 91 to get 2,219, which would be the weight of all 20 students if (A) were correct. When we divide 2,219 by 20, we get an average weight of 110.95 for all 20 students. So if the new student weighs 91 pounds, then the average weight of all 20 students is 110.95 pounds—not 111 pounds—which means choice (A) isn't correct. Now let's use this backsolving technique to check the remaining answer choices.

(B) $\frac{(2128)+92}{20} = 111$

If the new student weighs 92 pounds, then the average of all 20 students is exactly 111 pounds. This is what the question asks for, so (B) is correct. Of course, as trained test-takers, we know that we need to evaluate every single answer choice, especially when we backsolve, in order to give us the best possible chance to catch any mistakes we might have made.

(C) $\frac{(2128)+93}{20} = 111.05$

If the new student weighs 93 pounds, then the average of all 20 students is 111.05 pounds, not 111 pounds, so (C) isn't correct.

(D) $\frac{(2128)+101}{20} = 111.45$

A weight of 101 pounds for the new student would make the average of all 20 students be 111.45 pounds. This also isn't what the question asks for, so choice (D) isn't correct.

(E) $\frac{(2128)+110}{20} = 111.9$

If the new student weighs 110 pounds, then the average of all 20 students is 111.9 pounds. Again, this isn't what the question asked us to find, so choice (E) is also wrong.

At this point, we can see that only the value in choice (B) gives us the average weight that the question asked us for, so we know (B) is correct.

Now that we've approached the question in a concrete way, let's talk about how we might set up an equation to solve it. This is roughly what the College Board does in its own explanation on page 184 of the MSTB.

As we discussed above, we know the sum of the weights of the original 19 students is 112 × 19, since there are 19 students with a mean weight of 112 pounds. We can add x to that total to represent adding the weight of the new student to the combined weight of the other students. Finally, we can divide that new sum by 20 to represent the new average weight of all 20 students, and set that average equal to 111, since we're told that 111 is the new average weight. Then we solve for x to find the weight of the new student.

So we have this equation to work with:

$$\frac{(112 \times 19)+x}{20} = 111$$

Now we just do some algebra and solve for x:

$\frac{(112 \times 19)+x}{20} = 111$ \qquad (our original equation)

$\frac{(2128)+x}{20} = 111$ \qquad (multiply the numbers in parentheses)

$2128 + x = 2220$ \qquad (multiply both sides by 20)

$x = 92$ \qquad (subtract 2128 from both sides)

So the new student must weigh 92 pounds, which means, again, that (B) is the correct answer.

As you can see, the standard algebraic approach to this question is pretty straightforward if you're comfortable setting up the equation. But, as I mentioned above, there's actually one more way we could approach the question, even if it's generally not something that a lot of test-takers would want to do. I'll explain it here in case it resonates with you, but feel free to ignore this approach if it's confusing for you. I'm really only including it here as part of my never-ending campaign to help you realize that there are lots of legitimate ways to attack questions on this test.

We're told that the mean weight of the original 19 students was 112 pounds. With the addition of the new student, the mean weight of the class is 111 pounds. Notice that the new student brought the mean down from 19 students at 112 pounds to 20 students at 111 pounds—in other words, adding the new student dropped the average weight by exactly one pound. This means the new student must weigh one pound less, *per student*, than the original average weight—otherwise, the new student wouldn't be able to bring the average weight of the 20 students down by 20 pounds.

So the new student must weigh 20 pounds less than the original average of 112, which means the new student weighs 92 pounds, because 112 – 20 = 92. Again, we see that choice (B) is correct.

(Remember, if that last way of answering the question doesn't make any sense to you, don't worry about it! You can arrive at the same correct answer with total confidence by using either of the other two approaches I discussed above.)

By the way, notice that the values in answer choices (A), (B), and (C) form a series, and that the correct answer choice is in the middle of this series. As trained test-takers, we know that the College Board often (but not always!) puts correct answer choices in the middle of a series of numbers like this, so we can be partially reassured that we've thought about the question correctly when we see this pattern in the answer choices. Also notice that choice (E) has the number that can be averaged with 112 to give us 111—in other words, (E) is the result we'd get if we forgot that there were 19 students in the original class, and mistakenly thought there was just 1, because that would give us a setup like $\frac{112 + 110}{2} = 111$.

Page 166, Question 18

The College Board's solution to this question, which appears on page 185 of the MSTB, is actually pretty close to what I would recommend, which is fairly uncommon. I recommend you read it and consider following this kind of approach on similar questions in the future—as we discuss elsewhere in this Black Book, nearly all trigonometry questions on this test become a lot easier if we use our calculators, and we'll often find that the best way to use the calculator on a particular question might not be something that your teacher would allow in math class.

If your math teacher asked you a question like this, he might require you to start your solution by finding sin x given that cos x is positive and sin x must also be positive (since the question tells us that x is between zero and π on the unit circle). After that, you might have to use half-angle formulas to determine the sine and cosine of $(\frac{x}{2})$, so that you could then find tan $(\frac{x}{2})$.

But, as trained test-takers, we know that the College Board doesn't require us to use things like half-angle formulas to answer questions on the Math Level 2 Test; in fact, the only trig relationships we really have to know for the test are basic things like the definitions of sine, cosine, tangent, cosecant, secant, and cotangent. We should also always keep in mind that the test allows us to use a calculator in a lot of ways that are forbidden in school, because we never have to show our work—all we have to do is choose the correct answer from a list of supplied options.

As the College Board points out in its solution, the easiest way to approach this question is to skip the formal trig and use the calculator to find x itself, and then use the calculator again to evaluate $\tan(\frac{x}{2})$. When we do that, we see that (C) is correct.

Also notice how the College Board's own solution to the question acknowledges that some of the wrong answer choices for this question are designed to catch test-takers who make one or two likely mistakes in answering the question, such as accidentally leaving the calculator in degree mode even though the prompt gives the value of x in terms of π, not in terms of degrees. Let this be one more powerful reminder of the extreme importance of paying careful attention to small details on this test! As you can see, it's still very easy to miss a question by falling for a small mistake, even if you understand every concept in the question and the best way to approach it.

Page 166, Question 19

The College Board's explanation for this question appears on page 185 of the MSTB. That solution is technically correct, of course, but it leaves out some other approaches that are probably easier for most test-takers to deal with. If you'd like to see a formalized algebraic approach, you can take a look at the College Board's solution. Below, I'll go through the question the way I would actually choose to answer it on test day.

We're told that the percentage of "yes" votes is the same in both counties. This means we can take the following steps to answer the question:

1. Figure out what percentage of people voted "yes" overall, in both counties combined.

2. Apply the percentage in step 1 to the number of people in Lyon County, since that's the county that the question is asking about.

We can find the percentage of people who voted "yes" in both counties by creating a fraction and expressing that fraction as a percentage. To do that, we put the number that represents the total population in the denominator, and the numerator will be the number that represents the portion of the population that we're interested in.

So the denominator will be the total population of both counties, which is 30,744 + 20,496, or 51,240. When we put the number of "yes" voters in the numerator of our fraction, we get the following:

$$\frac{38,430}{51,240}$$

Evaluating that expression with our calculator gives us a result of .75, or 75%.

So we know that 75% of the population voted yes. This means that 75% of the people in Lyon County voted yes, because the question tells us that the same percentage of people voted yes in both counties.

Now we just need to multiply 0.75 by the number of voters in Lyon County, and we'll know the number of Lyon County voters who voted yes:

$$0.75 \times 30,744 = 23,058$$

That gives us 23,058 "yes" votes in Lyon County, which means (E) is correct.

As trained test-takers, we might almost be able to predict some of the wrong answers that the College Board is likely to provide in this question, since we know that the test often tries to anticipate the types of small, careless mistakes that most test-takers are likely to make.

One common mistake on this question would probably be to find the percentage of "yes" voters in *Saline* County, instead of in Lyon County, because a lot of test-takers will confuse the two counties. Sure enough, we see that (C) gives us the number of people who voted "yes" in Saline County, because it's 75% of the population of Saline County.

Similarly, we might expect some test-takers to find the number of "no" votes in Lyon County, instead of the number of "yes" votes. We can see that choice (A) is 25% of the population of Lyon County, which would be the number of "no" votes in that county.

Seeing these kinds of wrong answer choices can help us feel confident that we've approached the question correctly, because we can understand the kinds of small mistakes that the College Board was hoping we would make—of course, seeing that there are so many answer choices designed to take advantage of small mistakes should also remind us to re-check our answer, and make sure that we haven't accidentally made a mistake ourselves.

Page 166, Question 20

Most untrained test-takers will be intimidated by a question like this, because they've never seen an arrow symbol ($\rightarrow$) used this way before. But trained test-takers know that if a question defines the meaning of a phrase or symbol they've never seen before, then the best thing to do is to pay careful attention to the question and try to figure it out using the math we already know.

As will often be the case on the Math Level 2 Test, there are two primary ways that we can approach this question: we can go through the answer choices and plug in concrete values to test them, or we can try to reason through the question abstractly. As usual, we'll find that the abstract approach is probably faster if you feel comfortable with it, but the concrete approach is usually easier to work through if you feel like you don't totally understand the question. I'll start our discussion with the concrete approach, and then I'll walk you through the abstract reasoning approach.

When we try to pick values and plug them into a given expression like this, we have to remember that we generally want to avoid picking -1, 0, 1, or numbers that appear in the question, because those kinds of numbers are more likely to have unique properties that might cause more than one answer choice to seem correct. (For more on picking values, take a look at the article in this Black Book on Backsolving.)

Choice (A) says that coordinate pairs will stay the same if $x = 0$. So let's try plugging in (0, 3), and see if that meets the requirement from the question (I just chose 3 for the y-value at random, since the question doesn't specify anything about what the y-values can be for this answer choice):

$(x + 2y, y)$	(result of $\rightarrow$ according to the prompt)
$((0 + 2(3)), 3)$	(plug in $x = 0$ and $y = 3$ to test them)
$(6, 3)$	(combine like terms)

So plugging (0, 3) into $(x + 2y, y)$ results in an output of (6, 3). The question told us to find an (x, y) pair with an output equal to the original x- and y-values, but (0, 3) and (6, 3) aren't the same. So it doesn't look like (A) is correct.

Choice (B) says that coordinate pairs will stay the same if $y = 0$. So I'll try plugging in (3, 0)—again, I've just chosen 3 at random for the value of the coordinate that isn't specified in the answer choice:

$(x + 2y, y)$	(result of $\rightarrow$ according to the question)
$((3 + 2(0)), 0)$	(plug in $x = 3$ and $y = 0$)
$(3, 0)$	(combine like terms)

We can see that plugging in (3, 0) gives us an output of (3, 0), which means that the input and output are the same, just as the question asked. So choice (B) looks good so far . . .

But remember that we can't just stop checking answer choices because we've found one that we think we like! We always have to consider every answer choice, because that makes us more certain that we've understood the question correctly. So let's try choice (C).

(C) says that the outcome of the change will be the same as the original coordinate pair as long as $y = 1$. Let's try (3, 1) and see what happens:

$(x + 2y, y)$	(result of → according to the question)
$((3 + 2(1)), 1)$	(plug in $x = 3$ and $y = 1$)
$(5, 1)$	(combine like terms)

We can see that plugging in (3, 1) results in an output of (5, 1). (3, 1) and (5, 1) aren't the same. So (C) is wrong.

Choice (D) says that the output coordinate pair will only match the input pair if the input pair is (0, 0). We already know this isn't true, because we just saw that the output also matches the input when the input is (3, 0), which means that (0, 0) can't possibly be the only value that produces a matching output. But let's see what happens when we plug in (0, 0) anyway—if nothing else, it gives us one more way to test the idea that *any* pair with a *y*-coordinate of 0 satisfies the question.

$(x + 2y, y)$	(result of → according to the question)
$((0 + 2(0)), 0)$	(plug in $x = 0$ and $y = 0$)
$(0, 0)$	(combine like terms)

So we can see that the output value does indeed match the input value, just as the prompt asked for. But, again, this choice says that ONLY (0, 0) will produce an unchanged output, while we just saw in (B) that (3, 0) also produces an unchanged output. In other words, the real problem with (D) is the word "only," because we know that other coordinate pairs also satisfy the question. So (D) is wrong.

Now let's take a look at (E), which says that the output coordinate pair will only match the input pair at (-1, 1). (Just as with (D), we already know that (E) seems to be wrong, because we already know there are other coordinate pairs that produce matching outputs. But I'm going to work through (E) as well, because it only takes a couple of seconds, and because I want to make sure I give myself every opportunity to discover any mistakes I might have made.)

$(x + 2y, y)$	(result of → according to the question)
$((-1 + 2(1)), 1)$	(plug in $x = -1$ and $y = 1$)
$(1, 1)$	(combine like terms)

We can see that the output value doesn't match the input value, so (E) is wrong.

After testing each answer choice, we can conclude again that choice (B) is the correct answer. We've seen two coordinate pairs that satisfy the prompt and that are accurately described by (B), and we've seen that (A), (C), and (E) all mention coordinate pairs that don't satisfy the prompt.

Now that we've gone through the question in a concrete way, let's stand back from it a little and see if we can understand it from a more abstract perspective.

We can see that after the transformation described in the prompt, the *y*-coordinate portion of the output is still just *y*, exactly as it was in the original coordinate pair. In other words, the value of the y-coordinate remains unchanged. So we can ignore the y-coordinate portion of the output, and just focus on what happens to generate the x-coordinate portion of the output.

The x-coordinate part of the output is defined as $x + 2y$. So we need to figure out what kinds of x- and y-values would cause $x + 2y$ to be the same number as x by itself.

In order for $x + 2y$ to have the same value as x, it must be true that adding 2y doesn't change the value of x. The only way that adding 2y could leave the original value of x unchanged would be if y were equal to zero, because zero is the only number that you can add to a value without resulting in a new value.

So we need to find an answer choice that would allow the y-value of the input to be zero. That way, doubling the y-value and adding it to the x-value will leave the x-value unchanged in the output. (And remember that we don't need to worry about the y-value portion of the output, because we've already established that it's exactly the same as the y-value of the input.)

Choice (B) looks good at this point, because (B) would include all the points with a y-value of zero. But what about (D)? Choice (D) also includes a point with a y-value of zero. So now what?

Well, if we read carefully, we can see that (D) says the *only* point that would satisfy the prompt is (0, 0), while (B) says that *any* point with a y-value of zero satisfies the prompt. We know that adding zero to *any* number leaves the original number unchanged, not just adding zero to zero itself. So we know that (B) is the correct answer here—*any* point with a y-coordinate of zero will work. (If you wanted to, you could also prove that (B) is correct by testing out a point like (3, 0), as we did above when we walked through the concrete solution.)

Now that we've gone through the question in multiple ways, let's think over the answer choices, and see if we can figure out why the College Board chose them.

Notice that choice (A) says the statement is true when $x = 0$, while the correct answer says the statement is true when $y = 0$. We can imagine that a test-taker might easily confuse $x = 0$ with $y = 0$ and end up choosing (A) accidentally, so this wrong answer seems to be exactly the kind of thing the College Board likes to trick us with. (C) might also tempt some test-takers who make a couple of fundamental mistakes, because the y-value of 1 that's mentioned in (C) would be relevant to a *multiplicative* identity property, but the question is ultimately asking about the *additive* identity property—in other words, we're supposed to realize that we need to find a number we can *add* to a value without changing the value, instead of a number that we can *multiply* by a value without changing the value, which is what 1 is. Also notice that choice (D) describes a point that *does* make the statement true—but, as we discussed, (D) also says that "only" (0, 0) makes the statement true, which isn't accurate, because other points make the statement true as well.

Finally, notice that this set of answer choices actually follows the pattern of having a correct answer choice that has the most possible things in common with the other answer choices:

- Three of the five answer choices describe a set of multiple points, and the correct answer describes a set of multiple points.

- Of the three answer choices that describe multiple points, two of the three choices specify something relative to the y-coordinate, and the correct answer choices specifies something relative to the y-coordinate.

- Three of the five answer choices mention zero, and the correct answer mentions zero.

As we've discussed elsewhere, you should NEVER pick an answer choice based SOLELY on whether it conforms to a pattern like this, because these patterns aren't 100% reliable. But when we see that the answer choice we think is correct also happens to follow this pattern that commonly appears on the test, we can be more confident that we've probably understood the question from the College Board's perspective. This means it's more likely that we've found the correct answer without making any mistakes that could cost us the question.

Page 167, Question 21

This question provides another example of the many ways in which the College Board's own explanations often seem deliberately designed to make readers think the Math Level 2 Test is harder than it really is. The College Board's explanation, which appears on page 185 of the MSTB, is mathematically valid, but its approach is much more complicated and formal than necessary. As trained test-takers, we know that those kinds of approaches often provide more opportunities for us to make small mistakes that lead to incorrect answer choices, because formal approaches typically involve more steps and more reliance on memorized formulas.

So I'd like to discuss two approaches to this question that would allow most test-takers to find the correct answer more easily. For the first approach, we'll assume that you know what the term "geometric progression" means; for the second, I'll show how you might still be able to answer the question correctly with total confidence even if you didn't know what a geometric progression was when you first read the question.

(For the first approach, I'll remind you that a geometric progression is a series of numbers in which each term can be found by multiplying the previous term by a constant ratio.)

The first way to approach the question would be to go through each answer choice, add the corresponding amount to the numbers from the prompt, and see which answer choice results in a geometric progression. So let's do that:

(A) Adding 2 to each of the three numbers gives us 3, 9, and 21. We can multiply 3 by 3 to get 9, but multiplying 9 by 3 gives us 27, not 21. So choice (A) is wrong.

(B) Adding 3 to each of the three numbers gives us 4, 10, and 22. We can multiply 4 by $\frac{5}{2}$ to get 10, but multiplying 10 by $\frac{5}{2}$ would give us 25, not 22. So choice (B) is also wrong.

(C) Adding 4 to each of the three numbers gives us 5, 11, and 23. We can multiply 5 by $\frac{11}{5}$ to get 11, but multiplying 11 by $\frac{11}{5}$ doesn't give us 23. So (C) isn't correct, either.

(D) Adding 5 to each of the three numbers gives us 6, 12, and 24. We can multiply 6 by 2 to get 12, and we can multiply 12 by 2 to get 24. That means that 6, 12, and 24 form a geometric progression with a common ratio of 2, so choice (D) seems to be correct so far. Of course, as trained test-takers, we know that we always need to check every answer choice, even if we've found one that we think we like. We always have to remember that the College Board is going to present us with a lot of opportunities to make small mistakes that result in wrong answers, and we always want to take every reasonable step possible to make sure that we haven't fallen into a trap that could cause us to miss a question we could easily have answered correctly. So let's take a look at (E).

(E) Adding 6 to each of the three numbers gives us 7, 13, and 25. We can multiply 7 by $\frac{13}{7}$ to get 13, but multiplying 13 by $\frac{13}{7}$ doesn't give us 25, so choice (E) isn't correct.

So we can see that (D) must be correct, assuming we know that a geometric progression is a series in which each term can be found by multiplying the previous term by a constant value—in other words, a series of numbers with a "common ratio" between any two consecutive numbers. (If you don't feel comfortable with this concept, make sure you review the section on Series in this book's Math Toolbox.)

But what if we don't know what a geometric progression is? Let me be clear here—as trained test-takers, we *should* definitely know what a geometric progression is, because it's a concept with a decent probability of showing up on test day. But, for the sake of argument, I want to show that it might be possible to answer this question correctly with total confidence even if we don't remember the meaning of the term "geometric progression." I want to discuss this kind of situation because you might encounter questions on test day that ask you about concepts or scenarios that you've never encountered before, or that you've forgotten, and you may find that you can work around the gaps in your knowledge if you pay close attention to a particular question.

With that in mind, let's look back at the question from the standpoint of a test-taker who has momentarily forgotten what a geometric progression is. Such a test-taker could still try to approach the question by adding the quantities in the answer choices to the numbers in the prompt, just to see what happens. It probably wouldn't take very long to do this, and doing it might give us something we could work with; on the other hand, if it turns out to be pointless, we still won't have wasted much time on it, so there's no real harm that can be done. After we add each of the values in the answer choices to the original group of numbers, we get the following sequences:

(A) 3, 9, 21

(B) 4, 10, 22

(C) 5, 11, 23

(D) 6, 12, 24

(E) 7, 13, 25

At this point, if we reason that a "progression" in math is probably some kind of series of numbers with a pattern in it, we may notice that the only choice that seems to have a pattern at first glance is (D), where the second and third numbers are each twice as much as the number before them. We may also even notice that every answer choice creates a series where the difference between the first two numbers is 6 and the difference between the 2nd and 3rd numbers is 12, so it seems very unlikely that the "progression" in the correct answer choice will be based on addition, since every answer choice creates a set of numbers with the same differences.

By now, we may feel completely confident that we've correctly identified (D) as the only answer choice with a unique, clear pattern that could reasonably be called a kind of progression. (In fact, I've had some students tell me that they had begun working on this question without remembering exactly what a geometric progression was, but then had been reminded of the definition of the term when they saw that (D) was the only choice that created a series with a common ratio between any two consecutive numbers.) If we're sure (D) is correct, then we should mark (D) with confidence and go on to the next question. On the other hand, some test-takers may still not be confident marking (D) at this point, and also may not be able to think of anything else to try on this question. If that's where you find yourself, don't be upset at all—just recognize that this is going to have to be a question that you leave blank because you're not certain of the answer, and go on to the next item on the test. You're only losing the few seconds you invested in working through the answer choices. (Again, you really should know terms like "geometric progression" if you want to do your best on the Math Level 2 Test—you can see the Math Toolbox in this Black Book for explanations of those kinds of core concepts. We're discussing how this question might be approached by a test-taker who didn't know the term "geometric progression" because I want to show the kinds of work-arounds that are sometimes possible on multiple-choice College Board tests.)

It's also important to remember that the formal approach described on page 185 of the MSTB is still a perfectly acceptable way to solve this problem. I just think it's a lot slower and more complicated than necessary, and I want to make sure you're aware of faster, simpler ways to approach the test.

Finally, notice that the answer choices form a series where each number after choice (A) is 1 more than the number in the answer choice before it. As trained test-takers, we know that when we see a series like this in the answer choices, the correct answer is *likely* to be a part of the series, and it's *likely* not to be the first or last number in the series. This pattern suggests that either choice (B), (C), or (D) is likely to be the right answer, which means that our belief that (D) is the correct answer seems to fit the College Board's pattern. As I always say in this Black Book, you can never rely exclusively on these kinds of patterns when approaching the test, but you should learn to use them as tools to help you figure out what the College Board probably had in mind when it designed the question.

Page 167, Question 22

This is a great example of a problem that appears complex but can actually be solved quickly and easily if we read carefully and think a little bit. Like many Math Level 2 questions, this one isn't really set up to test our knowledge of some formulaic mathematical approach that we might have learned in class. Instead, the best approach to this question is to read everything carefully, identify the underlying math principles involved, and then try to think of a simple way to answer the question we're being asked.

When we read through the prompt and the answer choices, we see that all of the answer choices are integers—in fact, the choices form an arithmetic series of integers running from -2 to 2. This shows us that the question is asking us to find a numerical value for $a + b$, rather than an equivalent algebraic expression for $a + b$. As trained test-takers, we also know that the series in the answer choices tends to suggest the correct answer is more likely to be -1, 0, or 1, since the College Board tends to prefer not to make the correct answer be a number at the beginning of end of a series in the answer choices. (Of course, we know this is just a general tendency, and not a hard-and-fast rule, so we'd never decide to choose an answer or avoid an answer based purely on a pattern in the answer choices.)

With all of that in mind, we should now try to find a simple way to approach the question. Well, we're ultimately asked to find the sum of a and b, and we can see that each of those variables is mentioned in the expression we're given for $f(x)$, and that neither variable appears anywhere else in the question. All of this suggests that we're supposed to figure out something about a and b from the function . . . but what can we do with the function? The right-hand side of the function has four different variables in it, and we know that it can be hard to do anything with a function that involves more than one variable on the right-hand side. But we are told that $f(0) = 1$, and that $f(1) = 2$. These pieces of information might be especially useful, because we know that numbers like 0 and 1 have unique properties, and that those properties might be relevant to our situation.

So let's plug in 0 for x in the given equation, set $f(0)$ equal to 1, and see what happens to the rest of the function. There's a good chance that doing this will help point us in the right direction—in fact, it might be difficult to imagine anything else we could even try at this point. And if this doesn't help us, we'll only lose a little time finding that out.

$f(x) = ax^2 + bx + c$	(original function expression from the prompt)
$f(0) = a(0)^2 + b(0) + c$	(plug in $x = 0$)
$1 = a(0)^2 + b(0) + c$	(plug in $f(0) = 1$)
$1 = 0 + 0 + c$	(multiply variables by zero)
$1 = c$	(combine like terms)

From this, we now know that c is equal to 1. That seems like it might be useful, because the difficulty in the question seems to be related to figuring out values for variables, and we've just learned one of those values. (Even if the value we've just figured out isn't actually one of the variables we were asked about, it can probably still be useful, because it's in the same expression as the variables we're interested in.) So let's use the value of c to determine what we can learn from the fact that $f(1) = 2$. This time, we can plug in all of the following values:

- $x = 1$

- $f(1) = 2$

- $c = 1$

Now let's see what happens:

$f(x) = ax^2 + bx + c$	(original function expression from the prompt)
$f(x) = ax^2 + bx + 1$	(plug in $c = 1$)
$f(1) = a(1)^2 + b(1) + 1$	(plug in $x = 1$)
$2 = a(1)^2 + b(1) + 1$	(plug in $f(1) = 2$)
$2 = a + b + 1$	(multiply variables by 1)
$1 = a + b$	(combine like terms)

At this point, we realize that we've worked out the value of $a + b$, just as the question asked us to do. We can now see that the correct answer is 1, just like choice (D) says, so (D) is correct.

Even as trained test-takers, we'll frequently encounter questions like this one, where we may not be exactly sure what to do at first. But if we read carefully and try to gather all the information from the text, we'll usually find that we can figure out the answer—in fact, there's a good chance we'll discover that the individual math steps involved in the question are actually pretty simple, just as they were in this question.

Another important lesson to learn from this question is that many untrained test-takers will waste a lot of extra time on this question, and might miss it completely, even though it involves nothing more complicated than algebraic substitution and basic arithmetic. This is because they'll incorrectly assume that the only way to find the sum of two variables is to find the individual values of the variables first, and then add them, which is impossible in this question—we can know that the sum of the two variables is 1, but we don't have enough information to determine their individual values. This is yet another example of how the Math Level 2 Test isn't like a typical high school math test—the College Board likes to write math questions that look similar to things we might see in a math textbook at first glance, but that can't be approached in the same way we would approach questions in school.

Finally, notice that the correct answer does indeed fit the pattern of not appearing in the first or last position in a series within the answer choice, just as we thought it might when we first looked at the question. Although we know that we can NEVER pick an answer choice based SOLELY on these patterns, seeing that the pattern is followed here can help reassure us that we've probably thought about the question correctly.

Page 167, Question 23

There is a formal mathematical way to approach this question, and you can find that on page 186 of your copy of the MSTB. But it's also possible to answer this question in only a few seconds, doing almost no math. That's the approach I want to focus on here—NOT because there's anything wrong with the formal approach, but because one of my goals in this Black Book is to show you that test questions can often be successfully attacked in ways that your math teacher would be unlikely to reward in school, and these non-traditional approaches are often faster and easier than the formal approach would be.

We're asked for the measure of the largest angle in a triangle with sides of 6, 6, and 7. The first thing that I think of when I see those side-lengths is that they're almost equal. If the sides were 6, 6, and 6, then the triangle would be equilateral, and I know that an equilateral triangle has all three angle measurements equal to 60°. (We know this because the sum of the measures of the three angles of a triangle must always add up to 180°, and the angles of an equilateral triangle are all equal. This is a property of equilateral triangles that all trained test-takers should be immediately familiar with.)

But the triangle in the question has one side slightly longer than the other two, so the angle opposite that longer side will be a little more than 60°. (By the way, this means the other two angles will be a little *less* than 60°, but that isn't directly relevant to what the question is asking.) Only one answer choice is a little more than 60°, and that's choice (C), 71.37°. So (C) must be the correct answer.

There's a strong hint in the answer choices that makes us extra confident that we're right. As trained test-takers, we might expect that the College Board will provide a wrong answer choice that reflects the measurement of the other angles in the triangle, instead of the angle we were asked for. The College Board would do this because it knows that some test-takers will follow an approach to the question that involves working out the measurements of all the angles in the triangle, and some of those test-takers will probably choose a wrong answer that corresponds to the measure of one of the other two angles. Such an answer choice would be a little less than 60°, and when you multiply it by two and add it to the correct answer, you should get 180°. Sure enough, choice (B) is 54.31°, which is the measure of each of the two smaller angles. When we notice this wrong answer choice, we can be even more confident that we've understood the question from the College Board's perspective.

Notice that solving the question this way avoids a lot of complicated algebra and trigonometry, which also means avoiding a lot of opportunities to make mistakes. Not every Math Level 2 question can be answered using this kind of reasoning, of course, but many of them can. We just have to learn to pay attention to the questions *and their answer choices*, and to look out for these kinds of opportunities.

Also notice that this approach wouldn't have worked if there were several answer choices between 60° and 75°. It only works because the College Board has provided us with answer choices that allow us to use this approach—so make sure you always read the answer choices as you're deciding how to approach a question!

Page 167, Question 24

The College Board's explanation for this question (which is on page 186 of the MSTB) is, of course, technically correct—the main concept being tested in the question is that the quantity under the radical can be any real number, and all real numbers have unique real numbers as cube-roots, so the domain of the function is all real numbers.

But, as is often the case when a question on this test asks about the behavior of the graph of a function, the easiest approach is just to graph the function on our calculator, and then see which answer choice accurately describes the graph. If we enter this function into the calculator, we get the following graph:

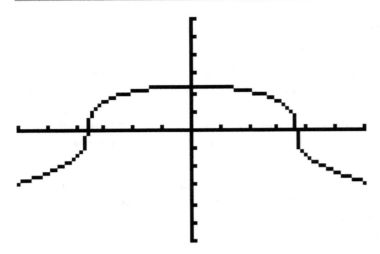

We can see that every value on the x-axis has a corresponding value on the y-axis, without any gaps, so we know that all real numbers can be plugged into the function as x-values. So (E) must be correct. (You could use your calculator to zoom out on the graph if you wanted more proof of this, but note that all of the possible ranges in the answer choices are already reflected in the graphing window above.)

This approach allows us to find the correct answer without actually doing any calculations, as long as we know that the domain of a function is the set of x-values that can be plugged into the function to produce a real number for a y-value. If we don't know that, it will be difficult to answer this question correctly. (Remember that the Math Level 2 Test often focuses on the properties and definitions of math concepts.) In fact, we may notice that most of the wrong answer choices reflect possible misunderstandings of the ways that the domain of a function could relate to key points on a graph, such as the x- and y-intercepts of a function: the y-intercept of the graph is roughly 2.35, which appears in choices (B) and (C), and the x-intercepts are roughly at -3.61 and 3.61, which appear in choice (D).

If you were unclear on the concept of a function's domain, or on any of the concepts in this question, make sure you review the relevant sections of the Math Toolbox in this Black Book.

Page 168, Question 25
The College Board's solution to this question, which appears on page 186 of the MSTB, is complicated and formal, which is what we'd normally expect from the College Board. And if you like that kind of approach, there's nothing wrong with it—it will still lead you to the correct answer, though it may involve more opportunities to make small mistakes or waste time than other approaches.

Rather than revisit the College Board's approach, we're going to look at two quicker, easier solutions that involve much simpler math, because I think those kinds of simplified solutions are the things that trained test-takers should gravitate towards.

(By the way, before we get started, notice that the question mentions a "radian value of x," so we know that we need to make sure our calculator is in radian mode!)

One solution would just be to graph y = cos x and y = tan x and then see which answer choice is an x-coordinate of a point where the two graphs intersect. Here's what that graph looks like:

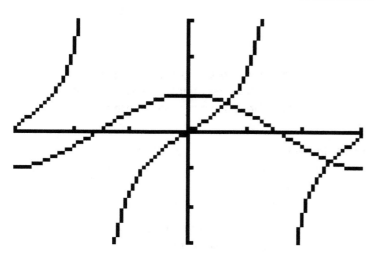

Noting that each mark on the *x*-axis corresponds to one unit, we can see that one point of intersection of the two graphs occurs somewhere between *x* = 0.5 and *x* = 1. When we look at the answer choices, we see that both (D) and (E) are in that range. The trace function on a graphing calculator allows us to see that the point of intersection of the two graphs is *x* = 0.67, which means (E) is correct. (Note that the graph shows multiple points of intersection, and that the question asks us to find "a possible radian value of *x*," as opposed to asking for *the* single radian value of *x*. All of this makes sense when we remember that cosine and tangent are periodic functions, which means they demonstrate patterns that repeat as we move from left to right across the *xy*-coordinate plane.)

Another solution would be to backsolve by taking the values from the answer choices and plugging them into both cosine and tangent using your calculator, looking for the answer choice whose cosine value is equal to its tangent value (bearing in mind that we may need to do some small rounding, since the answer choices are rounded to two decimal places, and since the calculator is using decimal approximations of the function values). Let's do that now:

(A) $y = \cos(-1) \approx 0.54$

$y = \tan(-1) \approx -1.56$

When we plug in *x* = -1, we get two different values for cos *x* and tan *x*. The question asks for an *x*-value that makes cos *x* equal to tan *x*, so choice (A) isn't correct.

(B) $y = \cos(-0.52) \approx 0.87$

$y = \tan(-0.52) \approx -0.57$

We also get two different values for cos *x* and tan x when we plug in *x* = -0.52, so choice (B) isn't correct, either.

(C) $y = \cos(0) = 1$

$y = \tan(0) = 0$

When we plug in *x* = 0, we get two different values for cos *x* and tan *x*. Again, since the question asks for an *x*-value that makes cos *x* equal to tan *x*, we know that (C) is wrong.

(D) $y = \cos(0.52) \approx 0.87$

$y = \tan(0.52) \approx 0.57$

When we plug in *x* = 0.52, we get two different values for cos *x* and tan *x*, which means (D) is also wrong.

(E) $y = \cos(0.67) \approx 0.78$

        $y = \tan(0.67) \approx 0.79$

When we plug in $x = 0.67$, we get two values for $\cos x$ and $\tan x$ that are very close together, but not quite the same. We can still tell that (E) must be the correct answer, since we know that we might have to account for some rounding, and since the cosine and tangent values we got for all of the other answer choices were so far apart from one another. So we can see that choice (E) is correct.

Yet again, we see that we can answer a question quickly and simply if we take advantage of the weaknesses in the test's design, even when the College Board itself provides a fairly complicated and advanced explanation for the same question. Remember that questions on the Math Level 2 Test are rarely as hard as they seem—and also remember that the test often rewards us for using our calculators in ways that wouldn't be allowed in school!

Finally, notice that the answer choices include -0.52 and 0.52. Often, when we see two opposites in the answer choices, we can expect that one of them is likely to be the correct answer, and the test is hoping we'll make some kind of fundamental mistake and choose the other. But in this case, neither of these opposite numbers is the correct answer. This is good time for me to point out that patterns in answer choices can be *helpful* for giving us alternative ways to think about a question and check our work, but we can never depend completely on answer choice patterns when we select our answer.

Page 168, Question 26

The presentation of this question is definitely unusual, but, as trained test-takers, we know that we shouldn't be put off by strange-looking questions. Most test-takers will panic when they see this question, because they don't know a formula for summing the areas of rectangles whose heights are defined by points on a function curve—but we already know that plenty of questions on the Math Level 2 Test just don't have formulas at all. So instead of being frustrated by the fact that we don't know a formula for this question, we focus on identifying the basic math concepts that are relevant to it, and then we use our knowledge of those concepts to attack it. When we try to do that, we'll see that the math in this question is actually pretty straightforward, as long as we proceed carefully.

The basic math concepts in this question seem to be the following:

- finding the area of a rectangle
- plugging numbers into a function
- addition

For a lot of test-takers, the best way to approach this question will just be to figure out the areas of the three rectangles, and then add them together. This is basically the College Board's approach in its solution on page 187 of the MSTB. We'll discuss that approach in a little more detail, and then I'll show you an approach that's more efficient because it exploits the test's design.

We know that finding the area of a rectangle requires us to multiply its base by its height. We can see that the base of each rectangle is 2 units wide. We can also see that the top-left corner of each rectangle is always a point on the function $y = 3^x$.

Now let's take a look at the first rectangle, the smallest one. Its top-left corner is the point on the function curve that corresponds to an x-value of 0. When we plug $x = 0$ into the function $y = 3^x$, we get a y-value of 3^0, or 1. That means the height of the first rectangle is 1. We already determined that the bases of all the rectangles are 2 units long, so the area of this rectangle is equal to 2×1, which works out to 2.

The top-left corner of the second rectangle has an *x*-value of 2. That means its *y*-value is 3^2, or 9. So the height of the rectangle is 9. Again, we know that the base of each rectangle is 2, so this rectangle's area is 2 × 9, which is 18.

Finally, the third rectangle's top-left corner has an *x*-value of 4. So the *y*-value of this point is equal to 3^4, or 81, which means the third rectangle's height is 81. Since this rectangle's base is also 2 units wide, its area is 2 × 81, or 162.

When we add up the areas of these three rectangles, we get 2 + 18 + 162, or 182. So (D) is correct.

Again, this is basically the approach the College Board takes for its solution, and it's a pretty straightforward way to attack the question.

But there's at least one other way we could think about this question, and I want to discuss it with you now—not because you'd definitely need it for this question, but because you may find this kind of approach useful on test day for a harder question.

My alternative approach begins by noticing that the answer choices would be relatively far apart from each other on a number line—in other words, we might be able to eliminate all the wrong answer choices if we can find some way to approximate the answer, because it may turn out that only one answer choice is anywhere near our approximation. This is the kind of thing that trained test-takers can often notice about a question, because they consider the answer choices along with the prompt before they start to attack a question.

One thing we might notice is that the sum of the areas of the three rectangles has to be less than the number we would get if we took the area of the largest rectangle and multiplied it by three, because the areas of the other two rectangles are smaller than the area of the largest rectangle. Similarly, we also know that the sum of the areas of all the rectangles must be larger than just the area of the largest rectangle.

One we figure out that the largest rectangle has an area of 162, we know that the correct answer must be greater than 162. That eliminates choice (E). We also know that the sum of the areas of the three rectangles must be less than three times the area of the largest rectangle, which would be 162 times 3, or 486. That means choices (A), (B), and (C) are all too large to be correct. So our approximation allows us to realize that only choice (D) can possibly be correct. Again, I'm NOT suggesting that approximation is the best approach for this question for all test-takers—it's just one more way we might choose to attack the question or check our work, once we realize that the College Board's selection of answer choices has made approximation a valid approach here. The main reason I wanted to show you this approach is that you might find it useful for other questions in the future.

(Notice that this kind of approximation is NOT the same thing as the traditional guessing approach that I said you should avoid earlier in this Black Book! In the traditional guessing approach, a test-taker who doesn't know how to answer a question correctly will trick herself into thinking she can reliably eliminate wrong answers and then guess randomly from the remaining choices without being influenced by what she doesn't understand about the question. But in the approximation approach that I just showed you, we fully understand all the basic concepts in the question, and we used our understanding to eliminate all four of the wrong answers with total certainty. Randomness and ignorance were never involved in our approach, but they're the cornerstone of the traditional guessing approach.)

Now let's talk about some mistakes an untrained test-taker might make on this question, and how those mistakes are reflected in the wrong answer choices. Notice that choice (B) is what you get if you accidentally use *y*-values of 2, 4, and 6 for the rectangles, instead of 0, 2, and 4. Choice (C) is the same as choice (B), with the added mistake of forgetting to multiply each rectangle height by 2, the width of the bases. Choice (E) is half of the correct answer, which is what you'd get if you did everything right but forgot to multiply each rectangle height by 2, the width of the bases.

Page 169, Question 27

Before we get started on this question, I want to point out that we shouldn't worry if we have no idea what the question is talking about when it mentions that "a certain radioactive element decays." We don't need any knowledge of chemistry or physics to answer this question. As we know by now, the College Board often likes to make questions seem harder or more complicated than they really are, and referring to scientific concepts like radioactive decay is one example of how that can be done.

In fact, this is probably one of the more straightforward math questions we'll ever see on a Math Level 2 Test. In order to answer it in the traditional way, all we'd need to do is read carefully, take the numbers from the setup and plug them into the function from the setup, and then do some algebra. (If we want to approach the question in a slightly different way, which would allow us to avoid working with e and natural log, then we could backsolve. This would involve trying out each value from the answer choices as t, and identifying which answer choice makes the function statement valid. I'll demonstrate this approach below, after we walk through the traditional approach first.)

We're given the function for the current amount of a particular element in radioactive decay:

$E(t) = ae\char`^(\frac{-t}{1000})$, where:

- t is the elapsed time in years

- a is the initial amount of the element

- $E(t)$ is the amount of the element at any time t

Then we're asked how many years it would take for an initial amount of 600 milligrams to decay to 300 milligrams. So let's plug those values into the function:

$E(t) = ae\char`^(\frac{-t}{1000})$	(given function from the prompt)
$300 = 600e\char`^(\frac{-t}{1000})$	(plug in $E(t) = 300$ and $a = 600$)
$\frac{1}{2} = e\char`^(\frac{-t}{1000})$	(divide both sides by 600)
$-0.693 \approx \frac{-t}{1000}$	(take natural log of both sides)
$-693 \approx -t$	(multiply both sides by 1000)
$693 \approx t$	(multiply both sides by -1)

So it takes approximately 693 years for 600 milligrams of the element to decay to 300 milligrams. That means the correct answer is (C).

If we want to attack this question without having to use the natural log, then we can approach the question in another way by taking the values from each answer choice and plugging them in to see which one makes the original function valid.

Again, we're given the following function:

$E(t) = ae\char`^(\frac{-t}{1000})$, where:

- t is the elapsed time in years

- a is the initial amount of the element

- $E(t)$ is the amount of the element at any time t

The question asks how long it would take for 600 milligrams to decay to 300 milligrams. So a, the initial amount, is 600, while $E(t)$ is 300. Just as we did in the other approach we'll plug that into the given function:

$$E(t) = ae^{\wedge}(\tfrac{-t}{1000}) \qquad \text{(given function)}$$

$$300 = 600e^{\wedge}(\tfrac{-t}{1000}) \qquad \text{(plug in } E(t) = 300 \text{ and } a = 600)$$

This tells us that the correct value for t will make the expression on the right side of the equation be equal to 300. So let's take that expression on the right, plug in each answer choice for t, and see which one gives a result of 300.

Choice (A):

$$600e^{\wedge}(\tfrac{-t}{1000}) \qquad \text{(right side of the original function after plugging in } E(t) = 300 \text{ and } a = 600)$$

$$600e^{\wedge}(\tfrac{-0.5}{1000}) \qquad \text{(plug in } t = 0.5)$$

$$599.7001 \qquad \text{(use a calculator to evaluate } 600e^{\wedge}(\tfrac{-0.5}{1000}))$$

So when we plug in $t = 0.5$, the expression on the right side of the equation is equal to 599.7001, which is basically twice as much as 300, the number we're looking for. So choice (A) is wrong.

Choice (B):

$$600e^{\wedge}(\tfrac{-t}{1000}) \qquad \text{(right side of the original function after plugging in } E(t) = 300 \text{ and } a = 600)$$

$$600e^{\wedge}(\tfrac{-500}{1000}) \qquad \text{(plug in } t = 500)$$

$$363.9184 \qquad \text{(combine like terms)}$$

When we plug in $t = 500$, the expression is equal to 363.9184. Again, we know that the correct value for t should make the expression equal to 300, not 363.9184, so choice (B) isn't correct.

Choice (C):

$$600e^{\wedge}(\tfrac{-t}{1000}) \qquad \text{(right side of the original function after plugging in } E(t) = 300 \text{ and } a = 600)$$

$$600e^{\wedge}(\tfrac{-693}{1000}) \qquad \text{(plug in } t = 693)$$

$$300.0442 \qquad \text{(combine like terms)}$$

When we plug in $t = 693$, the expression is equal to 300.0442. This is extremely close to 300, which is the value that we're looking for. If no other answer choice yields a result that's very close to 300, we can be confident that choice (C) is correct. This is because we know that our calculator is using a decimal approximation of e, which means we should expect that we might have to do some small rounding, like rounding 300.0442 to 300. Now let's take a look at the remaining choices.

Choice (D):

$600e\text{^}(\frac{-t}{1000})$ (right side of the original function after plugging in $E(t)$ = 300 and a = 600)

$600e\text{^}(\frac{-1,443}{1000})$ (plug in t = 1,443)

141.7308   (combine like terms)

When we plug in t = 1,443, the expression is equal to 141.7308. We know that the correct value for t should make the expression equal to 300, not 141.7308, so choice (D) must be wrong.

Choice (E):

$600e\text{^}(\frac{-t}{1000})$ (right side of the original function after plugging in $E(t)$ = 300 and a = 600)

$600e\text{^}(\frac{-5,704}{1000})$ (plug in t = 5,704)

1.9996   (combine like terms)

When we plug in t = 5,704, the expression is equal to 1.9996. So (E) isn't correct, because we need the expression on the right-hand side of the equation to equal 300.

After plugging each answer choice into the function, we've shown that choice (C) is the only choice that's basically equal to 300 (remember that we had to allow for a small rounding error because we were backsolving with our calculator, and the calculator relies on a decimal approximation of e). So (C) is correct.

As trained test-takers, we may find it interesting that the various wrong answers are actually *easier* to fall for if the question is approached in the traditional way; on the other hand, the backsolving approach that we just used makes it almost impossible to fall for the wrong answers, as long as we enter each expression into the calculator carefully. For example, choice (B) is the result if you only take the natural log of the side of the equation with e, instead of taking the natural log of *both sides* of the equation. Choice (A) is the same as (B), with the added mistake of not multiplying both sides by 1000. Choice (E) is the natural log of 300 multiplied by 1000, which we might find if we take the natural log before isolating the term with e. Again, these are all simple algebra mistakes that a test-taker might make if he tried a traditional approach to this question, but the backsolving approach neatly avoids them. To be clear, I'm NOT suggesting that you should always backsolve! I'm just pointing out that backsolving may have some advantages in some situations, and you shouldn't be afraid to try it just because your math teacher wouldn't allow it in class. We have to remember that the College Board often rewards approaches that wouldn't work in school.

Page 169, Question 28

When we see a question that asks about the behavior of the graph of a function, as this one does, we know that the quickest and easiest way to find the answer is usually to graph the function on a calculator. If we do that, we'll see that the graph of the given function looks like this:

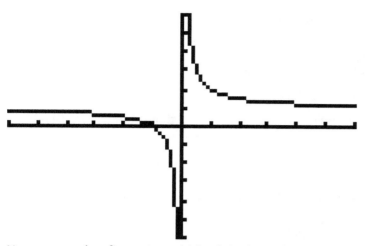

Now we need to figure out which of the lines described in the Roman numerals is an asymptote of the graph.

(Remember that an asymptote is a line that's approached by a function curve as the graph of the function goes off toward infinity on the x- and/or y- axes. An asymptote is NOT a part of the function curve itself.)

At this point, if you're comfortable with graphing, you may be able to look at the lines in the Roman numerals and figure out immediately which ones could be asymptotes. But if you're not comfortable with that, you could also try adding each of the lines from the Roman numerals to the graph of the curve from the prompt:

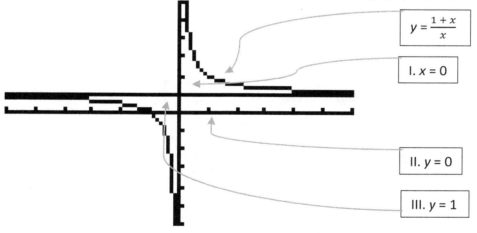

$$y = \frac{1 + x}{x}$$

I. $x = 0$

II. $y = 0$

III. $y = 1$

Let's consider each of the three lines from the Roman numerals in turn:

The first line is $x = 0$, which is a vertical line that lies on the y-axis. We can see that the graph of the function curve is constantly approaching this vertical line both from the left and from the right, but never touches or crosses it. (If you'd like to use your calculator to verify that the two lines never cross, you can zoom in on different parts of the graph, and you'll always see that the function curve is separate from $x = 0$, even though the two graphs get closer and closer to each other as you move towards positive and negative infinity on the y-axis.) So we know there is an asymptote at $x = 0$.

Now let's look at the second line, $y = 0$. We can see on the graph that $y = 0$ is a horizontal line that lies on the x-axis. We can also see that the curve of the function from the prompt actually *crosses* this line. That means $y = 0$ isn't an asymptote, because an asymptote of a curve must never cross the curve, by definition.

The third line we need to consider is $y = 1$. We can see that the graph of the function from the prompt continuously approaches $y = 1$ as the graph goes off to positive and negative infinity on the x-axis, but the two never meet. (Again, you can verify this in your calculator by changing the window and zoom settings to view different areas of the graph.) So $y = 1$ is also an asymptote of the given function.

Since I and III are asymptotes of the function, we know that the correct answer is choice (D).

This question is one more example of the importance of knowing properties and definitions on the Math Level 2 Test, because we'd have a very hard time answering this question if we didn't know the definition of the word "asymptote."

This question is also a great example of the way that graphing calculators can help us on the Math Level 2 Test. It's probably much easier for most test-takers to answer a question like this if they can see the behavior of the given function and the three lines at a glance, rather than having to calculate anything. Remember that it's perfectly okay to approach test questions in ways that your math teacher probably wouldn't allow, as long as you can arrive at the correct answer with certainty—in fact, the fastest and easiest approaches to test questions are often ones that involve exploiting the design of the test, as we just did in this approach. (Of course, if you prefer to approach the question without using a calculator, as the College Board explanation does on page 187 of the MSTB, that's perfectly fine. My point is just that other kinds of approaches can also work.)

Also notice the importance of checking out ALL of the given lines in the question. Some untrained test-takers might just check line I, see that it's an asymptote, and then mark (A) without checking the other two lines, possibly because they incorrectly assume that a function can only have one asymptote. This is one more reminder of the way we need to be in the habit of always considering everything in the question and answer choices before choosing an answer!

Page 169, Question 29

A lot of untrained test-takers will incorrectly assume there's some formal way to approach this question, and they'll panic because they don't know what that formal approach is. But the reason they don't know the formal approach to this question is that there isn't one.

On the other hand, trained test-takers like us always remember that a large number of questions on this test won't have formal solutions; when we see a question that looks a little strange, like this one does, we know that it's often possible—even necessary—to figure out the answer without relying on any specific, formal approach we might have seen before in math class. So we just read carefully, think about the properties and definitions of the concepts in the prompt and in the answer choices, and see what we can come up with.

As is often the case, there are two general ways we could choose to approach this question:

1. the concrete approach, which involves picking values for x and plugging them in to see what happens

2. the abstract approach, which involves thinking about the properties of the concepts in the question, without actually doing any calculations

The concrete approach is often easier for people who feel a little less confident in their math skills, while the abstract approach is often faster for test-takers who feel comfortable with it. Either approach can get you to the correct answer with total certainty. As we usually do in this Black Book, we'll discuss the concrete approach first, and then the abstract one.

For the concrete approach, we can take the following steps:

1. Choose an arbitrary number for x.

2. Plug that number in for x in the equation in the prompt.

3. Using the values from Step 2, take the value of the expression $2x + 1$ from the prompt, and plug it in as x in each answer choice.

4. Pick the answer choice whose value matches the value of $2x - 1$ that we found in Step 2.

(If that doesn't make sense yet, please keep reading through the explanation, and you'll see where we're going with this.)

When we choose numbers to plug in, we have to remember that we don't want to pick -1, 0, 1, or any numbers from the question, because those numbers might have unique properties relative to the question, which could result in more than one answer choice seeming to be valid. So I'll choose to use $x = 5$ here.

If $x = 5$, then $f(2x + 1)$ is the same as $f(2(5) + 1)$, which is the same thing as $f(11)$. Also, $2x - 1$ is the same as $2(5) - 1$, which is 9.

So we've figured out that if $x = 5$, then $f(2x - 1) = f(11) = 9$. In other words, plugging 11 into the f function yields a result of 9.

To figure out the correct answer to the question using this concrete approach, we need to know which answer choice will produce 9 when we plug in 11 as the x-value for function f. Let's try out each choice:

Choice (A)

$-x + 1$	(given expression)
$-(11) + 1$	(plug in 11)
-10	(combine like terms)

We figured out that when $x = 5$, $f(11) = 9$. But when we plugged 11 into this expression we got -10, not 9. So choice (A) isn't correct.

Choice (B)

$x - 1$	(given expression)
$(11) - 1$	(plug in 11)
10	(combine like terms)

We figured out that when $x = 5$, $f(11) = 9$. But when we plugged 11 into this expression we got 10, not 9. So choice (B) isn't correct.

Choice (C)

$x - 2$	(given expression)
$(11) - 2$	(plug in 11)
9	(combine like terms)

We figured out that when $x = 5$, $f(11) = 9$. When we plugged 11 into this expression, we got 9. So choice (C) appears to be the correct answer. Let's check the rest of the answer choices to make sure.

Choice (D)

$2x - 1$	(given expression)
$2(11) - 1$	(plug in 11)
21	(combine like terms)

We figured out that when $x = 5$, $f(11) = 9$. But when we plugged 11 into this expression we got 21, not 9. So choice (D) isn't correct.

Choice (E)

$\frac{1}{2}x - 1$	(given expression)
$\frac{1}{2}(11) - 1$	(plug in 11)
$\frac{9}{2}$	(combine like terms)

We figured out that when $x = 5$, $f(11) = 9$. But when we plugged 11 into this expression we got $\frac{9}{2}$, not 9. So choice (E) isn't correct.

After checking all the answer choices, we can see that choice (C) is correct.

Now, let's discuss the abstract, algebraic approach.

Answering this question in an abstract way requires an understanding of what we mean when we say $f(2x + 1) = 2x - 1$. In simple terms, that mathematical expression means that plugging $2x + 1$ into the f function will transform $2x + 1$ into $2x - 1$. In other words, the correct answer to the question will be an algebraic description of that transformation.

There's no formulaic way to figure out how the transformation will be described! Rather than lean on a formula, we just need to think about the information in the problem—as we've seen, this kind of flexible, detail-oriented approach is the key to scoring high on the Math Level 2 Test.

We should notice that the answer choices are all relatively simple expressions, which is reassuring, and not too surprising for a trained test-taker. The simplicity of the answer choices indicates the College Board isn't going to make us do anything complicated to find the answer. So let's think. Which of these answer choices reflects the difference between $2x + 1$ and $2x - 1$?

The difference between those two expression is just 2. If we subtract 2 from $2x + 1$, we get $2x - 1$.

This means the f function involves subtracting 2 from the input. So $f(x) = x - 2$, and (C) is correct.

When we look at the other answer choices, we see that the College Board seems to be trying to trap untrained test-takers in the usual ways. For example, choice (D) might trick someone who read the question too quickly, or who doesn't understand function notation, because (D) shows the same expression that was equivalent to $f(2x + 1)$ in the prompt, which means it can't be equal to $f(x)$ as well. (D) could also be tempting to someone who executes the concrete approach above in the wrong way, and mistakenly thinks the correct answer should be equal to the value that was found for $2x - 1$ in the prompt.

If we look at the table on page 178 of the MSTB, we see that only 54% of test-takers answered this question correctly, even though it involves relatively basic concepts like function notation, addition, and subtraction. Let this remind you, yet again, that the key to scoring high on the Math Level 2 Test is to be able to handle relatively simple concepts like this, even when they're presented in strange ways.

Page 170, Question 30

This question asks us to provide the coordinates for the center of a circle that would be tangent to both axes. A lot of untrained test-takers will assume that answering this question will require them to know something about the formal equations for describing a circle based on the circle's center and radius.

Trained test-takers, on the other hand, will realize that the question really requires us to understand the definitions of a few basic concepts:

- coordinate notation
- the center of a circle
- tangent
- x-axis
- y-axis

If we know these concepts, we can identify the correct answer choice without ever using a formula. (In fact, you could even find the correct answer without ever picking up your pencil, but I'll use diagrams in this discussion for the sake of illustration.)

One way to approach this question is to consider each of the points in the answer choices, and then try to use each given point as the center of a circle that's tangent to the x- and y-axes. So let's do that:

Choice (A): (-1, 0)

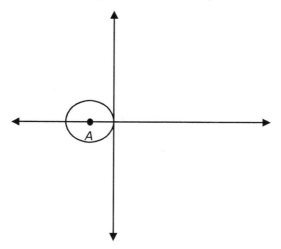

If we try to draw a circle with center (-1, 0), we'll find that we can make the circle tangent to the y-axis, but not to the x-axis—in fact, we can see in the drawing above that if the center of a circle is located on an axis, then the circle can't possibly be tangent to that axis, because the axis must intersect the circle in 2 points, and we know that a line is only tangent to a circle if both figures lie in the same plane and they only intersect in one point. That means choice (A) isn't correct.

Choice (B): (-1, 2)

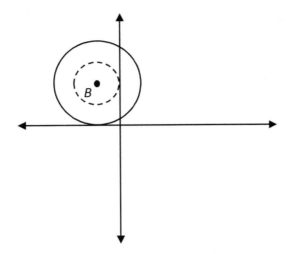

If we try to draw a circle with center (-1, 2), we find that we can make the circle tangent to *either* the *x*-axis (the solid circle) *or* the *y*-axis (the dashed circle), but not to both at once. (As the College Board's explanation points out on page 187 of the MSTB, this is because the center point is located at different distances from the two axes, which means that it's impossible for the radius of the circle to have the exact same length as the distance from the center to both axes.) So choice (B) isn't correct, either.

Choice (C): (0, 2)

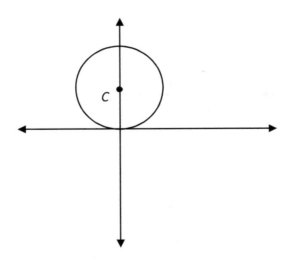

If we try to draw a circle with center (0, 2), we run into the same issue we had with choice (A), except that this time we see the center of the circle is on the *y*-axis, which means the circle intersects the *y*-axis twice, instead of the *x*-axis. That means choice (C) is wrong, too.

Choice (D): (2, -2)

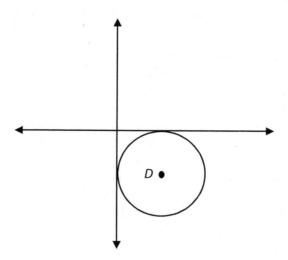

If we try to draw a circle with center (2, -2), we'll find that we can make the circle tangent to both the x-axis and the y-axis, because the center is the same distance from both axes, which means we can give it a radius that allows it to touch both axes in exactly one point each. So choice (D) is correct. Still, as trained test-takers, we know that we need to consider every answer choice before moving on to the next question, to help us make sure that we haven't made a mistake somewhere. So let's take a look at (E).

Choice (E): (2, 1)

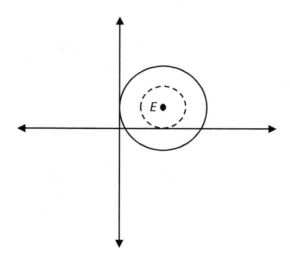

If we try to draw a circle with center (2, 1), we'll find that we can make the circle tangent to either the x-axis (the dashed circle) or the y-axis (the solid circle), but not both at one time—just as we saw with choice (B). That means choice (E) is wrong, just like choice (B) was.

Once we try out each answer choice, we can see that only choice (D) satisfies the question's requirements. So (D) is the correct answer.

You've probably never seen anything like this question on a high school math test before. But by now you should know that the College Board likes to present you with strange combinations of basic concepts, and you should be growing more comfortable with the idea of reading carefully, identifying the concepts that might be relevant to a question, and then using those concepts to identify the correct answer to the question, just as we did in this explanation.

I'd also like to point out that it's actually impossible to answer this question without considering the answer choices during the solution itself. In other words, there's no way to just read the prompt and know immediately which numbers should appear in the correct answer, because there's an infinite set of possible values that could appear—basically, any point whose coordinates have the same absolute value could be a valid answer to this question, because any point like that would be the same distance from both axes, just like (2, -2) is. So this is an example of a question that literally requires us to consider the answer choices as we try to figure out the answer. When we look at these answer choices, we may be able to realize that there are similarities among some of them—for example, as we mentioned above, (A) and (C) are both located on one of the axes. We might also see that only (D) has the property of having two coordinates with equal absolute values, and we might realize how that property is relevant to the question (in fact, it makes (D) the correct answer). But a big difference between trained test-takers and untrained test-takers is that the trained test-takers will consider the answer choices as part of the solution process *on every single question*, not just on questions like this one where it's required. Keep this in mind as you continue to prepare for the test.

Page 170, Question 31

In order to answer this question, we have to understand what the term "range" means in the context of functions. The range of a function is the set of possible *y*-values that can be produced by plugging in all possible *x*-values.

We also need to understand what a "piecewise" function is (although we don't have to be familiar with the name). A "piecewise" function is made up of pieces that are defined differently for different sets of *x*-values. In this case, $f(x) = x^{\frac{1}{3}}$ when $x > 2$, and $f(x) = 2x - 1$ when $x \le 2$.

(If we weren't familiar with this notation, we could probably have figured it out by reading the function closely. On the left side, we see "$f(x) =$," so we know that whatever is on the right side will be a function of *x*. Then we see a big bracket, which probably means that everything in the bracket is part of the function. When we see $f(x) = x^{\frac{1}{3}}, x > 2$, we could probably guess that the function is equal to $x^{\frac{1}{3}}$ when *x* is greater than 2. Along similar lines, we could probably guess from $f(x) = 2x - 1, x \le 2$ that the function is equal to $2x - 1$ when *x* is less than or equal to 2.)

(Remember not to be intimidated when you see something unfamiliar on the Math Level 2 Test! Just read carefully and think about what you're reading, and you'll often be able to understand enough of the question to be able to answer it with total confidence. Still, if you don't feel comfortable with the concepts from this question, or from any other question we talk about, be sure to review the relevant sections in this book's Math Toolbox.)

A lot of test-takers will probably feel more comfortable dealing with the part of the function defined by $2x - 1$, since it doesn't involve a fractional exponent, so we'll start with that.

We're told that 2 is the largest *x*-value that will be plugged into $2x - 1$. So let's try plugging that number in as a starting point—maybe we'll learn something valuable, or maybe we'll have to try another number. Either, way, it shouldn't take too long to plug in 2, and then maybe we'll have something to go on. When we plug in 2, we get a *y*-value of $2(2) - 1$, which works out to 3.

Any other *x*-value we plug in to $2x - 1$ will have to be less than 2, because we're told that the function is defined by $2x - 1$ only for *x*-values that are less than or equal to 2.

So let's think about what we can learn from what we've done so far. We can see that any *x*-value lower than 2 will produce a *y*-value less than 3, because we'll be multiplying a lower number by 2, and then subtracting 1. For example, 2(1) − 1 = 1, and 2(-10) − 1 = -21, and so on. There's no limit to how low the *x*-value can be, so in this part of the function there's no limit to how low the resulting *y*-value can be—either value could go all the way to negative infinity, so to speak. That means we know that the lower range for this portion of the function has to include everything from negative infinity to 3.

With this in mind, assuming we're correct so far, we can tell that (A), (C), and (D) are wrong, because they don't account for values extending to negative infinity.

Now what happens if we work with *x*-values above 2?

For *x*-values greater than 2, $f(x)$ is equal to $x^{\frac{1}{3}}$. For example, if $x = 5$, then $f(x) = 5^{\frac{1}{3}}$, which is approximately 1.71. If $x = 100$, then $f(x) = 100^{\frac{1}{3}}$, or approximately 4.64. So, as we can see, when *x* increases, we're just taking a larger and larger number and raising it to an exponent of $\frac{1}{3}$. That means $x^{\frac{1}{3}}$ increases without limit as *x* increases.

So the lowest possible value for *y* in this part of the domain is just barely more than $2^{\frac{1}{3}}$ (since $f(x) = x^{\frac{1}{3}}$ only when $x > 2$), and the highest possible *y*-value in this part of the graph is positive infinity, since $x^{\frac{1}{3}}$ will increase forever as *x* increases forever.

So the overall range for this function combines the range we found for the first portion of the graph (which was negative infinity to 3) with the range we found for the second portion of the graph (which went from $2^{\frac{1}{3}}$—or roughly 1.26—to positive infinity). Since the range includes all numbers from negative infinity to 3, and it also includes all numbers from $2^{\frac{1}{3}}$ to infinity, we know the range stretches from negative infinity to positive infinity—in other words, it includes all real numbers. So (E) is correct.

Another way to answer this question is to graph both functions on a calculator—this is probably the fastest and easiest approach for most students.

(If it were test day and you didn't know how to graph a piecewise function on your calculator, you could just graph both functions at one time, and look at the graph of $f(x) = x^{\frac{1}{3}}$ where $x > 2$, and look at the graph of $f(x) = 2x - 1$ where $x \le 2$, and ignore everything else.)

When you do that, you can see again that (E) is correct. The range of this function—the set of all possible *y*-values that the piecewise function can possibly have—is all real numbers, because the range extends from negative infinity to positive infinity.

Page 170, Question 32

The College Board's solution for this question, which appears on page 188 of the MSTB, is technically correct, of course. But it's a bit more complex than necessary—it involves the quadratic formula, for one thing. There's nothing wrong with taking that approach if you want to, but, as always, I want to make sure you're aware that the questions on this test can be approached in a variety of ways. So let's try an approach that will be less intimidating for a lot of test-takers.

In this question, we're given two equations involving *x* and *y*, and we're asked to solve for *x*. The basic mathematical challenge in a situation like this is that it's usually impossible to solve for the numerical value of a single variable when there are other variables in the same equation. So the first thing we'll want to do here (after reading the question and answer choices, of course) is to figure out a way to express y in terms of x, so we can eventually arrive at an equation that only involves x, without y. Then we'll use algebra to solve that equation for x.

As trained test-takers, we know that the College Board usually makes the steps in a calculation relatively simple and easy if we look at the question in the right way. With that in mind, we may be able to notice that the easiest way to express y in terms of x is to see that the second equation works out to $2y = x^2$, and the first equation has the expression $4y$ in it. Well, if $2y$ is the same thing as x^2, and $4y$ is twice as much as $2y$, then $4y$ must be equal to $2x^2$, right? That means we can switch out the $4y$ in the first equation for $2x^2$, which gives us this:

$3x - 2x^2 + 7 = 0$

This is where the formal mathematical explanation on page 188 of the MSTB tells us to rearrange the terms a little bit and use the quadratic formula. Again, that approach would work, of course, but it's probably not the quickest and simplest way for most test-takers to find the answer, especially if they don't remember the quadratic formula.

So, at this point, we could just take the values from the 5 answer choices, plug them into our equation, and see which one makes the equation valid. (Remember that the correct answer choice may end up being a rounded approximation, because we're dealing with squaring x.)

(A) $3x - 2x^2 + 7 = 0$ (our equation in terms of x)

$3(1.27) - 2(1.27)^2 + 7$ (plug in $x = 1.27$)

7.5842 (evaluate expression)

7.5842 isn't close to 0, so choice (A) must be wrong.

(B) $3x - 2x^2 + 7 = 0$ (our equation in terms of x)

$3(2.07) - 2(2.07)^2 + 7$ (plug in $x = 2.07$)

4.6402 (evaluate expression)

4.6402 isn't close to 0, so choice (B) is wrong.

(C) $3x - 2x^2 + 7 = 0$ (our equation in terms of x)

$3(2.77) - 2(2.77)^2 + 7$ (plug in $x = 2.77$)

$- 0.0358$ (evaluate expression)

$- 0.0358$ is pretty close to 0, so choice (C) looks like it's probably correct, because we're expecting some rounding to be involved, as I mentioned above. Let's take a look at the remaining answer choices.

(D) $3x - 2x^2 + 7 = 0$ (our equation in terms of x)

$3(4.15) - 2(4.15)^2 + 7$ (plug in $x = 4.15$)

-14.995 (evaluate expression)

-14.995 isn't close to 0, so choice (D) must be wrong.

(E) $3x - 2x^2 + 7 = 0$ (our equation in terms of x)

$3(5.53) - 2(5.53)^2 + 7$ (plug in $x = 5.53$)

-37.5718 (evaluate expression)

-37.5718 isn't close to 0, so choice (E) must be wrong.

After plugging in all the possibilities, we can see that only (C) gives us a result that's very close to zero, which means we can confidently choose (C) as the correct answer.

Notice that we didn't need to use the quadratic equation—or even be familiar with it—in order to answer this question in the way that we just demonstrated. As I've said repeatedly in this Black Book, and as I'll say again, the design of the Math Level 2 Test allows us to attack many questions in non-traditional ways, and it's important for us to keep that in mind at all times.

(Of course, there's nothing wrong with using the quadratic formula if that's what you prefer and you can do it correctly. But it's often possible to use a less formal approach on Math Level 2 questions, and less formal approaches often present fewer opportunities for error. And anyway a lot of test-takers just aren't very comfortable with the quadratic formula.)

There are still other ways to approach this question, of course. You could choose to skip the process of combining the two equations altogether, and test each answer choice by plugging in its value for x in the first of the given equations, obtaining a value for y from the first equation. Then you could take the same x and y-values from the first equation, and plug them into the second equation to see if they make that equation true. Only the correct answer choice will do that. And another approach would be to use your graphing calculator to graph both equations, and then see which answer choice corresponds to an x-coordinate of a point of intersection between the two graphs. Again, I'm not recommending any of these approaches over any other approach—the point is just that the College Board often writes multiple-choice questions so that they can be successfully attacked in multiple ways.

There are two other answer choices I'd like to discuss at this point, because they demonstrate test-design principles that we need to know about, as trained test-takers.

The first interesting wrong answer choice is (A), which is actually the opposite of the *negative* value of x that satisfies the equation. You may be wondering how a test-taker could possibly arrive at this value, but that's because we avoided the quadratic formula in the approaches I laid out above. But if you were to use the quadratic formula on this question, there's a chance you could make a simple mistake with the signs of the numbers involved, and accidentally end up with the value in choice (A). In other words, using the formal approach to this question actually makes it *more likely* that you could end up choosing one of the wrong answers. This isn't an uncommon situation on the Math Level 2 Test. Keep in mind that one of the benefits of using a less formal approach is that there are sometimes fewer opportunities to make mistakes like the one that might lead to choosing (A) in this situation. (Again, I'm not saying that it would be wrong to use the formal approach. It wouldn't be wrong to do that at all, as long as you use it properly. I'm just pointing out that some of the wrong answer choices on the test are designed to trap people who execute a formal solution incorrectly.)

Another interesting wrong answer choice is (E), which is roughly twice as much as (C), the correct answer (remember that the values in these answer choices are rounded to two decimals). We've talked a lot about how the College Board likes to use wrong answer patterns, and how one of the patterns we'll frequently encounter is a situation where a wrong answer is either twice as much or half as much as the right answer. Choice (E) is particularly interesting because there's no real way that a test-taker would be likely to make a mistake on this question that would result in doubling the correct answer accidentally, which strongly suggests that the College Board included choice (E) just because it tries to follow the halves-and-doubles pattern purely for its own sake.

Page 171, Question 33

I've had many students tell me that the College Board's solution to this question, which appears on page 188 of the MSTB, is more complicated than necessary. I have to agree with them. So I'd like to give you an easier way to think about this question without involving extra variables.

To answer this question, we need to be able to do the following things:

1. Recognize that $f^{-1}(x)$ is notation that indicates the inverse function of the $f(x)$ that appears in the prompt.

2. Know how to find the inverse of a given function (as many math teachers say, "switch x and y, then re-solve for y").

3. Know how to work with a logarithm algebraically.

Each of these concepts should be relatively simple for a math student who's planning to take the Math Level 2 Test. But, as always, the key to getting the question right will be paying close attention to details and avoiding mistakes. Let's take a look.

To find the inverse of a function, we switch the locations of the x and y variables in the original function, and then re-solve for y.

First, of course, we need to change $f(x)$ to y, or else we won't have a y to switch (remember that y and $f(x)$ are essentially equivalent concepts in function notation for the purposes of this test):

$$y = \log_2 x$$

Now we switch the x and y variables:

$$x = \log_2 y$$

Finally, we solve this new equation for y.

As you can see, the only expression involving y in the new equation is $\log_2 y$. So, in order to isolate y on one side of the equation algebraically, we need to make each side of the equation an exponent with a base of 2:

$$2^x = 2^{\log_2 y}$$

Then we just simplify the right-hand side of the equation, which leaves us with this:

$$2^x = y$$

(Another way to think of these last two steps is to note that $\log_2 y$ means, by definition, the exponent to which we'd raise 2 in order to arrive at y. So, in this case, $2^x = y$.)

Finally, we just switch y to $f^{-1}(x)$, because the y now represents the output of the inverse function we've found, and we can see that $f^{-1}(x) = 2^x$. So (A) is correct.

As will often be the case, the wrong answer choices represent many of the simple mistakes a test-taker could make.

Choice (B) is what we might get if we messed up the last couple of steps or forgot how logarithms worked, accidentally choosing x^2 instead of 2^x.

(C) is what we'd get if we made x the numerator in a fraction with a denominator of 2, instead of making x an exponent for a base of 2. Again, this is a mistake we could easily imagine some test-takers making if they got confused.

(D) is the reciprocal of the fraction in (C), so it kind of represents a mistake on a mistake.

(E) gives us still another way to make a mistake when we deal with the log expression. Here, the test is anticipating that some people will incorrectly think the inverse of $\log_2 y$ is $\log_y 2$, which would make the x side of the equation $\log_x 2$. An untrained test-taker might also guess that (E) was correct if she was incorrectly expecting the correct answer choice to include the word "log" because the prompt includes it.

(If you had difficulty with this question because of the logarithm involved, you'll want to make sure you review the portion of the Math Toolbox that deals with logs, because there's a very good chance you'll see at least one question on test day that deals with those concepts.)

Page 171, Question 34

This question gives us the definition for a term in a series and asks for x_3 in that series. Since we're given the zeroth term in the series and we're only asked for the third term in the series, we can just figure out the first, second, and third terms.

(As trained test-takers, we know that some or all of the wrong answer choices will probably be other terms in the series, because a lot of careless test-takers will accidentally mis-count the terms. So we need to be extra careful that the term we choose for our answer is really the third term, and not the first, second, fourth, etc.)

We're told that $x_0 = 0$, and that $x_{n+1} = \sqrt{6 + x_n}$. We're asked to find x_3. But what if we're not familiar with this kind of subscript notation? Well, let's just read carefully, think about the information in the question, and see if we can come up with anything.

We need to find x_3, and we have a formula to find x_{n+1} by using x_n. If we want to use that formula to find x_3, then we'll have to make x_{n+1} be x_3, which means x_n would be x_2 in that case. So we know that we can use x_2 to find x_3.

But how do we find x_2? If we need to know x_2 in order to find x_3, it makes sense that we'd need to know x_1 to find x_2. And, following that logic, we'll need to know x_0 in order to find x_1. The question does give us a value for x_0, though! So let's start there.

We can use x_0 to find x_1 using the given definition of x_{n+1}, and then we can use x_1 to find x_2, and use x_2 to find x_3, which is what the question is asking for.

So, if $x_{n+1} = \sqrt{6 + x_n}$, then x_1 must be equal to $\sqrt{6 + x_0}$. Since $x_0 = 0$, that means $x_1 = \sqrt{6 + 0}$, or $\sqrt{6}$, or approximately 2.449.

(By the way, notice that 2.449 is choice (A). But (A) isn't the correct answer—it's the value of x_1, and we were asked to find the value of x_3. The fact that we've run into one of the answer choices during our solution is probably a good sign that we're on the right track, though.)

To find x_2, we just go back to the formula. This time, we take the value we found for x_1 and plug it in as x_n:

$$x_{n+1} = \sqrt{6 + x_n}$$ 　　　　(given formula for finding the next term in the series)

$$x_2 = \sqrt{6 + x_1}$$ 　　　　(set x_2 as x_{n+1}, and set x_1 as x_n)

$$x_2 = \sqrt{6 + 2.449}$$ 　　　　(plug in 2.449 as the approximation of x_1)

$$x_2 = \sqrt{8.449}$$ 　　　　(add 6 and 2.449)

$$x_2 \approx 2.907$$ 　　　　(evaluate square root)

2.907 is answer choice (B) but, again, it's not the correct answer! We've only found x_2, but we still need to find x_3, because that's what the question asks for. To do that, we use the formula again, this time plugging in x_2 for x_n:

$x_{n+1} = \sqrt{6 + x_n}$ (given formula for finding the next term in the series)

$x_3 = \sqrt{6 + x_2}$ (set x_3 as x_{n+1}, and set x_2 as x_n)

$x_3 = \sqrt{6 + 2.907}$ (plug in 2.907 as the approximation of x_2)

$x_3 = \sqrt{8.907}$ (add 6 and 2.907)

$x_3 \approx 2.984$ (evaluate square root)

So x_3 is 2.984, which means the correct answer is choice (C).

A lot of people might choose (B) because they accidentally think it's the "third" term in the series—after all, it *is* the third number we encountered from the series! But we have to notice that the first term we were given in the question is actually the zeroth term, not the first term—we were given x_0, not x_1, and we were asked to find x_3.

Also, notice that choice (D) is equal to x_4 Here's a table with the values for the first five terms in the series:

x_0	0
x_1	2.449
x_2	2.907
x_3	2.984
x_4	2.997

(You don't have to generate this table to answer this question correctly, of course. I'm just providing it here for your reference.)

Notice that it's possible to do all the math correctly, but still miss the question if we get confused about which term is x_3. This is another great example of how careful reading is just as important as math knowledge on this test—we can do all the math right and still be wrong because of a reading mistake!

Also notice the series in the answer choices: choice (A), (B), (C), and (D) are x_1, x_2, x_3, and x_4, respectively. We know that when the answer choices contain numbers in a series, it's a little more likely that the correct answer will be a part of the series, and a little more likely that it won't be the first or last number in that series. That pattern would suggest that choice (B) or (C) is correct, and sure enough, (C) is the correct answer. Of course, we never rely exclusively on answer choice patterns, but they can often help point us in the right direction.

Page 171, Question 35

If you'd like to see an approach to this question that uses some complex trigonometry, you can find one on page 189 of the MSTB. But there's another way to approach this that involves much less trigonometry, and is probably faster and easier for most test-takers.

To start with, we need to recognize that a triangle inscribed in a semi-circle is always a right triangle, with the straight-line portion of the semicircle as its hypotenuse.

Then, we need to think about how we find the area of a triangle. The formula for the area of a triangle is one half the product of the base and the height, or $\frac{1}{2}bh$.

When we look at the answer choices (as we always should), we notice that they're all given in terms of θ. That lets us know that we need to come up with an answer that will also be in terms of θ. Is there a way that we can find the value of the base and height of this triangle in terms of θ? There is, actually. Let's start by kind of mentally rotating the triangle so that one of its legs is the base, and the other leg is the height, like this:

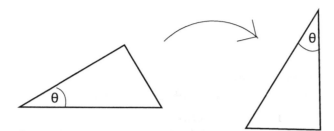

In this orientation, we can see that the side opposite θ is the base, and the side adjacent to θ is the height. So we'd like to be able to come up with a trigonometric equation that works out to something like $\frac{1}{2}$ opposite × adjacent, because that would be equivalent to $\frac{1}{2}bh$.

With this in mind, let's take a look at each answer choice.

Choice (A) is $\frac{\theta\pi}{2}$. This has the $\frac{1}{2}$ element we'd expect to see from $\frac{1}{2}bh$, but we have no reason to think that θπ would be equal to bh. So this answer choice doesn't look good so far.

Choice (B) also incorporates the idea of dividing by 2, but we have no reason to think that θ would be equal to the product of the base and the height. So (B) also looks like it has to be wrong.

Choice (C) is tan θ, which is what you get when you divide the length of the leg opposite θ by the length of the leg adjacent to θ (remember that SOHCAHTOA tells us tangent is "opposite over adjacent"). So the idea of tan θ doesn't seem to have any relevance to $\frac{1}{2}bh$ in this scenario, which means this choice doesn't seem likely to be right, either.

Choice (D) is sin θ, which is what we get if we divide the length of the opposite leg by the length of the hypotenuse. We've got no reason to think that dividing the length of the opposite leg by the length of the hypotenuse would be the same thing as multiplying half the base by the height, so choice (D) doesn't look good.

Before we consider choice (E), let's pause and remember something very important: as trained test-takers, we would never, *EVER* commit to an answer choice on the Math Level 2 without looking to see what it says first.

So we're going to give choice (E) the exact same kind of careful consideration we would give any other answer choice. If we think (E) is wrong, then we'll have to decide if we want to reconsider the entire question, or just skip it for now and come back to it, even after all the work we've put into it at this point. On the other hand, if we think (E) is correct, then we'll choose (E) and go on to the next question—but we'll only choose (E) if we actively think it's right, not just because we don't like the other four choices. This kind of mental discipline is extremely important if you want to maximize your score on a standardized test. Now that we've been reminded of this crucial fact, let's take a look at (E).

Choice (E) is 2 sin θ cos θ. Let's do what we've done with all of the other answer choices, and convert expressions like sine and cosine into the ratios they represent. When we do that, we get this:

2 sin θ cos θ   (original expression)

$$2 \times \frac{\text{opposite}}{\text{hypotenuse}} \times \frac{\text{adjacent}}{\text{hypotenuse}}$$ (substitute SOHCAHTOA ratios for sine and cosine)

Figure 2 tells us that the length of the hypotenuse is 2. Plugging in 2 for the hypotenuse gives us this:

$$2 \times \frac{\text{opposite}}{2} \times \frac{\text{adjacent}}{2}$$

That expression simplifies to this:

$$\frac{\text{opposite} \times \text{adjacent}}{2}$$

We've already established that the opposite leg was the base of the triangle, and the adjacent leg was the height, so this expression is the same as $\frac{\text{base} \times \text{height}}{2}$, which is the same as $\frac{1}{2}bh$, the formula for the area of a triangle. That means choice (E) is correct. We've already discussed all the problems with the other answer choices, so I won't revisit them here. I do want to point out once again, though, that the College Board has made it possible to answer a question on the Math Level 2 Test in a way that requires much less math knowledge than most test-takers would expect. What this approach does require, though, is a willingness to think in terms of definitions and properties, and an awareness of the set of answer choices. Keep this kind of thing in mind on test day.

Page 172, Question 36

This question is part of the minority of Math Level 2 questions that are straightforward enough that they could probably appear on the average high school math test. It's also an example of the kind of relatively basic probability concept that can be tested on the Math Level 2 Test. Since that's the case, the best approach is probably just to dive in.

To figure out the probability of multiple events happening together, we multiply the probabilities of each individual event. In this case, we're talking about 4 independent events—each "event" is a thermometer being in error by more than 1°C. The question tells us that each of these 4 independent events, on its own, has a probability of 0.2. So the probability that all four thermometers are in error by more than 1°C is $0.2 \times 0.2 \times 0.2 \times 0.2$, or 0.0016. That makes choice (A) the correct answer.

Notice that (C) is the answer we might get if we handled the decimal places incorrectly. (E) is the result if we accidentally multiply 0.2 by 4, instead of raising 0.2 to the fourth power. And choice (D) is what we get if we accidentally think we should just divide 1 by 4 (both of those numbers appear in the question, but nothing in the question indicates we should divide one by the other). Choice (B) is the result if we make an error using our calculator and accidentally enter something like 0.3^4 instead of 0.2^4.

These wrong answer choices should remind us of the importance of always reading and thinking carefully and avoiding careless errors. It would be very easy to understand the math in this question and still get it wrong because we weren't paying attention!

If you didn't feel comfortable with the concept of compound probability, you should review the section on Probability in the Math Toolbox of this Black Book.

Page 172, Question 37

This question provides another great example of the kind of small detail that can easily cause an untrained test-taker to pick a wrong answer. In this case, that small detail is the word NOT, in all capital letters. Many untrained test-takers miss questions like this because they make two simple mistakes in a row:

1. They don't pay attention to the word "NOT" in the question.

2. They commit to an answer choice as soon as they see a single choice they think could be correct, *without considering the other answer choices.*

As trained test-takers, we know that we have to read carefully, and we also know that we should consider all the answer choices in a question before moving on to the next one. On this particular question, if we accidentally overlooked the word "NOT," we might still realize that something was wrong in our understanding of the question when we looked at all of the answer choices and thought that more than one of the answer choices could be correct. Since we know that only one choice can actually be right, we'd know that we had made a mistake.

With all of that in mind, let's address the question. Our goal is to find the value that is NOT a possible value of vector (**b** − **a**).

If you've dealt with vectors in your Math classes, then you know that a vector represents a quantity with both magnitude and direction, and that there can be complicated rules for combining vectors. But vector questions are relatively rare on the Math Level 2 SAT, and the few vector questions we'll see on this test can typically be handled pretty easily if we just think of vectors as sides of a triangle, in the sense that two vectors being added have to produce a third vector whose value meets the following requirements:

1. The value *cannot be less* than the *difference* of the values of the other two vectors
2. The value *cannot be more* than the *sum* of the value of the other two vectors

(As you can see, this situation is very similar to the triangle inequality we discussed in the Math Toolbox, which is also the concept that the College Board invokes in its solution on page 189 of the MSTB.)

So, according to this idea, the "distance" between the endpoints of the two given vectors must be an amount ranging from 7 to 17 inclusive, because that range is defined by two numbers:

- the *difference* of 12 and 5, which is 7
- the *sum* of 12 and 5, which is 17

The only answer choice that falls outside that range—meaning that it's less than 7 or greater than 17—is (A), so (A) is the correct answer.

Notice that the biggest challenge in this question is probably just not being intimidated by the term "vector." Once we get past that word, we can focus on what we're being asked, and find a solution.

Also notice that the "triangle inequality" concept that we just talked about is simply the idea that the sum of any two sides of a triangle must be greater than the other side of the triangle. For example, what if we tried to make a triangle with sides of 15, 2, and 3? We couldn't, because the two shorter sides of the triangle wouldn't be able to reach each other; the triangle would be unable to "close." So we don't actually need to memorize the term "triangle inequality," and we don't need to use any formal notation that we see in the College Board's explanation for this question. We just need to understand that a triangle can only exist if the relative lengths of its sides allow the endpoints of those sides to touch. It's important not to get so hung up on memorization that we lose sight of the reasoning that supports the things we're memorizing.

(Of course, if you're unfamiliar with vectors, make sure you review the section on Vectors in the Math Toolbox in this Black Book, so you can be aware of the ways that vectors might show up on test day.)

Page 172, Question 38

The College Board's solution for this question, which appears on page 189 of the MSTB, is technically adequate, as far as it goes. The solution on that page accurately portrays the kind of pure-math solution that would be acceptable to most high school teachers.

But I want to say a lot more about this question, because it happens to combine a lot of interesting attributes that I want you to look out for in other questions on test day. (As we often discuss in this Black Book, you'll probably never see another question on an official Math Level 2 Test that's exactly like any given question in the MSTB, but you'll definitely see other questions that re-use the less obvious aspects of this question's design.) Knowing about some of these less obvious characteristics of the test can dramatically boost your score—which is the whole point of this Black Book.

First, let's amplify the College Board's solution a little bit by discussing the likely train of thought that would lead a test-taker to implement the College Board's approach, because the College Board has omitted any discussion of that train of thought, as it often does.

This question is essentially a test of whether we understand the fundamentals of logarithms. When a trained test-taker sees the prompt, the first thing he probably notices is that the question is asking him to compare two variables that are presented as exponents *with different bases*. This is significant because the relatively simple way to approach a question that uses variables in exponents is to modify the bases of the exponent expressions until those bases are equal to each other, but there's no real way to do that here. So a trained test-taker who is familiar with logarithms will recognize that the only way to approach the question mathematically is to take the log of both sides, because logarithms are often used to solve equations in which non-identical bases are raised to exponents.

The question tells us that $(6.31)^m = (3.02)^n$. Since these two numbers are equal, the log of the two numbers must also be equal, which means $\log(6.31)^m = \log(3.02)^n$. According to the properties of the log function, we know that we can take the exponents from our original expressions and multiply them by the log expressions without the exponents, so it must be true that $m\log(6.31) = n\log(3.02)$. From there, we can do some algebra to solve for the value of $\frac{m}{n}$:

$m\log(6.31) = n\log(3.02)$	(logarithm forms of the original expressions)
$\frac{m\log(6.31)}{n} = \log(3.02)$	(divide both sides by n)
$\frac{m}{n} = \frac{\log(3.02)}{\log(6.31)}$	(divide both sides by $\log(6.31)$)
$\frac{m}{n} = \frac{0.48001}{0.80003}$	(use a calculator to evaluate log expressions)
$\frac{m}{n} = 0.60$	(simplify fraction)

So we can see that the correct answer is choice (D), 0.60.

Again, this part of our analysis is largely similar to what the College Board has given us in its explanation for this question in the MSTB, except that the College Board's explanation never explicitly tells us that the key indicator that we need to use logarithms is the fact that the question equates two expressions with different exponents and different bases. If we know how to use logarithms properly, this question should be relatively straightforward.

But what if we don't feel comfortable with the key concepts related to logarithms? Obviously, the fastest way to answer this particular question is probably to use the log function. But there's another approach we can use if we don't feel comfortable with logs. This next approach involves a bit more work than the College Board's solution, but it can be done without needing to know anything about logarithms. I'm going to show this second approach to you now—NOT necessarily because I recommend it over the original approach, but because I want to help you see that most questions on this test can be approached in multiple ways, even if some alternate approaches involve creative problem-solving. I want you to be aware of these alternate approaches because you'll probably run into at least one question on test day where you won't be able to figure out a traditional solution, but you will be able to use the test's design against it, similar to what I'll show you now.

Now, in order to be aware of this second approach, we have to keep in mind that the Math Level 2 Test doesn't penalize us if we approach a question in a strange way, or in a way that our math teachers wouldn't like. All that matters is whether we find the correct answer to a question, using any approach besides cheating. We also need to be trained to notice small details, such as the fact that the question asks for the value of $\frac{m}{n}$, which is a ratio comparing the two variables in the question—*the question never actually asks us to identify the value of either variable individually!* As trained test-takers, we know that the College Board often asks us to find the value of an expression with multiple variables in situations where it would be impossible to identify the value of a variable on its own.

In other words, we may well find that it's possible to know $\frac{m}{n}$ without ever finding specific values of m or n individually.

This, in turn, means we can evaluate each answer choice to see if it's correct. To do this, we just pick an arbitrary value for one of the variables, and then we solve for the other variable, and then we can work through the answer choices to see which choice offers us the correct ratio, given the arbitrary value we picked for one of the variables. The might sound confusing, but let's give it a shot.

Let's say that we arbitrarily decide to make m = 5 for this approach. We'd start by plugging m = 5 into the given equation:

$(6.31)^m = (3.02)^n$ (given equation)

$(6.31)^5 = (3.02)^n$ (plug in m = 5)

$10{,}003.381 = (3.02)^n$ (use a calculator to evaluate $(6.31)^5$)

Now we know that when m = 5, the expression $(3.02)^n$ is equal to approximately 10,003.381.

Now, we go through each answer choice to see which one has a ratio that results in an acceptable value for n when m = 5. In other words, when m is 5, which answer choice's ratio gives us a value for n that satisfies the original expression in the prompt?

Let's start with choice (A). Choice (A) says that $\frac{m}{n}$ = -0.32. We can do some simple algebra to solve for n, given that we decided to make m be 5 for this approach:

$\frac{m}{n} = -0.32$ (set $\frac{m}{n}$ equal to the ratio from choice (A) so we can test choice (A))

$m = -0.32n$ (multiply both sides by n)

$\frac{m}{-0.32} = n$ (divide both sides by -0.32)

Now we can plug in the m value we chose, and we can solve for the corresponding n value:

$\frac{5}{-0.32} = n$ (plug in m = 5)

$-15.625 = n$ (reduce fraction)

So if choice (A) is the correct answer, then when $m = 5$, we would have $n = -15.625$. Let's see if those values make the original expression true:

$(6.31)^m = (3.02)^n$ (original equation)

$(6.31)^5 = (3.02)^{-15.625}$ (plug in $m = 5$ and $n = -15.625$)

$10,003.381 \neq 0.0000000316148784$ (evaluate both exponent expressions with a calculator)

The two expressions in the original given statement aren't equivalent when we use these values for m and n, so choice (A) isn't correct.

Now let's check the other answer choices using this same approach. We'll continue to use $m = 5$, because we arbitrarily set m equal to 5 when we began this approach. (Remember that we just chose 5 more or less at random, and you could solve this problem using a different value for m as long as you were consistent throughout.)

Choice (B) says $\frac{m}{n} = 0.32$. We decided that $m = 5$ for our purposes, so, again, we solve for n:

$\frac{m}{n} = 0.32$ (set $\frac{m}{n}$ equal to the ratio from choice (B) so we can test choice (B))

$m = 0.32n$ (multiply both sides by n)

$\frac{m}{0.32} = n$ (divide both sides by 0.32)

$\frac{5}{0.32} = n$ (plug in $m = 5$)

$15.625 = n$ (reduce fraction)

If choice (B) is the correct answer, then when $m = 5$, $n = 15.625$. Let's plug those values back in to the original equation:

$(6.31)^m = (3.02)^n$ (original equation)

$(6.31)^5 = (3.02)^{15.625}$ (plug in $m = 5$ and $n = 15.625$)

$10,003.381 \neq 31,630,676.735$ (evaluate both exponent expressions with a calculator)

The two original expressions in the prompt aren't equivalent when we use these values for m and n, so (B) isn't correct.

Now let's try the next choice. (C) says $\frac{m}{n} = 0.48$. Again, we solve for n, given that we've assigned the value of 5 to m:

$\frac{m}{n} = 0.48$ (set $\frac{m}{n}$ equal to the ratio from choice (C) so we can test choice (C))

$m = 0.48n$ (multiply both sides by n)

$\frac{m}{0.48} = n$ (divide both sides by 0.48)

$\frac{5}{0.48} = n$ (plug in $m = 5$)

$10.417 = n$ (reduce fraction)

So if choice (C) is the correct answer, then when $m = 5$, we would have $n = 10.417$. Let's plug those values back in to the original equation from the prompt:

$(6.31)^m = (3.02)^n$ (original equation)

$(6.31)^5 = (3.02)^{10.417}$ (plug in $m = 5$ and $n = 10.417$)

$10,003.381 \neq 100,053.509$ (evaluate both exponent expressions with a calculator)

Using these m and n values, the two original expressions in the given statement aren't equal, so choice (C) isn't correct.

Now we evaluate choice (D), which says $\frac{m}{n} = 0.60$. Again we solve for n:

$\frac{m}{n} = 0.60$ (set $\frac{m}{n}$ equal to the ratio from choice (D) so we can test choice (D))

$m = 0.60n$ (multiply both sides by n)

$\frac{m}{0.60} = n$ (divide both sides by 0.60)

$\frac{5}{0.60} = n$ (plug in $m = 5$)

$8.333 = n$ (reduce fraction)

This means that if choice (D) is the correct answer, then when $m = 5$, the value of n is roughly 8.333. Let's plug those values back in to the original equation from the prompt:

$(6.31)^m = (3.02)^n$ (given equation)

$(6.31)^5 = (3.02)^{8.333}$ (plug in $m = 5$ and $n = 8.333$)

$10,003.381 \neq 9,997.648$ (evaluate both exponent expressions with a calculator)

Using these m and n values, the two original values in the given statement aren't exactly equal—but notice that they're very close to one another. In fact, they're much closer to each other than what we've seen in any of the other answer choices so far. One is slightly more than 10,000, and one is slightly less than 10,000.

We know that we've had to do some rounding while taking this approach, which means that the numbers we get out of this process aren't going to be exact. In fact, when we found our n value just now, we rounded 8.3333… to 8.333. Let's see what happens if we use a slightly more accurate value for n. We'll raise 3.02 to an exponent of 8.333333, instead of to an exponent of 8.333:

$(3.02)^{8.333333} = 10,001.329$

We can see that with less rounding, we're getting closer and closer to $(6.31)^5$. So choice (D) looks like the correct answer. But, as trained test-takers, we know that we have to consider all of the answer choices in a question, especially when we attack a question by backsolving like this. So let's check the remaining answer choice to be sure.

Choice (E) says $\frac{m}{n} = 1.67$. Once again, we plug in our arbitrary value of 5 for m, and then solve for n:

$\frac{m}{n} = 0.1.67$ (set $\frac{m}{n}$ equal to the ratio from choice (E) so we can test choice (E))

$m = 0.1.67n$ (multiply both sides by n)

$$\frac{m}{1.67} = n \qquad \text{(divide both sides by 1.67)}$$

$$\frac{5}{1.67} = n \qquad \text{(plug in } m = 5)$$

$$2.994 = n \qquad \text{(reduce fraction)}$$

So if choice (E) is the correct answer, then n = 2.994 when m = 5. Let's plug those values back in to the original equation from the prompt, to see if they make that equation true:

$$(6.31)^m = (3.02)^n \qquad \text{(given equation)}$$

$$(6.31)^5 = (3.02)^{2.994} \qquad \text{(plug in } m = 5 \text{ and } n = 2.994)$$

$$10{,}003.381 \neq 27.362 \qquad \text{(evaluate both expressions with a calculator)}$$

Using these m and n values, the two original expressions in the given statement aren't equivalent, so choice (E) is wrong.

After using this method on all the answer choices, we see that only the m and n values from choice (D) come very close to making the original statement true. Since we had to round some very large numbers as part of this approach, and since none of the m and n values from the other answer choices even came close to making the original statement true, we know that choice (D) is the correct answer.

So that's one alternate approach to this question. You can probably find others.

As we often do, let's take a look at the wrong answers and see if we can figure out how the College Board might be trying to anticipate the mistakes that a test-taker would be likely to make. For me, the most obvious error—and also the most dangerous one, and the most predictable one—is in choice (E), which is the inverse of choice (D). In other words, (D) represents what you would get if you correctly found $\frac{m}{n}$, while (E) reflects what you'd get if you misread the question and found $\frac{n}{m}$ instead. (Of course, if you accidentally thought (E) was correct, and you still followed your training and paid attention to the other answer choices before making your selection, there's a good chance you'd realize that all of the other choices are less than 1, while only (E) is more than 1. This situation would strongly suggest to a trained test-taker that the correct answer should probably be less than 1, which might give you a second chance to look back over your work and realize your mistake.)

Page 173, Question 39

This question is basically testing our understanding of arccosine. Finding the arccosine of a value gives us the number whose cosine is the original value. For example, the cosine of 60° is 0.5, and the arccosine of 0.5 is 60°.

The arccosine function is essentially the inverse of the cosine function. So if we start with x, then take the cosine of x, and then take the arccosine of that cosine, we end up right back at x again.

In other words, the expression arccos(cos x) = 0 simplifies immediately to x = 0. So the correct answer is (A).

Even if we weren't sure of the relationship between cosine and arccosine, we can pretty quickly take the values in the answer choices and plug them into a calculator to see which answer choice satisfies the equation in the question. (Note that some calculators will have a button labeled "cos^{-1}," instead of a button called "arccos." Don't worry—"cos^{-1}" is just another way to notate the idea of the function that is the inverse of the cosine function, just like "arccos.")

$$\text{(A) arccos(cos 0)} = 0 \qquad or \qquad \cos^{-1}(\cos 0) = 0$$

(B) $\arccos(\cos\frac{\pi}{6}) = \frac{\pi}{6} \approx 0.524$ or $\cos^{-1}(\cos\frac{\pi}{6}) = \frac{\pi}{6} \approx 0.524$

(C) $\arccos(\cos\frac{\pi}{4}) = \frac{\pi}{4} \approx 0.785$ or $\cos^{-1}(\cos\frac{\pi}{4}) = \frac{\pi}{4} \approx 0.785$

(D) $\arccos(\cos\frac{\pi}{3}) = \frac{\pi}{3} \approx 1.047$ or $\cos^{-1}(\cos\frac{\pi}{3}) = \frac{\pi}{3} \approx 1.047$

(E) $\arccos(\cos\frac{\pi}{2}) = \frac{\pi}{2} \approx 1.571$ or $\cos^{-1}(\cos\frac{\pi}{2}) = \frac{\pi}{2} \approx 1.571$

As we work through these values, we'll see pretty quickly that the calculator just keeps giving back the original *x*-value we plugged in. Since the prompt tells us arccos(cos x) is 0, choice (A) must be correct.

By the way, notice that, in this case, if we had accidentally left the calculator in degree mode, we would still have ended up with the correct answer. This is because finding the arccosine of the cosine of a value gives us the original value, whether the calculator is in degree mode or radian mode. But you still need to make a habit of making sure your calculator is in the correct mode, because having it in the wrong mode can cause problems on this test.

This question gives me a good opportunity to remind you of a critical aspect of time management on the Math Level 2 Test. Notice that it's pretty realistic to think a test-taker could answer this question correctly in 5 or 10 seconds if she knew what arccos meant, or if she could figure out how to enter the expression from the prompt in her calculator with the different values from the answer choices. We should always keep in mind that some questions on the test will take much less time than most other questions, and some questions will take much more time. When we come across a question like this one, where we can be sure that we've read the question correctly and aren't making any small mistakes, we should view it as an opportunity to save up some time for other questions that might be more complex. In other words, it would be a mistake to budget a set amount of time for every question on the test beforehand, and then insist on spending all of that allotted time on each question, even if we didn't need to. Instead, we should try to spend as little time as possible on each question, *without sacrificing accuracy and attention to detail*. That way, we can maximize the benefit of a relatively simple question like this one, both by quickly getting it right, and by saving time that we can invest into other questions.

Page 173, Question 40

This question is actually fairly simple, but a lot of untrained test-takers make a small mistake that causes them to get the question wrong. These kinds of small mistakes are exactly the sort of thing we have to avoid when we take the Math Level 2 Test, because they can cause a test-taker to lose points on a question even when she knows all the math involved. Let's take a look.

We're told that the 20th term of an arithmetic sequence is 100, and the 40th term of the same sequence is 250. Then we're asked to find the first term in the sequence. We know an arithmetic sequence is one with a "common difference" between any two consecutive terms—in other words, an arithmetic sequence is one where each subsequent term is found by adding a constant number to the previous term.

Now let's think about how the concept of an arithmetic series applies to this question. If the 20th term of our sequence is 100, and the 40th term is 250, then we know that moving ahead twenty terms (from the 20th term to the 40th term) causes us to end up on a term that's 150 more than the term we started on.

In other words, we know that moving forward twenty terms in the series is the same thing as adding 150, because we just saw that moving from the 20th term to the 40th term is the same thing as going from 100 to 250.

Since moving *forward* twenty terms is the same thing as *adding* 150, and since the difference between any two consecutive terms is the same by definition, we know that moving *backwards* twenty terms must be the same thing as *subtracting* 150. So if the 20th term is 100, and moving *backwards* twenty terms is the same thing as *subtracting* 150, we know that the term that comes twenty terms before 100 must have a value of -50, because 100 – 150 = -50.

So far, so good . . .

At this point, unfortunately, many untrained test-takers will decide that -50 must be the correct answer, because they don't appreciate the importance of paying attention to small details when they read the prompt, and they don't realize that the relationships among the answer choices can often help us avoid making a mistake if we pay attention to them. So a lot of test-takers miss this question because they choose (A) without realizing that they haven't answered what the question was actually asking.

But we, as trained test-takers, will read the question carefully and notice that it asks us for the *first* term in the sequence . . . but counting backwards twenty terms from the 20th term doesn't land us on the *first* term in the sequence! In other words, when we figured out that -50 was the value of the term that came twenty terms before the 20th term, what we actually found was the "zeroth" term in the sequence!

Again, we need to realize that when we jump back twenty terms from the 20th term, we do NOT end up on the first term—we end up *right before* the first term, because 20 – 20 = 0, NOT 1.

So the term *before* the 1st term in the sequence is -50. To get the 1st term, we need to find the term in the series that comes immediately after -50. (You may be wondering how there can possibly be a term in a series that comes before the first term—it seems like the "first term," by definition, must be the earliest term in the series. But a series can go on infinitely in either direction unless otherwise specified, and we use ordinal numbers like "20th," "99th," and so on to refer to any position in the series. So a series can have a "1st" term and a "2nd" term, but it can also have a "0th" term, and a "-1st" term (called a "negative first term"), and so on.)

So how do we figure out the value of the first term in the series, as opposed to the value of the zeroth term? Let's go back to the information we were given and see what we can figure out. If going forward twenty terms is the same thing as increasing by 150, and the difference between any two consecutive terms is equal, then each term must represent an increase over the previous term of $\frac{150}{20}$, or 7.5. So if the 0th term is -50, then the 1st term must be 7.5 more than -50. We know that -50 + 7.5 = -42.5, so (B) is correct.

Notice, again, that choice (A) is what an untrained test-taker would pick after accidentally finding the 0th term instead of the 1st term. Also notice that (D) is the opposite of the correct answer, and (E) is the opposite of (A).

(If you had trouble with the concepts in this question, be sure to review series in the Math Toolbox in this book.)

Page 173, Question 41

This question is a perfect example of what really separates the Math Level 2 Test from the kinds of math tests we usually see in high school and college. Most test-takers will run screaming from a question like this, but trained test-takers view these kinds of questions as tremendous opportunities: if we think about a question like this in the right way, we can quickly come to a correct answer, and then take the time we've saved on this question and invest it in other questions.

By the way, before we go any further with this question, I just want to take a moment to point out that my explanation for this question is going to be pretty long. That's because I want to make sure we cover all the important stuff going on here—not just how to think about this particular question, but also how we can take what we learn from this question and apply it on test day.

An untrained test-taker will be intimidated by the way this question combines geometry and algebra, but a trained test-taker doesn't get scared just because a College Board math question looks strange at first. Instead of worrying, a trained test-taker reads carefully, and realizes that the individual concepts in this question are actually very simple, even if they come from different areas of math:

- The concepts of points, lines, planes, and intersection are all usually taught in the first week of a beginning geometry class.

- The concept of a variable (n, in this case) being used to represent an unknown number is usually taught in the first week of a beginning algebra class, or even in pre-algebra.

An untrained test-taker would probably also be bothered by the lack of a diagram in this question, since the question talks about geometric concepts. But a trained test-taker realizes that the question probably lacks a diagram because *a diagram might make the question easier to understand*, and the College Board doesn't want to give away too much on this question for some reason. So a trained test-taker simply prepares himself mentally for the possibility that creating his own diagram might be a helpful tactic on this question.

On top of that, a trained test-taker notices two common patterns in the answer choices:

1. Choices (A), (B), and (C) form a series, with the value for choice (B) in the middle of the series.

2. Choices (A), (B), (D), and (E) follow the halves-and-doubles pattern. (D) is half of choice (A), and (E) is half of choice (B).

A trained test-taker would realize that these patterns in the answer choices would tend to suggest that (B) is the correct answer, because it appears in the middle of a series, and because it's one of the answer choices with its half or double also present in the answer choices. Of course, a trained test-taker would NEVER conclude that (B) MUST be correct simply because it follows these patterns! We know that answer choice patterns on this test are just strong indicators of what's LIKELY to be correct, not guarantees of what MUST be correct.

There's one more thing we might want to think about when we see these answer choices. Notice that choices (D) and (E) involve taking an expression with n and dividing it in half. That means that if the expression in the numerator is odd, choices (D) and (E) could end up representing numbers that aren't integers. For example, if n were equal to 5, then (D) would be equal to $\frac{5}{2}$, which seems impossible in the context of the question—how could a line intersect with a half of a plane? Similarly, if n were equal to 8, then (E) would be $\frac{7}{2}$ and, once more, we'd have the impossible situation of intersecting half a plane. We know it's only possible for a line to intersect a whole number of planes, not a fraction of a plane. So unless we eventually figure out something about the situation described in the question that would mean the numerator in (D) or (E) could never be odd somehow, it doesn't seem possible for (D) or (E) to be the correct answer as far as we can tell right now, because the prompt for the question seems to allow n to be any number of planes, whether even or odd.

So, at this point, a trained test-taker would have read the prompt and the answer choices carefully. He would have realized that the question only talks about relatively basic concepts, even if those concepts are combined and presented in an unusual way. He'd also realize that it might be helpful to draw a diagram of the situation described in the question, and that the concept of $n - 1$ might be particularly relevant to the question, given the patterns in the answer choices. He probably wouldn't know the answer to the question yet, but he'd probably have a pretty good idea that he knew enough about the question to figure out an answer after some effort. After all, if the question talks about lines, planes, and points, and if we understand what those words mean, then it must be possible to answer the question—the answer has to come from some combination of the concepts related to lines, planes, and points.

Let's go ahead and try to draw a diagram of the situation being described in the question, to see if we can visualize the situation. A lot of test-takers might be a little put off when the question describes "distinct planes intersect[ing] in a line"—maybe trying to draw that situation will help us figure out what's going on.

We know that an intersection is the set of points that two geometric figures have in common. Let's imagine two planes intersecting, and see what that looks like. (I'll use parallelograms to indicate planes in my diagram, even though planes aren't actually parallelograms, of course—planes go on forever, while parallelograms have boundaries. But making the planes be parallelograms is probably the best way to try to represent multiple planes in a two-dimensional diagram, which is what I have to do here.)

Here's my diagram of two planes intersecting each other at 90 degrees (the clear plane is basically oriented like the sheet of paper you're reading this on, and the gray plane would be projecting straight out at you as you read this, and also away from you through the page, if the diagram could be in 3 dimensions):

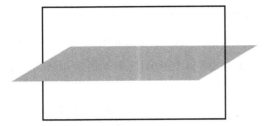

If we think about it, we realize that the set of points that are common to both planes is actually a line:

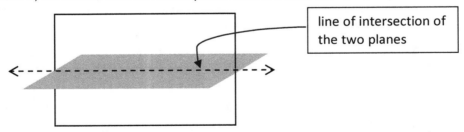

line of intersection of the two planes

The question actually says the planes "intersect in a line," so we're probably on the right track at this point, since we've noticed that it's possible to make two planes intersect in a line. But the question seems like it might be talking about the possibility of *more than two* planes intersecting in a line, since the question uses the variable n to describe the number of planes, and it doesn't say that n has to be below a certain number or anything.

So how could we get another plane to intersect with our two existing planes in the same line? We'll try adding a third plane to our diagram. That might look like this:

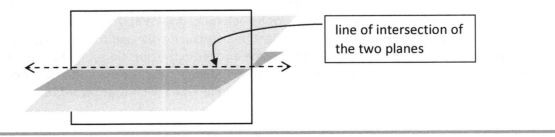

line of intersection of the two planes

Now we start to see that we could even add a fourth plane—or as many extra planes as we want, actually:

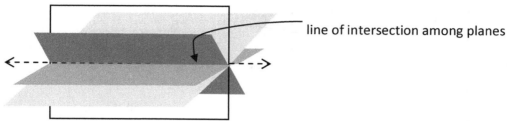

line of intersection among planes

So it seems to be possible to add an infinite number of planes to this setup, all intersecting along the same line. Okay, that makes sense. But the question isn't asking us how many planes can possibly be added! Instead, the question is asking us about a line that would intersect "one of these planes in a single point." When we try to imagine a line that intersects one of the planes in a single point, we'll see that it's impossible to add that line without having it intersect other planes, too . . . which seems to be what the question is getting at. So let's try adding a line and see what that might look like:

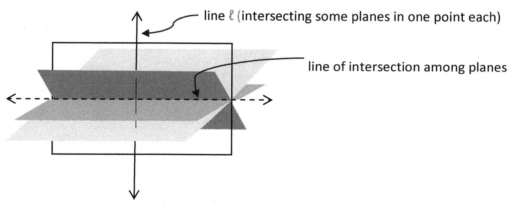

line ℓ (intersecting some planes in one point each)

line of intersection among planes

(This is probably a good time to point out that your diagram doesn't have to be nearly as complicated or precise as mine is—in fact, if I were doing this question on test day, my diagram would be a lot less polished than this, and it certainly wouldn't have any labels or anything, because I would know what each line represented. The only reason I'm making this diagram so detailed right now is to try to make it easier for you to understand what's going on in the question. Since the question is talking about figures in three-dimensional space, it can be a challenge to represent those figures in a single sheet of paper, so I'm trying to make my figure as clear as I can.)

So now we have an idea of what the intersecting planes could look like, and we have an idea of what line ℓ could look like. It looks like now might be a good time to try to figure out how to answer the question: if n is the number of planes, then how do we express the smallest number of planes that line ℓ could be intersecting?

In just a second, I'm going to "spin" my diagram 90 degrees horizontally, so that the line where all the planes intersect will be pointing directly towards the person looking at the diagram, and we'll see the "edges" of the planes (of course, planes go on forever, so they don't actually have edges, but we'll be looking at the diagram so that all the planes are coming directly toward us, and we're looking straight down the line of intersection). In other words, I'm going to show the system of planes and lines from the perspective of the eye in this diagram:

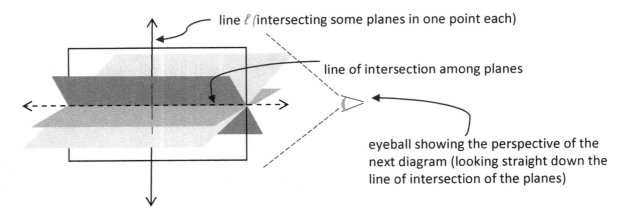

line ℓ (intersecting some planes in one point each)

line of intersection among planes

eyeball showing the perspective of the next diagram (looking straight down the line of intersection of the planes)

So here's what the whole system would look like if we were looking down the line of intersection (again, remember that real planes extend infinitely, but the ones in this diagram appear as line segments, because we're looking at them "edge-on," in a sense, like in a cross-section):

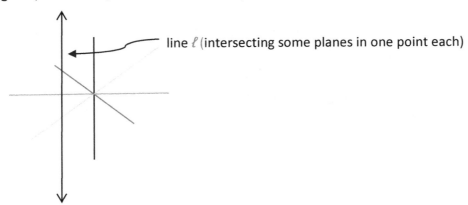

line ℓ (intersecting some planes in one point each)

Again, the question is this: if there are *n* planes, then what's the smallest number of planes that line ℓ can intersect?

Well, let's think about it. As we can see from the diagrams above, it's definitely possible for line ℓ to intersect many of the planes—most of them, in fact. At this point, we might wonder if it's possible for line ℓ to intersect *all* of the planes, depending on how we orient the line. If we think about it, we see that it is, indeed, possible to make line ℓ intersect every plane, if we tilt line ℓ the right way:

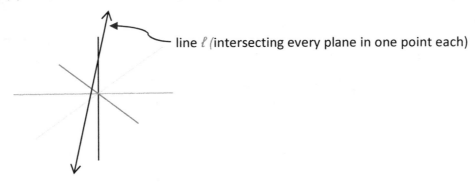

line ℓ (intersecting every plane in one point each)

So that's a starting point. If there are *n* planes, then it's POSSIBLE to make line ℓ intersect with all *n* planes, as we've just shown. But we're trying to get line ℓ to intersect with the *smallest* possible number of planes, because that's what the question asked us to do.

Could we get line ℓ to intersect with some number of planes that's less than *n*? Let's take the smallest possible step in that direction and try to get line ℓ to avoid just one of the *n* planes. If we can't figure out a way to make that happen, then we'll know that *n* seems to be the smallest possible number of planes that line ℓ can intersect. On the other hand, if we can manage to get line ℓ to intersect with only *n* − 1 planes, then that might show us a way to make it intersect with even fewer planes. So let's think a little bit.

Remember that a line goes forever in two opposite directions along one dimension, and a plane goes on forever in four opposite directions along two dimensions. As we just showed, it's easy to make a line intersect a plane: we just tilt the line a little bit towards the plane, and then the two must intersect at some point, since they're both infinite. That must mean that the only way for a line to avoid intersecting a plane completely is for the line and the plane to be parallel with each other. In other words, we have to position the line and the plane so that the shortest distance between the plane and a point on the line is always the same distance. This is basically how we drew line ℓ at first, actually:

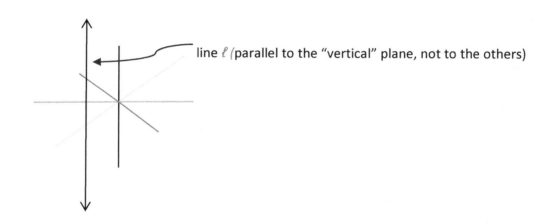

line ℓ (parallel to the "vertical" plane, not to the others)

So we can definitely position line ℓ so that it would never intersect *one* of the *n* planes in the system. That means it's possible for line ℓ to intersect *n* − 1 planes. But we'll have a problem if we try to make it intersect only *n* − 2 planes: since the planes all intersect with one another, no two planes are parallel to each other, which means it's impossible for line ℓ to be parallel to more than one plane at a time. This, in turn, means that the line ℓ can only ever avoid one plane at the most.

And that means that *n* − 1 is the smallest number of planes that line ℓ could intersect. So the correct answer is (B). (You may remember that we identified (B) as the answer choice that was most likely to be correct at the beginning of this discussion, based purely on the patterns in the answer choices. Those patterns turn out to be accurate here, as they often—but not always—are on this test.)

That was a long explanation to read on paper, but the actual solution to this question could have gone much more quickly in your head on test day, as long as you remembered the properties of geometric concepts like planes, lines, perpendicularity, and so on. The only reason my written explanation took up so much space is that I wanted my two-dimensional representation of the ideas in the question to be as clear as possible.

At the beginning of this explanation, I mentioned that this question was a great example of many of the design features we'll encounter in real College Board questions. I specifically pointed out the way the question manages to combine very basic concepts in challenging ways, and the way the answer choices follow common patterns that we often see in College Board math questions. But there are also other elements of this question that we should expect to see in some of the questions on test day:

1. The question doesn't involve any actual calculations. In fact, it would be extremely difficult to use a calculator to approach this question.

2. The question can be easily misread in a way that leads directly to a wrong answer choice. Many test-takers accidentally think the question is asking for the *greatest* number of planes that could be intersected, even though the question underlines the word "least." Choice (A) would be correct if the question used the word "greatest" instead of "least."

Unfortunately, many untrained test-takers who see this question in a practice session will think they should practice with other questions about lines intersecting planes, because they're used to the kinds of repetitive math tests that teachers give in school. But we trained test-takers know that we'll probably never see another question exactly like this one on a real College Board test, because the College Board typically doesn't re-use question setups in that way. Instead, we know that the basic elements of this question will appear in other questions on test day, and that untrained test-takers won't even be aware of the similarities. We'll probably see other questions that involve properties of lines and/or planes; we'll *definitely* see lots of questions that require careful reading, and we'll *definitely* see lots of questions that follow answer choice patterns like the ones we noted above. Those are the kinds of lessons you ultimately want to take away from a strange question like this one—or, for that matter, from any College Board math question.

Page 174, Question 42

The College Board's solution for this question, which appears on page 190 of the MSTB, refers to the idea of even and odd functions without really explaining what those terms mean. While I'm sure there are some high school math teachers who cover the concepts of oddness and evenness as they relate to functions, I know from my extensive tutoring experience that most teachers don't cover it. In fact, I've never once had a tutoring client who approached this question by stopping to reflect on which trig functions were odd or even, even though I've often had students answer this question correctly.

Luckily, we can answer this question easily without knowing what those terms mean. There are two general ways to do this. As I often do, I'll start with the concrete approach, and then give you a more abstract one.

A concrete way to approach this question might be just to plug in a single arbitrary value for θ—in the expression in the prompt and all the expressions in the answer choices—and see which answer choice comes out equal to the original expression from the prompt when we do that. (Of course, if we accidentally choose a value for θ that coincidentally results in more than one answer choice having a value that matches the expression in the prompt, then we can simply pick another value for θ and keep repeating the process until we see that only one answer choice always matches the expression from the prompt.)

Since the question doesn't indicate whether we're working with radians or degrees, we can use either type of value, as long as we're consistent throughout our calculations. We'll do this explanation in degree mode, just because I like degrees more than radians, for no particular reason. (I think it goes back to playing sports when I was a kid—people referred to "45-degree" angles all the time, but nobody ever really refers to a "pi-over-four-radians" angle in everyday life. But I digress.)

As always, when we pick an arbitrary number for a concrete solution to a question, we want to try to pick a number that won't have any special properties relative to the question. I see that the question deals with sine and cosine, so I don't want to pick values like 90 degrees (which has a cosine of 0 and a sine of 1, both of which are numbers with unique properties). I also don't want to pick a number like 45 degrees, because the cosine and sine of a 45-degree angle are equal to each other, which is also a rare property for an angle to have. So let's try θ = 30° and see what we come up with—30° angles have no special properties that should be relevant to this question:

sin θ + sin (-θ) + cos θ + cos (-θ)	(original expression)
sin 30° + sin (-30°) + cos 30° + cos (-30°)	(plug in 30° for θ)
0.5 + -0.5 + 0.866 + 0.866	(find approximate trig values)
1.732	(combine like terms)

So plugging in 30° for θ gives us 1.732 as a final value for the expression in the prompt.

Now we plug in 30° for θ for each of the answer choices, and see which one comes out to 1.732:

Choice (A) is 0 no matter what we plug in for θ, so it can't be right, since it doesn't equal 1.732 when θ is 30°.

Similarly, (B) is 2 no matter what θ is, and 2 doesn't equal 1.732, so (B) must also be wrong. (Now, it is true that 1.732 can be rounded to 2, and it's also true that we sometimes have to take rounding into consideration when we use decimal approximations of trig values. But any calculator that can handle trig functions will be precise enough that we won't need to round values to the nearest whole unit. In fact, a calculator that could only measure trig values to within a whole unit would be pretty useless, since all values for sine and cosine must fall on the range from -1 to 1 anyway.)

(C) gives us 2(0.5) when we plug in θ = 30°, which comes out to 1. That's not equal to 1.732, so (C) is wrong.

(D) gives us 2(0.886) when we plug in 30° for θ, which is equal to 1.732, which was the value of the original expression in the prompt when we set θ equal to 30°. So (D) is correct, assuming that we haven't accidentally chosen a value for θ that has a weird property relative to this question (if we've chosen a weird value, we'll know because more than one answer choice will seem to be correct). Of course, as trained test-takers, we know that we have to evaluate every single answer choice when we attack a question by plugging in a value, like we're doing right now, just in case we accidentally chose a value that results in more than one answer choice having the same outcome when we plug it in. So let's take a look at (E) now.

(E) gives us 2(0.5 + 0.866) when we plug in 30° for θ, which is a value of 2.732. Since we were looking for a value of 1.732 to match our original expression, we know this answer choice must be wrong.

So we can see that (D) must be the only answer choice that matches the original expression in the prompt for all θ, because (D) is the only choice that matches the original expression when θ is 30 degrees.

The more abstract way to approach this question is to think in terms of the unit circle. (If you're not familiar with the concept of the unit circle, don't panic—a lot of teachers don't seem to teach it anymore. The unit circle is a construct that helps us to understand how sine and cosine change as an angle gets larger or smaller. Strictly speaking, you don't have to know about the unit circle to answer this question, as we just demonstrated when we did our concrete approach to the question. But it can be helpful to know about the unit circle when you're taking this test. If you'd like more information on the unit circle, see the Math Toolbox in this Black Book.)

Since the sine of an angle is defined on the unit circle as the *y*-coordinate of the angle's point of intersection with the unit circle, we know that the sine of any θ must automatically be the opposite of the sine of -θ, since the original θ would open in one direction from the x-axis, and -θ would automatically open the same distance in the opposite direction, resulting in opposite sine values. Indeed, we just saw above that sine 30° and sine -30° came out to opposite values: 0.5 and -0.5, respectively.

On the other hand, the cosine of an angle is defined on the unit circle as the x-coordinate of the angle's point of intersection with the unit circle. So the cosine of any θ must be the same as the cosine of -θ, just as we saw above, when θ was 30°, and both cos 30° and cos -30° were approximately 0.866.

So we can see that adding the two sine expressions from the prompt will cancel each other out, since they'll be opposite values of each other, while the two cosine expressions from the prompt will have equal values. When we add all of that together, we'll have a value that's equal to twice the value of cosine θ. (Again, this is what we just saw when we plugged in θ = 30°.)

So we can see again that (D) must be correct. When we look back over the other answer choices, we can also see that the College Board seems to be playing its usual tricks in the various wrong answers. We see the idea of multiplying by 2 appearing frequently, which suggests that we were right to observe that at least one pair of values from the original expression will have identical values. We also see that (C) is there for test-takers who get confused about whether the sine or the cosine value will be the one that's doubled in the final expression. (A) would be an attractive wrong answer to an untrained test-taker who decided to plug in θ = 90° *and* who didn't test out each answer choice to see if there were any others with the same outcome. Similarly, (B) would trap an untrained test-taker who tested 0° for θ, and didn't check all five answer choices. (A) would also attract someone who incorrectly assumed that the cosines of opposite angles would cancel each other out just like the sines would, resulting in an incorrect sum of 0 for the entire expression from the prompt.

Yet again, then, we see that a College Board math question can be answered relatively quickly and easily if we read carefully and apply basic math principles correctly. We also see that there are multiple ways to attack the question, and that the wrong answer choices are clearly intended by the College Board to attract test-takers who make small, predictable errors. Remember to look out for these design features on test day, so you can use your awareness of them to turn them to your advantage.

Page 174, Question 43

As is often the case with College Board math tests, there are two basic ways that we can approach this question:

- We can attack it in a concrete way, by plugging in the same number for n in the original expression and each of the answer choices in order to find the choice that matches the original expression.

- We can attack the question in a more abstract way and do some algebra.

We'll start with the concrete approach, and plug in a number for n. Then we'll approach the question algebraically, to help you try to bridge the gap from the concrete to the abstract, because the abstract approaches to questions on this test are usually faster and easier if you're comfortable with them.

We know not to pick -1, 0, 1, or any number that shows up in the question, in order to give ourselves the best chance of avoiding a number that might result in more than one answer choice coincidentally coming out equal to the expression in the prompt. So let's pick 5, and plug it in to the expression:

$$\frac{[(n-1)!]^2}{[n!]^2}$$ (original expression)

$$\frac{[(5-1)!]^2}{[5!]^2}$$ (plug in 5 for n)

$$\frac{[(4)!]^2}{[5!]^2}$$ (subtract 1 from 5)

$$\frac{24^2}{120^2}$$ (evaluate factorials)

$$\frac{576}{14400}$$ (evaluate squares)

0.04   (divide numerator by denominator)

(By the way, if you don't remember that 4! is the same thing as 4 × 3 × 2 × 1, you can still just enter 4! in your calculator, and the calculator will tell you that 4! is equal to 24 anyway. You can do the same thing with 5!, or with any other factorial of a number you see on the test. But I'd recommend that you familiarize yourself with factorials if you don't remember what they are, because they can appear on the test in a variety of ways. See the relevant portion of the Math Toolbox in this Black Book if you need further help.)

So we've determined that the expression $\frac{[(n-1)!]^2}{[n!]^2}$ has a value of 0.04 when $n = 5$.

Now we'll go through each of the answer choices and plug in 5 for n, to see which answer choice also works out to 0.04 when $n = 5$. Remember that we have to evaluate ALL of the answer choices, in case we accidentally plugged in a number with some bizarre property relative to this question, in which case more than one answer choice might coincidentally generate the same value as the original expression:

(A) $\frac{1}{n} = \frac{1}{5} = 0.2$

(B) $\frac{1}{n^2} = \frac{1}{5^2} = \frac{1}{25} = 0.04$

(C) $\frac{n-1}{n} = \frac{5-1}{5} = \frac{4}{5} = 0.8$

(D) $(\frac{n-1}{n})^2 = (\frac{4}{5})^2 = 0.8^2 = 0.64$

(E) $(n-1)^2 = 4^2 = 16$

So we can see that (B) must be the correct answer, because it's the only answer choice that works out to 0.04 when n is 5, just as the original expression was equal to 0.04 when n was 5.

Now let's try the algebraic approach, which is basically the one on page 190 of the MSTB.

For this approach, we'd want to notice that all of the expressions in the answer choices are more simplified expressions than the one in the prompt, which strongly suggests that we should try to simplify the original expression and see which answer choice reflects that simplification. To do this, we'll need to remember that $n!$, or "n factorial," is the same thing as $n \times (n-1) \times (n-2) \times (n-3) \ldots$, and so on, until we multiply by 1.

Along the same lines, $(n-1)!$ is the same thing as $(n-1) \times (n-2) \times (n-3) \ldots$, and so on, until we multiply by 1.

We might notice that $(n-1)!$ is basically the same thing as $n!$, just without the first number being multiplied, which is n itself. In other words, $n(n-1)!$ is the same thing as $n!$.

So now let's go back to the original expression, expand it, and plug in $n(n-1)!$ for $n!$:

$$\frac{(n-1)! \times (n-1)!}{n(n-1)! \times n(n-1)!}$$

When we cancel out all the $(n-1)!$ terms, we're left with $\frac{1}{n^2}$, just as the MSTB describes. So, again, the correct answer is (B).

Now that we've worked through the question in the abstract, we can see that the wrong answers all come from simplifying the algebraic expression in the prompt incorrectly:

(A) is the square root of the correct answer, which we could arrive at by overlooking one of the n variables in the denominator at some point, or by incorrectly canceling one of them out, or even by not noticing that the numerator and denominator in the prompt were squared in the first place.

(D) is what we'd get if we messed up the process of reducing the numerator and the denominator by a factor of $(n-1)$, accidentally leaving $(n-1)$ in the numerator twice.

(C) is the square root of the mistake from (D).

(E) is what we'd get if we somehow thought we could totally eliminate the denominator without changing the numerator.

As trained test-takers, when we look at the answer choices, we should notice that the College Board is expecting a lot of test-takers to be off by a square or a square root, because there are two pairs of answer choices in which one choice is the square of another: (B) is the square of (A), and (D) is the square of (C). This should remind us that we need to be extremely careful in making sure that we haven't made a mistake in our approach that could involve incorrectly finding the square or the square root of what the question asked us to find. We always have to remember that the College Board loves to bait us into these kinds of score-ruining mistakes!

Page 174, Question 44

This is yet another great example of a question that combines relatively simple math concepts into a question that frustrates a lot of test-takers, even though it actually requires very little math to solve. We're told that a right circular cone has a radius of 6, and that a parallel cross section of the cone has a radius of 4. We're also told that the parallel cross section is 8 units away from the base, and then we're asked to find the height of the cone.

When we read through the prompt, we'll probably realize that we know the individual meanings of all of the words in the question, even if we've never been asked to work with a cone in this way before. By now, we should be familiar with the feeling of understanding all of the parts of a question even though we've never actually done exactly what the question is asking before.

When we encounter a question that involves geometry, and the question doesn't include a diagram, it can often be very helpful to sketch a diagram of our own. Let's do that:

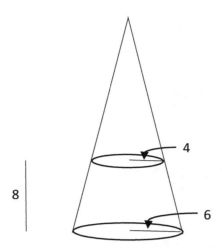

So what does this diagram help us realize, with respect to what the question is asking?

The phrasing of the question makes it clear that there must be some way to determine the height of the cone from the given information, and the diagram helps us see that there must be some relationship between these two things:

- The changes in the radius at different cross-sections
- The heights of the cross-sections

If the radius of the base is 6, and a cross section of the cone 8 units higher has a radius of 4, then we know that the radius of each cross-section decreases by 2 units every time we move 8 units up to make a new cross-section, because the cross-section of a cone gets smaller at a constant rate as we move up from the base of the cone. To determine the height of the cone, which is the same thing as the distance from the top of the cone to the bottom of the cone, we need to figure out the distance between the base of the cone, with a radius of 6, and the top of the cone, which will be a single point with a "radius" of zero.

So let's do that. As we said, the base has a radius of 6 units. When we move 8 units up from the base and take a cross-section, that cross section has a radius of 4. When we move 8 more units up (for a total of 16 units up from the base), the cross section at that level must have a radius of 2. Finally, moving up 8 units higher still (for a total of 24 units up from the base), the cross-section has a radius of 0, which means we've reached the top of the cone. Let's add this information to our original diagram:

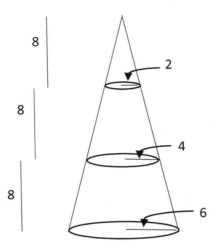

So we've just seen that if we start out with a radius of 6 at the bottom of the cone, we need to move 8 units up 3 times to reach the tip of the cone, where the radius of a cross-section of the cone is zero. And 3 times 8 units is 24 units, so 24 is the height of the cone. That means the correct answer is choice (E).

Notice that choice (C) is the answer you would get if you accidentally forgot about the first 8-unit distance mentioned in the question, and only counted the two 8-unit jumps between the horizontal cross-section in the prompt and the top of the cone—once more, we see that the College Board has deliberately created a wrong answer choice to take advantage of test-takers who understand the concepts being tested in a question, but make a small mistake in executing the solution.

Also notice that all the calculations in this question involve adding, subtracting, and multiplying single-digit numbers. The College Board could have made the calculations more challenging by setting the question up with numbers like 1.3842 and 29.0461 instead of 6, 4, 8, and so on. This is another example of the way that Math Level 2 questions tend to involve relatively simple calculations, even when the questions themselves are strange. These kinds of relatively simple calculations create opportunities for trained test-takers like us to notice shortcuts and patterns, which is all part of the underlying purpose of this test.

Page 175, Question 45

Answering this question requires us to be familiar with the term "indirect proof," and many test-takers won't know what that term means. (In fact, in all my work with clients, I've never had a single one who remembered what an indirect proof was when they first saw this question. Most math teachers don't dwell on the different types of proofs—or address them at all, actually.)

So for most test-takers, the smart way to handle this question is probably to read it carefully, realize they have almost no chance of answering it correctly, and then make the quick decision to skip the question and invest their time in questions they'll be able to answer with certainty. Remember that the Math Level 2 Test is designed so that test-takers can omit roughly 6 or 7 questions and still get a perfect 800 if they answer the remaining questions correctly. You don't need to get frustrated trying to answer the rare question that discusses an obscure concept you've never heard of; instead, you need to make sure that you lock down correct answers to every question that you *do* understand. (I realize that there are times when we can work around the meaning of an unfamiliar phrase to arrive at a correct answer choice with confidence, but, in my experience, most test-takers who don't know what an indirect proof is won't be able to figure it out from this question alone.)

With that important reminder out of the way, let's talk about what's actually going on in this question.

An indirect proof starts out by claiming the *opposite* of the conclusion it's actually going to prove, and then proceeds to show why that opposite must be *false*—meaning that the desired conclusion must be true. In this case, the conclusion that's ultimately going to be proved is ". . . $\sqrt{x}$ is <u>not</u> a rational number," since that's the phrase that comes after the word "then."

The opposite of that conclusion is "$\sqrt{x}$ is a rational number," or just "$\sqrt{x}$ is rational." That means choice (C) is correct. And that's really all there is to this question: if we know that an indirect proof starts out by claiming the opposite of what it wants to prove, then we can see that (C) is the only choice that contradicts the conclusion that $\sqrt{x}$ is not a rational number.

Again, a lot of people won't be familiar with the main concept in this question, at least not when they first see it. Now that we've discussed it, you may find that you can easily remember that an indirect proof proceeds by showing that the opposite of a desired conclusion is false, so the conclusion itself must be true. But there's an important catch with all of that—and if you've been reading this Black Book carefully, you probably already know what I'm about to say: you probably won't see the concept of an indirect proof on test day.

Instead, you're more likely to see one or two other questions with one or two other obscure concepts in them, and the smartest move you can make on test day when you see those questions—assuming you don't feel comfortable answering them—will probably be to avoid wasting time on them in the first place, so you can focus on making sure you answer the rest of the questions correctly. As trained test-takers, we know that the College Board typically doesn't re-use common setups in its questions, so we usually don't gain anything by memorizing the specific setup of a challenging question from a previous test. We try to appreciate the underlying design principles of the questions we encounter instead, so that we can look out for them on future questions.

So the major lesson to take from this question is that sometimes the best course of action is not to waste any time on a question, so you can invest the time you save on questions where it will actually pay off.

Page 175, Question 46

This question can be challenging for a lot of people, but, as we'll often see on this test, the challenge only arises from the fact that the question is combining relatively basic concepts in a specific way that most test-takers haven't ever seen before. As trained test-takers, we need to remember that our job is to read each question carefully, identify the underlying concepts, and then be ready to work with those concepts to find the correct answer, often in a way that might be new to us, and that might not involve doing much calculating—at least, not to the same extent that we typically calculate things in math class.

This is one time when the College Board's explanation of a question is actually pretty okay. It includes graphs of both f and g, along with a quick explanation of the mistakes that lead to the wrong answers. You can find that explanation on page 192 of the MSTB. And there's nothing wrong with using the College Board's approach to this question if you want to. In fact, it's probably pretty similar to the approach I would use myself, except that I would just use my calculator to help myself visualize the situation, rather than drawing all or part of it by hand. But that's only a small difference.

The College Board tells us in its explanation on page 192 that $g(x) = -(x + 3)^2 + 1$, which would be part of a more formal approach to the question. But the College Board doesn't really explain why we know that's the definition of $g(x)$. Since the College Board didn't really address that in the more traditional approach to the question, I'll do it now, in case you're curious. (If you're not curious, feel free to skip the rest of this explanation.)

One formal approach to this question would be to modify the original function of $f(x)$ to reflect the translations that account for $g(x)$, and then plug -1.6 in for x in $g(x)$. We know that horizontal translations involve addition or subtraction with the x portion of the function before it's raised to an exponent, while vertical translations involve addition or subtraction after the x portion of the function has been raised to an exponent. Further, for horizontal translations, we know that adding something to the x-value before it's raised to an exponent will result in shifting the original graph to the *left*, while subtracting from the x-value before raising it to an exponent will result in shifting the graph to the *right*. For vertical translations, adding a constant will shift the original graph *up*, while subtracting a constant will shift the original graph *down*.

We're told that the graph of $g(x)$ is 3 units to the left of $f(x)$, and 1 unit up from $f(x)$—and remember that $f(x) = -x^2$.

Let's account for the horizontal translation first. If $g(x)$ is 3 units to the *left* of $-x^2$, then we know that we'll be *adding* 3 to x before we do the squaring in the function. So the quantity being squared will be $(x + 3)$.

Now let's handle the vertical translation. If $g(x)$ is 1 unit *up* from $-x^2$, then we'll need to *add* on a constant of +1 after the squaring in the function is finished.

Combining those two translations to our original expression for $f(x)$, we see that $g(x) = -(x + 3)^2 + 1$.

Now that we've defined $g(x)$ this way, we can find $g(-1.6)$ by plugging -1.6 in for x in $g(x)$:

$g(x) = -(x + 3)^2 + 1$	(definition of $g(x)$)
$g(-1.6) = -(-1.6 + 3)^2 + 1$	(plug in -1.6 for x)
$g(-1.6) = -(1.4)^2 + 1$	(add -1.6 and 3)
$g(-1.6) = -(1.96) + 1$	(square 1.4)
$g(-1.6) = -0.96$	(combine like terms)

And we see that (B) is correct, and that the other answer choices reflect simple errors in understanding or calculation, as the College Board explains in the MSTB.

But there's another approach to the question, too, and it's one the College Board doesn't mention. I don't necessarily think this other approach is better—in fact, it's likely to be the most confusing approach for many test-takers. But it proceeds a little differently from what we've talked about so far, so I'll mention it now, for the sake of showing once again that most questions on this test can be approached in several ways, and many valid approaches are things that your math teacher would probably never think to show you.

We're told that the graph of $f(x) = -x^2$ is translated 3 units left and 1 unit up, and that the resulting graph is $g(x)$. The College Board's explanation and diagram on page 192 demonstrate this concept pretty clearly, and we've just gone through a formal explanation of what it means as well. But we haven't really worked things out in the other direction, so to speak—the College Board neglects to mention explicitly that each point on $g(x)$ could also be moved three units *right* and one unit *down* to find its corresponding point on $f(x)$.

Remember that the only function whose equation we're given is $f(x)$, so finding $g(-1.6)$ will require us to work in terms of $f(x)$.

The question makes it clear that $g(x)$ is three units to the left of $f(x)$. So any x-value in $g(x)$ is three units less than the corresponding x-value in $f(x)$. Well, the x-value in $g(x)$ that we're asked about is -1.6. So the corresponding x-value in $f(x)$ must be three more than -1.6. Since -1.6 + 3 = 1.4, our solution will be based (at least in part) on $f(1.4)$.

But we're not done yet. We've only accounted for the fact that g(x) is three units to the left of f(x). We haven't adjusted for the fact that g(x) is also moved one unit *up* from f(x). If g(x) is one unit higher than f(x), we'll need to add 1 to any f(x) value to account for that difference. So the answer to the question will be equal to f(1.4) + 1.

Let's think about why that is. As we just discussed, the question makes it clear that we can start at any point on the g graph, move 3 units to the right and one unit down, and find a point on the f graph. When we move 3 units to the right of -1.6, we arrive at 1.4 on the x-axis. After we plug that in to f, we just need to add 1 to the result, and we'll arrive at the value of g(-1.6).

f(1.4) is -1.96. Adding 1 to -1.96 gives us a result of -0.96. So g(-1.6) is -0.96, because if we start at (-1.6, -0.96) and move down 1 unit and right 3 units, we end up at (1.4, -1.96), which is the point on f that corresponds to g(-1.6).

So, again, we see that g(-1.6) is going to be the same thing as f(1.4) + 1, which is -0.96.

The College Board's explanation does an okay job of discussing most of the wrong answer choices, but I'd like to draw your attention to something that a trained test-taker should notice immediately on looking at the set of answer choices. There are two pairs of answer choices in which the values of the two pairs differ by one unit: (B) is one more than (D), and (C) is one more than (E). By now, we can probably guess which mistake the College Board was trying to prey on with these differences—it wanted to have wrong answers positioned for test-takers who forgot to add 1 to account for the vertical shift between g(x) and f(x).

On the other hand, if we actually *did* make the mistake of forgetting to add 1, we might realize that mistake when we quickly reviewed the other answer choices before making a selection and moving on to the next question, because we're trained to think about what the College Board is trying to accomplish at every step of the process. This is one more reason why trained test-takers make it a habit to think of the answer choices as a crucial part of the overall process of answering a question. As we've seen repeatedly throughout these walkthroughs, the relationships among the answer choices can often tell us a lot about how a question should be approached.

Page 175, Question 47

If we're familiar with this type of combination question, we can use the formal solution to find the answer—this is the approach we see in the College Board's explanation for this question on page 192 of the MSTB. When we read that explanation, we can see that the correct answer is choice (A), 120.

But what if we don't remember the formal approach to these kinds of questions? Or what if we never learned it?

In that situation, there are a few things we can try doing.

The easiest approach to this question is probably to use a calculator, if your calculator can handle combination questions. We'll be using the nCr function, for *n* things *combined* *r*-at-a-time. We want this function, as opposed to nPr, because nCr is what we use when we don't care about the order of things in the combination, and the question didn't say anything about order.

Now that we've identified the correct function to use, we ask ourselves, "What do we choose for *n*, and what do we choose for *r*?"

The question asks us how many ways we can make one group of 7 and another group of 3 from an original group of 10. So *n*, which represents the total number of possible things we can draw from to make our combination, will be 10. Now, do we choose 7 or 3 for *r*? Actually, as you may recall from math class, the value of the overall expression will be the same whether we use 3 or 7 for *r*. This makes sense if you think about it: whenever you would choose 7 things from a group of 10, you'd be leaving an unselected group of 3 things behind; if you chose 3 things from the group of 10, you'd be leaving an unselected group of 7 things behind.

So, using 10 for *n* and then either 3 or 7 for *r*, we'd enter *either of the following* into the calculator:

> 10 nCr 3
>
> 10 nCr 7

When the calculator evaluates either expression, it tells us the result is 120. So (A) is correct.

(Again, the nPr function on the calculator is for permutations, not combinations, so it can't be used for this question—remember that the difference between permutations and combinations is that permutations are concerned with order, while combinations aren't. See the discussion of permutations and combinations in the Math Toolbox of this Black Book if you don't feel like you're familiar with these concepts.)

Of course, some test-takers may not remember how to use a calculator to address combination questions on test day, and may also not remember the formula for combination questions that appears in the College Board's solution to this question. If you find yourself in that situation when you look at this question, I'd recommend that you skip it for the time being—there's no point in trying to figure out an answer to this question when you have so little to work with, because all of the other questions on the test count toward your final score the same amount as this one does. It would be much smarter to invest your time and effort in questions that you know you can answer correctly. Remember, as I've mentioned repeatedly, that you can still omit roughly a half-dozen questions or so per test and arrive at a perfect score if you answer everything else correctly. Use your time accordingly.

But let's pretend, for the sake of discussion, that you don't know how to answer this question in the formal way, and you don't remember how to answer it with a calculator—and let's also pretend that you've decided to skip this question the first time you saw it, because you're a trained test-taker, and now you've returned to this question, because you're certain that you've marked down the correct answers for all of the other questions on the test that you can handle. So now what?

We should remember that we can find the total number of combined outcomes for two events if we multiply the numbers of outcomes for each individual event. In other words, if I'm wondering how many ways I can pair a single hat with a single shirt, and I have 4 hats and 7 shirts, the answer is 28, because each hat has 7 possible shirts it can be worn with, and there are 4 hats. (If none of this is familiar, check out the discussion of counting problems in the Math Toolbox.)

So now let's think about the situation in the question: we have 10 people, and we're dividing them into one group of 7 people, and one group of 3 people. One way to start approaching this question, then, is to figure out how many outcomes there might be for selecting the 3-person group. (I'm choosing to focus on the 3-person group because 3 is a smaller number than 7, so I expect it to be less work—and, as we said earlier, every selection of a 3-person group also creates a 7-person group of people who weren't selected, and vice-versa, so we can focus on either group when we try to answer the question.)

There are 10 possibilities when we try to pick out the first person for the group of 3, because there are 10 total people in the group we're choosing from.

Once we pick the first person, there will only be 9 possibilities for the second person, because one of those original 10 people has already been selected for the group of 3.

Similarly, after the first two people are selected, there will be 8 people left in the original group who might be chosen as the last person in the group of 3.

That means there are 10 possible outcomes for choosing the first person, and then 9 possible outcomes for choosing the second person, and, finally, 8 possible outcomes for choosing the third person. So the total number of ways we can choose a first person, then a second person, and then a third person, will be equal to 10 × 9 × 8, which is 720.

But hold on a minute . . . 720 isn't one of the answer choices! How can that be?

The problem is that our approach of multiplying 10 × 9 × 8 only makes sense if we're assuming that the order of the selection makes a difference. But the question doesn't actually say that the order makes a difference—the question is only talking about a group of 3 people and a group of 7 people, without saying anything about the order of selection within either group.

In other words, if we call the people in the original group A, B, C, D, E, F, G, H, I, and J, then we could say that our idea of multiplying 10 × 9 × 8 would only have worked if a selection of A, B, C should be counted separately from a selection of C, B, A. But the question doesn't say that. The question only talks about selecting a group of 3 people. So, for this question, a group that contains A, B, and C should only be counted as 1 possible grouping, whether those people were chosen in the order A, B, C, or C, B, A, or B, A, C, or whatever.

So now we have to figure out how to modify our number of 720 possible *ordered* outcomes, so that it reflects the number of possible groupings if order doesn't matter.

There are a lot of ways we could do this. Obviously, we don't want to go through every one of the 720 ordered arrangements and figure out which ones are identical, because that would take more time than we have.

But what if we figure out how many ordered ways a single three-person combination could be counted? If we did that, we would know how many times larger 720 was than the correct answer. In other words, if it turned out that every group of three people was counted x different times when we calculated 720 possibilities, then we'd know that the total number of possible groupings of three people should be 720/x.

So let's imagine the three-person group of D, E, F. How many distinct orders can we select those three people in?

Let's think about this systematically. DEF is one possibility, of course. Are there any other possibilities that start with D? Sure there are—you could also choose them in the order DFE. Are there any other possibilities where D is first? No, there aren't—if D is first, then the next choice is either E or F, and the final choice has to be whichever person still hasn't been picked. So we've exhausted all the possibilities when D is first. How about when E is first? Well, then we could have EDF or EFD, which are the only two possibilities that start with E. How about when F is first? Again, two possibilities: FDE and FED. And that's all.

So there are 6 ordered ways in which we could choose the individual three-person grouping of D, E, and F:

DEF

DFE

EDF

EFD

FDE

FED

That means the individual group of D, E, and F was counted 6 separate times when we did our 10 × 9 × 8 calculation . . . which means that *every* individual three-person group was counted 6 separate times in that calculation.

So 720 is 6 times larger than the correct answer, because the calculation that we did to arrive at 720 was counting every three-person group six times. That means the correct answer is 720/6, which is 120. So, again, we see that (A) is correct.

Just to be extremely clear, I'm not suggesting that every test-taker should have the time, energy, and interest to go through everything I just described in order to answer this question. But I wanted to show this way of figuring out the answer for two reasons:

1. I wanted to show one possible approach that students might take if they were unable to remember the formal approach or the nCr command on their calculators, but still remembered the basic principles of counting problems.

2. I want to distinguish this question from questions like number 49 on the same College Board test, which we'll talk about in a few pages. Question 49 probably can't be answered by anyone who doesn't remember a formula, which is rare for questions on this test. This question, on the other hand, probably can't be answered *quickly* by people who don't know the formula, or who don't know how to use a calculator to do combinations . . . but it can, in theory, be answered by a test-taker who's willing to think about it logically and play around with some ideas, assuming time permits. It's important to realize that some questions can eventually be worked out if we don't already know the material, and a few just can't. (Remember that it's still possible to achieve a perfect 800 on this test even if we omit roughly half a dozen questions, so it's okay to admit that there are a small number of questions on any given test that a test-taker can't answer without knowing some relatively advanced or obscure material ahead of time.)

Now, as always, let's take a look at the other answer choices, and see if we can figure out what the College Board was thinking when it included them. Note that choice (C) is twice the correct answer, which is a common pattern, as we've seen many times by now. Choice (E) is the square of the correct answer, which isn't a common pattern, but kind of makes sense on this question—since any non-calculator approach to the question ultimately involves multiplication and division, it makes sense that someone might accidentally do something that amounts to multiplying the correct answer by itself, rather than adding the correct answer to itself, like we saw in (C). Choice (B) is what we'd get if we just multiplied the three numbers in the question for no particular reason. And choice (D) is actually equal to 7!, or $7 \times 6 \times 5 \times 4 \times 3 \times 2 \times 1$, which is a quantity you might run across in the process of approaching the question formally, but isn't the final answer to the question. (A sloppy test-taker might think that 7! could be correct because the question may seem kind of similar to the idea of picking 7 things from any group, but one way to realize that 7! can't be correct is to remember that the question can also be approached from the standpoint of choosing 3 things, and 7! isn't equal to 3!—there's no reason to think that either factorial makes more sense as an answer than the other one does, once we realize that the question can be approached either way.) We can imagine that an error in calculation or understanding might lead to any one of these choices.

Page 176, Question 48

This is yet another example of the way the College Board can take relatively basic concepts and combine them to form a question that seems pretty challenging to most test-takers. In this case, the concepts being combined are the following:

- the idea of one number being less than (and/or equal to) another number

- the idea of squaring a number

- the idea of positive numbers

- the idea of rational numbers

Each of those ideas, on its own, is something that most test-takers probably understand. But the question combines them in ways we probably haven't seen before, and many test-takers are unable to figure out what's going on. (In fact, the chart on page 178 of the MSTB shows that this question was the single question on the test that was missed by the largest number of test-takers.)

That's okay, though. As trained test-takers, we expect that kind of thing to happen sometimes. We also know that we can often figure out the answer to a question like this one by reading carefully and thinking carefully, rather than by applying a formula or doing some kind of calculation—in fact, as often happens on this test, there is no formula that could be applied to this question anyway, even if we wanted to do that.

So let's consider each of the sets in the question and see what we can come up with.

(Some test-takers might automatically make the incorrect assumption that *every* set, by definition, must have a single element that must be less than all other elements, so they'd expect the correct answer to be I, II, and III. But there's no answer choice to reflect that possibility, which means that at least one of the sets in the question must not have an element that's less than all the other elements.)

Roman numeral I is "the set of positive rational numbers." (Remember that a rational number is a number that can be expressed as a ratio of two integers. For example, 5 is a rational number because it can be expressed as 10/2 or 5/1 or 100/20, and so on. Similarly, 0.5 is a rational number because it can be expressed as 5/10, or as 1/2, and so on. But numbers like e, π, and $\sqrt{2}$, for example, are irrational, because they can't be expressed as the ratio of two integers.) So now we have to ask ourselves if there's a single positive rational number that's less than all the other positive rational numbers. One number we might think of right away might be 1, since it's the smallest positive integer. But then we have to ask ourselves if there are any rational numbers between 0 and 1. Of course there are—0.5 is one example that we just talked about. And once we remember that decimal numbers can be rational, we might think that 0.1 would be the smallest positive rational number . . . but we can actually keep putting zeros between the decimal point and the 1, and keep making our rational number smaller and smaller. Even when we get to something like 0.000000000000001, we can still keep adding zeros between the decimal point and the 1, and our number gets smaller and smaller, while still being rational, because we can still express it as the ratio of two integers. For example, 0.0000000001 can be expressed as 1/10000000000, and 0.0000000000000001 can still be expressed as 1/10000000000000000, and so on.

So now we have to ask ourselves something: would there ever come a time when we couldn't keep inserting zeros between the decimal point and the 1? No, there wouldn't. We can put as many zeros there as we like, and still always have a rational number, as we just saw.

So there actually *can't* be a single positive rational number that's smaller than all the others, because every time we think we might have found one, we can just insert another zero between the decimal place and the 1, creating a rational number that's even smaller. So the set in Roman numeral I does NOT contain an element that's less than all of its other elements.

Now let's take a look at Roman numeral II.

The set in Roman numeral II is "the set of positive rational numbers r such that $r^2 \geq 2$." We might immediately think that the smallest positive number in this set was $\sqrt{2}$, because that's the smallest r that would satisfy $r^2 \geq 2$ . . . but $\sqrt{2}$ is NOT a rational number! So $\sqrt{2}$ isn't actually a number in this set, since we're told that this set only contains rational numbers.

That means we need to figure out if there's a single positive rational number that's the smallest possible increase from $\sqrt{2}$. We might try to find such a number by working out a decimal approximation of $\sqrt{2}$, and then seeing where that leaves us. If we enter $\sqrt{2}$ into a calculator, we see that the approximate value is something like 1.414. So we might think of a number like 1.415 as a good candidate for being the smallest rational number after 1.414, which, in turn, is an approximation of $\sqrt{2}$. So 1.4145 is pretty close to $\sqrt{2}$, but plenty of numbers are even closer: 1.4149, for example, or 1.4148, or even 1.141422, and so on.

At this point we realize we're running into the same problem we had with the set in Roman numeral I: there's a number just outside of the set that defines the lower boundary of the set, and it will always be possible to insert another rational number between that boundary and the lowest rational number we can think of in the set. In the set from Roman numeral I, the boundary number was 0; in the set from Roman numeral II, the boundary number is $\sqrt{2}$. The infinite number of points on a number line between the boundary number and any rational number raises the same issue in both sets.

So the set in Roman numeral II also doesn't have an element that's less than all the other elements in the set.

Finally, let's take a look at Roman numeral III, which describes "the set of positive rational numbers r such that $r^2 > 4$." Here, we might immediately think that 2 could be a possible value for r, because $2^2 = 4$. But when we read carefully we see that r^2 must be *more than* 4, which means r must be more than 2.

So Roman numeral III is basically asking us if there's a single positive rational number that's greater than 2, but smaller than all other positive rational numbers that are greater than 2. And we find ourselves back in the same position we've been in for each of the other sets we've looked at so far: there's a number just outside the set that defines the lower boundary of the set, and we'll always be able to insert another rational number between that boundary and whatever is the lowest rational number we've thought of so far in the set.

So Roman numeral III doesn't contain an element that's smaller than all of the other elements in the set, either.

That means (A) must be correct: none of the sets will satisfy the requirement in the prompt.

As we might expect from a College Board math question, the other answer choices all reflect basic mistakes an untrained test-taker could make, whether in reading or in mathematical reasoning. The most common mistake that I've seen people make is to misread the phrase in Roman numeral III as though it said "$r^2 \geq 4$," instead of "$r^2 > 4$." Misreading it that way would make 2 the smallest positive rational number in the set, and would make (D) correct, because it would bring the "boundary number" we talked about above *inside* the set, and the "boundary number" in Roman numeral III is rational, unlike in Roman numeral II.

This question is one more example of the fact that paying attention to small details is often just as important on this test as knowing how to do math—in fact, you could argue that there was almost no "math" involved in this question at all, in the sense of calculations and formulas. Instead, we needed to know the properties and definitions of certain fundamental concepts, and then be willing to think about them carefully. The people who do well on this test are the ones with the ability and the willingness to do things like that.

Page 176, Question 49

This is one of those relatively rare Math Level 2 questions that simply requires us to know an obscure math concept. In other words, it's the kind of question that looks like it could appear on a typical high school math test on conic sections. So there really isn't any way that we might figure out this question without just knowing what the major axis of an ellipse is, and how to find it. You can find a formal, technical explanation of how to find the length of the major axis of this ellipse on page 193 of the MSTB.

(By the way, if we got sloppy, we might notice that choice (E) is twice as much as choice (B), and try to guess that one of those choices was correct, because of the patterns that the College Board often likes to follow, which we've discussed repeatedly in this Black Book. But in this case, the answer choice pattern doesn't hold up, because the correct answer is actually (D). This question is yet another good example of why we never rely solely on patterns when picking an answer, and why trained test-takers don't guess.)

Even though there isn't much for me to say about the actual solution to this question that the College Board hasn't already said in its description, there are actually a few important things we can discuss about this question as it relates to general test prep strategy.

Most untrained test-takers who come across this question will jump to the conclusion that they need to study ellipses in order to be fully ready for test day. But trained test-takers will recognize this question as an outlier. Instead of devoting time to learning more about ellipses, which are very unlikely to appear again on test day, a trained test-taker will continue to focus on the skills and concepts that matter: careful reading, awareness of the test's patterns and rules, and a strong command of the concepts that do appear frequently on the test.

We always have to remember that the College Board's SAT Subject Tests in Math are inherently different from the math tests you would expect to take in high school or college, and one of the major differences is that the College Board rarely re-tests math concepts in the same way that math teachers do. If you were trying to get ready for a math test in high school, and your teacher showed you a practice question you couldn't answer about ellipses, then you would have a reasonable expectation that the teacher's test would feature highly similar questions about ellipses, and you'd be right to practice those concepts repeatedly, until you could handle them almost in your sleep. But the College Board doesn't write standardized tests that way, for reasons we've discussed repeatedly in this Black Book.

Instead, the College Board follows its own (largely arbitrary) test-design standards, in order to ensure that each official test will reward the same skills, so that colleges can rely on the test to produce consistent results every year—and memorizing previous test questions isn't one of the skills that the College Board likes to reward. As we discussed earlier in the Math Toolbox, the subject matter for the SAT Math Level 2 Test can be roughly broken down into two groups of concepts:

- Relatively basic math concepts for college-bound students, such as the Pythagorean Theorem, the difference between positive and negative numbers, and so on. These concepts tend to include more definitions and properties as opposed to memorized formulas. **Questions that draw on this group of concepts account for the large majority of the questions on the Math Level 2 SAT Subject Test. You can't get an elite score without knowing at least the majority of these concepts.**

- Relatively obscure math concepts that focus more on memorized formulas from areas of math that would be relatively advanced for most college-bound students. Questions that draw on this group of concepts account for such a small minority of the questions on test day that it's usually possible to score a "perfect" 800 on the section even if we omit every single question from this group that we see on an individual test. Because the potential pool of formulas and other obscure concepts is so large, and because each official College Board practice test includes so few questions from this group, it's not common for concepts from this group to appear repeatedly in multiple tests. **Even if you omit all the questions that incorporate these concepts on test day, you can still usually get a perfect score on the test, assuming that you correctly answer all the questions based on Part I concepts.**

(Remember that the concepts in the first group described above are covered in this Black Book in Part I of the Math Toolbox, while the concepts in the second group described above are covered in Part II of that Math Toolbox.)

When it comes to your preparation for test day, the real lesson to be learned from this question is that you will almost certainly see *something* obscure on test day that you won't know how to answer, and that you haven't already seen in your practice work with official tests from the College Board—again, it probably won't be ellipses next time, but it will be *something*. And that's fine. You can leave those obscure questions blank and still get a perfect score if you answer everything else correctly.

So the best way for most people to "handle" this question isn't to panic over not knowing the material, or to commit themselves to spending hours on learning about ellipses, or to try to guess the correct answer by looking for answer choice patterns. The best thing for most trained test-takers to do when confronted with a question they can't figure out is to recognize it quickly for what it is, omit it, and then invest the extra time in making sure they've locked down correct answers to other questions that feature concepts they do remember.

For example, the page of the MSTB that contains this question also contains two other questions that many test-takers answer incorrectly. But question 48 deals with concepts like the definitions of terms like "positive," "rational," and "set;" question 50 deals with concepts like inequality, positivity, and negativity. The concepts in both of these other questions are ones that a trained test-taker should be well prepared for, because they're guaranteed to appear repeatedly on test day in a variety of forms. If a trained test-taker couldn't answer question 49 right away, because she had forgotten how to find the length of the major axis of an ellipse, then her instinct should be to omit 49 and make sure that questions like 48 and 50—which involve tricky presentations of concepts that appear frequently on the test—are answered correctly, or at least carefully attempted, time permitting.

If you read through the Math Toolbox and the walkthroughs in this Black Book, you can see the topics that come up over and over again: functions, triangles, basic arithmetic, etc. Make sure you spend your energy becoming completely comfortable with the material in Part I of the Math Toolbox in this Black Book (and the way that material is presented on the Math Level 2 Test) before you spend any energy learning more obscure material that's unlikely to appear on test day, which is covered in Part II of the Math Toolbox.

Finally, let this question—and the other official College Board questions on obscure topics that you encounter in your preparation—remind you of the paramount importance of avoiding unnecessary mistakes on other questions! As we've discussed on several occasions in this Black Book, the thing that prevents most test-takers from getting the score they want isn't a lack of math knowledge, but a lack of focus, discipline, and an awareness of how the test is actually designed. These are the things you should be concentrating on.

Page 176, Question 50

This is the last sample question in the College Board's book, and it's a very fitting example of the kinds of elements that the College Board likes to incorporate in the Math Level 2 Test. We see that the question doesn't necessarily involve calculating any particular value; instead, it requires us to think about basic concepts like subtraction, division, positivity, negativity, and inequality in a way that we might never have encountered before.

It should also be no surprise to you by now that the question will require us to pay careful attention when we read it, and when we select our answer choice. For example, if we confuse a and b, or if we accidentally misread a less-than symbol as a greater-than symbol, or a minus sign as a plus sign, we'll miss the question. (I've seen lots of people make each of those mistakes on this question, by the way).

This question is also pretty typical in the sense that there are two basic ways to approach it:

1. We can try a more concrete, backsolving-oriented approach, in which we assign values to a and b that conform to each set of relationships available in the answer choices.

2. We can try a more abstract approach, in which we focus on the different properties of the concepts of the question.

As usual, I'll start by discussing the concrete approach first, and then we'll discuss the abstract one.

When we look at the answer choices, we see that each choice offers a different possible inequality statement involving a, b, and 0. Let's look at (A) first.

Choice (A) says $0 < a < b$. To backsolve, we'll need to select numbers that satisfy this inequality, plug them into the original expression, and see if the expression is valid. I'll use $a = 2$ and $b = 3$:

$$\frac{a - b}{ab}$$ (original expression)

$$\frac{2 - 3}{(2)(3)}$$ (plug in $a = 2$ and $b = 3$)

$$-\frac{1}{6}$$ (combine like terms)

Since we arrive at a negative result when we plug in $a = 2$ and $b = 3$, we know that (A) must be wrong, because the question asked us for a scenario in which the original expression has a positive value.

Now let's try (B). The inequality for (B) is $a < b < 0$, so I'll use $a = -4$ and $b = -2$. (Remember that negative numbers run "backwards" from positive numbers, so -4 is a smaller number than -2, even though 4 is a larger number than 2. This is exactly the kind of basic math fact that we might easily mess up, which could cost us the question.)

$$\frac{a - b}{ab}$$ (original expression)

$$\frac{-4 - (-2)}{(-4)(-2)}$$ (plug in $a = -4$ and $b = -2$)

$$\frac{-2}{(-4)(-2)}$$ (combine like terms in the numerator)

$$\frac{-2}{8}$$ (combine like terms in the denominator)

$$-\frac{1}{4}$$ (reduce fraction)

Again, we get a negative result, so (B) must be wrong.

For (C), the inequality is $b < a < 0$, so I'll use $a = -2$ and $b = -3$ (again, I'm making a point of remembering to read carefully, and remembering that this answer choice is calling for a situation where b is now the smaller quantity, and both variables are negative):

$$\frac{a - b}{ab}$$ (original expression)

$$\frac{-2 - (-3)}{(-2)(-3)}$$ (plug in $a = -2$ and $b = -3$)

$$\frac{1}{(-2)(-3)}$$ (combine like terms in the numerator)

$$\frac{1}{6}$$ (combine like terms in the denominator)

Now, we've just learned that the value of $\frac{a - b}{ab}$ is positive when a is -2 and b is -3. A lot of untrained test-takers would stop working on this question at this point, and just mark (C) as their answer and move on to the next question. But we trained test-takers know that we should look at every answer choice before we move on, because we might discover something in another answer choice that could help make us realize we've made a mistake, and we know that one of the most important ways we can maximize our performance is by catching our mistakes. So let's take a look at choice (D) now.

The inequality in choice (D) is $b < 0 < a$, so I'll use $a = 2$ and $b = -3$:

$$\frac{a - b}{ab} \qquad \text{(original expression)}$$

$$\frac{2 - (-3)}{(2)(-3)} \qquad \text{(plug in } a = 2 \text{ and } b = -3)$$

$$\frac{5}{(2)(-3)} \qquad \text{(combine like terms in the numerator)}$$

$$\frac{5}{-6} \qquad \text{(combine like terms in the denominator)}$$

Just as with (A) and (B), we see that (D) leads to a negative result, so it's wrong.

Choice (E) must also be wrong, assuming we haven't made any mistakes in our reading or calculations, because it says that none of the other answer choices results in a positive value, but we saw that (C) gave us a positive value when we plugged in $a = -2$ and $b = -3$.

Of course, as trained test-takers, we'd definitely want to go back and review our work for this question before concluding that (C) is correct. We know that we should always try to work carefully and be alert to potential errors, but that's especially important now, because the approach we just used involved a lot of negative and positive numbers being used together in calculations, and we know how easy it would be to overlook a sign in our calculations and end up getting something wrong even though we understood the fundamental ideas behind the question.

Now that we've approached the question in a concrete way, let's discuss it more abstractly, so we can try to frame our understanding of why (C) is correct in terms of the properties of the concepts in the question, rather than in terms of specific calculations. (Of course, if you were answering this question on test day, it wouldn't be necessary to approach the question from multiple perspectives like this. I'm just doing it now because the discussion might help you understand how to approach future questions in a more abstract way, which is generally faster and more reliable than relying on concrete approaches where we plug in numbers.)

So let's think back over the question, in terms of properties and definitions. Choice (A) says that $0 < a < b$. How would that affect the value of the expression $\frac{a - b}{ab}$? Well, if a is smaller than b, then subtracting b from a has to give us a negative number. So the value in the numerator would have to be negative if we followed the conditions in choice (A). And if both a and b are greater than 0, then they're both positive, so multiplying them together will always yield a positive number when we follow the condition in choice (A). This means that $\frac{a - b}{ab}$ will give us a negative numerator and a positive denominator, which means that $\frac{a - b}{ab}$ will always be negative when we use the conditions in choice (A). So the condition in choice (A) can never result in $\frac{a - b}{ab}$ being a positive number.

Choice (B) says that $a < b < 0$. Just as we saw in (A), if a is less than b, then subtracting b from a will produce a negative number, which means the numerator of $\frac{a - b}{ab}$ will always be negative if we follow the conditions in (B). As for the denominator, if both a and b are less than 0, then they're both negative, and multiplying them together will always yield a positive number. So we'd always be dividing a negative numerator by a positive denominator, resulting in a negative quotient, just as we saw with (A). So choice (B) must be wrong, too.

Choice (C) says that $b < a < 0$. If b is smaller than a, then subtracting b from a will always produce a *positive* number, so the numerator of $\frac{a-b}{ab}$ must be positive under the condition in (C). And if both a and b are less than 0, then they're both negative, and multiplying them together must yield a positive number, so the denominator would also always be positive under the condition in (C). So, in this case, we'd have a positive numerator and a positive denominator, which means our result would always have to be positive. That means (C) must be correct, just as we saw when we plugged in values for it earlier.

Choice (D) says that $b < 0 < a$. If b is less than a, then subtracting b from a will produce a positive number, which means the numerator in the expression $\frac{a-b}{ab}$ must always be positive under the condition in choice (D). If b is negative and a is positive, then multiplying them together yields a negative number, which means the denominator of $\frac{a-b}{ab}$ must always be negative under the condition in choice (D). So (D) would have us dividing a positive numerator by a negative denominator, and the result would always have to be negative. That means choice (D) is wrong.

As we discussed earlier, when we talked about taking a more concrete approach to this question, choice (E) must be wrong, because it says that none of the answer choices would make the expression positive, but we can see that choice (C) is correct, because it makes the expression positive.

As always, let's take a moment to see if we can identify some of the mistakes the College Board was trying to get us to make on this question. Notice, in particular, that it would be very easy to make a careless error and pick choice (B) instead of (C) if we confused the two variables at some point in our solution, or even if we just weren't careful when reading the answer choices. For that matter, any of the wrong answer choices for this question might seem to be correct if we made the easy mistake of confusing positive and negative while working on one or more of the answer choices.

In fact, a lot of test-takers have difficulty with this question, but we've just seen that the individual concepts in this question are actually pretty basic in the context of high school math: subtraction, multiplication, fractions, inequalities, and signs. The key to answering this question has nothing to do with advanced math, and studying something like trig or calc in school would be unlikely to improve your performance on this question. Instead, the important thing on this question is simply reading and thinking carefully, and paying attention to details. As I've said repeatedly throughout this Black Book, and as this question demonstrates, we'll find that the Math Level 2 Test rewards careful, detail-oriented test-taking much more than it rewards sophisticated math knowledge.

Thanks For Reading!

I hope you've benefited from the strategies and examples in this Black Book, and that you'll put everything to work effectively on test day. I know that my readers take test preparation seriously, and I sincerely appreciate that you've put your trust in me at such an important time. I wish you the best of luck on test day, and with the rest of your educational career!

Appendix: SAT Math 2 Quick Summary ("Cheatsheet")

This is a one-page summary of the major Math 2 test concepts we've covered. You may want to consult it on test day to help you recall your training.

(For more information about any of these topics, please take a look at the corresponding sections in this Black Book. To see these ideas in action on 100 real Math Level 2 test questions from the College Board, consult the walkthroughs in this Black Book.)

The Big Secret: The SAT Math 2 tests relatively simple math ideas in unusual ways.

Here's an abbreviated version of the general SAT Math 2 process, or "Math Path:"

1. **Read the prompt carefully.** Note the concepts that appear, and the ways they're related.
2. **Read the answer choices carefully.** Note how the numbers, expressions, or words in the answer choices relate to the prompt, and to each other.
3. **Take note of any diagrams** and how they reflect what appears in the rest of the question.
4. **Identify the math concepts that could be related to the question.** Keep in mind the concepts in the Math Toolbox in this Black Book—don't look for things more advanced than those concepts.
5. **Look for an efficient solution.** Remember that questions can typically be answered in less than 30 seconds. Don't limit yourself to techniques your math teacher would endorse! Your solution might involve testing the answer choices, using your graphing calculator, considering patterns in the answer choices, and so on.
6. Execute your solution. **Remember that the College Board tries to put you in a position to make small mistakes that will cost you the question.**
7. Re-check your work. **Try to understand the College Board's perspective when it wrote the question.** If you understand how the question tests relatively basic concepts in strange ways, and if you see how an untrained test-taker might easily misunderstand the question or miss it because of a small mistake, there's a good chance you've correctly understood the question.

Wrong answer choices can contain valuable information. In some of the most common answer choice patterns you'll see, a **wrong answer may** . . .

- . . . be *half or double* the correct answer choice.
- . . . be the *opposite* of the correct answer in some way.
- . . . be an *"on the way"* answer.
- . . . be the result of finding the *wrong trig function*.
- . . . *imitate the correct answer choice* by containing similar elements.
- . . . be the *first or last item in a series* that contains the right answer.
- . . . be the *right answer to the wrong question*, like the area instead of the perimeter.

Remember the idea of working in passes! There's no reason to answer questions in the order they're presented. Your time should be invested in the ways that will get you the most points. No question is more valuable than any other question.

Don't guess. You can skip a handful of questions and still score 800 if all other questions are correct.

CPSIA information can be obtained
at www.ICGtesting.com
Printed in the USA
BVHW010052180919
558744BV00004B/26/P